Backpacker's Africa

Vervet monkey

Backpacker's Africa

East and Southern

Hilary Bradt

and other contributors

BRADT PUBLICATIONS

First edition published in 1977 by Bradt Enterprises. This edition published in 1994 by Bradt Publications, 41 Nortoft Rd, Chalfont St Peter, Bucks SL9 0LA, England.

Copyright © 1994

British Library Cataloguing in Publication data

A catalogue record for this book is
available from the British Library

ISBN 0 946983 85 2

Cover photos: Front, hiking Kilimanjaro by Kathryn Lewis; back, lion family by Peter Robinson
Maps by Caroline Crump
Typeset from the author's disc by Patti Taylor, London NW10 3JR
Printed by the Guernsey Press, Channel Islands

ACKNOWLEDGMENTS

Much of this guide has been compiled from the letters of travellers who have written from all parts of the globe and particularly Africa, keeping me up to date with changes and new information. Some were persuaded to write whole chapters or to share their specialised knowledge on aspects of natural history. Their names appear in the relevant chapters and are engraved on my heart in everlasting gratitude. Or something like that.

There are other dogs-bodies involved in the production of this Great Guide, beavering away in remote parts of North London and Buckinghamshire but I am resisting their efforts to be named here.

Major contributors

Simon Atkins (Zimbabwe) is a film-maker who has worked, lived and travelled extensively in Zimbabwe. He is co-author of Bradt's *Guide to Namibia and Botswana*.

Philip Briggs contributed chunks of South Africa, Tanzania and Uganda, based on his guides to those three countries published by Bradt.

Aisling Irwin & Colum Wilson (Sudan) are both journalists. Aisling is science correspondent to *The Times Higher Educational Supplement* and Colum is currently working as a civil engineer which allows him to travel to remote places.

David Else is a travel writer specialising in guidebooks about Africa. He contributed to the third edition of this book, providing large sections on hiking and travelling in various parts of the continent, and most of these sections have been retained in this fourth edition. He has also added new information on Sudan and Namibia.

Casper Hoebeek, from Holland, spent much of 1992 and 1993 in Rwanda and Burundi researching a Bradt guide to those countries. An abbreviated version of his work appears here, pending political stability in Central Africa.

Kim Naylor (Eritrea) is a professional travel writer and photographer with numerous travel guides and photographic essays to his name. He is co-author of the Bradt *Guide to Mongolia*.

Ian Redmond is a naturalist who has specialised in the study of elephants and mountain gorillas. He worked with Dian Fossey in Rwanda and played a major part in bringing gorillas and tourists together in Virunga.

Dr Jane Wilson has contributed her extensive knowledge of medical problems affecting travellers in the developing world.

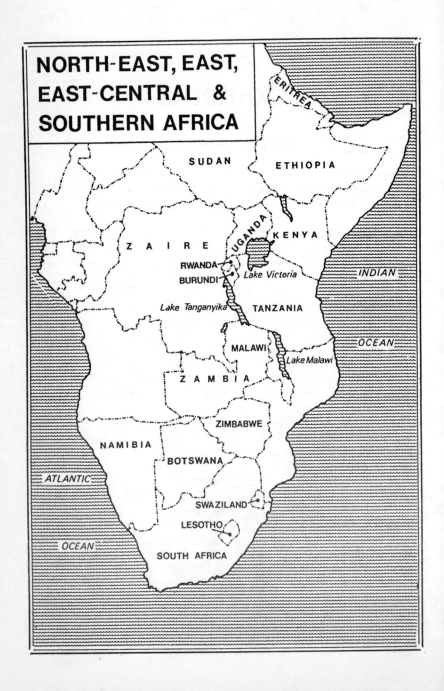

NORTH-EAST, EAST,
EAST-CENTRAL &
SOUTHERN AFRICA

Contents

SOUTHERN AFRICA

BOXES

Chapter 1

Preparations

Getting there cheaply

Africa is a popular long-haul destination, and there are many bargain flights from London. Those looking for the cheapest possible deal will probably do best to study the advertisements on the travel pages of newspapers and magazines.

If you are planning to visit the countries of East Africa (see the *Overview of regions* below), there are many cheap flights to Nairobi, the travel hub of the region. Good deals are often available on EgyptAir and Ethiopian Airlines. If you want to start at the top, in Khartoum (Sudan), Balkan Airways do a low-priced flight.

If you're visiting Southern Africa, Windhoek in Namibia is fast becoming an important regional centre with connecting flights on to Johannesburg, Harare and Victoria Falls. There are some good deals from London to Windhoek on Air Namibia. Australians can fly direct to Harare, with connecting flights to South Africa, from Perth or Sydney.

From the USA, your cheapest bet is probably to fly the USA to Europe leg independently, using a cheap trans-Atlantic flight, and arrange the flight to Africa in London.

A few travel agents in London stand out as specialists in travel to Africa, offering economical airfares and tours, plus advice, insurance, travel magazines, libraries...

STA: in the forefront of Africa know-how and an excellent source of information for independent travellers as well as cheap flights. STA has branches in the UK in London, Cambridge, Oxford, Bristol and Manchester, in Australia and the USA, and caters for anyone looking for an inexpensive flight or interesting tour. They offer the sensible 'open-jaw' option of flying into one African city and out of another. STA has a dedicated Africa Desk at 117 Euston Rd, London NW1 2SX, Tel: 071 465 0486. Two of the many US branches are: 17 East 45th St, suite 800, New York, NY 10017, Tel: 212 986 9470 and 7204 Melrose Ave, Los Angeles, CA 90048, Tel: 213 934 8722.

Africa Travel Shop: probably *the* experts on all aspects of travel to and in Africa, and catering specially for the independent traveller or small groups. African Travel Shop also offer some unusual – and tempting – options such as self-drive cars and walking and wildlife safaris, plus excess baggage and freight forwarding (ideal for expeditions). 4 Medway Court, Leigh St, London WC1H 9QX, Tel: 071 387 1211.

African Travel Systems: Another specialist company with some very good airline deals available. They can also arrange open-jaw tickets and regional flights between various African cities. 6 North End Parade, North End Road, London W14 0SJ, Tel: 071 602 5091.

Trailfinders: a company with long experience of helping independent travellers, Trailfinders are also agents for overland tours operators, as well as for well-priced air fares. They have a library, a vaccination centre, and an insurance scheme for travellers – in fact everything you need for your trip, under one roof. 42-48 Earls Court Rd, London W8 6EJ, Tel: 071 938 3366, or 194 Kensington High St, London W8 7RG, Tel: 071 938 3939.

Wexas: Also offer the combination of economical flights and low-priced tours in their members only 'Discoverers' programme (together or separately) and travel insurance. 45 Brompton Rd, London, SW3 IDE, Tel: 071 584 8113.

Planning your trip

Assuming you are in Africa for more than a brief holiday, you will need to plot out some sort of itinerary. Your decision will be based both on your interests and level of experience. The following overview will help.

If you are planning to travel the length of Africa, bear in mind that Southern Africa has the best infrastructure and the fewest hassles, and that North-East Africa has the worst and the most. The obvious decision may appear to be to start in South Africa and break yourself in gradually as you travel north to the more challenging countries. This means, however, that by the time you reach Ethiopia you will be travel-worn and home-sick. This country gives you the best of times and the worst of times, and you need to be fresh to cope with both.

An overview of the five regions

North-East Africa   This area is associated in most people's minds with war and famine. Although this is still sadly true for parts of Sudan, Ethiopia and Eritrea are finally at peace after a generation of warfare, with Eritrea emerging as Africa's newest independent country. For the experienced, patient, and truly adventurous traveller this area offers something completely, and spectacularly, different in terms of history, culture, landscape, and people.

East Africa   Historically speaking, and in this book, East Africa means the old East Africa Community of Kenya, Tanzania and Uganda.

Kenya and Tanzania are the Africa of films and tourist brochures, with acacia-dotted savannah teeming with game – and tourists. There are some fine mountain walks with afro-alpine vegetation (shown on the cover of this book) which should be seen by anyone with a taste for the exotic (you don't forget walking underneath something resembling a giant cabbage on a pole). There are also some very interesting tribal people who, after years of exploitation by tourists, have turned the tables and charge a fortune to have their photos taken.

Because Nairobi is a popular destination for bargain flights, almost everyone visiting East Africa starts in Kenya. And there is so much to see and do here, and living and travelling are so cheap, that many people look no further. However, Kenya is battling a highly-publicised crime-wave, and the fear of being robbed is encouraging many visitors to opt for Tanzania instead.

Tanzania is generally less scenic and rather more expensive, but has, arguably, the best game parks, including the incomparable Serengeti and the highest mountain, Kilimanjaro. And it is safer. Getting around on your own is more challenging than in Kenya, but the rewards are many, including the miles of unspoiled Indian Ocean beaches and the island of Zanzibar.

Uganda may be the Cinderella of the old Community. Occupying the western portion of the Great Rift Valley, it receives far more rainfall than most parts of Kenya and Tanzania, so is green all year round and exceptionally beautiful. The low number of tourists mean that the people are still genuinely friendly, so for scenery and people-contact Uganda is hard to beat. It also has Africa's outstanding animal attraction, mountain gorillas, and one of the continent's most challenging hikes, the Ruwenzori mountains. Uganda is now under a stable and enlightened government and is keen to forget the bloody excesses of the 1970s and '80s.

East-Central Africa The French-speaking (Francophone) countries of Burundi, Rwanda, and Zaïre also lie in the well-watered western part of the Rift Valley, and are stunningly beautiful in places; and often stunningly frustrating. You need good French and a lot of patience to enjoy travelling here, but the rewards are many for those who make the effort. The absence of tourists is one of them, and here you'll find some of the most beautiful scenery anywhere, the green lushness coming as visual relief after the savannah of East Africa. These are the areas for gorilla watching and for forest species of birds and mammals.

Central-Southern Africa This region is fast overtaking East Africa in tourism, with Zimbabwe deservedly leading the field with its good variety of attractions, all at a reasonable price. Botswana is not included in this book because it is not a country for hikers or budget travellers, though the Okavango Delta is an enchanting area for those who can afford it. Malawi attracts far fewer visitors, but is a superb country for hiking and backpacking. Zambia has the Victoria Falls and Luangwa Valley, an excellent game park.

Southern Africa Once the pariah of the continent, South Africa is now attracting plenty of tourists to its splendid scenery, wildlife, beaches, and numerous other attractions. At the time of writing, however, the political uncertainty and violence before the 1994 elections is putting some people off.

Namibia is set to become one of the major destination of the 1990s, so go there now, particularly if you are a budget traveller. The push is towards up-market tourism.

Southern Africa is particularly rewarding for hikers. Being further from the equator and the unique giant plants that flourish there, the mountain scenery and hiking trails are less exotic but no less beautiful, competing with the very best in Europe or North America.

One aspect of the majority of the countries in Southern and Central-Southern Africa which will attract some and repel others is that everything tends to work so well, you are deprived of the adventures that are commonplace further north. Don't despair, however; if you are travelling independently and looking for Zaïre-style experiences in the southern region, Zambia will do its best to meet your expectations!

The gateway country of the southern part of the continent is Zimbabwe. Positioned for perfect access to the other countries in the region and endowed with friendly people, excellent national parks for both hiking and game viewing, and plenty of campsites and other cheap accommodation, it is the ideal place to start. Namibia is also becoming a gateway country in this region, with direct flights from Europe and frequent regional flights to other Southern African destinations.

For some comparisons of hiking areas see Chapter 3.

Climate and seasons

Deciding when to go is as important as deciding where to go. The countries of East and East-Central Africa are close enough to the equator to have an equatorial climate governed by rainy and dry seasons, rather than the temperate climate we are accustomed to. There is not much temperature variation between 'summer' and 'winter' (temperature changes are governed instead by altitude, so the higher you go the colder it is. Don't, for instance, kid yourself that because it lies on the equator, Kenya must be hot. The highlands, where Nairobi and the game parks are located, are quite chilly at night).

Many people are restricted to certain months for travel, in which case they should read the *Facts* section of the countries that most interest them to check on the weather at that time of year. The lucky ones, with unlimited time and no fixed schedule, can try to visit each country at its optimum time, although there are definite advantages to hiking in the rainy season – less crowded, greener, more water, and rain anyway tends to fall in predictable heavy showers in the afternoon.

For best game viewing seasons see Chapter 5.   As you move south the climate becomes more temperate, with the tip of the continent enjoying four distinct seasons. The northern countries (of Southern Africa) have dry winters and wet summers, and the Cape reverses the trend by having wet winters and dry summers – hence the marvellous displays of wild flowers in South Africa's western Cape in the spring.

Here's a very rough guide to dry seasons: North-East and East Africa – June to September, December to March; East-Central Africa – June to September, January and February; Southern Africa (excluding the western Cape) – May to October; Western Cape – October to April.

Your itinerary

Once you have picked your region, get a good map (see page 14 for recommended maps) and decide on the route. One thing is certain: it will always take longer to go from A to B than you could possibly imagine! You will be held up as much by the delights of travel – the desire to stay longer at a particularly enchanting place – as by the transport breakdowns and other lets and hindrances to progress. Flexibility is all.

Until recently, a South African stamp in your passport prohibited your entry into many African countries. This no longer seems to be a problem, though you could still have some trouble at Tanzanian border posts. Your best protection is to be aware of the latest political events which may influence the attitude of border officials.

Suggested highlights

Successful travel depends, as much as anything else, on being flexible enough to go 'where the wind blows'. Rigid and unalterable plans will result in many missed opportunities, but so will journeying with no goals. Pick out a few treats for yourself, look them up in the index, decide if they really are your scene, then make damned sure you get there!

Game parks Samburu and Lake Nakuru (Kenya), Ngorongoro Crater and Serengeti (Tanzania), Murchisons Falls (Uganda), Luangwa Valley (Zambia), Etosha (Namibia).

Forest reserves Bwindi or Budongo (Uganda), Nyungwe (Rwanda).

Great apes Chimpanzees at Gombe Stream or Mahale (Tanzania), gorillas at the Virunga volcanoes (Uganda, Rwanda, or Zaïre).

Birds Lake Nakuru (Kenya), Rubondo and Saa Nane Islands, and Selous (Tanzania), Lamberts Bay (South Africa).

Wild flowers The Western Cape and Namaqualand (South Africa) in September and October. Namibia after the rains.

Equatorial mountains (moderate) Simien Mountains (Ethiopia), Mt Kenya and Mt Elgon (Kenya), Kilimanjaro (Tanzania).

Equatorial mountains (difficult) Ruwenzori (Uganda).

Highland walking Lesotho, Mt Mulanje (Malawi).

Coastal hikes Otter Trail (South Africa).

Time out Kenya coast and Lamu island, Zanzibar, Swaziland.

Strange sights Almost anywhere in Namibia.

Wow! Victoria Falls (Zimbabwe and Zambia), Lalibela (Ethiopia).

How to travel

Africa is a huge continent, and travelling overland is time-consuming. Once you have decided on your main areas of interest, you can select your means of transport (air travel is excluded here, but it makes a lot of sense in places such as Zaïre where road transport is very poor).

In a private vehicle

For many people this is the *only* way to travel. Few, however, will be bringing their own vehicle (for those who do, *Through Africa* published by Bradt Publications has all the information you need. *The Traveller's Handbook* – published by Wexas – also gives good advice). Many people hire a vehicle on arrival, and this is highly recommended in countries where roads are surfaced and vehicles are in good repair (South Africa), or where public transport is poor (Namibia), or in order to visit national parks.

It may be cheaper to arrange car-hire before you leave home. Africa Travel Shop in London is one company offering such a service.

Be wary of hiring a self-drive vehicle in countries where spare parts are a rarity, unless you are an excellent mechanic. It's much safer (and not much more expensive) to hire a driver along with the vehicle, and also gives employment to local people.

Packaged overland trips

Several companies based in Britain use converted trucks to transport 15 to 20 people thousands of kilometres through Africa. This is a sensible option for single people who, quite naturally, hesitate to disappear into the Dark Continent on their own, and for others who don't want the hassle of coping with border crossings, and so on. Travellers often find this is the only way to see a variety of sights within a relatively short period of time, and many enjoy the camaraderie. Kilometre for kilometre, it usually works out more cheaply than taking public transport.

Most companies run trips going from A to B so you can then explore on your own once you have gained confidence and perhaps met a travel companion on the truck.

Through Africa (Bradt) lists and evaluates a variety of overland companies. You can also check the travel pages of newspapers, or magazines such as *TNT* (distributed free in London), or contact Trailfinders or the Africa Travel Shop. Before settling on a tour, ask to be put in touch with someone who has done that trip. No good company will refuse and you can then find out what it's *really* like.

Hitchhiking and public transport

This book concentrates on these forms of transport so there is information in each chapter as well as in Chapter 4. In many countries the dividing line between hitchhiking and public transport is blurred, since when traffic is scarce you wave down any oncoming vehicle (which is likely already to be loaded with passengers) and expect to pay for the ride.

Motorbike or mountain bicycle

More and more people are choosing to travel through Africa by bike. Very few report any trouble, almost all had a wonderful time. *Through Africa* has practical details and anecdotes for both sorts of bikers. If you want to do a motor-bike trip in Africa contact the world expert, Bernd Tesch in Germany (he speaks English). Tel: 0241 33636; fax: 0241 39494.

Documents

Since most countries described here are members of the Commonwealth, British travellers will seldom have to worry about visas. Other nationalities will need to get theirs before leaving home or – better when on a long trip – from the appropriate embassy in a neighbouring country. Bring plenty of spare passport photos. Visa information is given under *Entry and exit* in each country's chapter.

Another document you are required to have, although you may never be asked to show it, is your international vaccination card.

You should have an international driving licence if there is any possibility that you will be renting or driving a car. This is also useful identification. Likewise a youth hostel membership card is not just valuable for YHA members but impresses quasi-officials who ask for an ID when you haven't got your passport on you.

Of course you'll need your passport; don't let it expire while you are travelling – it is easy enough to renew at embassies in Africa. A rubber band round the spine keeps all those currency declarations and other pieces of paper in place.

Money

The question foremost in anyone's mind when planning an overland trip through Africa is 'how much will it cost?' and it's one that's impossible to answer. So much depends on your interests, your needs, and your route. Certainly backpacking is the cheapest possible way of travelling, and when you're hiking in the countryside (outside national parks) you'll often spend nothing at all. On the other hand read the section on climbing Mount Kilimanjaro if you think all mountain walking is cheap! The problem with long distance hikes is that you return to civilisation with a voracious appetite for good food and the comforts of life and a spell in a city can break down your self control altogether.

Your daily budget will also depend on which countries you plan to spend time in. Currency rates, inflation and other factors which make countries expensive or cheap are always changing, so it would not be helpful to name such countries here (although it looks as though Kenya and Zimbabwe will continue to be popular with budget travellers for some time to come). As a very rough guide, the most frugal traveller should budget US$15 a day for all expenses except airfares.

Money will have to be carried in travellers cheques and cash. For British travellers it may be best to have your travellers cheques in sterling and your cash in U.S. dollars (smaller and lower denomination paper money). However, many people find it easier to think in only one currency, in which case stick to dollars.

If you are visiting Tanzania and Uganda you must have some cash dollars (in Tanzania park fees and lodges must be paid for in hard currency, and in Uganda the better class hotels have the same requirement). Since there are quite a few forged $100 bills in circulation, these are not always accepted. The rate of exchange for high denomination bills is usually better than for small ones, but you need a good supply of the latter for convenience if you run out of currency a day or so before leaving a country. Almost anyone in Africa will accept dollar bills in lieu of his local currency.

When you order dollar travellers cheques make sure your bank gives you American Express ones. These really are immediately refundable if lost or stolen and you can use American Express mail services (see *Mail* in Chapter 4). Trying to get a refund for the lesser known brands can be incredibly frustrating.

Credit cards are quite widely accepted and should be carried (don't forget to make a note of the number and who to contact if they are stolen) as emergency money, even if you are on a low budget.

Bring your personal cheque book. Many British consulates will cash a cheque (if supported by a bank card) in emergencies.

Travellers on an open-ended schedule will need to make an arrangement with their bank to have money sent out if necessary. Banks do not have a good record of doing this speedily and efficiently, so get it properly organised beforehand. Find out the name of corresponding banks in key cities, check that you will be able to collect the money in dollars or pounds not local currency, and make sure you are told of all the possible problems.

What to bring

'What should I bring?' is another difficult question. The short answer is 'Whatever makes you happy', bearing in mind that too much luggage will make you unhappy. What follows is general advice; for specific information on choice of backpack, sleeping bag, mountain clothing, etc., see Chapter 3, *Hiking and Backpacking*.

Long before you start your trip it's a good idea to keep a large box handy and put into it anything you realise you can't live without. You can collect all those items you come across when looking for something else and you won't then spend hours looking for them when the time comes to pack. You'll also need to make lists as things occur to you, so should keep a notebook handy at all times.

Bring diversions to sweeten those endless delays. Scrabble, a pack of cards or a chess set are marvellous value for weight. The latter two have the great advantage of having no language or cultural barrier, so can be played with local people. An electronic chess set will be much admired. Don't take too many books – you can exchange them with other travellers or buy them on the way – and don't take big fat novels. Shorter ones can be kept on you at all times for that unexpected delay. When we were detained in Uganda during the Amin era we had only one book, so one read a page then tore it out and handed it to the other. It provided a nice alternative to looking down the muzzle of the machine gun that was pointing at us.

Clothing   You can tell how experienced an overland traveller is from the number of clothes he brings in proportion to his total luggage. Some old hands bring a change of clothing only, knowing that replacements are easily and cheaply bought throughout Africa. For instance, those colourful East African wrap-around garments, *khangas*, can be made up into western-style skirts or shirts by local tailors who do an excellent job very cheaply. Personally, I think the one change of clothes philosophy is going a bit far since they are so light. It's worth bringing several tee-shirts, for instance, because they take up little room and those with a slogan written on the front make suitable presents or barter goods. Loose cotton shirts are often more practical than tee-shirts, however, because they protect you from the sun and insects and are cool. Bear in mind the dangers of sunburn around the neck; a collar privides good protection.

Trousers should be made from cotton or cotton-mix material and have deep, properly secured pockets (you can add these yourself). Rohan Bags are highly recommended because they dry so quickly and have plenty of zipped pockets including hidden ones on the hips. Phone 0908 216655 (UK). Jeans are not suitable; they're heavy, hard to wash and take ages to dry. Two pairs of slacks, one tough for hiking and one thin for hot weather, are far more practical. Men may wear shorts in many parts of Africa (the British Colonial heritage) providing they are not too short. Women will be cool and comfortable in a skirt, which will be essential in Malawi where they may not wear slacks. Add pockets if necessary. Women can bring shorts for out of the way places but do not cause offence by wearing them in towns, especially in Muslim areas. The same applies to scanty tops that expose the shoulders, or – worse – obviously bra-less breasts. A comfortable and modest alternative to shorts are culottes. If you bring cycle-clips you can keep them off dubiously damp toilet floors!

Give some thought to those chilly evenings and cold nights that you'll experience at high altitudes; not just on mountain tops, but in some towns. Nairobi, for instance, is at l,676 metres above sea level. You will probably find two wool sweaters (one thin and one thick) and a light nylon anorak (nylon shell) are more practical than a jacket. See Chapter 3 for how to keep warm at really high altitudes.

At any time of year you should bring rain gear, and during the rainy season a small umbrella is most useful.

For foot-wear many travellers wear rubber thongs (flip-flops) but they have their disadvantages: it's easy to stub your toe, your heels tend to dry out and crack, and they get sucked off if you walk in mud or water. Sports shops now sell good alternatives with rubber soles and nylon straps which secure the sandal properly to the feet. A worthwhile investment, especially for snorkellers. You can manage with just sandals and your hiking boots (footwear adds a lot of weight to your pack) but may want to bring trainers (running shoes) as well.

Don't forget your swimsuit and a small towel, and if you plan to spend much time on the coast you might want to bring a mask and snorkel for all those coral reefs, although they can often be hired.

A hat is essential, a cotton one being more practical than straw, and you'll need a bandana, or similar, to keep the dust out of your hair and the sun off your neck.

Warning Do not bring anything resembling military clothing, even to countries with no recent wars or disturbances. However trendy it may look at home, there are few advantages in being mistaken for a soldier or mercenary in Africa.

Presents In the first two editions of this book I recommended bringing 'presents for the locals' and – worse – 'sweets for the children'. I cringe when I read this. You will only have to be spend a few hours in a heavily touristed part of Africa to see the damage that tourists have done through indiscriminately giving out trinkets and sweets to kids. See *Exploits and exploitation* in Chapter 4 for more on the subject.

However, there will be times when you want to reward a particular kindness with a gift, or have to get yourself out of a tight spot with a 'gift' (often more appropriate than a bribe of money). Suitable offerings are beauty products, penknives, fish hooks, pocket calculators and other high-tech items. For children, rather than bringing sweets and balloons and doing nothing useful for them or their culture, bring a knowledge of cat's cradles, or origami, or a ball or a frisbee (which also doubles as a plate – very useful!). A small sketchbook and coloured pens can provide you with a far more rewarding record of Africa than photographs. If you stay in a village for a while ask the kids to draw their house or family or whatever for you. You can give them some photos from home in return; a good opportunity to clear out your photo drawer.

Other useful items A water filter, small torch (flashlight), with spare bulb and batteries, travel alarm clock, penknife (preferably Swiss Army type), tea-infuser, sewing kit, safety pins, large needles and strong thread for tent repairs, scissors, masking tape, Sellotape (Scotch tape), Magic Marker, pencils and ball-point pens, a small notebook for names and addresses, a large notebook for your diary and letters home.

Plastic bags, a plug for baths and sinks (the flat rubber sort that fits everything), clothesline and pegs, small scrubbing brush, shampoo, soap (in plastic dish, or better still, liquid soap), toilet roll, dental floss (excellent for doing running repairs as well as teeth).

Earplugs (a godsend in noisy hotels and on night buses), polaroid sunglasses, binoculars, spare glasses and contact lenses (note that very few Africans wear contact lenses – glasses are considered more fashionable – so you may find it difficult to buy saline solution, etc.).

Spare passport photos, pocket calculator, insect repellent, water purifying tablets, lipsalve and sunscreen.

An immersion heater (one of those gizmos that heats water in a cup to allow a brew-up in your hotel room can be very useful. Make sure it is fitted with a universal plug).

If you fish and are visiting Southern Africa bring your tackle. There is some excellent trout fishing in many of the rivers.

It's very useful to pack an extra bag – one of those lightweight nylon ones with a zipper is ideal – since invariably you end your trip with more luggage than you started with, and you can leave things locked in this bag in your hotel while you're backpacking.

A mosquito net is strongly recommended to avoid malaria. See under this heading in the Health chapter.

Medical kit   Don't bring too much – you can buy over-the-counter medicines in most places in Africa. A basic kit might include: antiseptic cream, butterfly closures for wounds that will later need stitching, gauze pads, small bandage, sticky plaster (band-aids) – the most practical comes in a roll rather than individual strips – vaseline (for cracked heels), 'moleskin' (for blisters), foot powder (for athlete's foot), aspirins, powerful pain killers such as Percogesic, diarrhoea medicine, decongestant, tetracycline, Ampicillin, topical anaesthetic cream (for stings), travel sickness pills.

A medical friend in South Africa, where wilderness hiking is popular, says the most essential item in her first aid kit are panty-liners. They make perfect dressings, being sterile, absorbent yet waterproof and are secured in place with a small bandage.

Photography

Photography pointers

Keep in mind that it is impossible to compress views of immense mountains and vast valleys into a small picture. Better to keep to details and record your overall impressions in a day-to-day diary. The combination of photos and diary is very satisfying.

The new compact autofocus cameras are ideal for backpacking, but for good wildlife photography you need a 200mm telephoto lens, which tends to be heavy. The standard 50mm lens that comes with most cameras is only moderately useful, its angle being too narrow for views and too wide for details.

Learn when to take photos. Avoid the mid-day sun, when there are few shadows and the light is flat. Early morning and evening shots are best, and the light is marvellous in the rainy season when the air is washed clean of dust particles. Clouds enhance a photo and some shadow lets the sun spotlight details in an otherwise rather featureless landscape.

When staying with villagers who don't mind the camera (many love it!) try using very fast film indoors using available light. ASA 400 can be pushed to 1600 ASA (make a note to tell the developing laboratory) to give a beautiful Rembrandt-like quality to faces.

African people are marvellously photogenic, but you should only take pictures with their permission. Muslims usually object, as do some tribal groups who have a superstitious fear of the camera, or – more likely – have learned that posing for photos can earn them big money. It is really more sensible to concede to their demands and pay once for a set of fine photos, than to try to sneak pictures with the danger of having stones thrown at you. Try not to introduce the concept of money-for-photos when it is not really expected. Greet the person, try to exchange a few words or interact in some way before producing your camera. If you promise to send a print of the photo you *must* keep that promise.

A good way of getting really natural, laughing photos is to give the local person your camera and have him or her take a photo for you. This is lots of fun for everyone concerned and works beautifully with big families, and if some of the subjects come out headless or crooked – well, so what?

Warnings　You should be very careful where you take pictures. Many African governments are quite paranoid about espionage and a perfectly innocent landscape may turn out to have military connections (see *Arrest* in Chapter 2). Don't take photographs at airports or near borders, and when you enter a country check with the border officials whether there are any restrictions on photography.

I never worry about airport X-ray machines and have never had a film damaged. Perhaps I've just been lucky.

Slide film is unavailable or very expensive in many African countries. Bring enough with you.

A radical suggestion

Why not leave your camera at home? Think of the advantages! You are no longer the focus for thieves, no more a walking logo for a tourist, never fussing with lenses and exposures while some amazing scene or animal passes by unnoticed. Imagine seeing Africa through your own eyes instead of through a view-finder! Think of relating to local people as fellow human beings rather than as paper or celluloid portraits!

Seriously, very few travellers have the equipment and expertise to take truly satisfactory photographs in Africa. The problem is we have become used to such a high standard from professionals that your wildlife photos will seem disappointing, the people (who are paid to pose) less exciting than the same face and costume on a thousand postcards, and few landscape photos will capture the feeling of space. Like any addiction, it takes will-power and courage to give up photography, but is well worth the effort!

Maps and guides

Don't expect to find specialist books and maps in your local bookshop. Unless you know exactly what you are looking for, go to one of the shops that specialises in travel. In London the best are: Edward Stanford Ltd, 12-14 Long Acre, London WC2 9LP (Tel: 071 836 1321); The Travel Bookshop, 13 Blenheim Crescent, London W11 2EE (Tel: 071 229 5260); The Traveller's Bookshop, 25 Cecil Court, London WC2N 4EZ (Tel: 071 8369132); Daunt Books, 83 Marylebone High Street, London W1M 4DE (Tel: 071 224 2295).

These shops have not only an excellent selection of guide books and maps, but knowledgeable sales staff and, for those who can't come in and browse, a catalogue of books and maps available for each continent (or region). Stanfords has the widest range of maps, Daunts a good selection of guides and travel literature in ideal browsing conditions, and The Travel Bookshop and Traveller's Bookshop sell out-of-print and second hand travel books (literature) as well as guides.

The obvious destination in London is the Africa Book Centre, 38 King Street, Covent Garden, London WC2E 8JT (Tel: 071 240 6649). They sell everything on Africa: travel, art, music...

In the US there is an excellent selection of hiking and travel guides available mail-order from The Backcountry Bookstore, PO Box 6235, Lynnwood, WA 98036-0235; Tel: (206) 290 7652; fax: (206) 290 9461.

Specific maps and guides are listed in each chapter, but here are some suggestions:

Maps

The evergreen favourites, and still probably the best general maps of Africa, are the Michelin series, scale 1:4,000,000. Sheet 955 covers the countries in this book.

For East Africa, there is the choice of four maps published by Bartholomew, Freytag and Berndt, Hildebrand, and TBLC, with scales varying from 1:2,000,000 (TBLC and Freytag and Berndt) to 1:7,000,000 (Hildebrand).

Central and Southern Africa is covered by Bartholomew's 1:5,000,000, and Southern Africa specifically by the 1:2,750,000 maps from Map Studio, and the South Africa Survey map scale 1:2,500,000.

Guides

There is now a good selection of guide books on specific countries in Africa which give more detailed information on accommodation, transport, etc than is possible in this book. I think the 17 Bradt guides are the best, but then I would say that, wouldn't I? You will have to decide for yourself, but go to page 331 for a complete list before visiting the bookshop.

"*So geographers, in Afric-maps,*
With savage pictures fill their gaps;
And o'er unhabitable downs
Place elephants for want of towns."

Jonathan Swift, 1667-1745

Chapter 2

Health and Safety

HEALTH

By (mainly) Dr David Snashall and Dr Richard Dawood, updated by Dr Jane Wilson.

Most of the countries described in this book have good private health clinics and hospitals, and of course the doctors are all experienced in recognising tropical illnesses. So don't become obsessed with your health. Enjoy yourself and take note of the following advice.

Before you go

Take out medical insurance. In addition to the standard coverage it's worth becoming a member of the Flying Doctors' Society of Africa. Your membership helps the society bring medical help to rural Africans, and, for a remarkably low premium, provides you with free air transport should you become sick or injured in remote areas of East Africa. You can join the society in Nairobi by contacting the African Medical & Research Foundation, PO Box 30125, Nairobi, Tel: 501301, Fax 502699. In the UK you can join in advance by contacting AMREF at 11 Waterloo St, Clifton, Bristol BS8 4BT, Tel: 0272 238424; in the US contact Flying Doctors' Society, PO Box 50756, Montecito, CA 93150.

Have a dental check-up — few things are more miserable than toothache when you are days from the nearest dentist. Take some temporary fillings.

Bring a good supply of any medication you need to take regularly. This includes contraceptive pills and condoms which are not always easily available.

Inoculations

There are two reasons for being properly inoculated. The first is to comply with international health regulations but the only jab in this category is against yellow fever. You need this for West, Central and East Africa but it may be insisted upon in North or South African airports if you have made even a brief stop-over in a country where the disease exists. It is obtainable at special centres only and is valid for 10 years. For travel to Africa you also need to be inoculated against meningitis. If you have not travelled abroad before you need to start organising immunisations at least six weeks before travelling.

A new vaccination against Hepatitis A, Havrix, is now available in the UK and is effective against this debilitating disease for ten years. More easily obtainable, but giving less overall protection, is Gammaglobulin.

If you intend travelling far from medical facilities, consider being immunised against rabies (see page 23). An effective vaccination is now available.

Although your GP can give travel inoculations there are several vaccination centres which specialise in this service. Their information is up to date and many also sell travel goods such as mosquito nets and dental first aid kits. British Airways run such clinics all over the country; phone 071 831 5333 for your nearest one. The Medical Advisory Service for Travellers Abroad (MASTA) is also an efficient source of information and can supply a written health brief. Phone the Traveller's Health Line on 0891 224100, or the Tropical Diseases Health Line on 0839 337733. For details of London vaccination centres see page 17. All these centres charge for their services, usually per inoculation.

Americans can get tropical health advice from the International Association for Medical Assistance to Travellers (IAMAT). Members receive a World Immunisation Chart and a list of recommended doctors all over the world. Their address is 417 Center St, Lewiston, NY 14092-3633. The Centers for Disease Control put out an annual booklet *Health Information for International Travel*; it can be obtained from the US Government Printing Office in Washington DC. Information is also available from their Atlanta office, phone (404) 332 4555. Herchmer Medical Consultants will prepare a personal pre-trip information pack giving the very latest requirements – but don't leave it too late before ordering it since some inoculations will need to be started several weeks before you leave. Phone 800 336 8334.

Malaria prevention

Malaria kills about a million people a year. You are 100 times more likely to catch malaria in Africa than in Asia (92% of cases imported into Britain are from Africa), and the situation is getting worse as the malaria parasite becomes resistant to drugs. You should therefore take every possible precaution against getting bitten by mosquitoes, as well as being meticulous in taking the course of prophylactic tablets. These should be started a week before reaching the malarial area and continued for six weeks after leaving it.

The situation regarding which tablets to take is constantly changing; it's best to phone the Malaria Reference Laboratory in London (0891 600 350) for recorded information specific to Africa (in the USA IAMAT can give you the same information). At the time of writing proguanil (Paludrine) daily and chloroquine (Nivaquine) weekly are being recommended. As an alternative the drug Mefloquine (Lariam) is now available in Britain on private prescription only. One tablet is taken weekly, so it is more convenient but it can only be taken short term and some side-effects have been reported and it is expensive.

Know your enemy: the female *Anopheles* mosquito is the only carrier of malaria (the male of the species does not suck blood but leads a blameless life sipping nectar). She emerges at dusk and tends to seek her prey at ground level. Bare ankles are thus particularly vulnerable. *Anopheles* mosquitoes can be recognised by the way they rest with their tail in the air.

Avoid being bitten by wearing ankle bands soaked in DEET (the strongest repellent) – you can make these yourself or MASTA sell them – and covering other areas of bare skin or thin clothes with repellent. Mosquito coils (available everywhere in Africa) are effective inside and outside. If enjoying a romantic sunset, burn one between your feet to deter the ankle-piercers. Remember that light attracts insects, including mosquitoes, so avoid leaving a light on in a badly-screened room. Most important, sleep under a mosquito net. It is better to bring your own than rely on the holey ones provided by some hotels. A good mosquito net should be self-supporting; most manufacturers assume there is something to suspend them from but this is not always the case. The best in my experience is made by Long Road in the USA (see advert on page 122). This 'indoor travel tent' is completely enclosed so keeps out not only mosquitoes but also bed-bugs and other nocturnal visitors.

If, despite taking the tablets, you develop the symptoms of malaria (headache, shivering, fever, joint pains) seek medical help straight away. You should get advice on *treatment* of malaria when you get your preventative pills, in case medical help is not available.

It is quite possible to develop malaria after returning home from Africa, in fact nearly 2,000 people do so every year in the UK. There are cases of people developing malaria several months after their return, so always keep this possibility in mind if you develop the symptoms long after you get home. Most – but not all – cases of malaria occur because people did not keep to a proper tablet-taking regime and poor tablet taking is no better than no tablet taking.

[Note: I was told by a manufacturer of mosquito nets, who certainly ought to know better, that malaria can easily be avoided by 'a healthy diet' and that chemicals are more dangerous. This is palpable nonsense, and it is worth emphasising that malaria is caused by a parasite (*Plasmodium*) which doesn't give a damn about what you eat, only what *it* eats, and that is you. H.B.]

Inoculation centres and useful addresses

British Airways Medical Department, 75, Regent St, London W.1. Tel: 071 439 9584. Hours 8.30 to 16.00. Best to book an appointment (without an appointment the waiting time is about an hour).

Thomas Cook Vaccination Centre, 45 Berkeley Square, London W.1. Tel: 071 499 4000.

Trailfinders Immunisation Centre, 42-48 Earls Court Rd, London W8 6EJ. Open 10.00 to 13.00, 13.30 to 16.30, Mon to Fri. Reduced fee for Trailfinders clients.

AIDS and Hepatitis B prevention kits (sterile needles, syringes, etc.) are available from MASTA and from SAFA, 59 Hill St, Liverpool, L8 5SA. Tel: 051 708 0397.

AIDS

AIDS, variously known as "Slim disease" or *ukimwi*, has had a devastating effect on Africa. Since it hits the sexually active at the peak of their working lives, it is leaving a disproportionate number of helpless dependents: the very old and the very young. Beside the harrowing human consequences of this epidemic, it is having a serious effect on the economies of the countries most affected.

Many Africans believe that AIDS reached their continent from America (just as many Americans believe the disease came from Africa). The devout in both continents wonder if it is the Wrath of God. Many African men are promiscuous by Western standards and there seems little likelihood that they will change their behaviour, apart from seeking out virgins because they will be "clean". Prevention of AIDS seems impossible here. Africa must wait for a cure.

Celibate tourists run little risk of contracting AIDS in Africa. Mosquitoes do not transmit the disease (proved, among other things, by the fact that children get bitten by mosquitoes but do not develop AIDS) nor do leeches (which spend several months digesting their meal of blood). There is some danger from contaminated instruments (so avoid going to the dentist, ear piercing and tatooing or having other invasive medical treatment, and bring your own needles). The bigger risk is a severe road accident needing a blood transfusion. Most blood is now routinely screened, but in the event of a serious accident your friends will need to be fairly forceful to ensure your wishes are adhered to in the bustle of a busy African casualty department. If you are travelling alone you will have to trust to luck.

For an excellent Africa travel book with an AIDS theme, read *The Ukimwi Road* by Dervla Murphy (John Murray).

Dr Jane Wilson adds:-

Some progress is being made in producing viricidal pessaries which women can use to protect themselves (condoms being unpopular amongst men) and this does offer some hope for control of the disease. Spermicidal creams and pessaries available in the UK are effective against AIDS but in women who are 'used' a great deal by men these can cause ulceration which promotes HIV transmission.

When you arrive

Heat problems

People flying into Nairobi will have no problems with the heat in this high, cool capital but in low-lying areas of tropical Africa you'll find the extreme heat and humidity quite tiring at first. Loose fitting 100% cotton clothes are ideal and a wide-brimmed hat will keep the hot sun off your face and back of the neck. Light colours are cooler than dark. Drink plenty of water and not too much alcohol. It's also wise to avoid extreme exertion early on as this can lead to heatstroke. Take plenty of tepid showers – this and the avoidance of tight clothing will protect against prickly heat which is the itchiest rash you're ever likely to experience and is caused by allowing your skin to become saturated in sweat. If you do get it, the best cure is an air-conditioned hotel.

Sunburn can be avoided by using a good sun-screen – factor 15 to begin with. Remember that sunburn may lead to skin cancer and certainly prematurely ages the skin, so avoid sunbathing, and never sunbathe in the middle of the day (in equatorial countries this is from about 10am to 2pm).

Travellers' diarrhoea

Few travellers escape this one, so be prepared for it. The cause is an infection of the bowel with germs to which you are not accustomed. As time goes by your system gets used to these germs and you tend to suffer less.

The condition comes on rather suddenly and consists of violent diarrhoea, stomach cramps, and sometimes bloating and nausea. It lasts from a few hours to a few days and can be very exhausting. Every traveller has his own story to tell on the subject. The basic treatment is rest and plenty of fluid to drink (not fruit juice, unless very diluted) with a pinch of salt or tea with sugar but no milk seem to be acceptable; so does coconut milk which has the advantage of being completely sterile (if drunk straight out of the shell). To avoid the dehydrating effects of severe diarrhoea it is sensible to make up and bring 'rehydration packs' of the type being used so successfully to treat babies and children in the developing world. These can now be bought commercially, but if you want to make your own the recipe is: three parts salt, two parts baking soda, one part potassium chloride, and 16 parts sugar or dextrose. Another simpler recipe, to be made *in situ* in Africa, is one teaspoon of salt to eight teaspoons of sugar in a litre of sterilised water (see below). If that is not possible, put a pinch of salt in any sweet drink (such as Coke). The secret is to drink a combination of salt and sugar, so add a little salt to sweet drinks or sugar to salty drinks. Drink a glassful after each bowel movement, but take in sips if you are feeling nauseous.

Most people make the mistake of not drinking enough. If you are not eating you need to drink three litres a day to compensate for fluids you normally absorb from food. If you have diarrhoea you need three litres *plus* all that you have lost via your bottom end. You need to drink at lot!

Only take blockers such as Imodium, Lomotil or Codeine Phosphate if you are likely to be stuck on a bus or in a similarly desperate situation. The abdominal pains associated with diarrhoea are caused by the bowel trying to expel bad food, and if the bacteria which cause these symptoms are deprived of food they will die out within 36 hours. Taking blockers tends to keep the poisons in your system so you will feel bad for longer. However, they are useful if the bowel cramps continue for more than 48 hours. If you pass blood with the diarrhoea, you may have dysentery and need to see a doctor. If that's not possible, take Ampicillin or Tetracycline tables, 250 mg every six hours for five days.

If the diarrhoea persists for more than a few days, try to seek medical advice or to get a stool specimen to a laboratory where they may be able to detect parasites, namely amoeba or giardia, which require specific treatment.

The germs which cause diarrhoea come to you from food or drink which have been contaminated by dirty food handlers, dirty water sources or dirty flies. Thus you should avoid food which has been left out for flies to walk on. It's important that all food is well cooked because cooking kills the germs. It is often safer to eat at roadside stalls where you can see the food well cooked on charcoal burners than in some hotels where food emerges lukewarm from kitchens you would rather not see. Do not eat salads, be very wary of shellfish and make sure you peel your own fruit.

Water may be safe in large cities because it is chlorinated, but outside such places it is wise to regard all water as contaminated either at source or during transportation.

Water can be sterilised in the following ways:

• Boiling. Bring the water to a rolling boil for a minute, then cool it. At high altitude, boil for five minutes.

• Filtering. There are several lightweight water filters on the market now. These are available from MASTA or from SafariQuip's mail order catalogue (Tel: 061 429 8700).

• Chemical sterilisation. This can be achieved by using chlorinating agents such as Puritabs or Sterotabs or even household bleach at a dose of three drops to one pint of water. Unfortunately, chlorine will not kill certain germs (those causing amoebic dysentery, for example) but iodine will – use one drop tincture of iodine to one pint of water or use iodine tablets.

Well known brands of fizzy drinks are usually safe unless you add ice to them, including carbonated mineral waters. It is not unknown for bottles of still water labelled with the names of French spas to be 'recycled' using tap or river water. Don't put ice in your drinks glass, put your glass on the ice.

Milk is not safe unless boiled or pasteurised and this applies equally to ice-cream, yoghurt and fresh cheese.

AIDS and Hepatitis B

As everyone knows by now, AIDS is rife in Africa where it affects women and men equally. There can be few readers who would consider having casual sex in Africa, but if you are one of the crazy few – bring condoms. That way you will also go some way towards avoiding Hepatitis B (not to be confused with the less-serious Hepatitis A or Infective Hepatatis) which is caught the same way as AIDS, and venereal disease.

Since AIDS is also spread through blood products, medical treatment could be a further hazard, but the health authorities in all countries are well aware of this and blood is screened and needles sterilised as a matter of course. If you are worried, bring a sterile needle kit and know your own blood group. It is *not* worth travelling with plasma or other intravenous fluids; most western embassies keep a register of blood donors who have been tested for AIDS.

See also Box on page 18.

Bilharzia or schistosomiasis

This disease is caused by worms which spend part of their life inside freshwater snails. It is widespread in Africa where it is picked up by swimming or even wading in slow moving or still water that is well oxygenated and well vegetated. This means most rivers and all lakes except Lakes Turkana and Malawi which are reputed to be free of bilharzia. The first symptom of infection is an itchy patch where the worm entered the skin, then perhaps a fortnight later, fever and malaise and, much later, blood in the urine or stools. It's a serious disease, and although easily cured if caught early, drug-resistance is emerging so it is sensible to avoid it. If you dry off promptly after spending ten minutes or less in the water, the parasite does not have sufficient time to penetrate your skin and so does not infect you.

Insects and arachnids

Apart from **mosquitoes** which are discussed in *Malaria* there are plenty of other tiresome or dangerous creepy-crawlies. When mosquitoes are around, especially between dusk and dawn, make sure your clothes cover as much of your body as possible. A can of knockdown mosquito killer is a satisfying weapon against any bug. The best repellents contain di-ethyl-toluamide (DEET). These repellents never last more than about four hours and are liable to dissolve your sunglasses. Burning pyrethrum coils repels mosquitoes and other insects.

Scratching mosquito bites is not a crime if you don't break the skin and introduce sepsis. But the more you scratch the more it itches.

Ordinary **houseflies** can drive you to distraction in Africa, and although they do not bite they spread disease. Devise and carry some sort of fly-whisk. Remember that an infected sore is a gourmet feast for flies. Their enthusiasm, plus the tropical heat can cause even a minor break of the skin to become infected and take ages to heal. Keep any cut or sore covered and disinfected. Antiseptic creams are not suitable since the wound needs to be kept dry; a dilute solution of potassium permanganate applied a minimum of twice daily is better, or iodine-based solutions. **Blackflies** and **sandflies** can be a severe nuisance especially near streams in mountain areas. They both carry disease.

In game parks you may come across **tsetse flies** which transmit sleeping-sickness. The fly is the size of a large, grey housefly, crosses its wings like a pair of scissors and tends to stick to the windows of moving vehicles. It gives a nasty sting but cases of sleeping-sickness in visitors to Africa are very few and far between.

Ticks are common in grasslands frequented by cattle and many transmit disease (tick-fever) to humans. They look like tiny spiders on your skin but once attached swell with your blood at an alarming rate. Do not pull them off but apply a lighted cigarette (tricky!) or paraffin and they will release their hold. The same goes for leeches, although salt works better with them. If you do not smoke or carry paraffin you can pull them off if you are very careful. Leaving any part of the beast behind will guarantee infection. The technique is to try to grasp the tick with finger and thumb as close as possible to the skin and pull steadily away from the skin. Do not twist or jerk.

In dry, sandy areas an annoying flea, the **jigger**, burrows imperceptibly into toes and remains there to enjoy its pregnancy and produce a lot of eggs. It grows to pea size. Hook it out with a sterile needle before the pea stage and treat the residual hole in your toe with antiseptic. These fleas can be picked up in the house, so don't go barefoot. Hookworm is also picked up by people who walk barefoot on soil contaminated by human excrement; the contamination need not be obvious however.

Another insect which can lay its eggs in your skin is the Tumbu or **Mango fly**. The adult deposits its eggs in clothes left to dry on the ground, so hang up your wet clothes in the sun.

Other more personal insects are often picked up by travellers; **fleas and lice** are common enough and so is **scabies**. Disinfect clothing or hair with 'gammexane' powder for lice and fleas and use benzyl benzoate emulsion all over your skin, except the face and head, for scabies. **Bed bugs** bite you in bed, make you bleed from the bites and smell horrible, so change your hotel or use an enclosed mosquito net. Cockroaches upset some people but are harmless, if filthy.

Spiders and **scorpions** sometimes sting but this is rarely serious. Medical aid should be sought if the bite area seems to be spreading.

Other animals

Some **fish** can cause severely painful stings. The best treatment is to immerse the area in very hot water (50°C).

Africa is home to a variety of **snakes**, some of them poisonous, but many visitors never see a snake let alone get attacked by one because they are elusive and timid creatures. All snakes are deaf and have poor vision; they mostly feed at night. When walking in snake country, wear boots and long trousers and proceed forcefully because snakes are very sensitive to vibration and will clear off the moment they feel you clumping through the bush. One of the most dangerous snakes is the puff adder – it is very sluggish and sometimes gets stepped on. Which it doesn't enjoy.

Snakebite is very rare and usually occurs when the snake is surprised or teased. If you are confronted with a snake, stand still and wait for it to go away or retire very slowly as quick movements alert the snake. [Good advice, but everyone I know who has been in that situation has shrieked and leapt a foot in the air. This seems to work just as well. H.B.]

Most snakes are non-venomous and in only about 50% of bites even by venomous snakes will any venom be dispensed. The chances are therefore if you do get bitten you will not come to any harm although very occasionally people have died of fright after being bitten by a non-venomous snake. The victim should keep still, the bitten part washed with clean water and soap and wiped gently with a clean cloth. This removes any venom from the skin surface. Since swelling is a feature of envenomation, it is wise to remove rings, watches, bangles, etc. The victim must then be prevented from moving the bitten limb preferably by splinting. This slows absorbtion of the venom and also reduces pain. The victim should then be taken promptly to a doctor or hospital (with the offending snake if it can be captured without risk of someone else being bitten). The victim will then be kept under observation so that if signs of envenomation begin, antivenin can be administered. Antivenin should not be given if there is no sign of the venom affecting the patient. Meanwhile: DO NOT give alcohol or aspirin but paracetamol is safe; DO NOT incise or suck the wound; DO NOT apply potassium permanganate; DO NOT panic – it is likely that no venom has been dispensed.

Scorpion stings are generally extremely painful but not dangerous to adults, and the same is true for large spiders and centipedes. Lethal species of scorpions do live in North Africa, Mexico and South India. All species can cause serious problems in infants and children and medical help should be sought in the case of children being stung.

Dogs carry **rabies**, and so do jackals, hyenas and other wild mammals including bats. Do not try to touch a suspiciously tame wild animal. If bitten by an animal suspected of having rabies, the wound should be washed very thoroughly with soap and plenty of water and the animal should (within reason) be captured and taken to a veterinary station for examination [It's hard to imagine complying with that standard advice. Can you imagine, 'Come here you cute little hyena, just climb into my rucksack and I'll take you to... let me see, are veterinary stations marked on the Michelin map?'. Actually, the domestic dog is by far the commonest culprit, and backpackers passing through villages are particularly vulnerable. Even so, the dog's owners are not going to take kindly to its capture, even if you manage to explain what you are up to, so heed the following advice from Jane Wilson. H.B.]

The immunisation against rabies is highly effective, but once symptoms show, rabies is incurable, and the way that you die is so very horrible that most doctors advise a post-exposure booster dose. If you have not been immunised and there is any possibility you have been exposed to a rabid animal (even a lick on broken skin is dangerous) you should get to a doctor as soon as you can. This should be organised promptly, but since the incubation period can be over a year, don't think that it's too late to get this done some weeks or even months after exposure. The incubation period is determined by the distance the bite is from the brain; if you are bitten on the face symptoms will appear in about ten days and you must seek medical help immediately. If the bite is on your hand you may have a month and if it is on your leg there is probably no need to disrupt your trip providing you get the injection as soon as possible. The message is, if you expect to travel extensively in remote areas or where the risk is known to be high, get immunised before you leave home.

Note: Animal bites also carry the serious risk of tetanus which kills in a few days if untreated, so ensure you are protected after being bitten even if you are not before.

Mountain health

In high mountains the main risk is Altitude (Mountain) Sickness (see box on page 24). Exhaustion also makes people more prone to accidents and to hypothermia. Trekkers, whose gear is carried by porters so inaccessible during the day, may be more at risk than backpackers who have the means for survival on their back. If you are trekking always carry warm, wind- and waterproof clothes in your daypack, and if you are backpacking resist the temptation to make it to your proposed destination if you are very tired and cold.

ALTITUDE SICKNESS

By Dr Jane Wilson.

Altitude sickness, or Mountain Sickness, is the principal danger to tourists in the high African mountains. There is less oxygen at altitude so people need to increase their breathing rate until other mechanisms have achieved some degree of acclimatisation.

Acute Mountain Sickness (AMS) is caused by a failure of the body's biochemistry to maintain the correct balance of acid and alkali which is normally controlled by carbon dioxide concentrations. It is carbon dioxide building up in the blood (not lack of oxygen) which stimulates any necessary increase in breathing rate, yet at altitude gas is more soluble so carbon dioxide takes longer to reach the concentration necessary to stimulate an increase in breathing rate.

Insufficient oxygen to the brain causes nausea and headache in the early stages of Mountain Sickness. If these danger signals are not heeded, mental confusion and ultimately loss of consciousness and death may follow. Lack of oxygen may also cause a build-up of fluid in the lungs and elsewhere, resulting in breathlessness and coughing up frothy or blood-stained sputum. This is a serious and quickly fatal condition. The only treatment is to descend to a lower altitude.

AMS is avoided by allowing plenty of time for acclimatisation and by ascending slowly, preferably not more than 300m per day. When slow ascent and proper acclimatisation is impractical, for example on Kilimanjaro, *acetazolamide* (Diamox) is an effective prophylaxis when used in conjunction with sensible ascent rates. (It is not possible to give a figure for a safe rate of ascent since people vary so much in their response to altitude but listen to your body.) In Britain it is available on (private) prescription. Take two 250mg tablets each morning for three days preceding the ascent and continue for two more days at altitude. It is also a treatment for AMS headaches. Side effects include tingling of the hands and feet and increased urination (it is a diuretic).

Young, fit people are more at risk from Mountain Sickness than middle-aged plodders because they are tempted to ascend too fast. But the condition is totally unpredictable. If you have suffered once you may be OK the next time, and if you escape the first time you may be affected later.

Since mental confusion is one of the symptoms of AMS (as well as hypothermia), it is up to other members of the party to make the decision to descend. The victim may argue that this is not necessary: an argument that could lead to his/her death.

"*Mountains should be climbed with as little effort as possible and without desire. The reality of your own nature should determine the speed. If you become restless, speed up. If you become winded, slow down. You climb the mountain in an equilibrium between restlessness and exhaustion. Then, when you're no longer thinking ahead, each footstep isn't just a means 8:(6 to an end but a unique event in itself ... To live only for some future goal is shallow. It's the sides of the moutain which sustain life, not the top*".

Robert M. Pirsig
Zen and the Art of Motorcyle Maintenance

SAFETY

Theft

Understandably, the very visible gulf between rich visitor and poor local has, in some countries, led to a variety of crimes directed at tourists.

Violent robbery is, sadly, on the increase and I can no longer say (as in the previous edition) 'You are unlikely to be harmed physically'. In areas where there are a large number of vulnerable tourists (Nairobi, beaches) mugging is common. You are generally safe in the countryside, and the basic rule is the remoter the area the safer you are from (human) attack. People have to learn to rob, and that education is lacking where there are few or no tourists to practise on.

The trick, when walking in a known dangerous place, is to be conspicuous in your lack of stealable items. If you have no camera, no watch, no bag, no bulging pockets, and an air of alertness about you, you will be pretty safe.

When staying in hotels, it is safer to leave money and valuables hidden in your room, rather than carry them on your person. I know numerous travellers who have been mugged or pick-pocketed, but very few who have had things pinched from a hotel room.

Items most likely to be stolen fall into two categories: those that can easily be sold, such as cameras, watches and passports (yes, there's a thriving market in stolen passports), and things the thief wants for himself, like penknives, clothes, food, and of course money. That doesn't leave much that you needn't protect, so follow these do's and don'ts.

• Do keep your valuables in a money belt, neck pouch, or secret pocket. I use a zippered bag, just big enough for my British passport, which can be fastened inside my slacks, round my leg, or deep within my pack. So far this has protected my valuables – which include my address book, plane ticket and anything else I'm particularly averse to losing. John Hatt, in his book *The Tropical Traveller* recommends Tubigrip to secure your valuables to your leg. Tubigrip is an elasticised tube bandage which comes in various sizes so you can experiment with the most comfortable and practical place to wear it. Bear in mind that to be seen with your hand deep inside the front of your trousers can be embarrassing.

• Do bring a combination lock (harder to pick than an ordinary padlock) to secure your hotel door or luggage. A chain is a useful and versatile addition.

• Do think of a way to protect your backpack. If you are creative, devise some sort of tough cover to protect it from being slit or the side pockets 'investigated' while it's out of sight on your back. Nylon mesh (which can be bought in gardening departments) is hard to cut and lightweight. Give the same thought to protecting your shoulder bag from the razor-slitters.

• Do select a hotel room which has bars on the window or one that can't be entered from a neighbouring room. Be wary of sharing a room with other travellers.

• Don't carry a handbag or any type of shoulder bag into known danger spots. That means markets, gatherings, crowded buses and trains. A leather bag is easily snatched or slit.

• Don't leave your money in your clothes when you go swimming, and try to have someone guard the clothes themselves.

• Don't camp in urban areas unless the campsite is well guarded.

• Don't resist armed robbers. It's better to lose your money than your life.

• Do keep identification (a photocopy of the first page of your passport plus driver's licence or similar) and a note of the numbers of your plane ticket, travellers cheques and credit cards separate from your valuables so that if they are lost you can more easily replace them.

• Don't become paranoid. As a backpacker in rural areas you will experience incredible honesty and generosity in the face of grinding poverty. It's a humbling experience.

Insurance

It's important to be well covered by insurance for medical expenses and loss of baggage. The premium will seem high if you're travelling for several months, but losing all your gear or being flown home with some nasty illness or injury is much more expensive. It's simply not worth the risk.

I buy comprehensive insurance from WEXAS (Tel: 071 589 3315) which I find very good value for under £100 for a year's travel. If you are doing a long trip there are other similar policies.

The travel agent of tour operator which sells you your air ticket will almost certainly offer insurance as well. Read the small print carefully.

Arrest

Arbitrary arrest is becoming a rarity in East and Southern Africa as the number of tourists increases. It makes me almost nostalgic for the Good Old Days in the 1970s when we were arrested three times during our Cape to Cairo journey. In retrospect each was avoidable. In Tanzania I was caught taking a sneak picture of a magnificent woman in a market, who I knew would object to being photographed. The charge should have been of violating her privacy, but it was photographing in an unauthorised area (in those days you were officially only allowed to take photos in game parks). The real reason was apparently suspected espionage, the market being not very far from an army barracks. Our film was confiscated and developed at the police station, where we waited three hours. Several officials examined selected 'blow ups' for incriminating evidence. We were released with the words 'You can go free', which we were to hear again in Kampala after our arrest as possible spies when we tried to visit a famous botanical garden. The trouble was the garden was in Entebbe, and this was July 1976, a few days after the Israeli raid to release airline hostages. It sounds unbelievably stupid to try to go there, but such was the abundance of censorship and the shortage of newsprint in Amin's time, we had only a hazy idea of what was going on. Our three hours on a disabled bus, guarded by a kid with a machine gun is not one I would like to repeat. Our final and most avoidable detention was in communist Ethiopia when we made the mistake of extolling the virtues of capitalism to an argumentative group of students. We didn't know the chap drinking beer at the next table was an army lieutenant. We felt lucky to get away with that one since, in contrast to the other two occasions, we were not innocent. In all three cases we were guilty of stupidity or ignorance.

As I said, times have changed, although North East Africa could still come up with some surprises, and that sort of incident is nowadays rare. That is not to say that many travellers do not deliberately break the law and end up paying the consequences. Their crimes vary from dealing on the black-market, carrying drugs, entering national parks without paying the fee... all unnecessary and unsociable in a foreign country where you are the visitor.

You can avoid arrest by finding out about and obeying the laws of the land, by being courteous to all officials, and by using your common sense.

If you are arrested (and have not committed a crime) the way you handle the situation will determine whether you are released in a few hours (as are the vast majority of travellers) or spend days or weeks in jail. There is nothing heroic about courting disaster by being abusive. Discretion is the better part of valour here, and this means patience, good humour, friendliness and truthfulness (assuming you have nothing to hide). You should also be firm without being arrogant, and insist on seeing a person in high authority if events seem to be turning nasty. It is sensible to stand up and shake hands with each new person who comes to speak with you; it indicates that you consider yourself a friendly equal. It's worth learning the names of key figures in the government. Nothing as obvious as 'I'm a personal friend of the president', but if you can say 'I went to school with Fifi N'bongo and I'm sure her father would be disappointed to hear about this,' you may secure your early release. Impressively headed notepaper (coats of arms score high) can also have a soothing effect, particulary if underneath they bear a glowing character reference and the request to 'grant the bearer all possible assistance'.

If things look really bleak remember you have the right to be put in touch with your embassy or consulate. But remembering that your rights may well be ignored will make you feel a lot bleaker.

Bribery

To bribe or not to bribe: that is the question in many travellers' minds. Some feel that it is immoral and imperialistic (it is) and therefore should never be used, others find that it smoothes the way so admirably you'd be crazy not to do it. I much prefer the former attitude – there's no doubt that the readiness of some visitors to pay bribes make it immeasurably more difficult for those that follow – but basically I think it depends on your personality. If you have an air of natural authority you can refuse to give the hinted-at bribe and will be doing a great service to other travellers and moral standards in general. But if you are by nature humble and subservient you'd probably better resign yourself to greasing palms and have done with it! In some countries, such as Zaïre, bribery is part and parcel of the travel experience and it's not worth fighting it. In any case approach the matter with subtlety. Often a 'present' is better than money.

War and revolution

Dramatic though these events may sound in the papers at home (the traveller's nearest and dearest usually suffer far more than he does), they present little danger providing you are sensible. Being sensible entails staying out of harm's way in a hotel and waiting the crisis out. Don't try to get to the airport – invariably flights will be cancelled, the border closed, or the roads will be jammed with people with the same idea. As a backpacker you are well equipped to stay well fed and comfortable in your room. One precaution you should take is to fill every available container with water, including the bath if you have one. Water supplies are often cut in a crisis and your dehydrated food won't then be much use. If there's a lot of shooting outside keep away from the window and draw the curtains to reduce the danger of being cut by flying glass.

Try to contact your embassy so they know who and where you are if things really get bad, but don't worry – tourists are almost never deliberately hurt in revolutions. The boredom of being stuck in a hotel room for a few days presents far greater problems!

Further reading

Travellers' Health by Dr Richard Dawood (O.U.P.). Frequently updated and comprehensive.
The Tropical Traveller by John Hatt (Penguin). Covers health and safety and a whole host of things besides. Meticulously researched and a marvellously informative and entertaining read. Invaluable for Africa backpackers.

"At last my experience in staring enabled me to categorize the infliction as follows. Firstly is the stare furtive, when the starer would peep and peer under the tent, and its reverse, the open stare. Thirdly, is the stare curious .... accompanied with irreverent laughter regarding our appearance ... and finally the stare cannibal, which apparently considered us as articles of diet".

Sir Richard Burton, 1857

Chapter 3

Backpacking and Trekking

Introduction

In its purest sense, backpacking means hiking in remote areas for several days at a time carrying all your requirements in your rucksack or backpack. Recently, however, the term has been used to describe independent overland travellers even if they are not prepared to be totally self-sufficient. This section is aimed at travellers who want to hike or climb in remote parts of Africa, either on their own or with an organised trekking group.

Backpacking in Africa – comparisons

The backpacking areas described in this book cover every type of terrain and trail, from expanses of semi-desert in the north of Kenya and Namibia to the ever-wet heavily vegetated 'Mountains of the Moon' on the Uganda/Zaïre border; from finding your own route in Lesotho to the well-maintained and hutted trails of Malawi and South Africa. In addition the 'new' countries of Sudan, Ethiopia and Eritrea offer some truly spectacular hiking, especially in Ethiopia.

Give some thought to the kind of hiking you are looking for. The overview in Chapter 1 of the regions covered in this book provides you with a summary of the topography and conditions you can expect, but here are some pointers relating to experience and fitness.

If you are not accustomed to backpacking, and are not particularly fit, you would do well to start with an area that has well-maintained huts and marked trails. Malawi and South Africa offer a perfect combination of excellent scenery, well-spaced huts and good trails. Backpacking here is very similar to using the well-established trails in North America or Europe, and the huts mean you don't have to carry so much.

For true backpacking, but still along easy trails and at a manageable altitude, try Zimbabwe. Here there are clear trails and good maps so there is little danger of getting lost.

When you are ready to strike out with a compass but not much else to guide you, there's Lesotho. The country is so small and the people so friendly that nothing bad is likely to happen to you, yet you have a wonderful feeling of adventure and freedom. Other countries offer this sort of open backpacking, but there is more possibility that you will run up against suspicion of your motives for tramping about in the middle of nowhere, so it is useful first to have gained some general experience of Africa travel.

The big mountains and massifs – Mt Kenya, Mt Elgon, Mt Kilimanjaro, the Ruwenzoris and the Simiens – are more challenging physically, with some trails which are easy to follow, and others which are a lot more serious. Because of the high altitude (much of the hiking is over 3,000m) and resulting freezing nights and danger of altitude sickness, you need to carry more (so you can keep warm and do it slowly) and be in good shape. Joining an organised trek with porters makes sense on these mountains. The toughest climb of all is in the Ruwenzoris; you must be prepared to be quite miserable some of the time here!

A different sort of tough hiking is found in Namibia. The Fish River Canyon is dramatic and different, hot, but not difficult.

Finally there is the combination of toughness and remoteness that make parts of northern Kenya the most challenging hikes mentioned in this book. By definition, such areas cannot be described in detail – you need a guide (of the human variety) plus strength and bush-sense. This can be the most exhilarating form of backpacking, but for an inexperienced or poorly equipped visitor to venture off the beaten path like this would be dangerous. For those prepared for it, the possibilities for wild walking in Africa are limitless.

Trekking

People join an organised trek for three reasons: they can only take a limited time off work so need to eliminate the delays that are inherent in independent travel; they do not wish to hike alone; they want to enjoy the climb without worrying about where to sleep, what to eat, and how to carry all that equipment. Trekking also enables climbers to take less usual, and often more scenic routes, with an experienced and trustworthy guide.

Many companies do treks in the mountains of East Africa, most centring their activities around Mt Kenya or Mt Kilimanjaro, but some have several other treks to choose from. Some of these companies have advertised in this book and most carry advertisements in the travel pages of national newspapers or specialist magazines.

Equipment and supplies

Serious hikers will need some additional items to those listed in *What to bring* in Chapter I. Most of these should be bought at a good outdoor equipment shop where the quality is reliable and salespeople knowledgeable. A list of such shops can be found at the back of walking magazines which always have a wealth of good information on outdoor equipment.

You can also shop mail order from catalogues: Safariquip (The Stones, Castleton, Derbyshire, S30 2WX, Tel: 0433 620320) are recommended since they cater specially for the tropical traveller, and Survival (Morland, Cumbria, CA10 3AZ) also have a good range.

Field and Trek provide the biggest range of competitively-priced outdoor equipment, combining catalogue sales with a chain of retail stores. They charge £1.95 for their 225 page catalogue which contains plenty of objective advice on choosing equipment. It is available from Unit 3, Wates Way, Brentwood, Essex, CM15 9TB, Tel: 0277 233122. Americans can get similar joy from REI (west coast) and EMS (east coast).

If you are starting your trip in South Africa and need to buy hiking equipment, think about buying it once you're there. Locally-made tents and sleeping bags are cheaper than equivalent models in the UK, and of comparable quality.

Good quality clothing and equipment is expensive but can often be bought second-hand. Try the Classified section of outdoor magazines. Resourcefulness is an alternative to money. We enjoyed a wonderful year of travel and backpacking in Africa with a home-made tent, second-hand backpacks and hand-made boots.

Clothes   For mountain climbing and hiking (especially in the southern winter or rainy seasons) you'll need a few extra clothes in addition to the wind-proof nylon anorak mentioned in Chapter 1. There are some very good sweaters made from synthetic fleece or pile, sometimes with a nylon (such as Pertex) layer attached. These are usually warmer, lighter and more versatile than wool. For the really cold days, or for sleeping, a down vest (body warmer) is excellent. It packs into a very small stuff-bag and will keep you cosy in freezing weather without hampering arm movements. Down is useless if it gets wet, however, so if you're planning to hike in very wet high areas (such as the Ruwenzoris), artificial filler may be more suitable. For heavy rain (likely at any time of year on the high mountains) you'll also need a good rain jacket, preferably made from a 'breathable' fabric which doesn't trap your perspiration. The Paramo range, made by Nikwax, is blissfully comfortable and keeps you warm as well as dry. Waterproof overtrousers are useful, and a rain poncho is versatile and keeps your pack dry.

Remember that in high mountains it can be hot, cold, dry and wet in the same couple of hours, so for extensive hiking choose clothing made from a combination of pile and Pertex which dries quickly, keeps you comfortable and is hard wearing.

The only additional warm clothing you'll need is a wool ski-hat, gloves, and thermal underwear for very cold nights.

Backpack   These days most backpacks have an internal frame and the leading manufacturers – Berghaus, Karrimor and Lowe – use highly sophisticated designs to ensure maximum comfort when carrying a heavy load. These tend to be very expensive, however, so the cheap, old-fashioned packs with an external, aluminium frame still have their devotees. Apart from the price advantage they allow air to circulate around your back so are much cooler. The frames are easily broken and cause problems on public transport, and they are not suitable for hiking in jungle where vegetation catches on the projecting parts of the frame.

The vital part of a good backpack is the padded hip-belt which distributes the weight between your shoulders and hips.

Look for a pack with double zippers which can be secured with a mini-padlock.

In addition to your main backpack you will need a small day-pack for short hikes or outings.

Sleeping bag   If you're expecting a lot of rain it would be best not to buy a down bag, although down is the lightest and warmest filler available. Some of the new artificial fillings are almost as light and compactable, and cheaper. A 'bivi-sac' cover will add a lot of warmth at high altitudes and can be left behind when you're hiking in lower areas.

A sheet sleeping bag is all you'll need in hot places and if used as a liner for your regular bag prevents it from becoming too grubby. YHA approved ones are fine, but you can easily make your own.

Mat   Some sort of insulation and protection from the cold hard ground is essential. Closed cell 'ensolite' foam pads are the most efficient, providing perfect insulation and tolerable padding even when less than a centimetre thick. They are bulky, however. I'm a devotee of Therm-a-Rest, a combination of air mattress and foam pad, which is lightweight, compact and comfortable. One problem inherent with Therm-a-Rest – sliding off the slippery surface when camped on sloping ground – has been partially solved with spray-on Slipfix which provides a non-slip coating for the mat.

An inflatable pillow is a useful addition, more as bum-joy on long, bumpy truck rides than to use at night when a sweater stuffed into a tee-shirt provides more comfort.

Tent and mosquito net   You'll need some sort of tent if you're doing any wilderness hikes, but note that many popular hikes and climbs in this book are in national parks where there are huts to sleep in. However, these are often in such poor condition that a tent is preferable anyway. What sort of tent depends on whether you are travelling alone or with a companion. If going solo, you will probably do better with the combination of self-standing mosquito net (see page 17), tarpaulin, and bivi bag. These will keep you comfortable in all conditions, and the item not needed for any one hike can be left in storage.

If there are two of you or you are planning to camp rather than use hotels, you will need a tent if only for privacy. Choose with care. Most tents are made of permeable nylon which allows moisture to escape, and have a separate waterproof fly. If you're travelling alone, weight will be the most important factor, but two people can pay attention to the various shapes on the market. The conventional ridge tent is usually the cheapest design, but tends to be cramped inside. Dome-shaped tents and tubular designs are more roomy and pricey. Whatever you choose, make sure it is easy to erect and well-ventilated. The ideal tent will be self-standing, with enough ventilation to use in hotels as a mosquito net and enough protection from the elements to use on the high mountains. It is worth spending a bit of money on the right product.

It is sensible to sew a ring onto the bottom of the tent so the zip can be locked closed with a mini-padlock. This deters both casual thieves and baboons.

Boots   Good ankle support and shock absorption are important here, as are solid rubber soles such as Vibram. New boot designs are appearing on the market all the time. Gore-Tex boots which are very light yet tough, and can 'breathe', and the soft boots, developed along the same lines as running shoes are very comfortable and popular – and cheaper than leather. They have the advantage of not needing to be broken in. In wet areas such as the Ruwenzoris, you will need leather boots, along with waterproofing/conditioner such as Nikwax.

Stove   Firewood is only occasionally available, so you'll need a stove. Since fuel availability varies, the most suitable is one that burns a variety of fuels and the most popular of these are manufactured by Mountain Safety Research (MSR) of Seattle, USA, and available in Britain. The X-GK stove burns the following (US and French names in parentheses): paraffin (kerosene, petrole), stove alcohol/Coleman fuel (white gas, petrole a bruler), petrol (gasoline, essence) and diesel. It weighs less than a kilogram, but the Whisper-lite (same company) is only half a kilo (but does not burn petrol/diesel).

The cleanest, easiest stove is the Bleuet 200 Camping Gaz, which operates off cartridges, but you may not carry them on aeroplanes, and you cannot always be sure to find the cartridges, although they are available in Nairobi.

Pots and pans   There's no need to spend a fortune buying special backpacker's lightweight saucepans. Perfectly suitable aluminium ones are sold throughout Africa.

Plastic plates and cups are better than metal – your food and drink stays hot longer. Bowls are more versatile than plates, and a frisbee is the most versatile plate of all (lots of fun in those high mountain meadows when you're not eating out of it).

A backpacker grill, which can be used with a campfire, is marvellous for cooking fish you may have caught or bought, and for an occasional meat treat.

Water containers   In addition to a canteen or litre water bottle, if there are two of you it's a good idea to have a soft plastic water container that will hold 4 litres (or a gallon). This not only provides a good supply of water at your campsite but ensures that you won't go thirsty during those long hot rides in open trucks or buses with a tendency to break down.

A water filter is an excellent precaution against waterborne disease and more effective (and less nasty-tasting) than water purifying tablets, but it's also heavier than tablets and takes more attention and time. Boiling your water is more effective and easier.

Light   In equatorial countries the nights are long, so bring a candle-holder (you can easily make one from a clear plastic bottle and some wire) that shields the wind. Candles, of course, can be bought anywhere, but slow-burning candles (available from outdoor stores) are very useful. Instead of a hand-held torch, try a headlamp. This will free your hands and is ideal for cave exploring or pre-dawn starts.

Other items   Waterproof matches, seam sealant for leaky tents, compass, whistle, nylon straps and strong cord. Lots of plastic bags and large bin liners (garbage bags) to cover your pack at night and in open trucks. A collapsible plastic bucket has endless uses, and a backpacker's trowel ensures a clean campsite. Plastic screw-top containers and tubes can be bought in camping shops and are useful for carrying honey, Marmite, margarine, or what you will.

Hiring equipment in Kenya   If you are hiking in Kenya, northern Tanzania or Uganda and don't have all the gear you need, Atul's Shop on Biashara St in Nairobi has a good selection of camping and safari equipment for hire. They are mainly a fabric shop (and can also make clothes to order), but are known for their efficiency and helpfulness. Other places in Nairobi selling and hiring climbing and hiking gear include Bushbuck Adventures and the Natural Action Mountain Centre (details in the Kenya chapter).

Choosing the menu

Some people (myself included) eat less than usual on the trail. I used to think that it's because your stomach is compressed when you're sitting on the ground or the effects of altitude, but now I do more trekking than backpacking I think it's psychological. Your stomach responds sympathetically to the thought of carrying all that weight and makes fewer demands. You'll probably find that dried soup padded out with extra dried vegetables and noodles is adequate for the evening meal. Remember weight is the important factor, so noodles are better than rice which is heavy and takes longer to cook so uses up more fuel. Dried food can be bought in all countries and package soups are usually available. Kenya and Malawi have all sorts of dehydrated goodies; peas, potatoes, milk, Vesta dried meals and so forth. You can buy these in supermarkets or even in general grocery stores.

Knowing that you can buy noodles in Africa, you can hedge your bets by bringing some spicy sauces from home. The package variety weigh very little and will ensure some tasty meals. I'm a devotee of Marmite and wouldn't dream of travelling without it (in a plastic tube, not the heavy glass jar). Australian travellers can be recognised by their jars of Vegemite.

Hot chocolate, tea or coffee rounds the meal off well. If you dislike the taste of dried milk in coffee, have tea with lemon instead; locally grown tea is often available. A tea infuser is more useful than tea bags.

The day should begin with a good breakfast, whatever your habits at home. Porridge is ideal, being readily available, quick to cook and lightweight. You can add raisins, cinnamon, brown sugar or honey to vary the flavour.

Lunches should not be elaborate. Bring bread and crackers to eat with cheese (when available), and tinned sardines or other snacks (sometimes you have to break the 'no tins' rule). It's nice to end with something sweet like honey or cookies.

Purify your drinking water unless you're quite sure it comes from an uncontaminated source. Powdered drinks make treated water much more palatable.

Bring trail snacks such as nuts, raisins, chocolate and so on. They give you energy and an excuse to sit down and rest for a while. Fruit should be carried as a refreshing snack when water is in short supply, but otherwise it is too heavy. Sometimes you can buy it along the trail.

On arduous hikes you'll find your body craves sugar so take twice as much as you think you'll need.

Pack enough food for the number of days you think you'll be hiking plus two extra, just in case.

Minimum impact

If your camping has hitherto been limited to organised campsites with flush toilets and hot showers, you may not know how much damage wilderness camping can do to the environment. Here are some basic rules:

- Avoid contaminating the water supply. Washing should be done downstream, using biodegradable soap (liquid soap sold in small plastic tubes is ideal).

- Do not build a campfire on grass. Find a bare patch which can then be returned to its previous state before you leave.

- When you need to defaecate, go well away from the trail, campsite and water, and dig a hole. If you have room for a backpacker's trowel (they are small and light) that's ideal for the purpose, otherwise use a stick or remove a large stone. Burn the paper.

- Dispose of rubbish properly. Not only does litter spoil the enjoyment of the people who follow you, but it is potentially harmful to wildlife. Paper should be burned (carefully – don't start a bush fire) and foil wrappers and tin cans should be carried out with you. Some people bury tins, but they are often dug up by animals attracted to the smell. Where campsites are littered when you arrive, you can be noble and clear up. In this situation it may just be a case of hiding the rubbish in the bushes and burning the paper. Carry extra plastic bags for collecting rubbish.

SAFARI TOURISM IN KENYA — GOOD OR BAD?

By Cindy Morey.

On Safari:

When tourists on safari drive their own vehicles or allow their tour guide driver to go off-road so they can get closer to the animals, they destroy the terrain and interfere with the natural boundaries and movement of the wildlife. I witnessed many drivers making new roads which then causes erosion and kills plant life. On several occasions in the Maasai Mara I saw drivers and tourists following cheetahs too closely while they were on a hunt, cutting them off from their prey. In some cases they have separated mothers from their young, which are then either killed by larger predators or die of starvation. The same is true for any animal that provides a good photo opportunity. Tour guide drivers that are extremely knowledgeable about the wildlife and their natural habitat usually have more respect for the animals' boundaries.

Safari code:

- Do not allow your driver to go off-road to view the wildlife
- Do select a knowledgeable and reputable tour
- Do obey the park rules.

Local People:

Some Good News ...

Local people that live on the outskirts of the game parks are finally beginning to reap the rewards of tourist dollars. For example, in the Maasai Mara, a Community Conservation Program has been developed by Friends of Conservation to ensure that a percentage of the gate revenue will be shared with the local people. These dollars help to build schools, provide medical care, and other needs. In return, the local people are becoming more involved with park management, making souvenirs for sale at tourist lodges, and helping with wildlife protection. The people now have more incentive to protect their wildlife because they are benefitting by their well-being.

Friends of Conservation has a similar program in the Serengeti National park. They also provide excellent guide books for viewing birds and wildlife that are full of useful conservation ideas for tourists.

and some bad news ...

Some of the lodges in the game parks and many of the hotels along the coast have polluted the natural water systems and the sea by the inadequacies of their waste system.

Several of the game lodges still use wood to heat their cabins. The local people must also have wood in order to cook and heat their dwellings. Game lodges have other alternatives for heat and energy but the local people are in critical need of firewood. Forests are being cut to build tourist facilities inland and along the coast, creating erosion and soil run off which both destroys the land and pollutes the waterways.

Responsible tourism:

- Do support the local people: buy indigenous not imported souvenirs
- Do ask whether gate revenues help local communities
- Don't pollute, and only stay at hotels/lodges with adequate waste systems
- Do inquire if your lodge uses wood and how this effects the local people.

Chapter 4

On the Road

Transport

Public transport was touched on in Chapter 1 and details specific for each country are given in Part 2.

Transport exists in all shapes and forms: trucks, buses, trains, steamers and a variety of planes. There always seems to be something going where you want to go, even if you have to wait a few days now and then. The only problem is actually to fit into the vehicle you've chosen.

These days most countries have a reasonable bus service, but where there are none trucks fill the gap and travel to very remote areas. It's best to arrange this transport in advance by going to the truck depot, the area of town where the vehicles spend the night. Ask around until you find one going to your intended destination and settle the price and time of departure. Get there early even though it's unlikely to leave on time.

Even the hardiest overlanders shouldn't ignore the possibility of flying. If you calculate the money spent on food and lodging, and then add that to the bus fare you may find the price the same as flying.

Note that where first class travel is available (trains, lake steamers and river boats) it is often booked up for months in advance.

When hitching, don't stick your thumb out – in some places this is a rude gesture – but wave down a vehicle. In most countries it is courteous to ask 'how much?' when getting into a car and leave it to the driver to charge or not, although there will obviously be situations when you know it would be inappropriate to pay (when offered a lift by expatriates, for instance).

Warning If flying out of a country, expect to have to pay an airport tax. This is usually about $20 and payable in hard currency. Check the amount when you arrive and make sure you have it when you leave.

Food and rest

Eating With the exception of Ethiopia there are few dishes unique to Africa, and no great African culinary traditions. The colonial powers imposed their cuisine, and this is what you'll find: rice, beans and spices from the Arabs; bananas, oranges, maize and potatoes from the Portuguese; lamb, wheat and chips from the British; chips (but call them French fries) from the Belgians; samosas and chapatis from the Asians. And of course the greatest influence of all in recent years – American fast food!

Game, such as zebra steaks, is occasionally served in tourist lodges but is not available to the ordinary African. He is more likely to eat maize in a variety of forms – *Ugali*, *Nzima* or *Mieli* – or potatoes or rice (*Mcheli*), served with meat (*Nyama*) if he can afford it.

Tea – *Chai* – is ubiquitous and often very good, with cinnamon and other spices added.

In most countries the traveller can at least read the menu which is usually chalked up on a blackboard in English, French or Swahili. Make your choice but here are a few recommendations: avocado pears are excellent and cheap in Malawi; talapia is a delicious lake fish plentiful in Lakes Malawi, Tanganyika, Victoria and Turkana; chips (French fries) are great in Burundi, Rwanda and Zaïre; curries and other Indian dishes are the best choices in Kenya, particularly in Mombasa, and Tanzania.

Finally, don't hesitate to point to some delectable dish being devoured at an adjoining table and say, 'I want one of those'.

Sleeping   When you're not hiking you can still camp in one of the many organised campsites in towns and holiday spots, particularly in countries geared to tourism. However, although you may plan to camp out the whole time, unless you have your own vehicle you will often end up in a hotel simply because your possessions are safer there than in a tent. Most African towns have hotel beds costing a few dollars. Cleanliness may leave much to be desired, but this sort of accommodation is perfectly adequate and comfortable. In most countries even 'good' hotels are much less expensive than in Europe or the U.S.

There are Y.M.C.A.s throughout Africa which offer accommodation of various standards. If you are travelling the full length of the continent, Youth Hostel membership is worthwhile, there being good hostels in South Africa, Lesotho, Zimbabwe, and Kenya.

Try to use your initiative in finding places to stay; excellent new places are opening up all the time and by slavishly following the advice in your guide book you will miss out on one of the original delights of travel – venturing into the unknown and making your own discoveries. If your initiative has reached a low point, remember that the most reliable source of accommodation information is the travellers' grapevine.

Hospitality

In the town   Some people depend on 'posh' hospitality during their travels in Africa, and many abuse the goodwill of their hosts. Many expatriates are genuinely delighted to meet and talk to their fellow countrymen, or anyone from 'outside', and there's no shortage of residents who love showing their country to foreigners and meeting new people. The point is to give them the option, so avoid phoning from the airport or wherever saying you have nowhere to stay that night, and never just arrive on the doorstep. Write well in advance with the dates you expect to be in their area, and say you'll phone when you arrive. Then at least their invitation, if it is offered, will be genuine and not the result of being taken by surprise.

If you have made arrangements to stay, and your plans change, have the courtesy to let the people know that you will not be coming.

Once invited, you should be sensitive to your hosts' pace of life. If they are frantically busy, keep out of their way and entertain yourself. If, on the other hand, they are rather bored and looking for diversion, do your best to be entertaining (but not by expounding your views of their country's politics or by talking non-stop about yourself and your travels). There won't be many opportunities to be helpful since they will almost certainly have servants, but you can always offer to cook one of your country's typical dishes, or take them out to dinner, or teach the children a new game. Don't outstay your welcome. In our western cultures most people find it impossible to ask a guest to leave and will automatically press him to stay longer, so be attuned to non-verbal communication.

The servants should be tipped when you leave, and you should always write and thank your hosts. Best to send a brief card first, then a longer letter later describing some of your adventures since you left.

It's a nice gesture to send a gift when you get home, but find out whether they'll have to pay exorbitant customs charges to receive the parcel.

The considerate traveller doesn't save much money by accepting hospitality, but has the chance to make new friends and really learn about a country from the inside.

In the country Backpackers and overlanders are sure to be invited to share the village life of the local people in remote areas. This is a wonderful opportunity to get to understand another culture, but it has its pitfalls. Not that you will come to any harm but that you may inadvertently harm your hosts with your western ways. Most people find it difficult to shed their own culture and blend into another with quite different priorities and values, so if you don't think you can adjust, you'd do better to avoid such encounters. Pass through the village and greet the people, but camp away from settlements.

If you do stay with a family, you will want to give presents when you leave. But be careful – there is little you can give that is really of use in an alien culture. Eventually it will break, or stop working, or – consider this – be so marvellous that the recipients will never be quite so happy again and will always yearn for another one.

Bring something to share: a frisbee, for instance, delights both children and adults; cat's cradles is a popular game and can be played by anyone anywhere; there are books showing all sorts of novel string patterns. Origami, the art of paper folding, is another entertaining diversion.

When arriving in a remote village, you should ask to see the chief. It is etiquette to ask his permission to camp in the area, and he may well allocate a hut for you to stay in. Be prepared to eat and drink whatever is offered, however unappetising, and join in any local festivals however flamboyant. (If you are offered something really repulsive it's better to say that eating it is against your beliefs/religion than simply to refuse it, which would be rude.)

See box on page 77 for a discussion on the ethics of providing medical help in remote areas.

Borders

As more travellers visit Africa, so border crossings are becoming easier. These days most difficulties are restricted to those taking a vehicle across. Drivers know they are completely at the mercy of the official there who may deny them entry or at least subject them to a long delay. Any likely difficulties for backpackers are given under *Entrance and exit* in each country's chapter.

Before you approach a border, be absolutely sure that all your papers are in order and that you have the necessary visa or that it is definitely obtainable at the border. If you think you may have trouble entering a country, chat up the border officials of the country you are exiting to make sure they will let you back in if necessary.

Some countries ask you to fill in a currency declaration form at the border. This is to prevent you changing money on the black market.

Other border formalities include questions on your financial status (even without currency declaration forms you may be asked to show that you have enough money to support yourself) and perhaps a ticket out of the country. At present South Africa and Zimbabwe insist on this, and Kenya officially requires it, so overlanders may want to travel with an M.C.O. This Miscellaneous Charges Order is basically a credit slip for an air ticket, and can be exchanged for one or cashed in. It's usually acceptable in lieu of an air ticket, and of course much more versatile.

Your luggage may be thoroughly searched by customs officials, especially in countries with strong moral laws such as Malawi. They are looking for 'subversive or pornographic literature' and drugs. Don't carry either.

Always arrive at a border as clean and neatly dressed as you can manage. You will be subjected to much less harassment if you look likely to spend a reasonable amount of money and behave yourself. And talking of money, it's a good idea to bring some local currency with you to each country, although you are usually only allowed to import a very small amount. There are often unexpected expenses to be met before you can get to a bank, and border money-changers may give you a bad rate. Travellers coming in the other direction often have left over money they're only too happy to change.

Mail

For communication with your loved ones you will have to rely on Poste Restante. This means your letter will be held at the main post office until you collect it. Ask your friends and family to write your last name in capitals to make it easier for the clerk to put it in the right pigeon-hole. Important letters should be photocopied and mailed twice. Aerograms tend to arrive faster and disappear less often than regular letters.

When mailing out a quantity of letters or cards, try to work out beforehand how much the stamps will cost. It is a popular ruse to punch in an extra amount on the calculator and overcharge the bemused tourist. You may want to mail home parcels of handicrafts etc. bought en route. This is rarely a problem, although post office staff sometimes want to see the contents before you secure the parcel. See *What to buy* in each country's chapter for further information.

Shopping

Bargaining is a way of life when buying souvenirs direct from the maker or in markets, or some other items in touristy areas. Some shops in towns also allow bargaining although here you may want to be a bit more subtle and ask for a 'discount'. As usual, the travellers' grapevine is your best guide to an appropriate price for an article, but generally speaking you start at about two-thirds the starting price. Since the vendor needs the money more than you need to save a few shillings it seems unnecessary to expend a large amount of energy on bargaining unless you truly enjoy it. Just shop around then pay what you feel is fair.

While you can safely assume that curio sellers are fair game, you will generally find that outside of tourist areas people selling fruit and other foodstuffs do ask a fair price initially. It may be possible to beat them down with sufficient petulance, but is it really worth exploiting the vendor's urgent need for cash just to save a few pennies? It's difficult to generalise, but if someone is unwilling to quibble over a shilling or two they probably asked an acceptable price in the first place, and on the whole it's better to err on the side of generosity.

Do not buy ivory or other wild animal products.

Language

There are over eight hundred distinctive ethnic groups in Africa, and the division of the continent into separate countries ruled by various colonial powers took no account of the geographical distribution of tribes. Since most countries have several tribes speaking a variety of languages or dialects, the official languages are still mostly European and spoken by the people themselves as well as foreigners, although Swahili is widely spoken in East Africa. So the most useful languages for travellers are English and French. Many readers will be surprised to know that in Africa 23 nations are Francophone; more than those with English as their mother tongue. However, of the 15 countries described here, only the former Belgian colonies of Zaïre, Rwanda and Burundi speak French. Otherwise it's English.

The African English you will hear is often charmingly formal and rather Victorian. In Lesotho a distinguished village chief offered us hospitality by saying 'I would be most condescended if you would visit my humble abode', and in Uganda a young black face materialised out of the darkness outside our window with the request 'To give me, please, a cigarette?' Some of the cultural difficulties between Europeans and Africans have a linguistic basis. Many African languages do not have the shades of meaning that ours have. In West Africa there's a saying '"Perhaps" prevents the white man from telling lies'.

You will hear English (or French) spoken in very remote areas, and by quite young children, but it is an obvious courtesy to learn some basic greetings and questions in the native language, Swahili being the most useful.

Swahili, or KiSwahili is not in fact a native language but was developed by Arab merchants who traded up and down the East African coast for well over a thousand years. It is derived from the coastal dialects with the addition of many Arab words, and is the *lingua franca* of East Africa and parts of Central Africa. It is easy to learn, and it is well worth bringing a Swahili phrase book. Lonely Planet publishes a good one.

Exploits and exploitation

I once received a trip report from a Dutch mountaineering expedition which had travelled throughout Africa. Their account included the following passage: 'Our stock of spare leaf-springs dwindled quickly and after one month we had to buy new ones whenever available. Often this was not the case... we had to barter them for some of our costly or irreplaceable goods. Sometimes they bluntly refused to help us out at all... Once, in a small capital, one of our team climbed the barbed wire of a luxurious western-style hotel. He looted the leaf springs from under a car belonging to a neo-colonialist and left the vehicle stripped down on a couple of loose stones.' An extreme example of loutish behaviour, but we travellers all have our ways of getting something for nothing and saving money at every opportunity. Many of us consider that this makes us 'real travellers' as against 'tourists'. Yet when Africans or their governments try to do the same to us, we are outraged.

My own attitude to cheap travel has changed considerably since the first edition of this book. One reason was a letter from a Zambian woman who wrote: 'I am one of those millions for whom Africa, warts and all, is home... I, too, have had the misfortune to travel far from home, in Europe, and have lived and worked in the UK. I can tell you, for a black woman, that country is dangerous (the National Front and other racist groups), uncomfortable (the weather is awful) and unpleasant (dog shit all over the streets) and the officials are obtuse and unhelpful.' She goes on to point out that 'your attitude towards the black market and bribes, for example, is not only irresponsible but alarming for its lack of analysis of the implications of what you are recommending that these young people do, especially since for most of them this will be their *only* experience of Africa... To justify the black market on the grounds that it makes your trip cheaper in fact also justifies, to me, all the hardships you encounter at borders, with officials, etc. They, the officials, know that you are out to screw every penny out of the countries you travel through, and avoid foreign exchange regulations... so why do you complain when officials treat you badly? To travel cheaply is your maxim, regardless of the laws you break, the insulting attitudes towards the people who live there, and the underlying arrogance that makes you believe that Africa only exists for you to travel across. You are therefore surprised that there are countries (with laws) and people (with their own lives and priorities) in the way.'

Think before you give   Handing out sweets or trinkets to children is a selfish activity. Rural Africans rarely visit a dentist, so tooth decay is the gift that lasts, not the sweets. Children clamour for ball point pens, and if they can convince the tourist it's for school, they'll acquire a status symbol and a toy, but there's little chance they'll have paper to write on, or even know how to write. If you really want to help, give the pens to the school teacher who can then hand them out as appropriate.

Presents are acceptable, or even required, in return for services or friendship; that is a different matter.

Tourism Concern As more and more people take 'long haul' holidays to the Third World, so their effect on the local people increases. The UK has lagged behind the rest of Europe in actively promoting a more thoughtful attitude towards the people in the countries we visit. West Germany, Switzerland and Holland have for many years been raising consciousness (and consciences) on this issue, and now a British group called Tourism Concern has joined this network. Membership costs £15 and includes an excellent magazine, *In Focus*. For more information write to Tourism Concern, Froebel Collage, Roehampton Lane, London SW15 5PU, Tel: 081 878 9053. This organisation would particularly like to hear from people with experience and information on what is happening to communities and environments in tourist receiving areas.

The equivalent organisation in the USA is the Center for Responsible Tourism, P.O. Box 827, San Anselmo, CA 94979.

Homesickness

Awareness of travellers' responsibilities means that most readers will set out for Africa with impeccable ideals. They will be aware of the dangers of ethnocentricity and cultural imperialism, and they vow to shed their western trappings and become part of Africa. Few achieve this and the conscientious feel pangs of guilt at their failure.

I think we are asking too much of ourselves and the subject deserves some reflection. All human beings feel more comfortable as a member of a tribe or group and most feel somewhat uncomfortable with people who are different. From the safety of one's own tribe, 'Otherness' is interesting but this feeling of curiosity can easily slip into one of insecurity; then the people who are different are seen as a threat. There are sound evolutionary reasons for this.

For many Africans the tribe is still the focus of their lives, dictating their behaviour and responses, and giving them that exuberant self-confidence that delights visitors. In the West we form more subtle groups based on class, interests, region, religion or race, but our tribal instincts are still intact and we are just as vulnerable to feelings of insecurity when dropped into another culture.

Only a few lucky travellers feel genuinely at one with Africa. If you experience occasional unease or frustration it will do you a power of good to give in to homesickness from time to time. Read the novels you brought, revel in the discussions with other travellers over your favourite London or New York restaurants, don't be ashamed about buying Time Magazine or listening to the BBC World Service, enjoy English language movies, eat occasionally in a Macdonalds, take tea in an international hotel, chat with expatriates. Best of all spend a day at the British Council or the American Cultural Center (or equivalent for your own country). You will recharge your tribal batteries and be ready once again to marvel at the Otherness of all you are seeing and experiencing.

GAZELLE

It is nice — and of useful snob value — to be able to tell the two similar gazelles apart. **Thomson's gazelle** ("Tommies") are smaller than **Grant's gazelle** and have a distinctive black stripe along their side and a black tail which is constantly wagging. Apart from the absence of the black stripe, the white rump of Grant's gazelle is characteristic, especially as it runs away. The tail is also white.

Tommies are strongly territorial, and having small territories have to make a big show of defending their area. They scent mark twigs and grasses by rubbing them with a tar-like substance from a gland just in front of the eye (which gives gazelles the conspicuous "tear mark") and by defecating and urinating as conspicuously and frequently as they can manage.

These territorial signs are easily seen by backpackers walking through Tommy country, and are something to look out for on foot safaris. Despite all this, border disputes are common, but nature has guarded against serious injury by placing the horns close together to minimise injury. Females generally have no horns.

Like their similar-looking cousins in the south, the **springbok**, Tommies indulge in stiff-legged bouncing, known as "stotting" or "pronking", even when predators are around. This is thought to be a way of showing their attacker how powerful and energetic they are, and so persuade it to give up all idea of gazelle for dinner. To the casual observer it looks more like high spirits.

Tommies very rarely drink water and Grant's gazelles have never been known to take a drink. This has obvious advantages.

Compared with Tommies, Grant's gazelles have larger territories, are more selective feeders, and do less fighting. Territories are not marked with the pre-orbital gland.

Being larger, with more potentially lethal horns (set wide apart) the Grant's gazelle avoids actual conflict which might result in death or injury. Most territorial defence is done by threat rather than fight. The animals face each other, arch their necks, and shake their horns from side to side. Then they pretend to graze ("ceremonial grazing"), or scratch, or groom (all the sorts of activities we indulge in if embarrassed) and only interlock horns for the real thing if all else fails.

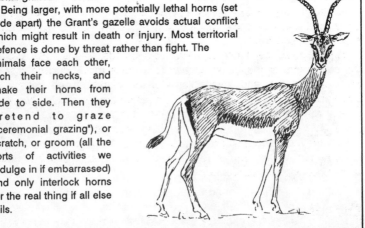

Chapter 5

The Animal Kingdom

Wildlife and national parks

There are more large wild animals in Africa than in any other continent, and the biggest concentration is found in East and Southern Africa, where that geological accident, the Great Rift, has created the ideal environment for a plentiful and diverse wildlife. The countries endowed with this wealth realised the commercial benefit, first in hunting then by protecting the animals in national parks. Wildlife now accounts for much of their foreign exchange earnings.

The major game parks (for convenience I've used 'game parks' to denote parks that protect 'game' animals rather than forest or mountain environments) in East Africa are savannah grasslands, and their success in feeding the vast herds depends partly on the great variety of plants and grasses growing in the shallow volcanic soil which supports few trees, and partly on the climate. Near the equator there are two rainy seasons, so two growing seasons.

Birds are as abundant as mammals, and are a very rewarding area of study for backpackers. In Africa they are frequently spectacular and may be observed in city parks and gardens and around popular campsites as well as in national parks or protected areas. If you carry only one field guide, it should be a bird book.

National parks aren't just for mammals and birds. Marine parks, protecting the coral reefs of the Indian Ocean, provide a mind-boggling display of multicoloured fish and invertebrates which can be seen from a glass bottomed boat or by snorkelling. Then there are the reptiles and insects, usually disregarded by tourists seeking the 'big five' (elephant, lion, leopard, rhino, buffalo) but often far more intriguing because less familiar.

Knowing more about an animal than its appearance greatly increases your enjoyment of an encounter; to this end I have scattered short pieces on animal behaviour throughout the book.

On safari

Safari is a Swahili word meaning 'journey' but nowadays it is associated with big game viewing.

To travel in Africa without visiting a game park is like going to Egypt without seeing the pyramids. The question is not whether but how, since you generally need a vehicle. Independent travellers need not miss out, however. There are some parks in Africa which can be visited on foot, but to get close to the Big Five you must be in a car. Now, to my mind the fanatical interest in animals that take no skill to see (they are easily visible either because of their size, or – in the case of the big cats – because they will be surrounded by a ring of minibuses) is rather sad. Most vehicles only stay long enough for the occupants to take photos, and there is no chance to study behaviour. Even the best safari drivers are so conditioned to what the majority wants that they are reluctant to stop to look at smaller animals. That said, however, no one wants to come back from Africa without having seen a lion, and for that you will need to take an organised safari (which can be arranged locally or in your home country) or to hire a car. In East Africa it's generally best to join a group safari since the drivers are expert in spotting animals and knowing the most likely spots for the elusive ones. In South Africa and Namibia the reasonable cost of car-hire makes self-drive a realistic option for budget travellers. You can ask a company like the Africa Travel Shop (see Chapter 1) to arrange a self-drive car in advance.

Which parks?

All countries charge a high fee for visiting their game parks, and combined with vehicle hire this ensures that you are selective. Chapter 1 gives a few suggestions, and in Part 2 the main game parks or parks of particular interest to backpackers are briefly described. Bear in mind that East Africa is the place to see huge herds. If you can be in Serengeti from December through May, you could see around a million wildebeest massing for the annual migration which begins in late May or early June as the animals head for the wetter grazing grounds of the Maasai Mara. The distance covered is over 800km. In late June they give birth (all calves in the herd are born within three weeks of each other). In the Maasai Mara the herds are best seen from September to November.

As you move south the character of the game parks changes with the climate. The two rainy seasons (the 'short rains' and the 'long rains') of the equatorial countries give way to a prolonged dry season when grass becomes parched, waterholes dry up, and the land supports fewer animals. Those that remain are concentrated near rivers and waterholes, providing some outstanding wildlife viewing in the more open areas such as Zambia, west South Africa and Namibia in the right season (usually June to September).

The southern habitat is different: the grasslands give way to semi forest where the thorny *brachystegia* and acacia trees conceal the animals. There are some different species here, though, including nyala and (in Zambia) the rare lechwe antelope.

Foot safaris

Seeing animals from the safety and isolation of your vehicle doesn't compete with walking quietly through the bush suddenly to confront a grazing white rhino and her calf, or sitting near a popular watering hole and watching the animals come down to drink.

Obviously such safaris must be carefully controlled. You travel a set route seldom frequented by the park's dangerous species and a rifle-carrying gamewarden leads the group while another brings up the rear. You see fewer animals (their instincts of fear are aroused by the sight or smell of humans not vehicles) but your basic instincts of hunter and stalker are also out to the fore – your senses are keener, you are more observant and you feel far more in touch with the Real Africa.

These safaris are leisurely affairs, designed for wildlife enthusiasts rather than hikers. Food will probably be part of the package. Everything else is provided and a camp crew do all the actual work. Luggage is carried on donkeys or by jeeps which take a different route so the wildlife is not disturbed.

Foot safaris should be taken in the dry season, when the grass is short and visibility good. Animals also congregate at known watering places.

The main parks allowing this type of safari currently include the following. Kenya: Samburu; Tsavo. Tanzania: Selous. Zambia: Luangwa Valley. Zimbabwe: Mana Pools. South Africa: Umfolozi (and several others).

Close encounters of the furred kind

By Ian Redmond

A pack rides comfortably on your back as you stride along in the crisp mountain air; afro-alpine flowers carpet the moorlands and mountain chats call from every bush. Suddenly you round a corner and with a snort, a big bull buffalo lumbers to his feet and stands, yards away, glowering at you with lowered head ... what do you do?

Situations such as this are not uncommon when wandering in the wilds of Africa, and while they often send the adrenalin surging, the actual danger is less than might be imagined. American hikers may be used to occasional encounters with large animals (having bears, moose and the like in their wilderness areas) but to your average British fell walker, such an experience is novel to say the least! It is impossible to generalise for different species and different circumstances, but the following hints may help to defuse a potentially explosive situation.

The first tip for when meeting big beasties on their home ground must be simply DON'T PANIC! Don't let your mind exaggerate the danger just because it is unfamiliar. Try to understand the psychology of the situation; almost every confrontation between different species (or between members of the same species) ends with bluff and counter-bluff, thereby avoiding actual violence. Contrary to the Hollywood image, the last thing that the average lion/buffalo/snake wants to do is to maul/charge/bite every passing human. Hence the buffalo, or whatever, will also be thinking 'How can I get out of this confrontation without danger to myself?'. So the second tip must be STAND STILL and give both yourself and the buffalo time to weigh up the situation. If you turn tail and run, the animal will see that he is in no danger, and he might just be tempted to chase you – good for his ego but not for your health!

At this stage, I usually *very slowly* raise my camera, whilst watching the animal (but not with an aggressive stare) and almost invariably the beastie, seeing that I'm not afraid of it, crashes off through the bushes before I get a picture but just occasionally it works. Alternatively you might prefer to begin to back off *very slowly*, keeping an eye out for climbable trees just in case. All movement you make must be slow so that there is no chance of it being misinterpreted as a threat. Some species, such as gorillas and elephants, like to bluff charge (if they feel confident enough) but if *you* look confident, and just stand quietly, it is very unlikely that they would be bold enough to call your bluff and touch you.

Finally, PREVENTION IS BETTER THAN CURE. Two or more people seldom see much game at close quarters because they are usually talking. Any animal (unless sound asleep) will hear your approach and move out of your way. If you are on open savannah or moorland they will see you approaching and avoid you (unless they are not afraid, in which case they will expect *you* to avoid *them*). Even if they do not see or hear you, if you approach from up wind or in a valley where wind eddies, they will smell you and flee.

What to do to avoid such encounters must now be clear (make a noise, keep to open places and don't wash!), but if you actually relish the prospect of seeing wildlife unimpeded by bars or windscreens, the converse applies. Make use of any cover available to break up your outline; never break the skyline with your silhouette when topping a mound or slope; walk alone or, if silence can be maintained, in pairs; keep all your senses alert – it surprises me how often I come across an animal a few yards ahead and am able to freeze before it becomes aware of my presence; occasionally I have stood in full view of shy, forest duikers for up to half an hour watching them feed or groom, just because I saw them before they saw me; remember – a camera in the hand is worth two in the rucksack (but also remember that camera and binocular lenses look like giant eyes, and may be interpreted as an aggressive display and provoke a 'flight or fight' reaction).

In general, though, walking in the wilds can begin to get you down because *everything*, from the tiniest of birds to the biggest buffalo, flees in abject terror at the approach of man. The zebra that runs from the hunting lions pays no attention to them after they have fed; not so with our kind – however benign our intentions we are always assumed to be deadly. Indeed, man *is* the most dangerous animal; the backpacker in Africa has more to fear from his own species than from any other. Personally I feel far safer walking though a forest full of gorillas, elephants and buffaloes than through Nairobi at night...

Conservation

Because of the importance of wildlife to the economy of many African countries conservation is encouraged at government level, as can be seen by the proportion of land set aside for national parks. But these far-seeing governments are beset with problems, not least the population explosion which is unlikely to be stabilised for many years. In a protein-deficient land it is hardly surprising that some wildlife falls victim to poachers, nor will most westerners condemn the practice of taking the odd antelope to feed a hungry family. Of much greater concern is the killing of animals such as rhino and elephant because their horns and tusks have an artificial value to the wealthy nations. No-one needs ivory or rhinoceros horn, yet these animals are in danger.

There is much you can do to help: by joining the East Africa Wildlife Society, you not only get an excellent bi-monthly magazine, *Swara*, but are giving active encouragement to locally run conservation efforts. The address is P.O. Box 20110, Nairobi, and copies of *Swara* may be read and purchased at the Society's headquarters in the Hilton Hotel complex in Nairobi. You can also support conservation groups at home, such as the World Wide Fund for Nature and the Flora and Fauna Preservation Society. If you visit lesser known national parks and pay the park fee without resentment you are helping as much as when you don't buy ivory or other animal products (including coral and shells).

Field Guides

Nature-loving travellers in Africa have an excellent selection of field guides to choose from. Here are some, but for a complete list of all natural history books pertaining to Africa, send for a catalogue from the Natural History Book Service, 2 Wills Rd, Totnes, Devon TQ9 5XN.

You'll find other more specialised titles for sale in Africa. South Africa has a particularly good selection of locally published guides. These may be obtained mail order from Russel Friedman Books, P.O. Box 73, Halfway House, 1685 RSA. Tel: (011) 702 2300; Fax: (011) 702 1403.

The leaders in Britain are the excellent series published by Collins, with these titles:

A Field Guide to the Birds of East Africa by John G. Williams.
A Field Guide to the Birds of Southern Africa by O.P.M. Prozesky.
A Field Guide to the Mammals of Africa (including Madagascar) by Theodore Haltennorth.
A Field Guide to the larger Mammals of Africa by Jean Dorst and Pierre Dandelot.
A Field Guide to the Butterflies of Africa by John G. Williams.
A Field Guide to the Snakes of Southern Africa by V.F.M. Fitzsimmons.
The Wildflowers of Kenya by Michael Blundell.
A Field Guide to the National Parks of East Africa, by John Williams.

Equally useful guides have been published in America. Here are a couple:
Birds of Africa by John Karmali (foreword by Roger Tory Peterson).
Animals of East Africa by C.T. Astley Maberly.

A few from South Africa:
Robert's Birds of South Africa by G.D. Maclean.
Trees of Southern Africa by K.Palgrave Coats. (Struik, Cape Town).
Succulent Flora of Southern Africa by D.Court. (A.A.Balkema, Cape Town).

And published in all three countries is the invaluable guide to animal behaviour:

The Safari Companion by R.Estes. (Chelsea Green, USA; Green Books, UK; Russel Friedman, S.A.)

Two other excellent guides to animal behaviour are:

Portraits in the Wild by Cynthia Moss (University of Chicago Press).

A Wildlife Guide: a natural history of Amboseli by David Western (self-published in Kenya; usually available in Nairobi).

And for those clear nights round the campfire, how about:

The Safari Star Guide by Alex and Joy MacKay (self-published in Kenya; usually available in Nairobi).

Finally, the funniest bird guide in Africa!

Birds of East Africa and *More Silly Birds of East Africa* by David Bygott (self-published in Kenya; usually available in Nairobi).

BABOON

As with all apes, watching a troop of baboons is endlessly interesting because most of their behaviour is so recognisably like our own. There are some differences, however, which are useful to know; aggression, for instance, is conveyed not only by the obvious "yawn" showing the fearsome dog-like teeth, but also by staring, or head bobbing, with raised eyebrows, using the white upper eyelids to emphasise the threat.

Baboons have a wide range of vocalisation, and can indicate to the rest of the troop whether the danger comes from above in the form of an eagle, in which case they will take cover on the ground, or from a predator such as the leopard, when they rush for the trees.

Baboon troops consist of both males and females. They are very easy to tell apart – the male is much larger, with a pronounced mane, and the female has areas of pink skin on her bottom which becomes greatly swollen when she is receptive to mating, and, of course, is a constant source of interest to the resident males. Male baboons take a great interest in the babies, playing with them and grooming them. Sometimes a subordinate male will grab an infant if threatened by a dominant baboon; the presence of the youngster always inhibits attack. Babies cling to their mother's bellies at first, but later climb up to ride piggy-back.

Baboons are omnivorous, eating plants, seeds, roots, insects and even small mammals. They have become very partial to tourist menus, and have the intelligence to find their way into most things and the assertiveness to grab what they want from your very hands. Baboons have become a menace in many campsites, unzipping tents and taking anything that appeals to them.

NORTH-EAST AFRICA

Sudan
Eritrea
Ethiopia

THE ROUTE THROUGH EGYPT

By David Else.

Overland travellers beginning a length-of-Africa journey in Egypt may appreciate a few notes on this country. Egypt, with its unique antiquities and special tourist attractions, is well covered by other guidebooks which will show you the way in detail. But for planning purposes, here's how you go:

To reach Egypt, there are cheap flights from London to Cairo, or you can travel through Europe and take a ferry from Athens to Alexandria, and travel to Cairo by road or train through the fertile fields of the Nile Delta. From Cairo take the train southwards along the Nile Valley to Luxor (where you can visit the Valley of the Kings). From there you can travel on by train, road or *felucca* (sailing boat) to Aswan, a beautiful town with a fascinating market, good cafes and coffee shops, and calm and dignified people.

Just south of the town is the Aswan High Dam, where you embark on the three-day voyage across Lake Nasser by overcrowded boat (provide your own food, bedding and entertainment) to reach Wadi Halfa, the first town in Sudan and the beginning of this book.

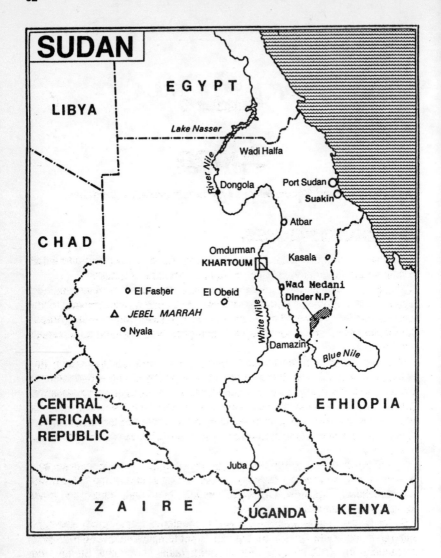

SUDAN

LIBYA

EGYPT

Lake Nasser

Wadi Halfa

River Nile

Dongola

Port Sudan

Suakin

Atbar

CHAD

Omdurman

KHARTOUM

Kasala

El Fasher

El Obeid

Wad Medani

Dinder N.P.

△ *JEBEL MARRAH*

White Nile

Nyala

Damazin

Blue Nile

CENTRAL
AFRICAN
REPUBLIC

ETHIOPIA

Juba

Z A I R E

UGANDA

KENYA

Chapter 6

Sudan

By Aisling Irwin and Colum Wilson, with contributions by David Else.

FACTS AND FIGURES

Sudan is the second largest country in Africa, with an area of two and a half million square kilometres, making it 10 times the size of Britain.

At this cross-roads in Africa, colourful people and civilisations have risen and fallen – from the Biblical Kingdom of Kush, through Pharonic empires, to the establishment of Islam and the Fung and Fur dynasties. Slave-traders, Arabs, Coptic Christians and colonisers have struggled over this land, and have all left their mark.

National identity can be traced back to the rise of a spiritual leader (the Mahdi) in the 1880s. His popular revolution led to the bloody end of General Gordon, and the intervention of Kitchener to shore up British imperialism in Sudan. Sudan finally gained independence in 1956, encompassing within its borders the predominantly Arab Muslims in the north and the black African Christians and animists in the south. Unrest and civil war have ebbed and flowed ever since.

In the south, the government is currently locked in an expensive and indecisive war against the Sudanese People's Liberation Army (SPLA) and two breakaway groups, although recent inter-tribal attrocities have complicated these distinctions further.

Sudan's size means that the climate is equatorial in the south, and sub-Saharan in the north. On the border with Egypt temperatures vary from 25°C in January to 42°C in July and it rarely rains. In central Sudan, the temperature is often in excess of 40°C in Khartoum before the wet season starts in June, although it may rain on the Red Sea coast at other times of the year. In the south the rains fall between April and October, with temperatures in Juba of about 32°C, increasing to 37°C in the dry season.

People

The population of Sudan is about 22 million, and comprises some three hundred tribes, many of which have been converted to Islam, mostly in the north. Sudan also shelters the victims of various wars: Eritrean, Tigrean and Somali refugees in the east and Chadean refugees in the west.

Arabic is the official language. In the south and parts of the west, the first languages are tribal. English is spoken mainly by older people and those who have had higher education, although we are told that if you penetrate the Christian south, English is more widespread.

TRAVEL

Impressions

Sudan is a great, brown flatness. From a glance at the atlas, it seems to hold little promise compared with mountainous Ethiopia. Through the centuries the lure of gold and the hunt for the elusive source of the Nile have attracted travellers here. Today, Sudan's attraction still stems from its inaccessibility. It is remote, it is unknown, vast and unvisited.

Until the bloody war in Sudan is over, you will never see some of its most beautiful and fertile parts, or the bulk of its African Christian and animist peoples. Instead you will see its Muslim people, governed by Sharia law and mostly of Arab descent. They are quiet, generous, dignified, law-abiding – a relief from the insistent badgering you may have encountered in North Africa.

Much of the land is parched and dusty, deforested and almost ugly. Infrastructure such as railways and irrigation, installed in the fifties, gradually decays. But this landscape is the most dramatic setting for the eruptions of mountains in the west and the east. Sudan will be one of the most difficult countries you will travel in, but you will feel proud and rewarded when you have done it.

Entry and exit

Everybody needs a visa. The Sudanese Embassy (3 Cleveland Row, St James, London SW1, Tel: 071 839 8080) will issue a three month visa if you submit two forms, two photos, pay £50 and demonstrate that you are taking £300 of travellers cheques into the country. Allow three weeks for processing. Get your visa in London (or your home country) even if you are planning to enter Sudan from Egypt, says the embassy, 'in case the embassy in Egypt is suspicious about why you didn't get the visa in London'.

Overland, you can enter from Egypt on the Lake Nasser steamer from Aswan to Wadi Halfa in Sudan. A border dispute between Sudan and Egypt means that crossing elsewhere is probably inadvisable. Other border crossings are at Kasala for Eritrea; at Am Dafug for the Central African Republic (on the road from Nyala to Birao); and across to Chad. Boats from Port Sudan go to Port Suez (Egypt) and Jeddah (Saudi Arabia). There are occasionally cargo boats between Port Sudan and Mombasa (Kenya). Contact the Red Sea Shipping Line in Port Sudan.

In 1993, Ethiopian visas were being issued in Khartoum with 'by air only' written on them, but several travellers have reported being able to cross the border overland at Kasala. Beware, however, of difficulties when you try to leave. You could end up with a fine if you entered the country 'illegally'. It costs US$266 single to fly to Addis Ababa.

For Chad you need to take a letter of recommendation from your own embassy in Khartoum to the Chad embassy.

You must register at the Ministry of the Interior Aliens' Office within three days of arriving in Khartoum.

Money

The monetary unit in Sudan is the Sudanese pound, written £S. In 1986 there were £S4 to US$1. By 1991 the rate was about £S25 to US$1. In June 1993, US$1 officially bought £S200. The exchange rate is likely to carry on increasing, as inflation continues to be high. The government recently introduced the dinar (1 dinar = £S10), to make the bundles of notes more manageable.

You can change travellers cheques in most towns where there is a bank, but be prepared to wait.

There is a healthy black market in dollars and even in dollar travellers cheques. In Khartoum, loiter on the north side of Sharia El Gamhuriya and moneychangers will soon home in. You take the risk that some may be plain-clothes policemen. Don't accept torn notes as no-one will accept them from you. Official exchange receipts are no longer required by airports.

Permit

You cannot travel anywhere south of El Obeid. While this puts out of bounds the Nuba Mountains and the rainforests and game parks of the deep south, it is still possible to get to some extremely remote and spectacular areas to the east and west of the country.

A permit is necessary for each journey outside Khartoum. Permits are only available in Wadi Halfa and Khartoum (at the Aliens' Office). Some travellers who get their permits in Wadi Halfa just add destinations to them as they travel, which is possible because the destinations are inscribed in English. In Khartoum they are written in Arabic.

Accurate permits are vital. Some travellers reported having permits that read 'Khartoum - Kasala - Khartoum'. At Kasala they were prevented from crossing to Eritrea because their permits did not allow them to travel the small distance from Kasala to the border.

Take lots of passport photos to Sudan for sticking onto permits.

Warnings

Sudan hosts one of the bloodiest civil wars in Africa, has a human rights record that is the focus of huge international criticism and is run according to Sharia (Muslim) law, which takes some getting used to.

Photography requires, in theory, a permit. In practice, you should not photograph anything 'sensitive' like dams, bridges, or anything military. Remember, too, that Muslims often dislike being photographed.

You cannot buy maps of Sudan in Khartoum unless you have proof that you need them for business reasons. Check at the Government Survey Department next to the Presidential Palace in case the situation has changed.

All tourist offices have closed except one that offers no useful information.

It is possible to get moonshine date spirit ('Aragy'), but bear in mind that Sudan is a strictly 'dry' country. The penalty for being caught is severe – as recently as 1990 a Westerner was flogged and deported for 'dealing in alcohol'. Khartoum is full of shifty individuals selling bottles of 'Johnny Walker Black Label', but don't be tempted. It is estimated that one in four of the Sudanese are linked to Security, and it's probably not the real thing anyway.

Muslims dress modestly, and expect visitors to do the same. Women do not need to wear headscarves, but should cover arms and legs. Shorts are acceptable when you are hiking in the remoter parts.

Travelling during Ramadan requires extra patience. No tea or meals are sold during daylight and life is even slower than usual. The dates of Ramadan vary from year to year, according to the lunar cycle. Find out the dates before you leave home.

Accommodation

Wherever there is habitation you will find somewhere to sleep, ranging from a selection of hotels in a large town to a single hut reserved for visitors in a large village ('Lakonda wain?' means 'Where is the guesthouse?'). At small settlements, you may be offered floorspace in someone's hut, or at least a place at their fire.

Eating

Markets sell oranges, grapefruit and tomatoes (season permitting). There are generally bread, peanuts and a few other staples. Restaurants in the market areas of towns serve *ful* (brown beans), *bayd* (egg, generally omelette) and *la'am* (beef cooked directly on hot coals). Eat with your fingers (right hand only). Men, plus *khawaja* (white foreign) females, eat together from one bowl, scooping up liquids with bread or pounded sorghum.

Tea (*chai*) is served everywhere, except during Ramadan. Unless you direct its preparation, you will receive a mixture of one quarter sugar and three quarters very strong black tea. 'Mumkin chai bidoon sukre?' means 'Is it possible to have tea without sugar ?' [I used to carry lemons to make lemon tea. H.B.]

Transport

All that remains of the railway system is a skeletal service which is infrequent and unreliable.

Roads run along the courses of the Nile with branches going east and west. Frequent fuel crises send prices up and vehicle numbers down but you can still get anywhere if you try hard enough. Full information can be obtained at the bus stations in Khartoum and Omdurman (both called Souk A'Shaabi). Buy your ticket a day in advance.

Travel on the well-metalled roads in the north-east of the country is quick – you can travel from Khartoum to Port Sudan in a day. Journeys further south are more gruelling. To travel west from El Obeid to Nyala can take up to six days, and you have to go by lorry as there is no road.

Lorries and buses stop every so often at roadside refreshment posts, where you can buy food and *chai* and refill your water-bottles.

The cheapest transport is by slow, open lorries. It took us 15 hours and an overnight stop in the desert to travel the 450km road from Khartoum to El Obeid (by bus it can be done in a day). For company there were 52 assorted men, women and babies, as well as bags and unlikely bits of household furniture, including doors and rickety tables, all perched on top of bags of cereal.

The softer option is to fly: Khartoum to Nyala (£S8,000 return, 6 flights per week); to Port Sudan (£S6,000 return, two flights a day); to Atbar (three per week); to Wadi Halfa, Kasala, Dongola, El Obeid and El Fasher. Buy tickets, as far in advance as you can, from the Sudan Airways Office in United Nations Square.

TOWNS

Khartoum

Khartoum straddles the junction of the Blue and White Niles, and is sometimes referred to as the 'three towns'. The main administrative centre is Khartoum, an untidy mixture of dilapitated colonial buildings and badly-made modern blocks. The Mahdi's old capital is Omdurman, full of dusty little shops selling daggers, pots of old coins and medals, elaborate gold jewellery and plastic flip flops. The industrial centre of the capital is Khartoum North.

Sleeping and eating

The cheapest place to stay is the youth hostel, at £S80. Travellers say it is clean and safe. It is in Extension 2 near the airport and near to the Save the Children offices. There are many mid-range hotels, for example the Hotel Haramein at £S670. There are four international hotels, including the Meridien Hotel at $US156 single, $US192 double.

There are many basic restaurants in the souk/cheap hotel area south of the presidential palace, including some excellent places that specialise in Eritrean cooking. Try the vegetarian Brahmin restaurant on Sharia Gandhi, next to the bus station in Omdurman; the boat restaurant on the Nile near the Grand Hotel; and the international hotels, which do all-you-can-eat meals for a set price on certain days. The Chinese restaurant on Airport Road is good, but over-priced.

Places to visit

The **Sudan National Museum** is full of dusty and badly-labelled exhibits, but would be interesting to anyone who knows anything about Sudanese history. It is in a lovely setting overlooking the Nile.

The Whirling Dervishes   These dancers whirl at the tomb of Hammad El Nil every Friday (except during Ramadan) from 4pm till sunset. It is a difficult spot to reach by bus, so share a taxi. The performance has deep religious significance for those involved. Believers dance in a circle for many hours until they reach a semi-hypnotic state which brings them closer to God.

Tuti Island   This island is in the middle of the Nile, between Khartoum and Khartoum North. It is best to go there one day when you are fed up with the noise of the city. The island's village is full of quiet and confusing streets and is surrounded by relaxing woods and vegetation. The ferry goes from near the National Museum and costs £S5.

Friendship Palace Hotel   On the banks of the Nile, in Khartoum North, this well-kept, empty hotel has luscious gardens with a pool and tennis courts. It is another good place to escape to. We are told that there is a fee for using the facilities, but no-one asked us for money.

Omdurman Souk   A colourful market place in the old city. Each street seems to dedicate itself to particular merchandise. Try some of the exotic incense (it looks like gungey tree sap), or buy yourself a 'genuine' antique sword. It is rumoured that you can occasionally find old colonial swords here.

German Club   Following the demise of the Sudan Club, which boasted a pool and provided a focus for ex-patriot British social life, you can still get a swim in European surroundings at the German Club.

Wadi Halfa

The gateway to Sudan, this town is where you arrive if you come by boat from Egypt. There is one hotel, or you can sleep outside near the station or customs sheds.

Trains to Khartoum usually wait for the boat from Egypt to arrive and vice versa. But frequent breakdowns mean the train often arrives many days late. A Land Rover service runs the 5km between the port and the railway station.

Instead of the train, you can take a lorry south, sticking closer to the Nile. Lorries to Dongola or Kerma (from where you can get transport to Dongola) leave Wadi Halfa about once a week, usually the day after the boat arrives.

El Obeid

West of the Nile and on the main route between Khartoum and Nyala, this town was the Mahdi's southern stronghold in the 1880s. For a place without its own supply of water or electricity, it is colourful and lively.

There are regular buses and lorries from Omdurman. Travelling onwards, buses depart daily from the souk near the railway goods yard for El Fasher and Nyala. From Souk A'Shaabi, slightly out of town, buses go to Dubeibat (for Kadugli) and other towns.

The Hotel El Medina, by the main souk, charges £S300 per night, the same as the grimy Hotel International next door. The Hotel Kordofan, on the outskirts, is smarter (£S500 per night).

To while away the time waiting for transport, you can visit the huge souk or even the British Council Library. Near the football field is an imposing Catholic Cathedral recommended for its Sunday music. At the foot of the radio mast, an open-air cinema shows American films sub-titled in Arabic.

Nyala

In western Sudan, this is the nearest town to Jebel Marra (see *Hiking*). Nyala was the capital of the Mediaeval Fur Sultanate, and thrived in splendid isolation well into the last century.

Nyala is a two-hour flight from Khartoum. Alternatively, the marathon, six-day truck ride from El Obeid costs about £S2,500.

The Hotel Darfur is cheap (£S150 a night) and popular but smells of sewers. The Hotel El Ryan (the old government resthouse – 'Istra'a') costs £S300 a night and is clean and well-run.

Buses and lorries leave Nyala every day for El Fasher (1½ days), Zalingei and El Geneina (one day by tarmac road) and for Khartoum two or three times a week. In the dry season you should be able to find transport to Birao in the Central African Republic. Transport for Jebel Marra and Nyertete leaves from a small bus terminus on the outskirts of town called Souk El Geneina ('Magtuf' El Geneina).

El Fasher

In western Sudan, to the north of Nyala, El Fasher is built on small hills around a wadi. Be careful what you drink as there is little running water.

The Hotel Darfur is quite expensive but the Rest House, on the other side of the wadi from the souk, is cheaper.

There are frequent buses and lorries to El Obeid and Khartoum and a good road to Nyala, with buses every day.

Port Sudan

Port Sudan was once a bustling colonial port, kept spic and span by the British, who established the city in 1905. Since then it has largely fallen into decay. If you do end up in Port Sudan, you will find that the hotels are not cheap. The Hotel Africa and the Hotel Cardif (sic) in the city centre have been used by travellers. There is also the old colonial style Red Sea Hotel which is pleasant but expensive.

The Red Sea (British ex-patriots) Club on the sea front sometimes offers temporary membership, and with that comes food, a swimming pool, cold pepsi and other luxuries.

There are buses every day from Souk Deim Suakin (on the southern outskirts of town near the main road) to Kasala.

See *The Red Sea Coast* for places to visit.

Kasala

Kasala is in the east of the country, on the main road to Port Sudan, and close to the Eritrean border.

For accommodation, the Hotel Africa is reasonable. Around the souk and near the Shell petrol station are several cheaper hotels.

Give your palate a holiday by tasting the variety of the food sold in the souk. Also in the souk, men of the Rashida, a nomadic tribe originally from Saudi Arabia, sell weapons; their women, often in decorated black cloaks, sell silver and amber. Ethiopian refugees often have jewellery to sell – they need the money to eat. Far better to buy direct from them than from an Arab merchant acting as a middleman, and making his profit from their suffering.

Just outside the town is Jebel Kasala (see *Hiking* section).

Damazin

Damazin is remote, interesting, and about as far south as you can go safely. The town was built in the 1960s for the workers on Roseires Dam, which supplies 80% of the country's power. The dam is impressive, rising to about 50m, and holding back a vast reservoir.

Damazin is at the end of the road from Wad Medani through Sennar and Singa, near the border with Ethiopia. The journey takes about 10 hours by bus, although this will be reduced when the last 100km of road into Damazin is metalled.

There is a government rest house (£S600 a night), and a cheaper hotel called the Elsidiek.

For sightseeing, start at one of the four souks selling everything from woven baskets to baobab fruit (white and crunchy). Near the central souk, you can get a lorry to Roseires, a green and shady place across the river.

A lorry can take you the five or six hour journey to the Ingessana Hills, a ring of impressive mountains surrounding a plateau. The people here do not speak Arabic, and will be as curious to see you as you are to see them.

A longer lorry journey takes you to Belgoa, a tatty gold-prospecting settlement. Gold-bearing quartz is recovered from rabbit-warren pits and crushed by little boys with rocks. The gold dust is painstakingly separated and displayed in heaps by traders. It is bought by Damazin merchants. If you are a serious gold-buyer, bring your own weights and someone who knows about gold. Dollars are unknown here.

HIKING

Most people consider Sudan to be composed entirely of flat, featureless desert, so it is not renowned for its hiking. But if you are prepared to make the effort to get into the mountains, you will be able to enjoy some of the most unusual and untouched country in Africa.

Jebel Marra

Introduction As our lorry crawled along the road towards Thur, I was scanning the horizon for my first glimpse of Jebel Marra. An old man nudged me and pointed up at an angle far steeper than the one I had been searching for. And there, towering above us, was a faint grey outline in the evening light, the outline of a mountain more massive than I had ever believed possible in this flat land.

At more than 3,000m, Jebel Marra forms part of the jagged rim of a vast volcano crater. The lower foothills are cool and wooded with enough villages within a day's hiking distance to make the going very pleasant. The people who live here are Fur, a Muslim tribe distinct from the Arabs and with its own language and customs. The women dress colourfully and wear gold studs in their noses. They bow slightly when they greet you.

Higher up, the terrain is hostile and parched, with steep gorges. Inside the crater, it is a dry and lonely place, home to baboons and a few solitary camels. There is a network of footpaths linking villages across the mountains. Try to time your visits with the once-weekly markets at each village.

Kilometres do not mean very much to the locals. Far better to ask 'How many hours to...?' ('Cum sahr ila..?'). The answer you get is the time taken by a fit, wiry Sudanese: allow about half as many hours again. You can buy a donkey, or hire one for about £S200 a day, to carry you or your rucksack.

Guides cost about £S600 a day, but are indispensable although you should also bring a compass. Wait till you are near or in the mountains to hire a guide. We heard from some travellers who hired one in Nyala and discovered, after two days lost in the mountains, that he had never been to Jebel Marra. Eventually they had to return to Khartoum to catch a pre-booked plane without ever seeing the volcano.

Preparations   In Nyala you must get permission to walk in the mountains from the Immigration Office, near the airport. Inter-tribal fighting and insurgents from Chad mean that the mountains are sometimes closed to visitors. Ex-pats in Nyala (if you can find any – all the English teachers have been expelled so there is just a clutch of aid workers) can update you.

You should aim to be self-sufficient as far as food is concerned, bearing in mind that what you can buy in mountain villages on non-market days will be extremely limited. Should you be fortunate enough to be offered food and lodging while you are on the trail, remember that, while the generosity of the local people is unlimited, they have next to nothing to share with you. The village Sheikh at Torantonga requests that hikers bring their own water as well as their own food.

You should buy your provisions in Nyala. Some shops stock welcome but expensive tinned food. Plastic water containers are also available here, but you should check for leaks. In the dry season (Nov-June) water supplies in the mountains are unreliable, and you should carry at least two days' supply with you. In temperatures of up to 40°C, you will need at least five litres a day.

At night, the temperature can drop by as much as 30°C, so bring a sleeping bag and waterproofs in the wet season.

Directions   The usual way to approach the crater of Jebel Marra is from the village of Torantonga (also spelt Tarantonga, Tora Tonga), which can be reached from several points along the (tarmac) Nyala to El Geneina road.

1) At Kass a new road leads to Torantonga, although transport is infrequent so only take this route if you can arrange a lift all the way in Nyala.

2) From Nyama you can walk to Torantonga via Kalu Kitting and Genditoor (two days).

3) Another option is to spend the night at Thur and catch the early morning lorry to the German reforestation camp at Golol. It is a ten hour walk to Torantonga, though locals say it takes them six.

4) Although most people end their route here, it is possible to set out from

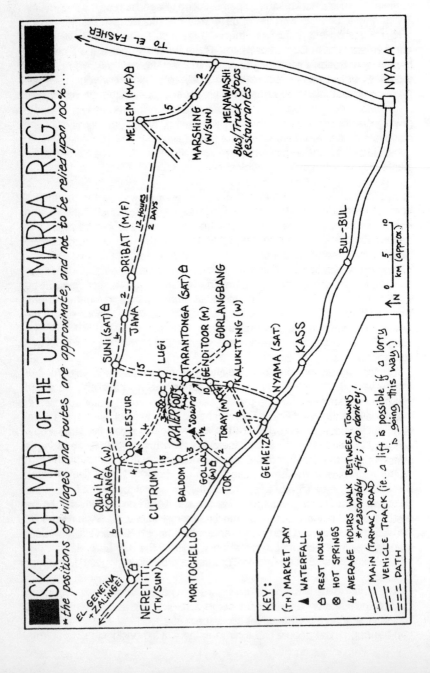

SKETCH MAP OF THE JEBEL MARRA REGION
*the positions of villages and routes are approximate, and not to be relied upon 100%....

KEY:
(TH) MARKET DAY
▲ WATERFALL
⌂ REST HOUSE
⊗ HOT SPRINGS
4 AVERAGE HOURS WALK BETWEEN TOWNS
   *reasonably fit; no donkey!
═══ MAIN (TARMAC) ROAD
──── VEHICLE TRACK (ie. a lift is possible if a lorry
      is going this way.)
─ ─ ─ PATH

Neretiti to Koranga (six hours), and approach the crater from the west.

Alternatively, you can take the El Fasher road to the lorry stop at Menawashi. From there you can sometimes find transport to Mellem or Dreibat on the north-east side of the mountain. You may even find a truck that goes directly to Suni from Nyala.

On the trails

You can spend as much time as you like in the Jebel Marra region walking from village to village tying in your hike with the once-weekly markets in each village. Even just a few days walking is well worth the effort of getting there. Below is a description of some possible routes.

1) We got a lift in a lorry to Kalu Beri, a few kilometres from Torantonga. We stayed the night here then walked up to Torantonga early next morning.

From Torantonga the path to the crater starts behind the village school. It was a hard, four-hour walk along a meandering path to a gap in the crater rim. We dropped down onto the crater floor, which was covered in pumice stones. The water in the large lake is salty and brackish and definitely undrinkable but a spring, which is difficult to find, comes up in the mud at its southern end producing water that can be drunk if you're desperate. We spent two nights camping in the crater, and on the day in between walked over to the small lake called 'The Eye of Jebel Marra' at the base of a secondary crater to the west of the large lake.

The path out of the crater heading towards the hot springs and Quaila is marked by a couple of cairns and some Arabic 'graffiti' carved on the rocks nearby. We climbed up the steep path, crossed over the rim at the top, then wound our way down to the hot springs at the foot of Jebel Idwa. The path was sometimes indistinct, and the journey from the crater floor to the springs took about five hours. From the springs to Quaila took another four hours (including a stop for a quick dip at the waterfall near Dillesjur, about 1km before Quaila). There we slept in one of the market shelters, with the village headman's permission.

On the last day it was an easy walk following the river down to Neretiti. It took about seven hours and by the afternoon we were walking through woods. Neretiti is a beautiful, peaceful little town. The rest house is on the outskirts near the Quaila track. The next morning we walked through the town to the main tarmac road and waited for a ride back to Nyala. (David Else)

2) If you insist on scaling Jebel Idwa, the ascent will take you about half an hour. The top is surprisingly green, with large trees offering welcome shade. The view takes your breath away – the emptiness and hugeness made me feel very insignificant. You can just make out a patch of green at the foot of the western slope of the jebel. This marks the hot springs, and is on the route to Quaila.

3) From Torantonga we headed towards the crater. After two hours, we reached a beautiful settlement just before the gap in the crater wall. There was a cold clear stream running over rocks, irrigating perfectly laid-out

terraces where onions and potatoes are grown on the valley floor.

We descended to the water and followed it down to the left, crossing it just before it became a waterfall. Ahead there was a steep path leading up the almost vertical wall on the south side of the gap in the crater rim. We found a scrambling route up the cliffs from this path after only a few minutes (but we were assured that if you keep to the path you will eventually reach the top). It was then a hard two hour scramble to gain the crater rim. The views from the rim, along the ridge and down into the crater were sudden and dramatic.

On the rim, we turned left (south-west) along the ridge-crest to reach the highest peak of the ridge (3,019m) which took another three hours. The air was thin and the sun merciless, but the occasional light breeze brought relief. To get to the highest peak of all (3,042m), slightly south-west of the rim, would take an hour's diversion.

Leaving the peak at 3,019m, we walked to the next peak (with two white painted rocks on the top). We then struck a cold and sloping camp down one of the shoulders, but the serene grey and orange of a perfect sunrise the following morning was more than compensation. To persevere northwards along the ridge is impossible without ropes and climbing equipment. Resist the temptation to descend down a shoulder away from the crater, as the gorges will mean that you will end up doing far more scrambling up and down than you need to. We retraced our steps around the rim and found a steep route into the crater just before the gap. From there, it was a gentle walk back through the gap for another night on the valley floor by the waterfall.

4) We have heard that you can walk from Toga, a village to the west of the crater, up to the highest peak of the mountains (3,042m) and back down to Toga in one day. Golol may be a good place to set out from for this route. Take a guide, and check with the Germans at the Golol forestry station. (Aisling Irwin, Colum Wilson)

OTHER PLACES OF INTEREST

Dinder National Park

Don't go to this park if you want sophisticated facilities or lots of varied wildlife. Although the game wardens here are armed to the teeth, poachers have severely depleted the game. Do go if you want to experience the vastness and remoteness of a tract of land the size of Wales and home to just a few isolated tribes. The park is in eastern Sudan, 250km south east of Wad Medani, near the border with Ethiopia.

If you can get from Sennar or Singa to the village of Dinder, we are told that you pay US$50 per day for a guide, a vehicle and accommodation in the park. Dinder village is a three hour drive from Gallegu, a camp on the Dinder river, where you will see any game if there is any to see.

Kasala Mountains

The mountains are massive, sugar-loaf towers that rise spectacularly above the desert. Kasala is a one-day coach trip from Khartoum. There are cheap hotels in the town. You can stay here and do day trips into the mountains.

You can get a bus to the village of Katmir about 5km out of town, nestling at the foot of the jebels. You can walk round the foot of these mountains or scramble (rather than walk) on them. The views from the top of the scree plateaux between the peaks are spectacular. The peaks themselves need full mountaineering gear for climbing. You can stay the night on the plateau between the two largest jebels. Bring food, water, firewood and warm clothes.

Nuba Mountains

Due to continued fighting in this area, travellers are not allowed here, but this information is provided in case the situation changes.

These fertile hills have become one of the most documented regions in the Sudan. They are the site where the worlds of Arabia and Africa meet. They are beautiful, green and cool.

Directions   The mountains are south of El Obeid, in the province of Kordofan, centred around the town of Kadugli. Kadugli is a day's journey on a good road from El Obeid. From Kadugli you can travel to surrounding villages by lorry. Some travellers have rented bicycles in Kadugli for travelling along the hard, dirt mountain tracks. Alternatively, a hotel in Kadugli could be your base from which to do day trips into the mountains.

The Red Sea Coast

Red Sea Diving

Some of the best diving in the world can be found near Port Sudan on the unspoilt coral reefs of the Red Sea. One traveller said: 'The sea is beautiful – completely untouched. If you start diving here, you've started with the best. People compare it with Australia.'

A German called Harry has opened a diving centre 55km north of Port Sudan. For US$65 a day, you get to dive twice a day, with accommodation and three meals a day laid on. Look for the travel agent next to the Bohein Hotel in Port Sudan. He will organise your papers and lay on transport.

For other snorkelling and boating trips, ask at the Red Sea Hotel.

Suakin

Before the British built Port Sudan, Suakin was Sudan's main Red Sea port, built on an island joined to the mainland by a causeway. The buildings were constructed from brilliant white rocks cut from a coral reef. The island has been abandoned but is fascinating to visit. You may be able to sleep in the ruins of the old fort. People may take you boating and snorkelling, and you can swim here, but beware of jelly fish.

Avoid Port Sudan and Suakin during Haj – the season of pilgrimage to Mecca.

Chapter 7

Eritrea

By Kim Naylor.

Note: As befits a new country, this chapter breaks the format of the rest of the book to give a more detailed account of the history and people.

INTRODUCTION

A long history of colonialism followed by a destructive 30 year war has come to an end: In 1991 the Eritreans ousted the occupying Ethiopians from their territory to win their liberation. A new country is emerging.

Eritrea is presently in a state of flux as it repairs the damage of war and rehabilitates its victims. And there is constant change in all aspects of life as the nation is moulded and shaped.

The war isolated Eritrea for decades and the country is an unknown entity lying off the beaten track. Tourism has yet to be developed, though there is potential in the white sandy beaches along the Red Sea, the underwater diving off the Dahlak Islands and hiking in the high plateau of the interior. The major historical sites of the ancient Kingdom of Axum are across the border in Ethiopia and nature parks are still to be created. There is beauty in the hills and coast, though the charm of Eritrea is the warm, easy-going character of the people and their positiveness and hope for the future. There is no danger in the street, but beware, mines still lie undetonated around the countryside.

FACTS AND FIGURES

Eritrea is approximately the size of England, covering 124,320 sq km between latitudes 12 N and 18 N in the northern quarter of the Horn of Africa. Its eastern limit is a 1,000km stretch of coast overlooking the Red Sea, to the south the country borders Djibouti and Ethiopia, while to the west and north it is neighbours with Sudan. During its recent occupation Eritrea served as Ethiopia's outlet to the sea; now with Eritrea's liberation the door to the coast is closed and Ethiopia is landlocked.

Narrow in the south, broad in the north, Eritrea comprises four main geographical regions: Danakil, a long sliver of desert coastal strip running northwestwards from Djibouti; the high plateau, an extension of Ethiopia's highlands with an average height of 1,500 metres, which covers 30% of the country, forming the backbone of central and northern Eritrea, and which includes Hamasien province and Asmara, the country's capital; the mainly flat potentially fertile lowlands of Barka province spreading west of the highlands into Sudan; the Sahel, a region of rugged hills in the far north of the country which, to the east, gives way to a narrow fertile lowland and then the coastal plain.

June to September is the main rainy season for most of the country. On the high plateau the average temperature is around 18°C with an annual rainfall of around 500mm. Down on the coast temperatures average 30°C and rainfall is below 200mm. There are the unpredictable 'little rains' between October and March along the northern coastal region. The best time to visit is during the winter months: it is hot down on the coast – but by no means as sweltering as in summer – and warm but fresh on the high plateau where it can get cool and chilly at night.

PEOPLE

Eritrea was a European colonial creation and in drawing the boundaries in the late 19th Century the colonists brought together within one country, as they did elsewhere in Africa, a large diversity of peoples and cultures. The two main language groups are the Tigrinya and the Tigre, highland Christians and lowland Muslims respectively, whose Semetic languages are closely related and, along with Amharic, originate from the ancient Ethiopian language of Ge'ez; today the three tongues are mutually unintelligible.

About half the population are Tigrinyan-speaking Christians (their small Muslim minority are called Jabarti), who live on the high plateau and have similar language, faith and other customs to their neighbouring highlanders across the border in the Tigre province of Ethiopia. The Tigrinya are primarily sedentary agriculturists and cultivate the small grain tef (*Eragrostos abyssinia*) as well as maize, wheat millet and barley and a variety of vegetables; cattle and other herds of animals are sometimes kept and provide supplementary income.

Tigre-speaking Muslims account for over a third of the total population and tend to occupy the western lowlands as well as the northern hills and coastal regions. Traditionally they are nomadic pasturalists and they include peoples such as the Beni Amer, the largest group, who have historical ties with the Beja of Sudan and can also speak the Beja language. Through history there have been trading and other links across the Red Sea with Arabia, and Arabic is spoken at the main centres down on the coast.

Eritrea's other Muslim peoples include the Danakil, the nomadic herdsmen of the harsh Danakil region, who are related to the Afar of Djibouti; the Rashayda, who are Arabs; and the Tukrir, whose distant forefathers left their homeland in Nigeria with their sights set on the holy city of Mecca, but, en route, found Eritrea to their liking and chose to go no further.

The Italians also had an eye on Eritrea and they came, saw, conquered and stayed. But as the heyday of colonialism waned most returned to the motherland leaving behind a small community who, because of marriage to locals, successful business or lack of options in Italy, decided to allow their roots to dig ever more deeply into Eritrean soil. Today the Italian Eritreans number several hundred and most live in Asmara and congregate regularly at the Casa d'Italia in the heart of the capital. In 1991 the Italian Consulate was reopened.

More conspicuous than the Italians themselves are the legacies of their presence: their roads, cars (Fiats), beers (Melotti) survive; their predilictions and passions – Catholicism, pasta, expresso and cappuccino, ice cream – have become part of Eritrean culture. Many older Eritreans have at least some knowledge of Italian and words such as *ciao* are daily parlance for all.

The evidence of British presence in Eritrea is scant, with the British cemetery outside Asmara being one of the few signs to indicate they ever passed this way. English is spoken by the educated, not because it is a colonial inheritance, rather because of its importance as an international language. Due to popular demand the British Council in Asmara has moved to larger premises and is constantly enlarging its library.

HISTORY

The region of present-day Eritrea was part of the Kingdom of Axum, one of the great empires of the classical era, which spread from Meroe in Sudan across the Red Sea to Yemen during the 3rd and 4th Centuries AD. Axum was founded by Semetic peoples, who had originated from Arabia, and had its capital deep in the highlands of Tigre (the northern province of present-day Ethiopia) and its port, its gateway to the outside world, at Adulis (present-day Zula on the Eritrean coast). Along with the thriving flow of commerce there came Christianity, the faith Axum adopted.

With the rise of the Persian empire in the 6th century and then the expansion of Islam, the Kingdom of Axum began to wane. In 710 AD Muslims destroyed Adulis and converted the lowland populations; Axum became an isolated, remote enclave of Christianity surrounded by Islam.

After centuries of introspection Axum re-emerged as Abyssinia (later Ethiopia). The Abyssinian kings or their vassals were usually the rulers of the Eritrean highlands with Christian Tigrinyan agriculturists forming the population, while the lowlands remained Islamic and a separate world predominantly populated by the Tigre and Beja peoples. In 1517 the Ottoman Turks won the coast and its inland plain; they were overthrown by the Egyptians in the 1860s, who went on to control all the lowlands of Eritrea. Once again, there was contact between highlands and lowlands. The governor on the plateau was allowed access to the sea – he was known by his peoples as *bahr negash* (lord of the sea) – but he had no authority on the coast.

In September 1869 a group of Italian missionaries arrived on the coast of Eritrea and stayed 18 months before returning home. The information they gathered interested their government, who consequently authorised the Rubattino Shipping Company to buy the port of Assab from the local ruler as a fueling and trading base. The Italians had gained their foothold in Africa.

It was the era of the European 'scramble for Africa' and the British, keen to

VICTIMS OF WAR

Eritrea has a population of roughly 3.5 million. However the war has had its toll: it created over 750,000 refugees, the vast majority of which ended up in camps on the Sudanese borders, while others found asylum in the Middle East, America and Europe; many are now returning home. More than 100,000 people were made homeless and sought refuge in the hills. Around 50,000 Eritrean fighters and 10,000 civilians lost their lives; 60,000 were handicapped; 50,000 children lost their parents. The current force of 100,000 EPLF fighters (men and women) is maintained — they are conspicuous by their khaki or green jackets — and, without pay, they are helping rebuild the country; the Asmara contingent is based in Kagnew Station.

offset the ambitions of their French rivals in this region, encouraged the Italians to extend their influence in Eritrea. In 1881 the Italian government bought Assab and designated it the Colonia di Assab under the rule of the King of Italy; four years later they captured Massawa.

By now the Egyptian occupation was on the decline. The powerful Emperor Yohannes of Abyssinia, in control of the highlands, saw opportunity and moved down to the lowlands and defeated the Egyptians. Meanwhile, the Italians, with their own colonising ambitions, moved inland. They clashed with the Abyssinian force led by Ras Alula, Yohannes' general, and were soundly defeated at the Battle of Dogali in 1887. It was the first victory over a European power by an African army.

Other wars diverted Yohannes from Eritrea and so the Italians faced little opposition when they relaunched their mission into the interior. They occupied the lands as far as the River Mareb, the traditional frontier with Abyssinia, and on 2nd May 1889 they established the Treaty of Wichale (Ucciali) with Menelik II, Yohannes' successor, which endorsed their presence in Eritrea. On 1st January 1890 the Italians officially declared Eritrea (the name is derived from Mare Erythraeum, the Roman name for the Red Sea) as their colony. For the first time since the heyday of the Kingdom of Axum these lands came under one ruler and for the first time ever these lands, with their different peoples and cultures, were defined within these frontiers of Eritrea as a country.

The Italians tried to extend their rule across the Mareb into Abyssinia, but they were soundly defeated at the famous Battle of Adwa on 1st March 1896. Their next attempt, in 1935, was more successful when, under orders from Mussolini, they conquered Abyssinia which by now was ruled by Emperor Haile Selassie. With this victory, the Italians decreed in June 1936 that their acquisitions of Eritrea, Italian Somaliland and Abyssinia constituted 'Africa Orientale Italiana' (Italian East Africa).

World War II heralded the beginning of the end of European colonialism. In East Africa, the British defeated the Italians and occupied their colonies. Eritrea came under British command from 1941, while Abyssinia was restored to Emperor Haile Selassie.

The victors of World War II could not decide amongst themselves how to dispose of Italy's former colonies and so the problem was left to the United

Nations who eventually, in 1952, passed Resolution 390-A (V) which declared an autonomous Eritrea should be federated with Abyssinia, now called Ethiopia.

However, Ethiopia soon violated the terms of the federation as it increasingly encroached upon Eritrea's rights as an autonomy. G.K.N. Trevaskis, a former British Administrator in Eritrea, warned: '...[Ethiopia's] temptation to subject Eritrea firmly under her own control will always be great. Should she try to do so, she will risk Eritrean discontent and eventual revolt, which, with foreign sympathy and support, might well distrupt both Eritrea and Ethiopia herself'. Haile Selassie never heeded such advice and in November 1962 he actually annexed Eritrea as a province of Ethiopia. The revolt and disruption Trevaskis had feared became a reality: The Eritrea-Ethiopia conflict which 'officially' started in 1962 continued until 1991 and became, during its time, the longest war in Africa.

Initially the Eritreans were split on ethnic, religious and ideological differences and they fought amongst themselves. Meanwhile, in Ethiopia, Haile Mariam Mengistu, an army officer, deposed Haile Selassie in 1974 and intensified the war. In the 1980s the Eritreans were finally able to unite as one people and rally as a nationalistic force, the Eritrean People's Liberation Front (EPLF); when Mengistu himself fell from power in the summer of 1991 they were able quickly to defeat the crumbling Ethiopian army.

TRAVEL

Entry and exit

A valid passport and an Eritrean visa is required for entry into Eritrea. Visas are available from EPLF offices (effectively embassies) around the world; speed of delivery and cost vary, but in European cities it is common to obtain a visa within 24 hours at a price of £25. If there is an EPLF office/embassy in your own country, it is necessary to get your visa there. You will not be issued one in Addis Ababa (Ethiopia). If there is no office in your own country, an Eritrean visa in Addis costs 10 birr, available from the EPLF office, in a villa on the south side of the road between Meskal Square and the railway station.

Visitors are required to have been vaccinated against Yellow Fever.

Money

The Eritrean currency is still the Ethiopian birr, though the Eritreans do plan to introduce their own money.

Hard currency must be declared on entry into Eritrea and receipts and statements showing exchange at officially recognised bureaux are usually demanded on departure. These, plus unspent money, should of course tally with the sum brought into the country.

Eritrea is in great need of hard currency in its drive to rebuild the country. But though the government tries to ensure all foreign money does pass through its authorised channels there is a lucrative black market, with the US dollar – the most favoured currency – fetching two to three times the official rate on the street.

The main branch of the government bank, where money can be exchanged, is on National Avenue in Asmara. The top hotels also have official money exchange desks. The US dollar is the advised currency to bring to Eritrea, though the English pound, Italian lire, German mark and Japanese yen can also be exchanged; other currencies are not so quickly identified. Travellers cheques are accepted. It is best to exchange money in Asmara before travelling the country, or at least find out where there are suitable banking facilities beyond the capital.

The 15 minute taxi ride from the airport to the centre of Asmara costs about $7.

What to buy

There has been little demand for souvenirs in recent years. Textiles, ceramics, woodwork, silverware and basketry can be bought in Asmara's main market. There are a few shops around town selling and making old and new ethnic and religious artefacts. The majority of Eritrea's Christians are Copts (Abyssian Christians) and now, with greater freedom to practise their faith, there is a desire for religious symbols; the distinctive Coptic cross, for example, is a unique souvenir from this part of Africa. Haile Gebrehiwat is a craftsman and dealer in cultural curios; his shop is at the end of Ras Mangesha Street, near the Karen Hotel.

Accommodation

Asmara has several good hotels, with the Ambasoira, in particular, being of an international standard. In Massawa they are rebuilding their better hotels; a room at the better hotels ranges from $8-13, but here, as in the other provincial capitals, there is also a choice of simple, inexpensive accommodation.

Eating

The Italian cuisine has been absorbed into the Eritrean eating habits, at least at the restaurant level. The standard 'Italian Menu' starts with a choice of pastas and is followed by a meat or fish dish and completed with ice cream or fruit. The traditional Eritrean food, including *injera*, the large pancake served with a variety of meat or vegetable sauces, is available at local eating places. Fish is naturally a main dish down on the coast. A meal at a restaurant is about $4.

Local wines, beers – the famous Melotti – and spirits, notably *araki*, the colourless aniseed brew, can be found at most bars. Scotch whisky, European beers and other alcohol are imported.

Whether or not the water is safe to drink depends on personal constitution. Local bottled spring water is readily available.

Transport

The main bus depot in Asmara is near the market, though buses to some destinations leave from the stadium end of National Avenue.

There are fairly frequent buses or collective taxis/mini buses to Massawa, Dekamere, Adi Keyeh, Mendefara and Keren (from here public transport continues along the Agordat and Nakfa routes); these places can be reached within hours or at most a day. The tiring land journey to Assab is currently via Ethiopia and takes several days. Asmara to Addis by road is also possible; it is about a five day trip along a poor road.

The Asmara to coast railway was destroyed during the recent war and will probably remain defunct for quite a while.

Chauffeur driven vehicles – Fiat cars, Land Rovers, mini buses – can be rented, though in the months after liberation there was a shortage of such vehicles. The Africa Garage at 29 Ras Wole Butul (tel: 111755) rents cars. Alternatively ask at the Tourist Office (see below).

Ethiopian Airlines operate a daily flight between Asmara and Addis Ababa at a cost of about $100 one way. Increasingly, Ethiopian Airlines' services between Addis and Europe and being routed via Asmara. The airline's office is on National Avenue.

Further Information

There are bound to be changes in regulations – and life in general – as Eritrea gets back on its feet and plans its future. For up-to-date information contact the Eritrean People's Liberation Front (EPLF) or other Eritrean representatives in your home country. Once in Eritrea the valuable source of information and issuer of permissions is the Department of Protocol; the office is currently in the Ambasoira Hotel. The fledgling Department of Tourism has an office in the Post Office square. Various Western aid agencies have set up branches in Asmara and their workers can provide sound advice and useful tips. Italy is at present the only country with an embassy; it is at Villa Roma (Box 220), near the Ambasoira Hotel. The Italian community, with their club at Casa d'Italiano off National Avenue, can also be enlightening. It is easy to orientate yourself around Asmara and people are always willing to help you find your destination. You are made to feel at home very quickly.

Photography   There are surprisingly few rules for a new country so fresh from war – you are free to photograph what you wish (save for military installations) and nobody questions your intentions.

TOWNS

Asmara

Capital of Eritrea, Asmara is situated on the eastern edge of the high plateau at a height of 2,325 metres; the city has a clement air with an average temperature of 17°C and an approximate annual rainfall of 510mm.

Asmara's war wounds are superficial compared to some Eritrean towns: Buildings may be shabby after years of neglect, but few bear the scars of bullets and bombs. The city is small, clean, pleasant and exudes an easy-going, warm, friendly atmosphere. Half way along National Avenue – Asmara's wide palm-lined central boulevard – is the imposing Catholic church; a kilometre or so beyond, the tower and dome of the Kidane Mehret Orthodox church sprout above the market; on the hill slope on other side of the market is the city mosque and the Coptic cathedral. Spreading over a large area, the market – abundant in fruit, vegetables, spices, animals and much more – is itself a main attraction of Asmara.

Occupied by the Ethiopian Dergue but not destroyed by battle, Asmara does have other legacies of the war: The city's population has swelled to around 300,000 partly due to the influx of refugees from around the country; Kagnew Station, the military base on the edge of town originally built by the Americans and now home for the EPLF fighters, has hundreds of captured tanks and armoured vehicles in its backyard awaiting to be scrapped; on the same side of town and now open to the public is Mariam Gimbi, the prison where Mengistu's men tortured EPLF sympathisers. Memories of older wars are less brutal: the British and their allied soldiers, who died fighting the Italians in 1941, are neatly buried in a well kept cemetery outside Asmara, near the zoo on the road to Massawa.

Sleeping and eating   There are five hotels in Asmara which are deemed suitable for visitors (most have a restaurant): the **Ambasoira** (32 Dejatch Hailu Street, Tel: 113222) is the best and most modern hotel in town, a few blocks from National Avenue; rooms at 65-75 birr; the **Nyala** (67 Col. Belay Haileab Street, Tel: 113111) is a high-rise hotel, a little far from the main downtown with rooms at 45-65 birr; the **Ambassador** (36 National Avenue, Tel: 116544) is another high-rise hotel on the city's main thoroughfare, earmarked for refurbishment with rooms currently at 25-45 birr; the **Karen** (7 Victory Street, Tel: 110740) is an old colonial building with faded charm of a bygone era – decorative urns and a chandelier in the salmon pink dining room – a few blocks from National Avenue (other side of it to the Ambasoira) with rooms at 30-40 birr; the **Hamasien** (30 Dejatch Hailu Street, Tel: 110233) is a large rambling colonial building next to the Ambasoira; in need of refurbishment, but with character and rooms at 25-35 birr.

Other less expensive hotels and lodges do exist, but they tend to be for local travellers; one such place – it does not appear to have a name – is in an old villa near the Italian Consulate (just down the road from the Ambasoira) which is set in a garden with colonial Romanesque statues and tumbling bougainvillea.

Asmara's hotel restaurants tend to serve Western dishes. Elsewhere in town there are the **San Giorgio** and the **Asmara**, both near the Post Office in the side streets off National Avenue; they serve the typical Italian menu as well as traditional Eritrean food. On the other side of town and not far from the Nyala Hotel, is the **Caravelle** – serving the 'Italian menu' – which is also a disco on Friday nights.

Some cafes serve Italian pastries and small pizzas for breakfast. For example there is **Cafe Alba** – still run by the Italian family who founded it – in the street behind and parallel to National Avenue; several blocks up the street is one of the best pastry cafes, newly decorated in pink, lilac and candy green.

There are numerous cafes and bars serving coffee, beer, wines and spirits. These are a popular rendezvous and the ones along National Avenue – such as the **Cafe Royal** with its pavement seating – are usually packed in the evenings when people promenade this central boulevard. They are fun places in which to while away a few hours.

Some of the hotels organise evening entertainment. The Caravelle has its disco and there is weekly dancing and live music at the Mocambo club just off National Avenue.

PLACES OF INTEREST

East to the coast

Eritrea's main road runs east from Asmara and wends a gradual and dramatic path down the plateau to the coastal plain and the port of Massawa. Built by the Italians, it is a highly strategic route – the link between the inland and the sea and the country's two main cities – and it was damaged as both sides fought for its control during the recent war. The road is tarmac and is currently undergoing repair; along the way lie burnt out tanks and destroyed villages awaiting clearance and reconstruction.

Massawa, Eritrea's largest port and main outlet to the world, was ruined by the war. Haile Selaissie's palace, the colonial residences, the mosque, the waterfront, and the Dahlak Hotel were all destroyed. The ageing dockyard is back in operation and is handling an impressive tonnage of merchandise given its dated equipment. There are simple restaurants serving fish and the hotels are being restored. About 15 minutes drive out of town is Massawa's resort, a simple hotel-restaurant complex on a white stretch of sand where you can swim in the warm waters of the Red Sea. Off shore are the **Dahlak Islands**, once an Ethiopian military base with an Israeli built air strip, where the scuba diving is reputedly comparable with the best in the Red Sea.

South of Massawa is the **Danakil** – one of the hottest, least hospitable places on earth. The strip of land measures 15-80km in width and, at the Kobar Sink, lies 116m below sea level; there are no proper roads through this region. At the far end, near the border with Djibouti, is the sweltering port of **Assab**, capital of Danakil province, which may become a Freeport and the all important outlet to the sea for Ethiopia.

South towards Ethiopia

Two southbound roads lead out of Asmara and pass through hill country to Ethiopia.

An hour or two to the southeast of Asmara is **Dekamere**. For a time the town was in the frontline of the fighting. Dawit Wolde Giorgis, an Ethiopian posted as governor of Eritrea by Mengistu in 1980, went on a fact-finding mission prior to taking office; he was greatly saddened by the damage his side had inflicted:

'The hardest part for me was my visit to Dekamere, a once beautiful little place 25 miles (40kms) south of Asmara. The Italians used to call it "Secondo Roma" because it looked so much like a small Italian town. I had lived here for two years in the early 1960s when I was assigned to the nearby military training centre. Dekamere meant a lot to me; a part of my youth was spent here. I knew every restaurant, every bar, and had many friends ... It was a lovely city of fruit trees, parks, small factories and vineyards which produced the best wine in the country ... It had been nine years since I had last visited, and what I saw now sickened me. Dekamere was half destroyed and what remained was a ghost town'.

Today Dekamere still lies half destroyed, but at least life and optimism has returned to the town.

The road proceeds from Dekamere through spectacular hills to **Adi Keyeh**, a small oasis of a town and provincial capital of Akele Guzai province, with irrigation schemes nuturing nurseries and market gardens. The route continues into Ethiopia.

The other southbound road out of Asmara descends to Adi Ugri before entering a hilly region and the town of **Mendefara**, provincial capital of Serae. The border with Ethiopia is approximately 25km further south.

West and north towards Sudan

A road northwest from Asmara runs through the hills of the high plateau of Hamasien province and serves as the link to west and north Eritrea. It is about 130km along this route to **Keren**, capital of Senhit province, and here the road divides:

The route to the southwest cuts across the lowlands of **Barka** province through Agordat, the provincial capital, and on to Barentu and Tessenei, before crossing the border into Sudan.

The way north is rough and leads through rugged, arid hills to Afabet and Nakfa, the capital of **Sahel** province, and onto Karora on the northern border with Sudan. During the liberation war, this route was the essential line of communication between 'free' Eritrea and the outside world.

For much of the war, the southern part of Eritrea was occupied by the Ethiopians and only the far north – the hills of Sahel – remained as 'free' Eritrea. The EPLF resettled in these hills, a relative safe haven from where they despatched fighters to the front lines around the country. Furthermore, these harsh hills became home for their families, orphans of the war and many EPLF members serving in a civil capacity. Away from the centres of fighting, these hills were still within range of the Ethiopian MiG jets. The new dwellings, schools, orphanages, hospitals, factories, bakeries, canteens, printing presses, a library and a radio station were built in caves or dug into the ground and camouflaged. Steep narrow valleys, such as those around Orota to the west of the north-south route and just below the Sudanese border, were chosen as they were more hazardous for the jets to negotiate. Always alert to the very real possibility of air raids, the inhabitants continued their lives as normally as possible under these difficult and strange conditions.

WHITE MAN'S MEDICINE

Travellers off the beaten path in Africa will sooner or later be approached by villagers asking for medicine. This poses a difficult problem: even if you have the applicable drug for the illness you cannot stay to supervise the treatment, so the chances of it doing the trick are small. And if it doesn't, you will be undermining the villagers' faith in western medicine and so perhaps making the job of government doctors or rural clinics more difficult. More importantly, if it does work you may damage the villagers' faith in traditional healing practices or village-based medicine which is probably all they have. It is hard not to try to alleviate the suffering you see, but it may, in the long run, be the responsible reaction.

One incident in Ethiopia is etched in my memory. When we hiked past a remote village in Wollo, the poorest of provinces, the villagers ran to us for treatment of their horrible sores and ulcers. We were busy painting them with iodine when a woman led a young boy to us. His closed and bulging eyes were infected; he would soon be blind. All we could do was shake our heads, and recognise the futility of our "treatment" which, in truth, was provided to make us feel better, not the villagers.

Dr Jane Wilson adds:-

If you have any intention of interfering with systems of village health care, you should consider carefully what you are doing and do some homework. The disease that you are most likely to see (and be asked to treat) are skin infections which get a hold so much easier in the tropics. You should find out what antiseptics are available locally (potassium permanganate and gentian violet are often available very cheaply; creams like germoline are less effective) and dispense these explaining that next time they could do this themselves. This demystifies western medicine and will also do good in the long term. That boy's blinding infection might have been prevented by early, appropriate, cheap treatment like this.

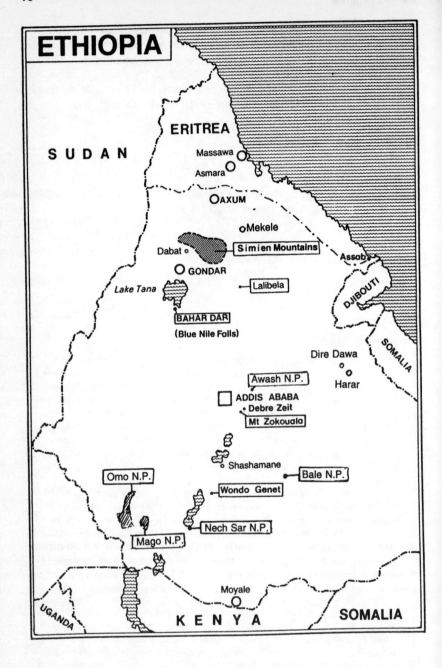

ETHIOPIA

SUDAN

ERITREA

Massawa

Asmara

AXUM

Mekele

Dabat

Simien Mountains

GONDAR

Lalibela

Lake Tana

BAHAR DAR

(Blue Nile Falls)

Assab

DJIBOUTI

SOMALIA

Dire Dawa

Awash N.P.

Harar

ADDIS ABABA

Debre Zeit

Mt Zokouala

Shashamane

Omo N.P.

Bale N.P.

Wondo Genet

Nech Sar N.P.

Mago N.P.

UGANDA

Moyale

KENYA

SOMALIA

Chapter 8

Ethiopia

Revised and expanded by Ron Barak, Conrad Hirsh, Bryan Hanson, Val and Gavin Thomson, and Javier Grinfeld and Liora Donskoy.

FACTS AND FIGURES

Ethiopia is the tenth-largest country in Africa with an area of 1¼ million square kilometres (twice the size of France). Broadly speaking the country is a high plateau, with an average elevation of 2,500 metres, surrounded by low lying desert. The north and centre are mountainous, with more than 25 peaks rising to over 4,000 metres.

The climate is dominated by rainy and dry seasons. The small rains (*kremt*) fall from late February to early April and the big rains from late June to early September. (The *Maskal* ceremony at the end of September marks the end of these rains.) The *bega* are the warm dry months, with April, May and June being unpleasantly hot in the lowlands. The highlands are always a comfortable temperature in the dry season but very unpleasant in the big rains.

Agriculture is the main economic activity and most people are subsistence farmers. Principal exports are coffee (which originated from here) and oil-seeds. It's common to see villagers roasting the coffee beans before grinding them for a freshly brewed drink.

The Ethiopian years are determined by the pre-Julian solar calendar, which is similar to the one used in ancient Egypt and quite different to our Gregorian one. The year is divided into 12 months of 30 days each, with a 13th month of five or six days days tacked on at the end. Hence the tourist posters' claim of 'thirteen months of sunshine' (although this seems a sad joke in the middle of the rainy season). Ethiopia is about seven years and eight months behind the West, but all Ethiopians and all documents in English make the necessary adjustments.

Ethiopia and Eritrea were at war for 30 years until Tigrean and Eritrean rebels toppled Mengistu Haile Mariam, the Ethiopian leader, in 1991. Mengistu had overthrown Emperor Haile Selassie in 1974. After the April 1991 revolution, the EPRDF came to power. Local elections were carried out in June 1992, but may have to be run again as there was suspicion of rigging. General elections have been promised.

Ethiopia's flora and fauna are of outstanding interest, with the highest rate of endemicity in Africa.

People

As a country that was never colonised, Ethiopia is almost unique in Africa. True, the Italians made their presence felt during the late 19th Century when they annexed Eritrea, and again in 1935 when they invaded the whole country, but in general the various tribes have developed their own distinctive cultures unimpeded by outside influences. As the historian Edward Gibbon (1737-1794) wrote: 'Ethiopia, encompassed on all sides by the enemies of its religion, slept near a thousand years forgetful of the world by whom it was forgotten.'

Ethiopia has a population of 45 million, with a growth rate of about 2.5% per year. There are three main tribal groups: the Oromo, the most numerous and found mainly in the south, the Tigrinya in the north, and the Amhara who live in the central highland areas around Addis Ababa, the capital.

Amharic is the spoken language in and around Addis Ababa, but it is no longer the official language of the whole country. TV broadcasts are now in Oromo, Tigrinya and English, as well as Amharic. In the north and northwest Tigrinya is the primary language while in the south Oromo (also known as Gallina) is predominant.

Both Amharic and Tigrinya descend from Ge'ez (the same relationship that French and Italian have to Latin) which is an ancient Semitic language that is now used only by the Orthodox Church of Ethiopia. Amharic and Tigrinya are totally different from Oromina, which is a Hamitic language. Amharic has its own unique script, made up of 33 consonants with variations to signify the vowels, and Oromina is written in roman script.

About half the population are Muslim, and many people are members of the Coptic Church (Orthodox Christian) or practise traditional religions.

Ethiopia used to have a small minority of Jews, called *Falashas*, who for centuries thought themselves to be the only ones of their faith in the world, but, since the 1985 mass evacuation known as Operation Solomon, almost all *Falashas* have emigrated to Israel.

SOME USEFUL AMHARIC PHRASES

Hello/goodbye	*tanastalin*	Please	*ibakih* (to men)/*ibakish* (to women)
Thank you	*amsagenalu*	Yes	*awoh*
No	*yelem/aydelem*	Okay	*ishi*
Very	*batam*	Very good	*batam tiro*
Mr/Mrs	*ato/waziro*	Foreigner	*farangi*
Food	*mugub*	Water	*wuha*
Tea	*chai*	Milk/	*wa'tat*
Ethiopian coffee	*buna*	European coffee	*makiato*
Bread	*dabo*	Banana	*muz*
Sauce	*wat*	Egg	*enculal*
Chicken	*dura*	Expensive	*wud*
Cheap	*rekash*	Road	*mengad*
Village	*serfer*	House	*bet*
Hut	*tukul*	Toilet	*shintabet*
Right	*kan*	Left	*graa/chrmachina*
Tomorrow	*nega*	Tomorrow morning	*nega twat*
Which is the road to...?	*ye...mengad yet no?*	Where are you going?	*wadyet teheduluh?*
How much is it?	*sint no wagaw?*	Where is Gondar?	*Gondar yetno?*
What is it?	*mindeno?*	What's your name?	*sumu mano?*
Go away!	*hid!*	Give me (I want)	*seten* (to men)/*sichin* (to women)
One tea please	*and chai ibakih* (to men)/*and chai ibakesh* (to women)	How are you?	*danane* (to men)
I want...	*afellegum*	I don't want...	*alfellegum*
(Hailing a taxi)	*warach bakah*		
1	*and*	2	*hulet*
3	*sost*	4	*arat*
5	*amist*	6	*sidist*
7	*sabat*	8	*simint*
9	*zeten*	10	*assr*
20	*haya*	25	*haya amist*
30	*salassa*	40	*arba*
50	*hamsa*	60	*silsa*
70	*saba*	80	*samana*
90	*zetana*	100	*meto*
1000	*shi*		

TRAVEL

Impressions

In the first edition of this book (1977) I wrote: 'After the relative sameness of East Africa we were at first enchanted by Ethiopia. The people are so varied, their religion so different, their clothes and jewellery so beautiful, the scenery so magnificent and travelling so cheap we were completely bowled over. Inevitably disillusionment set in, and after eight weeks we wanted only to escape from the filth, the constant begging, the cheating and political bickering. The bargain hotels turned out to be full of fleas and the countryside so full of *shifta* that for the first time in Africa we feared for our lives. Ethiopians are either unbelievably nice or remarkably unpleasant. Many people have reached a high level of competence in manipulating foreigners. It was the need to be constantly on our guard that finally made us crack. That, and the incessant cry of "Faranji!" echoing round our ears from morn til night. And yet kindness and helpfulness were abundant, and the hospitality more open-handed than any we received elsewhere.'

This politically incorrect reaction has been echoed by some recent travellers, including Val and Gavin Thomson, who were driving their own Land Rover, so open to more hassles than backpackers but also able to see more of the country. Some of their impressions: 'We passed through a stream of peasantry returning from the market. Weather-beaten faces under wide-brimmed hats, becloaked horsemen cantered by in the rain, loads of thatch or produce bent the walkers' backs – it was truly like driving through a scene in *Henry V*!... On the way to the next town there were numerous wrecked tanks, trucks, missile launchers. These became all-too-common sights, uglifying the truly breathtaking mountain scenery which Ethiopia has in abundance. We could only reflect on the incongruity of the best of modern technology being used to destroy one of the most backward places in the world.... We headed north through the Simien Mountains – yet another range of utterly spectacular peaks, chasms, cliffs and hair-raising roads. Whole ridges of peaks like church spires would dominate the horizon...'.

In contrast to the trials of independent travellers, two tour operators checking out the country had very favourable impressions: 'I found the new Ethiopia much more free, open, *laissez-faire* and relatively free of obstacles.' (Conrad Hirsh). 'What we found was progress and happiness; an astonishing *joie de vivre* that you could almost touch.' (Stephen Dallyn, Exodus).

For budget-minded, independent travellers it seems that the main requirement for fully appreciating the wonders of Ethiopia is the right frame of mind, and the knowledge that after years of war and famine a real effort at rehabilitation is being made. If you are physically or psychologically exhausted from too much travel perhaps you should give it a miss. This exceptional country requires exceptional travellers. Those unsure of their ability to cope with the hassles should consider an organised tour.

Entry and exit

All foreigners need a visa, which is given in 48 hours in Nairobi. It will be valid for a month. An exit visa, which gives you a further month, is required if you stay for longer than 30 days. This is obtainable from the Immigration Department in Addis Ababa, near the post office (the old Ministry of Justice).

Visas are stamped 'by air only'. Officially you are not allowed to enter overland, but Conrad Hirsh, a Nairobi based tour operator, reports: 'Some people have been getting across from Moyale (from Kenya), and the situation is likely to normalise and become easier. There is no problem crossing to/from Eritrea, providing you have a visa' *which must be obtained in your country of origin*. Others have managed to enter from Sudan but have had a problem leaving because of the exit visa requirement. Try to check the situation with other travellers before making your plans.

There is an international airport tax of US$10.

Money

The monetary unit in Ethiopia is the birr (a nice word to say!), divided into 100 cents. The official rate for one US dollar is 5.56 birr (November 1993).

Currency declaration forms are issued on arrival. These must be used to record all money exchanged, or any purchases made with foreign currency. You should save all bank and shop receipts for this. Theoretically, excess birr can be changed back into hard currency when you leave if your currency declaration form is in order.

Telephone

The system is very good. Many public phones exist, in working order and unvandalised, and many kiosks have phones available at 50c a call. Faxes and international calls can be made at the Telecommunications offices. In Addis this is near the Ras hotel.

What to buy

Ethiopian handicrafts are among the most beautiful and interesting in Africa. There is an enormous choice ranging from lovely hand-knotted rugs in natural wool colours and traditional designs, to silver jewellery and amber.

There used to be a thriving business in religious art, robbing the country of its rich religious heritage. The trade was supported by the Marxist government. Since religion has gained its former status, no religious artefacts should be taken out of the country.

Maps and brochures

In Addis ask at the ETC (Ethiopian Tourism Commission) office on the ground floor at Meskel Square, both for maps and the excellent and attractive brochures. Maps and information on the national parks may be obtained from the Wildlife Conservation Organisation by the Mobil station at the other end of Meskel Square (5th floor, tricky elevator). Or ask at bookshops.

Warnings

There are no official travel restrictions but since the revolution (and the turbulent transition period which has followed), road travel has been unsafe at times, with groups of armed bandits regularly attacking vehicles in some areas. You should carefully check the current situation before leaving Addis Ababa. In general, however, violent crime is much rarer than in Kenya.

In Addis beware pickpockets on city buses.

Ethiopian officials (including police and military) are still pretty paranoid about photography. Do not use your camera in any area which might be considered sensitive: near public buildings, bridges, dams, stations, and so on.

Be particularly careful not to contract malaria; few cheap hotels are properly screened against mosquitoes. Flies have been described as 'The national bird of Ethiopia!'.

When Ethiopian people agree with you they breathe in as if they are choking. Do not be alarmed.

The time of day is measured from dawn (6.00am). Thus if your bus ticket says you leave at 2.00 it probably, but not invariably, means 8.00. Always check with the ticket clerk.

Accommodation

Large towns and cities have tourist hotels which tend to be expensive (about $20 a double) and sometimes require payment in hard currency. Chains that crop up all over the country are the Ras and Bekele Mola hotels, but there are some new private hotels that offer clean, bright, self-contained rooms at very modest rates, not to mention a warm welcome and good service. They also have lively bars, delicious coffee and both European and Ethiopian food. For those on a tight budget, very cheap local-style hotels are easy to find; they are usually painted pink or green. Rooms here are around 5 birr.

Eating

People, myself included, get very excited about Ethiopian food. It is totally different from anything served in other parts of Africa. In the first edition I wrote: 'Ethiopian national food and drink are unique so deserve a special description. When you first eat at a typical Ethiopian restaurant you'll be amazed to be confronted by a large disc of thin, grey foam rubber. It's dotted with various colours of sludge, all meant to be eaten without cutlery! *Injera* is unleavened sour bread and *wat* is a spicy vegetable or meat stew. When we say spicy we mean hot enough to make you choke, cry and pant a lot. Fortunately we loved it from the start, and even suffered severe withdrawal symptoms all through the Sudan. While the *injera* is a constant, the *wat* varies enormously. Vegetable *wat*, made from chick peas or maize, is always good and cheap and quite mild. Meat *wat* is pricier, hotter, tougher but almost always delicious.' Gavin and Val are more succinct: 'Sometimes it is labelled as bug wat, sometimes kuk wat, but invariably it tastes like guess wat.'

If you never acquire the taste for *injera* and *wat* many European and

Eritrean restaurants have recently opened.

The national drink is *tej* or honey mead, of varying strength and flavour. We loved it, so did Conrad Hirsh: 'It has been known to produce some happy, giggly highs as well as the occasional headache when imbibed overabundantly. *Tej* is preferably quaffed from the traditional glass *birille* while seated on long wooden benches in a rustic *Tej bet*, where the hostess repeatedly fills your *birille* deftly from the spout of a big teapot at high elevation. The *birilles* are placed on similar long benches with anti-sliding rims, and the trick is to make your exit over same without knocking everything ass over teakettle. *Tella* is a lighter drink brewed from barley that can be a good thirst-quencher on trek – it is frequently sold at shady places at strategic points of market-going trails.'

Transport

Ethiopia has the French to thank for the 780km railway link between Addis and Djibouti (currently being modernised), and the Italians for a fine network of roads, bridges and tunnels through the mountainous north.

Buses and **minibuses** are generally in good condition and driven soberly. They are also very crowded. Try to go to the bus station the day before departure to book a ticket; if you can get an Ethiopian to help, do so. (In 1976 the only way we could get on a bus from the Kenyan border was to pay a ragamuffin child to fight his way on, so we could pass our backpacks through the window, then shove our own way on board.)

Although the bandit (*shifta*) problem has eased, they are still a danger, and though they will not kill you for your property they might leave you naked (literally) on the road. The situation is improving; check with other travellers before planning an itinerary.

Currently the **train** is running, but terrorists could alter the situation at any moment. The EPRDF forces are spread too thin throughout the countryside to give any real protection.

Air travel is the safest form of transport, and Ethiopian Airlines operate an extensive domestic network, although many towns have dirt airstrips which can be closed during the rainy seasons (travel to Lalibela, for example, can be affected by this). Departure is on a flexible basis; check and recheck the official departure time. Sometimes domestic air tickets bought in Addis have to paid for with foreign currency, but birr are accepted in other towns, so you can save money by getting two single tickets.

Sample prices (June 1993): Addis to Axum, 212 birr ($52); to Gondar or Lalibela 161 birr ($32).

For domestic flights out of Addis you need to get to the Domestic terminal, where you'll see several unmarked queues. Ask which is the one for your destination. As a foreigner, when you *do* find the right queue, you'll probably be shoved to the head of it and it'll be a breeze. Planes run like buses: seats are not numbered and conditions are spartan. Be sure to dress warmly as there may be no heating and it can get very cold during the flight. Try to choose a seat at the back of the plane, as the noise of the propellers at the front can be quite loud.

On landing at any airport outside Addis, find the local representative of

Ethiopian Airlines (most easily found at the airport rather than in the town) to reconfirm your flight back; even if your ticket was confirmed in Addis, you might find your name absent from the return flight list.

There is a 5 birr airport tax on every domestic flight.

Because of the danger of highjacking, there is strict security and baggage check-in, frisking, etc, which require an early check-in time.

Organised tours

It is well worth considering booking a tour of Ethiopia if your time is short or you want a proper holiday.

In Britain Experience Ethiopia Travel (211 Clapham Rd, London SW9 0QH; tel: 071 738 3197) works with Ethiopian self-help organisations, local authorities and local business people to create tours which will benefit local communities. They deserve support.

Conrad Hirsh, a contributor to this chapter, organises his own adventure trips including rafting the Omo and Awash rivers. Contact him at PO Box 59622, Nairobi; tel: (254 2) 891331. Other operators specialising in Africa are starting to add Ethiopia to their itineraries; several have advertised in this book.

A recommended tour operator in Addis is Nile Touring Co, with an office opposite the stadium in the road between the Ghion and Harambee Hotels. Box 3228. Tel: 513553/518403.

The Ethiopian National Tourist Organisation (NTO) organise (expensive) tours to various sites around the country. Contact their office in Addis Ababa for details: PO Box 5709, tel: 153827.

Festivals

The visitor to Ethiopia will encounter strong local traditions in food, drink, dress, and manners. Traditional national holidays are celebrated from the heart. It can be a special treat to be present, whether in a small town, a historic place like Lalibela, or even Addis Ababa, for the Ethiopian New Year, Meskel, Genna, Easter, or Idd. These festivals are celebrated by feasting, dancing and general merriment.

THE COPTIC CHURCH

The Coptic Orthodox Church of Ethiopia is the oldest Christian church in the world, dating back to the 4th Century.

The lavish trappings associated with this church make a fascinating spectacle for tourists, as do the beautiful paintings of the saints that decorate the church walls. These Coptic saints seem to have led much more interesting lives than ours. There's St Eostateos, who managed to float up the Nile on long stones, St Gabre Manfas Kiddus, who wandered around for 300 years dressed in furs and preaching peace to wild animals, and St Abuna Samuel who befriended a lion. Most admirable, however, is St Tekla Haimanot, who spent seven years standing on one leg, surviving on one seed a year, fed to him by a bird. How this promoted Christianity is not made clear.

TOWNS AND PLACES OF INTEREST

Note: because there is so little information on Ethiopia available to travellers, this section has broken with the format of the rest of the book to give more coverage of regular tourist sites.

Addis Ababa

This is the modern capital of Ethiopia. All international flights arrive here, and most travellers can't wait to get out. The city has no redeeming features, although the largest open-air market in Africa (Mercato) is worth visiting, and some of the restaurants will give you a very enjoyable evening out. If you are stuck in the city, check the bulletin board at the Hilton Hotel for outings and cultural events. Streets are seldom named.

The focal point in the city is Maskal Square which was formerly known as Abiot (Revolution) Square. Streets are seldom named.

Sleeping and eating There are plenty of cheap local hotels around, but best get your bearings in one of the better ones first. Recommended in the middle range of hotels are the Yordanos (on the Asmara Road, 5 mins walk from Meskel Sq) rooms $20-$30, and the Extreme (200m west of Tewodros Sq on the road to Tekla Haymanot and the Mercato). $17 for a large room.

Under the new government, small free enterprises are springing up: several pastry and coffee shops have been opened, along with some new restaurants. Try the fried fish at The Cottage restaurant on the avenue between the Ghion Hotel and the GPO, just off the junction near the Ethiopia Hotel. Other recommended restaurants are Castelli's and Blue Tops (Italian) opposite the National Museum. Favourite Ethiopian places include The Sheraton (no relation) and Tiru Migib (opposite the Yordanos).

There is some lively nightlife. Quite a few new discos have opened. A bar with lots of character, offering drinks, food, and occasional live music is The Coffee House, near Sidist Kiloo. Also try Cheers, on the Debre Zeyt Road.

Getting around 'Contract taxis' are blue and white. You will have to bargain hard to get a fair price. Minibuses are much better. You are charged according to distance travelled. Private taxis are blue and you will need to bargain over the fare. 5 birr should get you to most places.

White taxis are operated by the National Tourist Organisation (NTO), and found at the airport and outside major hotels. You pay in advance at a nearby booth. Do not pay the driver.

Gondar

Gondar was the capital of Ethiopia from the time of its founder Emperor Fasiladas, known as Fasil (1632-1665) until the mid-19th Century. It is part of the so-called Historic Route, and its castles and churches are very impressive. The main place of interest is the Imperial Precinct, a compound which contains several castles built by various emperors during the 200 years that the city flourished, and there are also some interesting churches.

Getting there   Gondar can be reached from Addis by road or plane. The bus ride is very long. If you're flying you can go direct (161 birr) or via Bahar Dar. The airport is some 17km out of town, and usually some local taxis wait to meet the plane. The ride should be about 30 birr but you'll need to bargain hard.

Sleeping and eating   Gondar has many hotels. The Goha Hotel (part of the Ghion chain of government hotels) is by far the best in town, in a magnificent location on a hill overlooking the northeast outskirts of town. Double rooms with toilet and bath cost about 110 birr. The meals are excellent. The Quara Hotel is right in the Piassa, east of the telecommunications building and within 10 minutes walk of the castles. Double self-contained rooms cost 65 birr. Cheaper local hotels abound.

Getting around   In addition to the regular blue and white taxis, Gondar is also full of horse-carts which can be used like taxis.

Bargaining is the name of the (transport) game in Gondar. Taxi drivers generally settle for half of their initial asking price.

Sightseeing

The Imperial Precinct and castles   The centre of Gondar is called the *Piassa* (Piazza), and from there an avenue leads south (past the offices of the NTO, Ethiopian Airlines and the city cinema) to the Imperial Precinct and the castles.

To save you any disappointment you should note that these 'castles' are very small: some are no more than 200m square. They do have a distinct style however, marked by high wooden doors and dome-capped towers.

Before you go into the castle compound, walk around the outer walls to get an impression of their size and layout. Entrance is 30 birr and the ticket also gets you into Fasil's Bath (see below). Tickets do not seem to have been updated for some time as the inscription reads: *Imperial Ethiopian Government, Antiquities Administration, Gondar Branch*.

As you walk into the compound (aiming south) from the entrance you'll see on your left several cages: one contains a very bored and weary lion. Nearby stands **Tsadiku Yohannes's Castle**, and south of this is the library and chancery that are attributed to Yohannes I, Fasiladas's son and successor. The inscription on it reads: *A-Alef Seghed Tsadiku Yohannes's Castle 1667-1682*. (*A-Alef* means 'To whom there are countless bowings'). The building is in very good repair and serves today as the compound's office.

The oldest building in the compound is **Emperor Fasiladas's Castle**. It is still in good condition and you can climb up onto the roof (beware the precarious wooden planks) to reach the look-out tower and get a fantastic 360-degree view over Gondar. The inscription on the castle reads: *Alem-Seghed Fasil's Castle 1632-1667*. (*Alem-Seghed* means 'To whom the world will bow'.)

In the northeast end of the compound stands a castle which is larger than most of the others, but not in a very good state of repair. This is **Birhan-Seghed Kuaregna Iyasu and Itegue Minitwab's Castle**, 1730-1755. (*Birhan-*

Seghed means 'To whom the light will bow'.)

Finally, to the east of the lion cage is **Adbar-Seghed Dawit's Castle** (1716-1721). (*Adbar Seghed* means 'To whom all the abstract things will bow to'.) So that just about wraps up the bowings.

Fasil's Bath Emperor Fasiladas's bathing pavilion (where in January the *Timkat* festival takes place) is another attraction. Entrance tickets cannot be bought at the gate here, you have to use the one you bought at the Castles. The main attractions are the place to set the Emperor's crown, the fire-places, and, on the northern side near the compound wall, the royal stable for Zovel, the emperor's horse, which is now buried in a small building about 70m away from the eastern gate.

Debre Birhan Salassie Church This lies on the southeastern outskirts of Gondar. It was built during the reign of Emperor Lyasu (1682-1706), Fasiladas's son, and is well-preserved and, although not very impressive from the outside, is tiny but magnificent inside, the walls being entirely covered in vivid paintings of biblical stories, Christian myths and Crusader epics while the ceiling has a famous motif of rows and rows of angel faces.

To reach the church, take the paved road from the Total petrol station leading south, past the Road Transportation Authority on the right. As the paved road makes a turn to the right (west), leave it and continue straight ahead on a dirt road. You will cross one paved road and then the dirt road will end at a second paved road. Take this road to the left (downhill) and after about 300m, where it starts to climb uphill, the church is on your right.

The church is about 350 years old, as are some of the trees in the compound. Around the church stand twelve towers. Those that still have roofs are lived in by monks. On the south of the compound, near the outer wall, there is a small house that accommodates the bibles of the church. On the roof of the church are two crosses decorated with white balls which are actually ostrich eggs. The bell near the entrance was donated by the Catholic church. According to the local guide, the painting on the church walls and ceilings were completed in 1682 using natural colours from soils and plants. The designs were painted on to *shema* (traditional Ethiopia white cloth) which were then glued to the wall.

Local legend tells that in the year 1888 the *Derbush* from Sudan came to destroy the church, and were driven away by bees living in the compound.

Bahar Dar, Lake Tana and the Blue Nile Falls

The Blue Nile Falls flow out of Lake Tana which lies to the northwest of Addis. This is Ethiopia's largest lake and a major source of the Blue Nile, which joins the White Nile in Khartoum and then flows through Egypt to the Mediterranean. The best time to see the falls is at the end of the rainy season, (September - October), when they are full of water.

Bahar Dar

Getting there The town lies on the southern shore of Lake Tana. It is possible to go by bus, but this is over 600km, and requires an overnight stop (probably at Finote Salem – literally 'The Peace Road' – some 86km north of Debre Markos). On the way from Addis, halfway between Goha Tsiyon and Dejen, you'll pass over the Blue Nile on an impressive modern bridge – photography prohibited!

You can fly to Bahar Dar for 153 birr. A local taxi from the airport into town is 30 birr.

Eating and sleeping   The best hotel in Bahar Dar is the Tana Hotel on the shores of that lake. Double rooms cost about 210 birr per person. The Ghion is cheaper at 170 birr, and the location in the centre of town convenient.

The Blue Nile Falls

From Bahar Dar to the Blue Nile Falls is about 35km. Transport can be arranged in town. Get a group together and bargain hard (Ron Barak paid 125 birr – half the starting price, Bryan Hanson settled for 250 birr, but he found a bus (3 birr) to take him there). Head for the village Tis Isat (meaning 'Smoky Flame' in Amharic), which is on the lake. The falls themselves are called either Tis Isat or Tis Abay. (Abay is the name of the Blue Nile in Ethiopia.) In the village you will be swarmed over by children, seeking employment as guides to the falls, but you can find your own way if you want. There are two possibilities:

1) (In the wet season.) Take the road out of Bahar Dar towards the hydro-electric plant. About 50 metres before the plant, take a track on the right across a small wooden bridge, and follow this out of the village past the hydro plant on the left and a church on your right and parallel to a small creek. After about 200m the track descends towards the Blue Nile which you cross on an old bridge. (According to my guide it is more than 350 years old).

On the other bank the path turns right along the river, and immediately there is a fork in the road. Go left, up the hill, and after a few metres left again to go upstream parallel to the river. As you go uphill, you pass through a small village, and soon you hear the roar of the falls. When you get level with the hydro plant on the other side of the river, you can leave the path and go towards the noise of the river for a breathtaking view of three of the four falls.

If you continue on the path you will see the fourth fall, plus the tropical vegetation created on the islands in the river. You may be lucky and spot the rainbow.

2) (In the dry season.) From the Hydro-electric plant at the end of the road from Bahar Dar, go through the village taking the trail leading northeast. After about a half kilometre you'll reach the bank of the Blue Nile. Here papyrus boats are available for crossing the river. Bargain hard (Ron paid 10 birr). On reaching the other bank go downstream and after about 200 metres you'll reach a cliff. In the wet season this is the top of the Falls!

Lake Tana Island

Lake Tana has several islands with old churches on them, one of which can be reached from Bahar Dar. To get there you have to go to the Lake Authority opposite the Telecommunications building and hire a boat. This costs 150 birr per hour, regardless of how many people are renting, and has to be booked for four hours, but you get a refund if you come back sooner. The boat holds about 30 passengers and the ride takes about 45 minutes. There is also a speed boat which costs 300 birr.

Once you arrive at the island it is a pleasant walk through dense bush to a church that has traditional Ethiopian paintings on the inner walls depicting events from the New Testament. Entrance is 4 birr per person, payable to the monk at the door. Do not forget to remove your shoes.

You can also ask the monks to show you the treasures, which are kept in a building near the church. These include the crowns of some of the ancient kings of Ethiopia and the vestments the monks wear on special occasions.

You can also spend some time wandering through the thick vegetation on the island, a refreshing change from some other parts of the country where trees are so scarce. The trails are good and it is almost impossible to get lost, but if you are in a hurry and wish to support the local economy, you can hire a local guide.

The Lake Tana Viewpoint

Another interesting place to visit in the Bahar Dar area is the Lake Tana Viewpoint, where the late Emperor (and the deposed Mengistu) had a palace, which offers a spectacular view of the lake and falls.

To get there, travel east through the main avenue of town, pass the Tana Hotel (on the left) and cross a bridge over the Blue Nile. Then take the road leading to the right and follow it up for 1km, after which you turn right up the hill to reach the view-point.

You are not allowed to enter or even photograph the palace but this is no great loss. It has little tourist appeal.

Axum

Axum is the ancient capital of Ethiopia, and rich in history. The Axumite civilisation had some great achievements (most scholars agree that the builders of the great pyramid in Giza were of Axumite descent), and the old church of Saint Marion of Zion was the Ethiopian kings' coronation place for centuries. It is a shame that there is no money for investment in tourism and archaeology, as only about 5% of the area has been excavated, but even this small portion is quite impressive.

Getting there   Several buses go to to Axum, but as the distance between Addis and Axum is about 800km you may prefer to fly. The return ticket costs about 212 birr, via Mekele. Both Mekele and Axum have dirt landing strips, so it might be impossible to fly there in the rainy season.

As you land, you will see the wreck of an Ethiopian Airlines aircraft near the airport buildings. This was the royal plane of Haile Selassie until it was converted to a commercial aircraft after he was deposed. When the rebel forces of the EP attacked Axum, the plane was stuck there due to mechanical problems. Fearing that the rebels might take the plane, the Mengiistu government bombed it.

There are no taxis in Axum, so you have to walk from the airport into town. Local children will offer to carry your bag for about 1 birr.

Sleeping and eating   The Axum Hotel (part of the Ghion chain) is about 2km from the airport, along the paved road to the east, with double rooms for about 110 birr. There will be no water in the taps during the dry season, so you'll have to make do with buckets of water in the bathroom. Electricity is available only from the afternoon until midnight.

The antiquities   To get to the sites, start walking from the Axum Hotel towards the west. At the road fork go right, past a school on the left, to reach a big square with a large tree in the centre. On the northwest corner of this square is the local branch of the Ministry of Culture, which is in charge of the archaeological remains. Ask there for a guide to see the area, for which you pay 5 birr plus 2 birr for entrance to the sites.

From the square, start walking north, and on the left are the Saint Mariam of Zion churches. The new church was built by Emperor Haile Selassie I so that women could also pray (women were barred from the old church). On passing the churches on the left, you'll see in front of you the **Stelae and Obelisks garden**. In the middle of the compound there is a stelae, shaped like a high-rise building and decorated with carvings of nine floors of windows, and a door at the bottom (complete with lock and door-knob). To the left of it there is a collapsed broken stelae that stood 33m high.

On the west side of the compound you can get to underground chambers. One of these contains an interesting rock that gives a hollow sound when knocked. The stones were held together by metal hooks in the shape of dumbbells, some of which can still be seen.

From the compound, continue in a northeast direction, along the left bank of the stream (which may be dry) and you will see some more fallen stelae along the walls of the church. One of these has carvings representing the tablets that Moses brought down from Mount Sinai.

On the opposite bank of the stream you will see an endless line of (mostly) women going up and down the hill, carrying water containers (ranging from the traditional terracotta to the contemporary oilcan). Crossing the stream you will see their destination: a large reservoir attributed to the Queen of Saba (Sheba) full of water, covered mostly by algae. You can still see the ancient staircase leading to the water's edge, but more recently some concrete steps have been built. Order is maintained by an old man wielding a whip. It is quite amazing to watch the women wait patiently for his signal, and then rush down the steps to get a good spot to fill their water containers, then help each other pick them up and start the long walk home.

Continuing uphill along the road in a northeast direction, after some 300m you will see a small shack on the left of the road. The guide will open it for you and inside is what may be considered the **Rosetta Stone** of Ethiopia (after the original stone in Egypt), which has the account of a victorious Ethiopian battle written in Greek, G'ez and Sabian.

On top of the hill, there is the restored **King's Palace** with underground chambers where Christian carvings can be seen on the walls (bring a torch). The Axumite way of building is reminiscent of the South American Incas, the stones being accurately cut so that they fit perfectly with no mortar. Also just off the top of the hill you can see a hole in the ground in the shape of a cross that was probably some sort of water holding place. From the top of the hill you can also see in the distance the **Battlefield of Adwa**. This is the site of another great Ethiopian victory (over the Italians in 1896), which is still celebrated to this day.

Back down the hill, you can visit the **Saint Mariam of Zion church**. Walk east along the road from the entrance to the Obelisks Garden for about 40m, and on the left there is the entrance to the garden outside the two churches. Inside the garden, on the right, are some huge lumps of stone. These are the remains of the **Judgement Place** of the king and his court.

At the gate of the old church there are two Egyptian-Turkish cannons that were taken after a battle some 100 years ago. There is an inscription on the cannons with the Arabic figures 1241, which is probably the year (in the Islamic calendar) when they were built. The church itself is built of a special kind of cement (of unknown ingredients) which gets harder as the years go by and now resembles stone in its solidity.

Wherever you go little children will shout *Babini!*, which is probably their version of the Italian *Va Bene*. In the Tigrinya vernacular of the children it has probably come to mean 'foreigner'.

Lalibela

This is the jewel in Ethiopia's crown and one of the wonders of the modern world. Built in the 13th Century, on the religious inspiration of King Lalibela, the churches are hewn out of solid rock. In this respect they resemble Petra, in Jordan, but whereas Petra's buildings were cut from rock buttresses and cliffs, incorporating the rock into the design, most of Lalibela's churches are below ground level, entirely separated from the rock from which they were hewn. A mammoth task.

The legend surrounding the Lalibela churches give them added appeal. When the future king was a baby in the town of Roha (now called Lalibela) his mother saw a swarm of bees descend on her son. With the knowledge that the animal kingdom can prophesy the fortunes of man, and believing the bees to be angels in insect form, she declared that the baby would grow up to be king, although that position was held by his elder brother. She called the child Lalibela, which means 'The bees manifest his majesty'. The king, Harbay, was not happy about this and plotted his brother's death. Lalibela survived the poison and was summoned to visit God: angels took him to the first, second and third heavens, where God ordered him to build 10 big churches, giving him detailed architectural plans, and put his mind at rest over his safety and ascent to the throne – these were assured by his agreement to build the churches. God's word was kept as soon as Lalibela returned home; Harbay met him outside the town, asked forgiveness and stated that he would abdicate in favour of his young brother.

King Lalibela set to work to build the churches. He even bought the land (the normal practice of the day was to confiscate it). His building schedule was much helped by the fact that angels carried on the work at night, achieving twice as much as the human workers during the day. The 10 churches (11, actually, but two are adjoining on the inside) were completed in 23 years.

These churches are not unique – there are other examples in other parts of Ethiopia, some built as early as the 6th Century – but they are the most impressive. A common motif is the swastika, an oriental symbol, which has been used in Ethiopia some 6,000 years.

Getting there   During the dry season the easiest way to get to Lalibela is by plane, although these Twin Otters may not go if there are insufficient passengers, so prepare to be patient. Bring something warm to wear – the heating is often inadequate. The 1993 fare from Addis was 161 birr, from Bahar Dar 90 birr, and from Gondar 72 birr.

From the airport there is a NTO bus which climbs the very steep hill to the town, which lies at an altitude of 2,600m. The distance is variously reported as being 13km or 9km. Having the monopoly of the route, they charge a whopping 60 birr.

An alternative to flying, and the only way to get to Lalibela in the rainy season, is to go by public transport plus three days hiking. It's a wonderful walk taking you through some dramatic scenery. Choose your time carefully; after heavy rain the rivers may be too deep to cross. You will be plagued by flies and perhaps by children (who like to throw stones at *farangies*) but it's well worth these discomforts. Here's how you do it.

Go to Weldia (Weldiya), which is either 1½ days by bus from Addis, or fly to Dese (Dessi) and take a bus from there (3-4 hrs). From Weldia take a bus along the 'Chinese Road' towards Werota, but get out at Dlib (about 2 hrs). Start walking from here. A vehicle might pass you and offer a lift, and shepherds or farmers along the route may well offer the services of a donkey to carry your backpack. It is about 24km to a small town where you will find basic accommodation and provisions. Near the town is one of the rock churches, Gennata Maryam, off up the hills to your right. If you've missed it, ask someone in the town to show it to you (it is probably only open in the morning and there will be an admission charge). Also ask for the path to Lalibela. This is 30-40km rather than 70km on the winding road. There will be plenty of animal tracks to guide you.

Sleeping and eating   The Seven Olives is reported to be a better hotel than the new Roha. There are plenty of budget hotels. Ask one of the children who will fasten himself to you as a guide to find one.

The churches   Though all churches have their similarities, each is unique. Geographically they are divided into three groups: six are clustered together north of a small stream (dry most of the year, and fancifully called the Jordan) and four to its south. The most beautiful and famous, St George's church, in the shape of a cross, stands alone to the south east.

Apart from its shape, **St George**'s is notable for the rows of windows at eye level which were uncompleted: either the budget ran out or the angels went on strike. Their shape is indicated on the wall, but they are not cut through the wall. Outside **Bete Mariyam** (House of Mary) there is a small pool where barren women can submerge themselves to ensure fertility. Near **Bete Qedus Gabriel Rafael** there is a narrow wall which rises very steeply. It is known as the Ascent of Heaven and walking up it guarantees you a place in Heaven. Unfortunately a slip means you will plummet to Hell. And it is a very slippery wall! Entrance to all the churches is 50 birr.

Another church, **Yamrehanna Krestos**, is a day's trek from Lalibela town. The spectacular trek and cave church, quite unlike the others, should not be missed. Unless you are an extremely fit hiker it is best to hire a mule (about 50 birr).

Harar

Harar is worth visiting because it has an entirely different atmosphere from other towns in Ethiopia, being strongly Muslim.

The journey there is probably more rewarding than the actual town which has seen better days.

Getting there   Harar can be reached by bus, a spectacular journey which takes the whole day, or by air or train as far as Dire Dawa from where there is plenty of transport. The train is supposed to leave at 2pm, arriving in the early morning. First class (the only sensible option) is 90 birr. Take food and water, and try to check whether the hi-jackers are still active on this line.

Sleeping and eating   The Ras hotel is overpriced with poor food, but there are several good value smaller places. The Lam Lam hotel costs 9 birr and was flea and bed-bug free. It is near the Lam Lam market past the Shoa gate and down a bad track, just before a cafe on the left.

Sightseeing   Harar is still more or less a walled city and contains some attractive Muslim houses. You will need a guide; they can be found near the police station in the church square. The Emperor's House has a faded glory but is now a clinic. The French poet Rimbold lived here for a while last century.

Dire Dawa

This low-lying town seems hot and dusty after the highlands but it has a good market and reasonable accommodation including the Sai Hotel (66 birr). From here you can continue to Djibouti by road or rail.

"The tourist seems to go by plan and is a bit dismayed to leave it. The curious traveller, though, moves a lot by whim, by imagination, and creates departures, seeks experience in unusual places."

Jefferson Coleman
Curious Travels in America, 1924

HIKING AND NATIONAL PARKS

In additional to the hike to Lalibela described earlier, there is some spectacular hiking in Ethiopia and some excellent national parks. Very good brochures and guide books to the Simien and Bale National Parks are available from the ETC office in Addis.

Mount Zokouala

Mount Zokouala is a volcano, lying southeast of Addis, complete with a crater lake and monastery on the top.

From Addis you have to get to the town of Debre Zeit, which is about 50km southeast of the capital. As you enter the town you will see a large bar on the right of the road. Just beyond the bar a dirt track leads to the top of the mountain, a distance of about 10km. (A military installation has recently been built on the road – so you need to circle around it. Keep your camera out of sight.)

From the base of the mountain to the top you gain about 1,000 metres in altitude. It takes about three hours, but it is not a very hard climb as the track to the peak was repaired recently. The local village boys will be glad to carry your luggage (for a fee) and show you the various short cuts. But beware: these shorten your way but also your breath! However, they do offer more shade and less dust.

On the way up you have glorious views of the valley below, and you may spot some of the mountain's population of baboons. The route is particularly beautiful during the blossom season – October to November. Picturesque villages can also be seen. As you reach the summit you can see the monastery and crater lake between the trees. The water in the lake is considered holy so (if you dare risk it) you could try a taste. Although you could ask the monks in the monastery to fill your bottle, it is best to bring enough food and water from Debre Zeit.

The monastery on the mountain is a few hundred years old. The main chapel is a sextant-shaped building with a tin roof. It is the inside which impresses, with traditional paintings adorning the inner walls. A contribution of a few birrs will allow you to see them. Near the church, in the living quarters, there is a small store room that contains everyday artefacts (lamps and candles) and some holy utensils (including crowns and robes).

Wondo Genet

By Jan Peter Smith.

This area of hot springs provides excellent birding and is within easy reach of Addis. Wondo Genet is essentially a forest on a hillside that remains green and cool throughout the dry season and that overlooks a steamy, swampy lake. One of former Emperor Haile Selassie's daughters had a summer residence here which has now been turned into a hotel. The nearby forest contains some large podacarpus trees which are a remnant of the extensive forests that covered 60% of Ethiopia less than a hundred years ago.

The hot springs are a short walk from the hotel and were refreshing after

Silvery-cheeked hornbill

the dusty trip from Addis Ababa. One pool with a couple of pipes pouring in hot water is free to the public, and many of the locals seem to spend all day here. When we arrived early one evening, everyone hopped out with laughter and excitement in order to watch us bathe. It made us feel quite immodest despite the bathing suits we wore. We eventually discovered, and retreated to, a fenced pool carved out of the rock. A caretaker charges a small entrance fee, and we found the privacy worth it.

Several trails lead up and away from the hotel, crossing a few fields before reaching the forest which still contains many animals and birds. Colobus monkeys are fairly numerous and can be spotted at a distance by their dangling fluffy white tails. Anubis baboons are abundant, and we spotted bushbucks bolting away into the underbrush, and huge silvery-cheeked hornbills are everywhere. The hornbills are easily recognised by their large casqued bills and noisy wingbeat, and they usually spend their days eating figs in the treetops. Looking back over and down onto the plains the views are magnificent.

Below the hotel and on the other side of the village, there is a trail along the edge of Shallo Swamp which has an extensive papyrus bed and numerous boiling hot springs. Hippos and crocodiles come to feed here, and the nearby cliffs are splattered white from the hundreds of roosting white-backed and Ruppell's griffon vultures.

Getting there   Several buses leave Addis Ababa daily for Shashamane which is about 250km south of the capital. To get from Shashamane to Wondo Genet (13km) either catch a local bus or hitch a ride. The road to Wondo Genet turns left (west) off the main highway just at the south end of town near a telecommunications building and ends at the village of Wondo Genet. From Addis the ride is a slow descent into the Rift Valley and can be quite dry and dusty during the dry season. The loss in elevation is about 1,200m to Shashamane. The road passes through agricultural country and near several Rift Valley lakes. By the time you reach Wondo Genet you have gone up 300m and the nearby hills are as high again, making this area cooler in the evening than the surrounding country.

Just as you enter the village of Wondo Genet take the only left turn, which goes up the hill to the hotel about one kilometre away.

Eating and sleeping   There are many small hotels of dubious quality along the main road in Shashamane. It is a popular trucker's stop between Addis and the south, so if you plan to stay here, reserve a room early. Stores and eating establishments are also numerous. If you plan to camp in the hills of

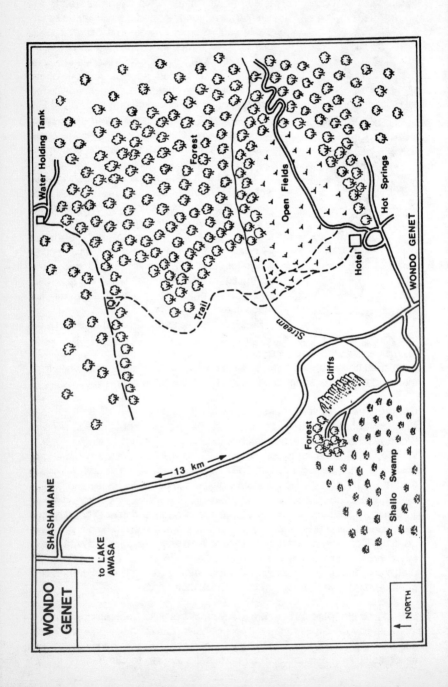

Wondo Genet and cook for yourself, this is probably the last place to stock up on food, although fruit can be bought in Wondo Genet. The Wondo Genet hotel also serves meals and has moderately priced accommodation. On weekends it is popular with the Addis crowd, so advance reservations are advisable, but on weekdays it is usually empty. If you are prepared to camp, there should be no problem, although you should check and ask permission at the hotel. Although hyenas are generally shy here, it is important to remember that they can be dangerous and are quite common at night not far from the hotel.

The trails   Behind and above the hotel to the east is a wide track that leads up through some open grazing fields for a couple of kilometres. A few fig trees are scattered around, and there are some coffee bushes at the upper end. No one lives here, although a few people may be working in the fields or tending animals. At the high end of the field, the track narrows to a trail and leads into the forest and down into a gorge with a rushing stream at the bottom. It is a cool, shady walk, and it is possible to wander 3-5km up the hill on the far side and eventually come to a rather barren scrub. We were busy looking at the monkeys and the birds and never left the forest. Getting lost is difficult as you can almost always look down and back on where you have come from. Watch for bushbucks here. Dusk is a good time to watch for larger mammals, and pigeons and parrots fly off to roost in small groups. This 12km walk can easily be done as a day hike.

To the north of the hotel are many trails across planted fields and banana groves. Eventually they all converge and descend to cross a rushing stream in two places. While it may seem easy to get lost in the maze of trails which go past several huts, it is almost always possible to see the forest ahead as it is a fairly steady uphill slope. After crossing a couple of irrigation channels we reached the forest and found a track leading up to a water tank. From here short trails branched off in several directions and the terrain became fairly steep. Large trees loomed overhead, and in the heat of the day we found it quiet and solitary. Our total elevation gain was about 300m and this walk could easily be done as a day hike.

Another pleasant and interesting walk is along the edge of Shallo Swamp down below the hotel and on the other side of the village. To get there, walk down the hill on the road on which you entered, turn right on the road toward Shashamane and look for a dirt track leading off to the left. This track passes though the lower end of the village and through the fields for three or four kilometres before turning into a trail that runs along the side of the swamp. On your right will be a stretch of jagged cliffs where the vultures roost (some are sure to be there at any time of day). On your left will be the edge of Shallo Swamp, where the water is so hot that it will be boiling in places. Don't be tempted to take a dip because there are hippos and crocodiles in the reeds. Several villagers were fishing from shore, and we watched one man land a six foot Nile perch. Birds including hornbills, hawks and vultures, and shorebirds are numerous. Eventually the trail comes to a small but interesting patch of forest which contained a family of martial eagles. The trail led for several kilometres further before we turned back. Total distance was about 8km each way from the hotel.

All of the hikes described can be done within a day of walking from the hotel. It is possible to hike in and camp, but carrying water becomes a limiting factor since drinking water is extremely scarce in the hills. Because of the heat and bright sun, the elevation changes (totalling perhaps 500m from the hills down to Shallo Swamp) should be taken slowly, and you should bring a hat and plenty to drink. The hotel water should be purified.

Awash National Park

Located only 210km from Addis Ababa on a tarmac road this is easily accessible and very beautiful. The dramatic volcano of Fantalle and its associated hot spring oases, the Ilala Sala plain, with sizeable herds of oryx and Soemmering's gazelle, and the big waterfall near the park headquarters, and the shady banks of the Awash River upstream from the falls make this park well worth a visit.

In the northern sector of the park are the Filwoha Hot Springs, which have lots of palm trees and lots of biting sand-flies. Another hot springs resort is Sodere, which has an Olympic-sized hot pool.

Sleeping and eating   The campsites in the southern section of the park are beautifully situated under huge fig and acacia trees on the banks of the Awash river. Kereyou Lodge is on the edge of Awash Gorge. It is actually a group of caravans, is overpriced, but commands a lovely view.

Simien National Park

The Simiens are dominated by Ras Dashan (4,620m), the fourth highest mountain in Africa. Much of the area is national park, protecting the walia ibex, found only on the escarpments of the Simiens and thus one of Africa's rarest species. There are also gelada baboons inhabiting the crags. Far more noble and lovely to look at than the common baboons, these long-haired, pink-breasted creatures make fascinating study. You may also see the Simien fox. The majestic lammergeyer, or bearded vulture, is commonly viewed once you get to high ground.

In addition to these special animals there are dozens of flowers in alpine meadows. In a few square metres of field we counted 15 species without much

Walia ibex

effort. On still higher ground there are plenty of giant lobelia.

With all these attractions, plus well-maintained huts, good trails, the availability of guides, horses and mules for hire, the Simiens offer a unique experience. It's well worth five days at a minimum, or even a week, but two day hikes may be made to the first shelter where you may see an ibex or two.

Getting there and getting organised The park headquarters are at Debarek, 100km north of Gondar (3-4 hours by bus). The efficient park wardens make all necessary arrangements for visitors. 1993 prices were 40 birr per day for a guide, 20 birr for a game scout, 10 birr for a muleteer and 10 birr for his mule. The park entrance fee is 10 birr. You will probably need to bring backpacking food with you from Gondar, but try to check in Addis on the current availability of food/cooking equipment in the Simiens.

Sleeping and eating In Debarek the Simien Hotel is recommended; 10 birr per bed, with good food, coffee and spiced tea.

The trails *The following description, taken from the first edition of this book, is for flavour rather than a sure-to-be accurate description of the route. Recent reports suggest that little has changed, however.*

Heading northeast, towards Ras Dashan, the first night is spent in Sankobar in a good hut with a splendid view. The next day takes you into the very heart of the plateau, along precipices with gossamer waterfalls and through alpine meadows. After about six hours you arrive at Geech. The view from this hut, situated in the middle of a plateau, is unspectacular, but as you walk to the edge you will see incredible drops down into the valley below. It's on these precipices that the walia ibex and the baboons may be seen.

We spent our night at Geech poring over the map and plotting our route along the edge of the plateau to the next camp at Chenek. Our guide and pack animals took the regular route, while we struck out to the north. Once we hit the edge of the plateau we walked east along the prow of our rock-ship to a pinnacle like the highest and most spectacular crows-nest imaginable. To the east and beneath us, we could see Chenek camp glinting in the strong sun. Neither of us had spent a more magnificent day anywhere. We saw baboons, ibex, lammergeyers, and literally carpets of flowers. Every step offered new and stunning views down into the valley, or of a particularly lovely sculptured group of rock towers once joined onto our plateau.

Bale National Park

Bale is pronounced Bah-lay. This park lies at 3,500m and is very rich in wildlife and has some of the most beautiful highland forest in existence (the Harema Forest on the southern escarpment). Gavin and Val Thomson saw several endemic mammals including Menelik's bushbuck, mountain nyala, and Simien fox. From Dinsho the highest all-weather road in Africa takes you to the Sanetti Plateau at 4,100m where you can see bearded vultures (lammergeyer), and vegetation typical of that altitude including giant lobelia.

The park is well-run and the warden will organise horses, game-scouts, and everything necessary for trekking. One excursion worth doing is to the Caves of Sof Omar. The trout-fishing in this park is excellent; a friend of Conrad Hirsh caught one weighing 7 kilos!

Sleeping and eating   The self-catering guest house set up with Swedish assistance is excellent, but popular, so be prepared to camp. Bring your own food and warm clothing – it gets bitterly cold at this altitude. The guest house has a sauna (extra charged for both the sauna and the wood to fire it). Alternatively there's the Ras Hotel in Goba or the seedier Bekele Molla in Robi.

The Rift Valley Lakes National Park

The main feature of this park is its lakes, which attract a good variety of waterfowl. Conservation has not been enforced here in recent years. 'As far was we could see the park has been set aside to protect the only remaining populations of cows, donkeys, goats, sheep and people.' (Gavin and Val Thomson). Camping is allowed at the Bakele Molla Hotel on the shores of Lake Langano.

Nech Sar National Park

Described by Conrad Hirsh as a small gem with a good variety of habitats, including an extraordinary but over-exploited ground water forest with many fresh springs, the 'Bridge of God', which is the neck of land between Lakes Abaya and Chamo, where thick bush provides cover for many greater kudu, and the wide plains of light-coloured grass to the east where you can find herds of zebra and Swayne's hartebeeste. The shores of Lake Chamo offer one of Africa's great reptilian spectacles: a collection of huge crocodiles can be approached (with care) either by land or by boat, the latter arranged through the Maritime Office in Arba Minch, the nearest town. Take all precautions against malaria in this area.

Sleeping and eating   In Arba Minch the Bekele Molla Hotel is decaying gracefully in a splendid location; excellent fried Nile perch is available at the Shell station not far from the hotel.

Mago National Park

The access town for this park is Jinka. It is suitable for hiking, with a very steep 35km track leading from Jinka to a campsite near the Neri River and a sparse network of tracks which allows for some wildlife viewing. South of the park is another reserve where wildlife is more visible. Oryx, Grant's gazelle, and hartebeeste exist in profusion.

Omo National Park

This park is very hard to get to but immensely rewarding. There is lovely scenery, and a good mix of wildlife including large herds of eland.

Hiking in the Tigray region

By Javier Grinfeld and Liora Donskoy (Israel).

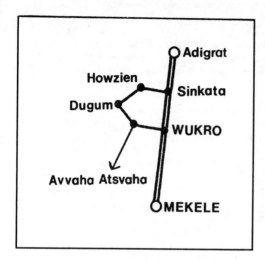

This is a land of stone pinnacles and stone-hewn churches. The houses in the Tigray area are also built of stone, and the farmers use stone terraces to prevent soil erosion. The sandstone pinnacles, cliffs and mountains are some of the most impressive we've ever seen. The hike is mostly on the plains or small hills, between huge rock formations. The churches seen on the way are rock-hewn like Lalibela but usually less impressive from the outside. They are most interesting on the inside, however. We didn't take guides, just asked advice from the locals.

The hike starts in a village called Wukro, between Mekele and Adigrat. In Wukro itself there is the first church, called Cherkos. It is almost a monolith, being hewn on three sides from the rock. From Wukro it is 5-6 hours walk to Avvaha Atsvaha. Here there is a big church with fine carvings and paintings on the inner walls. From there 5-6 hours takes you to the village of Dugum. Around here there are 30-40 churches. Of the three we visited, Debre Zion was the most special with its carvings and shape. More information is available from Mekele tourist commission in the centre of Mekele town.

From Dugum a 5-6 hour trek brings you to Howzien, a big village in which you can find transport to Sinkata, a village on the main Mekele-Adigrat road.

Further reading

In Ethiopia with a mule by Dervla Murphy (John Murray). A wonderfully evocative and exciting account of travel on foot in the Ethiopia of Haile Selassie.

"A traveller! By my faith you have great reason to be sad; I fear you have sold your own lands to see other men's; then, to have seen much and to have nothing, is to have rich eyes and poor hands."

W. Shakespeare
As You Like It

ELEPHANT

The social life of elephants is based on a matriarchal society, with the oldest female taking the lead, particularly in defence. Females stay with the herd or family unit into which they were born; young adult males leave to form transient bachelor groups, visiting female herds to look for mates. You may see huge herds of up to 300 animals; these are composed of a number of family units that have come together to make the most of good feeding places. The big animals will be males: females stop growing when they are 20 or so, but males continue to grow throughout their lives, sometimes reaching a massive 5,500kg by the age of 40. It is not always easy to tell a young male from a female since the testes are internal and the penis hidden in a sheath (a sexually excited male is, however, unmistakable and unforgettable!).

A large elephant eats about 130kg of vegetation a day, spending up to 18 hours on the job. Their size and appetite makes them only second after man in their impact on the environment, particularly when confined to small areas such as game parks. Another characteristic that elephants share with man — or woman — is that the female lives long after she ceases to reproduce which allows her to devote her time to leadership.

Gestation is 22 months and the family, particularly older sisters, look after the infants with loving care. It is interesting to note that elephant teats are between the front legs — an unusual arrangement in non-primates. The young do not use their trunks to suckle, and indeed, have very little control over this unique appendage at first. An elephant's trunk is amazing in its versatility. It can pick up a pea, wrench a branch off a tree, gently guide a baby, smell the sexual receptiveness of a female or the approach of a human, function as a shower-head or a snorkel, and broadcast its owner's intentions from afar. It is surprising that evolution has only equipped one species with such an effective piece of equipment.

Bull elephants periodically come into *musth* (the word derives from the Urdu for 'frenzy'). This is a state of high sexual activity, and is easily recognised by the secretion from the temporal gland above the eye, and a constant discharge from the penis. It's an altogether smelly affair, which alerts females and non-musth males that this is the sexual boss. They may stay in musth for several months during which time their one-track mind leads them to eat less and lose condition.

Note: Place names on maps or brochures can be spelt in a variety of ways in Ethiopia. Since the original was in the Amharic script there is no 'right' or 'wrong' spelling.

EAST AFRICA

Kenya
Tanzania
Uganda

African wild dog

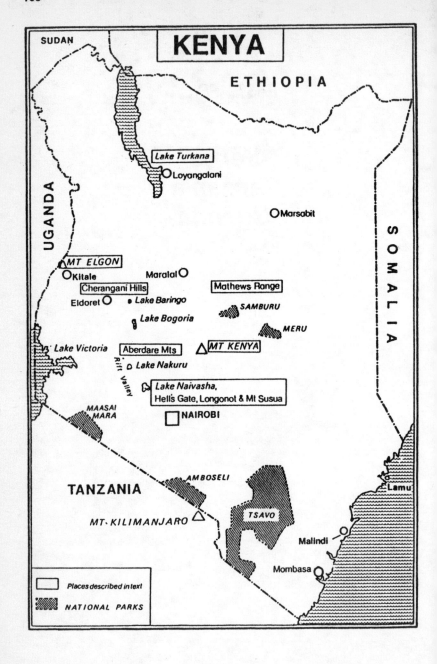

Chapter 9

Kenya

Updated by David Else and Jill Bitten, with Jack Clayton, Paul Hunt, A Warndorff, Steve Hullett, John Hillan, Jim Noakes and Claudine Combrie.

Extra information for this edition from Scott Morgan, Patrick Frew, Lluis Tort, Jaume Tort, Joan Masoliver, Javier Grinfeld, Liora Donskoy, Yoel Jurgeman and Philip Briggs.

FACTS AND FIGURES

Kenya gained its independence from Britain in 1964, and has since become the most popular destination in Africa for tourists, even with the recent 20% drop in tourist figures.

Kenya is blessed with outstanding geographical variety. From sea level to 1,000 metres the country is semi-arid and, apart from the lush well-watered coastal strip, supports only low scrub and baobab trees. Savannah grasslands predominate over 1,000 metres and above 2,000 metres are extensive evergreen forests rising to afro-alpine vegetation near the snowline.

Kenya's weather is equally varied. On the coast the rainy months are April and May; June and July are relatively cool and pleasant and January, February and March exhaustingly hot. The mean annual temperature in Mombasa is 27°C. In the western highlands the rainy season is longer, between March and September, with May and August the wettest months, and the eastern highlands and Nairobi expect 'the long rains' between March and June, and 'the short rains' in November. The high seasons (when prices are highest) are December to March, and June to October.

People

The ethnic diversity of the people of Kenya is fascinating. There are over a hundred tribes of pure-blooded Africans, along with Asians, coastal Swahili-speakers with their Arab blood and a sizeable number of Europeans.

The dominant tribe in government and business used to be the Kikuyu but with the election of President Moi from the Tugen tribe the political balance has changed, although the Kikuyu are still the most numerous tribe. Asians are very active in commerce, and despite efforts at 'Africanisation' in the mid seventies, most small and middle-sized businesses seem to be Asian-run.

For tourists the most interesting tribes are the Maasai and Samburu, pastoralists who retain their traditional way of life and clothing (or lack of it), and the El Molo, a very small tribe found on the east bank of Lake Turkana.

Muslims dominate the religious scene, although there are many Christians.

TRAVEL

Impressions

Kenya is satisfying in so many ways it's tempting to spend months there. Many people find the game parks almost too well organised, but it's easy enough for backpackers to leave the package tours behind and visit the lesser known places — Kenya is a large country.

Entry and exit

Most Commonwealth citizens do not need a visa, nor do Scandinavian and West German passport holders. Australian and North American visitors must have a visa, and may be asked to show a return or onward air ticket. Visas are usually valid for three months and renewable in Nairobi. Overland visitors not needing a visa may be asked to show a return or onward air ticket at the border. Residents of South Africa, or those who have stayed in South Africa for longer than three months in the last year, must have a visa whatever their nationality.

The majority of Africa travellers arrive in Nairobi by air. There is a Kenya Airways bus which runs between 06.00 and 20.00 to the city, and costs around $2. The airport tax on departure is $20.

Money

The Kenyan shilling (Ksh or /-) is broken down into 100 cents. Kenyan currency can only (legally) be obtained in Kenya; you may not take more than 200/- in local currency in or out of the country. Currency Declaration Forms are no longer used. Keep your bank receipts so you can change surplus Kenyan shillings back into hard currency when you leave.

What to buy

A large selection of goods and handicrafts are available, with baskets, jewellery and precious stones, silver, kikoi fabrics and khangas (traditional African wrap-around skirts) all being good buys. It is now illegal to trade in animal products in Kenya, and, thankfully, the animal skins and carved ivory that used to dominate the souvenir stands have disappeared.

'Makonde ebony carvings are a good buy if you are not going to Tanzania. Best prices are in the coastal areas: Mombasa's Ebony Factory, located near the matatu station, is great. Also Tiwi Beach and Diani Beach. Bargain hard.

Barter works well – I brought digital watches from England and came away
with 15kg of great carvings.' (J.Clayton)

Maps and guidebooks

Good maps of Kenya's National Parks are published by Survey of Kenya, and
are available from Nairobi bookshops, or from the map office on Harambee
Ave, Nairobi, next to the International Conference Centre. Each sheet contains
pictures of the common animals found in the park and a list of birds. The
following are available: Meru, Tsavo East, Tsavo West, Amboseli, Shimba
Hills, Marsabit, Samburu and Buffalo Springs, and Maasai Mara. Maps are
sometimes available from bookshops and the National Museum.

Survey of Kenya road maps and topographical maps are no longer officially
available, though some bookshops still have old stocks. To get good maps
in Nairobi takes some perseverance. Intrepid traveller Scott Morgan wrote to
tell us the procedure for Survey of Kenya maps:
1) Go to Public Map Office to find what sheets you want. 2) Write an
application to buy the maps, stating reason as 'mountaineering, walking or
tourism' and deliver to the Director of Surveys, Ministry of Lands on the
corner of Ngong Road and 1st Ngong Ave. 3) They will type out an
application, which is best for you to deliver by hand to the Department of
Defence on Lenana Road. 4) In 3-4 working days, hopefully, authorisation
comes through back to the Director of Surveys, who then informs you to
come and collect a document allowing you to purchase the maps. 5) Take
this form and purchase the maps at the Public Map Office (near the
Conference centre) at 25/- each.

Good road maps are published by Macmillan (1:750,000), Nelles
(1:1,000,000), Bartholomew (1:1,250,000), and Freytag & Berndt (1:1,500,000).

Mountain Walking in Kenya by David Else (published in the UK by McCarta,
distributed by Cicerone) is an ideal addition to this guide, with a selection of
long and short walks.

The *East Africa International Mountain Guide* by Andrew Wielochowski
(West Col) is mainly on technical mountaineering and rock climbing in Kenya,
Tanzania and Uganda, but it also contains some information on Mount
Kenya's walking routes.

Camping Guide to Kenya by David Else (Bradt) has details on every
campsite in Kenya, in towns, national parks and on the coast, as well as 'wild'
camping in the mountains and around the country. Surely a 'must' for all
backpackers!

Warning

Gangs of panga-wielding thieves make Nairobi a dangerous place after dark.
It is unwise to walk around any large town at night, and at all times you
should be on the look out for pickpockets and handbag slashers. Always
walk quickly and purposefully, and avoid carrying a daypack or handbag.

Accommodation

Nairobi and other large towns have plenty of inexpensive hotels (called Boarding and Lodgings, or B&Ls, in provincial towns), and there are various favourites much frequented by travellers which are excellent places to exchange tips. More details in the *Towns* section.

Eating

The large number of Asian-run restaurants means a large number of curries (including vegetarian meals in Sikh restaurants). In large towns you can find food of international standards, and local African dishes everywhere.

Transport

The **train** from Nairobi to Mombasa is a fine experience; treat yourself to breakfast in the dining car and listen to the exotic babble of tongues as you eat a traditional English breakfast off EAR china and silver. The train runs through Tsavo National Park and if you get up early you have a good chance of seeing wildlife from the safety of your compartment.

There are two trains per day – both running through the night – leaving Nairobi at 17.00 and 19.00. The latter tends to be very crowded. The journey takes about 13 hours.

There are many **buses**, from the very fast services between Nairobi and Mombasa which compare favourably with the UK, to the EAR service which is very slow but cheap. Buses run just about everywhere (in inhabited regions) and where they don't, **matatus** fill the gap. Matatus are cheap, overcrowded minibuses that are driven at breakneck speed. They have their devotees although they are quite dangerous. **Matatu** is Kikuyu for '30' – the original fare.

Shared **taxis** are safer, though more expensive. These Peugeot 504 seven-seater station wagons run between major towns and cost two or three times the bus fare.

Hitchhiking is easy on the main roads although Africans may expect you to pay.

When quoted a departure time for transport, check that it is not Swahili time, which begins at 6.00am, the hour of sunrise.

Contacts and equipment

Climbers and walkers can get guide books, maps, and sometimes second-hand kit from the Mountain Club of Kenya, which organises outings for its own members and may be willing to include visitors. Tel: 501747 (evenings).

Another option is the Natural Action Mountain Centre in the Museum Hill Shopping Centre, opposite Nairobi's National Museum. This place is run by a group of experienced local guides. They organise treks on Mount Kenya and several other mountains, plus Kilimanjaro and the Ruwenzoris. They sell and hire new and second-hand kit, supply a range of gas cartridges, and have a message board for climbers and backpackers looking for companions.

Another place where you can buy or rent safari equipment and hiking gear is Atul's shop on Biashara Street in central Nairobi. They also do repairs to tents and rucksacks and, if you need to lighten your load before catching a plane home, Atul's will buy any equipment that you no longer need.

TOWNS

Nairobi

A large modern city well able to cope with the thousands of tourists who make it their base. The cool climate and wide main avenue invite wanderers, and there is a sufficient number of places of interest (not to mention bookshops, restaurants and the latest movies) to make an enforced stay in the capital pleasant enough. Particularly recommended is the National Museum (more for Joy Adamson's marvellous paintings of tribal peoples than for the stuffed animals and birds), and the adjacent reptilarium. The National Museums of Kenya purchase, maintain and protect the country's heritage, and control the 7,000 archaeological sites in the country.

The market (off Muindi Mbingu St, two blocks north of Kenyatta Ave) is rewarding, but there is a better one on the eastern side of town near the country bus station: very African with no souvenir sellers.

Worth a visit is the railway museum behind the station, even if you are not crazy about trains, for the macabre fascination of learning all about 'The Man Eaters of Tsavo' – lions (or a lion) which dined on railway workers (28 of them) during construction of the Mombasa to Nairobi railway (the lion entered a compartment and pulled one man from the train).

Outside town is the Langata Giraffe Centre (where you can meet and feed the elegant creatures at eye level) and the Karen Blixen museum. Further details about places of interest in Nairobi can be found in the booklets *Tourist's Kenya* and *What's On*, available free in hotels, or from *Nairobi – things to see and do* which can be bought at most bookshops.

The Ministry of Tourism and Wildlife is located at Utalii House, Off Ururu Highway, PO Box 30027, Nairobi. Tel: 331030.

Sleeping and eating   The Iqbal hotel (Latema Road, off Tom M'boya Avenue) is a perennial favourite, but there are other less popular, so cheaper, hotels on the same road. Try The Nakuru, The New Kenya Lodge, the Sunshine Lodge or the Tropical Valley Hotel. The Dolat Hotel on Mfangano Street is slightly more expensive but very good value. Even more popular is Mrs Roche's Guest House, which is 4km from the city centre on 3rd Parklands Avenue, opposite the Aga Khan Hospital (frequent matatus run there from Latema Road). Traveller hang-outs such as these have notice boards full of items and tickets for sale, requests for travelling companions, and so on. (The Thorn Tree Cafe, near the New Stanley Hotel, which also has a famous notice board, now discourages loiterers.)

On arrival in Nairobi, it is not a bad idea to select a better class hotel for the first night, since luggage can then safely be left there. The Jacaranda (Tel: 335807), in the suburb of Westlands and set in four acres of garden, has been recommended for a splurge (about $35 double). Cheaper ($20) is the Hotel Boulevard (near the Norfolk Hotel and the museum) and cheaper still (around $15), also set in a garden and very British, is the Hurlingham (Tel: 723001), in the northern part of town.

There are plenty of restaurants of all classes, from the outstanding – and very pricy – Tamarind, to cheap and cheerful curries at the Curry Pot (on Moi Ave) and the Satkar (Dodo St, off Moi Ave). Another good Nairobi restaurant is African Heritage (off Kenyatta Ave) – quite expensive, but an interesting all-you-can-eat menu. The Lord Delamere bar at the Norfolk Hotel is a pleasant place to spend the evening.

Nakuru

Kenya's fourth largest town, and accessible by rail as well as by good road, Nakuru has a good selection of places to stay, and is perhaps the best place near Nairobi to buy handicrafts – there are numerous street traders and prices are lower than in the capital.

Mombasa

Kenya's main port is, as you would expect, a lively town, though most people move out to the nearby beaches after a day's sightseeing in the Old Town and Fort Jesus with its museum.

A good value budget hotel (with fans) is the Cosy Hotel up Haile Selassie Rd, not far from the railway station. The New Britannia Hotel and the YWCA have also been recommended. The Cosy Tearoom (corner of Digo and Nkrumah Roads) is good for daytime snacks.

Of the more popular beaches (south of Mombasa) Tiwi is quieter, and Diani best for partying. Dan Trenches has been recommended for accommodation at Diani, but security is a problem. Far better is Twiga Lodge on Tiwi Beach.

Malindi

The main attraction here is the Malindi Marine National Park, where you can go snorkelling from a glass-bottomed boat. It's best to have your own snorkelling gear, although it can be hired, and bring sneakers, (*not thongs*), to protect your feet from sea urchins, and an old tee shirt to protect your back and shoulders from sunburn.

Accommodation is limited and noisy in town; your best bet (if you have a tent) is the Silver Sands campsite, 2km south of the town. Malindi also has a youth hostel. A beach hotel in the mid-price range ($15 double, peak season) is Ozi's (Tel: 20218); recommended.

Watamu

About 24km south of Malindi, this smaller resort also has a Marine Park, and is quieter than Malindi. Mrs Simpson's, Plot 28 (Tel: Watamu 23) offers excellent value: for about $18 you get full board with sail boat privileges and free snorkel trips. Gedi ruins are only a few kilometres away.

HIKING

Kenya's high mountains and rolling hills make hiking and climbing a popular pastime with Kenyans and expatriates as well as visitors. There are more choices here than in any other East African country.

Mount Kenya National Park

Introduction   The nation of Kenya is named after its great mountain, the second highest in Africa; Kenya means 'Mountain of Whiteness' in Kikuyu. Mt Kenya actually refers to the entire massif; the highest peak is Batian (5,199m) followed by Nelion (5,188m), with Lenana (4,985m) coming third. Point Lenana is accessible to all fit and acclimatised hikers, needing no special climbing skills, while the higher two should be attempted only by competent and well-equipped mountaineers.

A hike up to Point Lenana and back can be done in three days, but four or five is much more appropriate. The great popularity of this hike is partly because, unlike Mt Kilimanjaro, you are not compelled to use a guide and porters although the latter are available if you want to make the ascent easier.

There are three main routes up Mount Kenya. The Naro Moru Route is the most popular, followed by the Sirimon Route and the Chogoria Route (see map). The Mount Kenya Circuit Route joins the top sections of these three, making a complete circuit of the central peak area.

The vegetation is characteristic of Africa's high equatorial mountains, with bamboo jungle giving way to giant species of heather, lobelia and groundsel. Above 3,800m the vegetation is very scarce on the dry valley walls and the ridges. There are plenty of animals, although these are becoming increasingly shy: buffalo (potentially dangerous) and elephants are occasionally seen. Of the smaller mammals, you'll see several species of monkey, and in the high areas the endemic Mt Kenya rock hyrax, which may look like a rodent but is probably a relative of the elephant. You'll see – and hear – rodents galore in the huts. African dormice prefer the high altitude ones, and rats the lower ones.

December to March are the best months for the trip (when it's dry and clear), but June to September are also usually dry.

Visitors must pay the standard park entrance fees of 540/- per day (around £9 or $15), plus a daily camping fee of 180/- per person, at the park gates. These fees must be paid at the park entrance, whichever access route you choose. If you stay longer than anticipated, extra payments must be made on your way out.

Huts

There are several huts varying in quality and price. Some are owned by the Mountain Club of Kenya and are open only to members so are not described here. Privately run huts and lodges are usually well-maintained, but tend to be expensive and crowded; others (still officially the property of the MCK although no longer effectively administered by them) are in a very poor state of repair, rodent infested, and dirty. A summary of the huts available to the general public follows.

Naro Moru route   Met Station; bunkhouses sleeping 40, piped water, pit toilets, kerosene lamps. 250/- a night. Camping plus use of facilities, 50/-. Teleki Lodge at Mackinder's Camp; bunkhouse sleeping 80. Toilet, water, commonroom, kitchen. 200/-, camping 30/-. Both are owned by Naro Moru River Lodge. Bookings: PO Box 18, Naro Moru, or through Let's Go Travel, (PO Box 60342, Caxton House, Standard St, Nairobi, Tel: 29539/29540/340331).

Chogoria route   Meru Mount Kenya Lodge; self-catering bandas with kitchen, toilets, electricity. Comfortable and good value at 300/-. Bookings through the manager, PO box 365, Chogoria, or through Let's Go Travel, Nairobi. Urumandi Hut, a small wooden hut, in bad repair, off the main route between Chogoria Gate and the Chogoria track roadhead. Minto's hut; an MCK hut in rapidly deteriorating condition.

Sirimon route   Old Moses Camp; bunkhouse with kitchen and basic facilities, 250/- per night. Camping, with use of facilities, 50/-. Liki North Hut, a small wooden hut in bad repair with no facilities. Shipton's Camp; bunkhouse with kitchen and basic facilities 250/-. Both bookable through Mountain Lodge (formerly Bantu Lodge), PO Box 333, Nanyuki, or through Yare Safaris, (PO Box 63006, Union Towers, Moi Avenue, Nairobi, Tel: 214099).

Mt Kenya circuit   Huts here were built by the MCK but abused over the years; Two Tarn and Kami Huts are small, dirty and dilapidated, but usable. Austrian Hut is larger, with room for about 30 people, still in reasonable condition, with fine views of Point Lenana, the main peaks and the top of the Lewis Glacier. (Top Hut is beside Austrian Hut and completely unusable.)

Because the huts are either dirty, small, crowded or expensive many backpackers will prefer to bring their own tent. This gives you a lot more freedom to choose where to stop each night. You can camp near one of the huts and use the facilities, or anywhere else that's suitable (see route descriptions).

Preparations

Most food items can be bought in Nairobi, which has several well-stocked supermarkets and a good market. If you want to carry special items (eg freeze-dried) these are not available. Remember that tins are heavy and you must carry the empty ones out with you, so dried or fresh food is much better. (If you are hiring porters, the extra weight will not be a problem.) Lentils and rice do not cook well at high altitudes - pasta is better. Packet soups are invaluable.

Bring a stove; you are not permitted to make fires.

You'll need warm clothes for the very cold evenings and nights (below freezing). You should also have thermal underwear and gloves. Pay attention to your footwear. You have to tackle the 'vertical bog' and other marshy areas. Don't forget sunscreen and lipsalve, water-purifying tablets (or filter), candles, a torch (flashlight) and spare batteries, and your compass. String and plastic bags are useful, since you'll need to hang your provisions out of reach of the hut rodents. Bags are also useful for bringing rubbish down again.

In the dry seasons, you do not normally need an ice-axe and crampons for Point Lenana if approaching from Austrian Hut (ie the usual way). You will be climbing a steep slope (200m or so) of permanent snow and ice which is, of course, slippery, so extreme care should be taken, especially when heading for the peak in the half-light to see the sunrise.

Porters and guides can be hired at Naro Moru or Chogoria. They are not available at the start of the Sirimon Route itself but can be arranged for this route at Mountain Rock (Bantu) Lodge. When you hire guides and porters you pay them a daily fee (100 - 200/- per day) and also have to pay their park fees (50/- per day). Tipping is expected – usually an extra day's pay. If you descend by another route you must pay an extra day's fee plus transport costs back to the starting place.

You are not allowed to enter the park alone. This is a sensible regulation, as every year several hikers do get lost on the mountain, and some are never found. Solo hikers can hire a porter, or team up with other visitors at the park gate. Experienced hikers, with map and compass experience, will not need a guide.

Warning Many cases of cerebral and pulmonary oedema occur on Mt Kenya. Part of your preparations should be acclimatisation. To avoid this sometimes lethal complication of altitude sickness (see Chapter 2) you should plan on a leisurely ascent.

Map The Kenyan government map is out of print. Others available include one by Andrew Wielochowski and Mark Savage, scale 1:50,000. This is a good, up-to-date map showing the main access routes and mountain trails, with useful information on the back. It is available from the Mountain Club of Kenya and Nairobi bookshops, or from the publisher, West Col Productions, Goring, Reading, Berks RG8 9AA, England.

Approach The most popular approach is the Naro Moru Route, but the longer and less crowded Chogoria Route is favoured by many backpackers – for the wildlife and acclimatisation. The Sirimon route is more undulating, so strenuous.

The best plan is to use different routes for ascent and descent. Most people favour ascending via Chogoria and descending on Naro Moru. The 25km walk up the Chogoria track is necessary acclimatisation, and the Naro Moru's Vertical Bog is easier on descent. On the other hand, those with the time may prefer to acclimatise at Mackinder's, at 4,225m, and do the 25km Chogoria walk when less heavily laden.

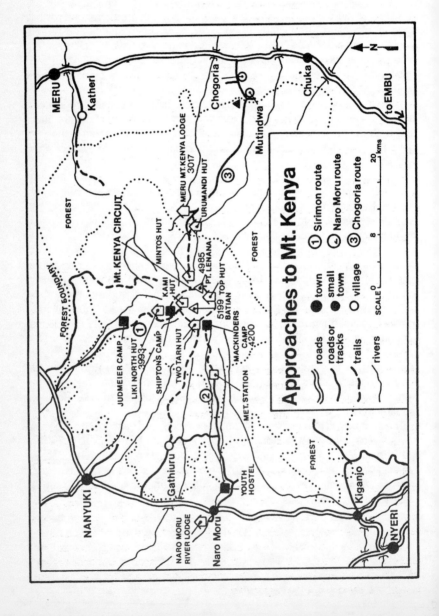

Approaches to Mt. Kenya

Naro Moru Route

Numerous buses, matatus and shared-taxis run to Naro Moru from the River Road area of Nairobi, reaching the town in about three hours. This is the centre for climbing Mt Kenya, and here you can hire equipment, porters and guides (but cannot buy food) at the comfortable Naro Moru River Lodge.

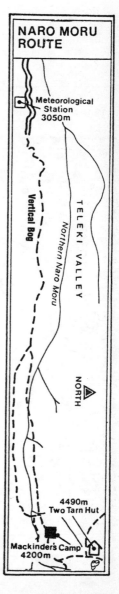

The bunk house at the lodge is recommended for accommodation, and there is also a campsite. Naro Moru Youth Hostel is about 10km from Naro Moru town on the track leading to the park, and is served part way by matatus from town. If you want a lift all the way to the gate, you'll have to pay extra!

You may be able to hitch a ride to the Met Station (3,048m), 26km from Naro Moru, or arrange a lift in the lodge's 'shuttle bus', although this is not really advisable as the walk is useful for acclimatisation.

From Naro Moru town head towards the mountain for 8km, turning left at the first junction and passing the track to the Youth Hostel. About 5km more brings you to the entrance to the National Park, where you must pay your fees. This walk is not without interest − it is here that you are most likely to meet large mammals and see forest birds.

Met Station is a further 8km from the park gate, with bunk house accommodation and a campsite. If you don't have your own tent you should spend the night here, as the next hut − Mackinder's Camp − is a good six hours away.

The forest continues above Met Station for a few kilometres. Above the forest the moorland starts, and the notorious 'vertical bog'.

The bog is actually a beautiful area of lichen, moss and ferns, just above the tree line. Above the bog the trail splits, running each side of the valley to Teleki Lodge at Mackinder's Camp. The views open up and on a clear day the peaks of Batian and Nelion can be seen at last.

The setting off place for Point Lenana is Austrian Hut (4,790m), a 3-4 hour climb from Mackinder's. From here it is about an hour up the ridge on the right side of the Lewis Glacier to the summit at 4,985m. You must make a pre-dawn start in order to be on Point Lenana at sunrise and before the snow melts making the descent difficult. Like most of the world's glaciers, Lewis Glacier is receding fast, halving in size since the beginning of the century.

For your return, the Naro Moru Lodge has vehicles running between the lodge and Met Station, so you might be able to arrange a lift down the last bit. This can be expensive but, if the vehicle is not already booked by other hikers, the price might be negotiable...

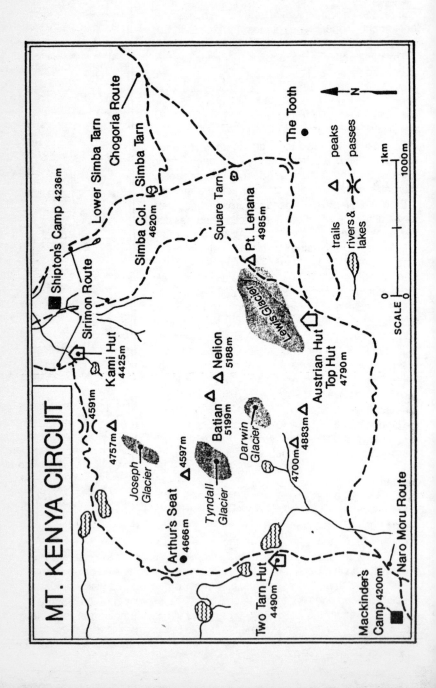

MT. KENYA CIRCUIT

The Tooth

N

Chogoria Route

Lower Simba Tarn

Simba Tarn

Shipton's Camp 4236m

Simba Col. 4620m

Square Tarn

Sirimon Route

Pt. Lenana 4985m

peaks

passes

trails

rivers & lakes

1km

1000m

SCALE

Kami Hut 4425m

4591m

4757m

Nelion 5188m

Lewis Glacier

Austrian Hut Top Hut 4790m

4597m

Batian 5199m

Joseph Glacier

Darwin Glacier

4883m

Arthur's Seat 4666m

Tyndall Glacier

4700m

Two Tarn Hut 4490m

Naro Moru Route

Mackinder's Camp 4200m

From Austrian Hut you can also take the Mt Kenya Circuit round to the top of the Chogoria Route and Minto's Hut. (3 hours – details below.)

Mt Kenya Circuit From Mackinder's Camp, instead of going direct to Austrian Hut, Point Lenana can also be approached 'the long way round' by continuing the circuit route around the north of Mt Kenya. This is a tough but exciting hike. There are few sign posts so a map and compass are essential. Unless you're particularly fit, it's best to take two or three days on the Circuit.

From Mackinder's keep left at the head of the valley and take a steep, rough path up to Two Tarn Hut (4,490m), nicely situated near a lake, with a superb view of Batian. Head for Kami Hut (actually two huts), by going over a col, dropping to pass between two lakes (tarns) and over the Hausburg Col (3 hours).

From Kami Hut drop to Shipton's Camp then go up the valley to Simba Col and Simba Tarn. Alternatively, from Kami you can keep your height and work round the head of the valley to reach Harris Tarn, then drop to Simba Tarn. Here the trail divides: to the left is the descent to Minto's Hut and the Chogoria Route; to the right leads to Square Tarn, Tooth Col and Austrian Hut (5 hours).

Sirimon Route

This route starts near the small town of Timau, on the main road between Nanyuki and Meru on the north side of the massif. Buses from Nairobi to Isiolo (via Nanyuki) will drop you at the junction where a drivable and well signposted track runs 9km from the main road to the park gate – a pleasant forest walk.

There's a campsite at the park gate, with water and toilet, but no other facilities. From the park gate to Judmeier Campsite is a 3-4 hour walk. The Old Moses Camp bunkhouse is nearby. 4WD vehicles can reach Judmeier and Old Moses.

From Judmeier and Old Moses a path leads southeast, then bears south, still following the track. Where this finally peters out you cross a small stream and the trail divides.

Most hikers go right here, as the route is more level. (The old route via Liki North Hut is hard and not used much.) You cross another stream, then

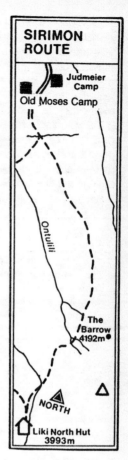

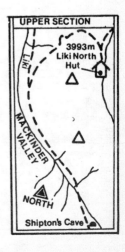

contour round a broad ridge, before crossing the Liki North river. From here the path climbs over another ridge – great views of the main peaks form the top – and drops into the Mackinder Valley, to lead straight up the valley to Shipton's Camp. (From Judmeier to Shipton's by this route is 5-6 hours.)

Near the head of the Mackinder Valley, half an hour before Shipton's Camp, the path climbs steeply up past Shipton's Caves. The grassy area below the caves makes a good campsite.

At Shipton's Camp you have several choices: straight up the scree to approach Point Lenana by its steep north face (very hard – especially after snow – and not advisable without a good guide); to Kami Hut (steep) and the Mt Kenya Circuit, on which you can continue to Two Tarn Hut and Mackinder's Camp to join the Naro Moru Route; or the other way round the Mt Kenya Circuit by Square Tarn and Tooth Col to Austrian Hut.

HYRAX

The hyrax is a familiar sight to hikers all over east and southern Africa. It looks like a large guinea pig, and belongs to the Procaviidae family, which means "almost guinea pig". Almost is the operative word: scientists believe that these attractive little creatures belong to an ancient group of "near-ungulates" which includes the elephant and aardvark. They retain several elephant-like characteristics: internal testes, rasp-like cheek teeth and incisors modified to tusks, rounded nails instead of claws, and teats between their forelegs. Their ancestors were the size of large pigs but once true ungulates appeared the only niche available was among the kopjes and cliffs of the savannah, so evolution designed them to expoit this habitat, and also life in the trees.

Hyraxes fall into two main groups: the rock hyrax (dassie), genus *Procavia* and similar bush hyrax, *Heterohyrax*, and the tree hyrax, *Dendrohyrax*. Rock hyraxes live in social groups and whistle their alarm calls, and tree hyraxes are solitary and live in hollow trees. Their (nocturnal) call is a spine-chilling scream.

Female dassies outnumber males three to one. This is because the unfortunate young males are kicked out of the maternal home once they reach adolescence and have to cross open savannah looking for an unoccupied kopje or cliff. They are likely to be eaten during the search.

One male and a harem of females occupies each nest site. After a long gestation period, seven or eight months, the young are born ready to go: active, with fur and open eyes. They are able to eat the adult diet of flowers, seeds, etc. within a few days. Hyrax diet, and the proliferation of the animal, has caused problems in heavily-used mountain areas, such a Mt Kenya. They feed on food left by hikers, then go on to nibble the rare afro-alpine plants. This is leading to large-scale destruction of the giant lobelia and groundsel that are characteristic of these altitudes.

Judith Rudnai, a Kenya-based scientist who has studied the hyrax, points out another of their dietary likings: liquor. "An economical way to bait them is with cheap sherry, although a rare old whisky, if not beyond your budget, may do a quicker job."

Rock hyrax (dassie)

Chogoria Route

This is the gentlest and longest approach route. It starts at the village of Chogoria, about 150km from Nairobi and reached by OTC bus and frequent matatus (it may be necessary to change buses at Embu). The road has been recently tarred and hitching is possible.

In Chogoria village is the Transit Motel, where porters and guides can be organised. The Motel can also provide a vehicle for a lift up to the Chogoria Gate. Things are more casual here than at Naro Moru; make sure your guide is familiar with the route and that he has sufficient food and equipment for himself. If you descend by another route you will have to pay him an extra day's fee and transport costs back to Chogoria. Unless you have a tent, spend the night at Chogoria; it is a full day's walk – about 25km – to the Park Gate and accommodation in the Meru Mount Kenya Lodge bandas or camping at nearby Parklands. Those with a tent can be more flexible, camping at the Forest Gate Station, 5km from Chogoria, then walking 14km to Bairunyi Clearing (the only feasible camping place along the track). Water is a problem here, however, the stream being some way from the camping area. From Bairunyi Clearing to the park gate is another 8.5km. The thick forest along this track provides excellent bird watching and the chance for wildlife viewing.

Shortly after the Park Gate there's a choice of two routes to the roadhead:

a) To the left a drivable track goes to the Parklands/Park Gate campsite, then continues (an hour's walk) to Urumundi Hut. This is a MCK hut but visitors can stay there by pre-booking with the club. You can also camp here. From the hut a path leads to the roadhead – a 1-2 hour walk.

b) To the right a drivable track leads directly to the roadhead. After 2.4km Urumundi Special Campsite is on the left, in the beautiful Urumundi Glade. This campsite has water, a toilet and a wooden shelter. From here it is a further 4.5km to the roadhead, up an increasingly steep track. From the park gate to the roadhead is 3 hours.

At the roadhead there is room to park vehicles and pitch a few tents. A stream provides water. This is a good place to rest up for a day; a good hike in the area is to the Giant's Billiard Table (6 hours there and back), or to the nearer Lake Ellis or Mugi Hill (about 4 hours).

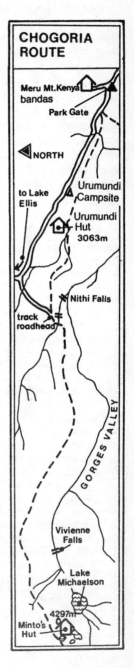

From the roadhead a single path leads up a large ridge to Minto's Hut, 6 hours walk with no water. You can camp here but it is more pleasant further up the valley. Beyond Minto's the path follows a valley and water is more plentiful with a number of places to camp. About an hour from Minto's the path divides: to the right it climbs steeply to Simba Tarn; to the left it zig-zags up the valley side to Square Tarn.

From Square Tarn go through Tooth Col, between Point Lenana and The Tooth (a prominent pinnacle), to reach Austrian Hut (Minto's to Austrian Hut takes 3-4 hours). Point Lenana can be climbed from here. It cannot be approached direct from Square Tarn.

From Simba Col you can descend via Shipton's Camp and the Sirimon Route, or bear west to Kami Hut (keeping high to avoid streams in small valleys) and continue on the Circuit Route round to Two Tarn Hut and Mackinder's Camp.

These are very long days, but with early starts they are possible for fit hikers carrying light loads.

The Rift Valley, with Mt Susua, Mt Longonot and Hell's Gate

By Ian Redmond, updated by David Else

Introduction The East African Rift Valley is part of one of the largest geological wonders of the world – a rift system that extends for more than 5,000km (more than an eighth of the earth's circumference). Long narrow sections of the earth's crust have sunk, leaving the valleys with associated volcanoes and strings of lakes along the floor. From the road from Nairobi to Naivasha, the viewpoint on the rim of the Eastern Escarpment presents a stupendous view towards the two large volcanoes and the Mau Escarpment, hazy in the west. Mt Longonot rises to 2,776m from the floor of the valley just south of Lake Naivasha (l,884m) and has an almost text-book volcanic cone with a crater on top. 30km further south lies the lower peak of Mt Susua with its crater within a crater. These mountains and the spectacular cliffs at Hell's Gate are accessible to hikers and offer some really unusual sights.

People This is Maasai land, and being by-passed by the main tourist trade offers the opportunity for the traveller on foot to meet uncommercialised pastoral herdsmen and women. These tall, proud people are well known for having resisted the tide of Western civilisation. They take what is useful to them (torches, radios, etc.) but shun Western dress and culture. Don't be put off by their vastly different way of life; many young *morans* (warriors) speak English and a few hours' conversation can be an enlightening experience. Away from the roads there are many traditional *manyattas* (compounds) where snotty-nosed kids run amongst the legs of their beloved cattle. The decorated gourds they carry are used to mix their staple diet – cow's blood and milk which is then curdled with cow urine – yummy!

Fauna and flora In Kenya the floor of the Rift Valley is typical East African savannah – hot and dry for much of the year. Despite the cultivated parts, there is still some wildlife around – giraffe, zebra, gazelle, baboon, cheetah and leopard (even a few elusive lion may survive). Hell's Gate offers the best chance of seeing lammergeyer (bearded vulture) nesting on the cliffs, along with a fantastic number of swifts. Flora includes the gaudy flame tree, aloes, whistling thorn acacias (with round, ant-filled galls on every twig) and the cactus-like *Euphorbia candelabra* trees. The prickly pear cactus (*opuntia*) is an introduced species which continues to spread everywhere and threatens to become a real nuisance.

Geology The many volcanic features in the area include steam vents, hot springs, lava tubes and innumerable cones and craters. Inside the 12km wide outer caldera of Mt Susua is a circular inner crater 5km in diameter; inside that is a raised plateau, a tilted plug of lava 4km across. This is known to the Maasai as the 'Lost World'. The terrain consists of angular chunks of jagged lava laced with *sanservaria* – spear 'cacti' which cause septic wounds. Oddly, it supports the only cedar forest for many miles in any direction, and twice the number of plant species found in the outer caldera. There are many

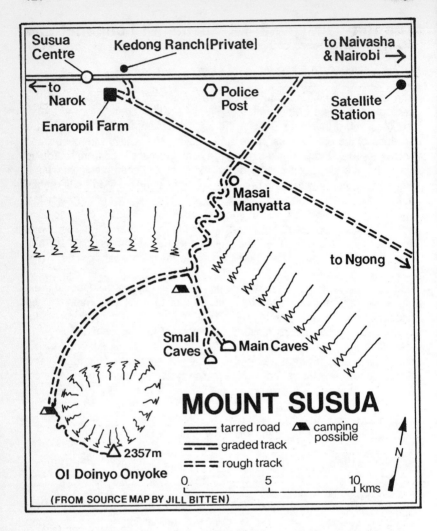

Susua Centre

Kedong Ranch [Private]

to Naivasha & Nairobi →

← to Narok

Enaropil Farm

Police Post

Satellite Station

Masai Manyatta

to Ngong

Small Caves

Main Caves

MOUNT SUSUA

Ol Doinyo Onyoke

2357m

tarred road   camping possible

graded track

rough track

N

0   5   10 kms

(FROM SOURCE MAP BY JILL BITTEN)

lava tubes under Mt Susua – caves formed when a flow of lava cools and solidifies on the outside but continues to flow on the inside leaving a hollow tube. Where the roof has collapsed you can climb into these caves and see amazing lava 'stalactites' where the liquid rock solidified in mid-drip all down the walls. Early risers will see the steam vents at their best, puffing clouds of white steam into the chilly dawn air and smelling of sulphur.

Preparations Hiking in this part of the Rift Valley is not difficult, and except on high ground the weather is warm or hot the year round (but nights can be very cold, with frost recorded).

Water is sometimes hard to find, particularly on Mount Susua. If you have a car, bring what you can from Nairobi. Food supplies can be bought at the small villages, but it is safer to bring some with you. A tent is necessary for serious hiking.

Survey of Kenya maps of this area are no longer available.

Organised hikes   A Kenya-based company, Kentrak, runs a four or five day backpacking trek in the Great Rift Valley, as well as day walks in the area. Contact David Furnivall, PO Box 47964, Nairobi, tel: 27311, 339094, or his agent Special Camping Safaris, Gilfillan House, Kenyatta Ave, Nairobi.

Mount Susua

Mt Susua rises above the floor of the Rift Valley south of the main road to Narok and the Maasai Mara, about 60km due north-west of Nairobi. The plains around the mountain are full of grazing giraffe, zebra, hartebeest and gazelle.

To reach Mt Susua from Nairobi take the old A104 road towards Naivasha (the lorry route). This road drops spectacularly down the rift valley escarpment to the small town of Maai-Mahiu (pronounced 'Mai-Mayu'). Buses and matatus run this way or you can hitch.

From Maai-Mahiu take the main B3 towards Narok. After 12km you pass a satellite station on the left, then, after 2.5km, a track on the left signposted Kedong Ranch. Ignore this. The track you want is a further 5km. It is not signposted. Follow this track towards the mountain which looks long and deceivingly low, crossing another road after 6km. After passing a manyatta, the track begins to climb steeply to the crater rim, 6km further (allow at least 3 hours' walking). Because this track is drivable (just) Mt Susua is popular with week-end trippers from Nairobi and you may get a lift to the top.

Once you have reached the top the crater is surprisingly large. The track branches at the rim: to the right the track continues across the crater plains for a further 11km to a grassy roadhead (camping possible), from where a footpath follows the inner crater rim up to the peak of Ol Doinyo Onyoke (Maasai for 'Red Mountain') at 2357m; to the left the track passes through trees (ignore a branch to the right after 3km – this leads to smaller caves) to reach a grassy area outside the entrance to the main Susua caves. A path drops to the cave entrances hidden by trees.

There are some places (especially on the north rim) where you can fairly easily clamber down the inner crater into the moat and up onto the central plateau. In the caldera, a clump of trees and bushes often denotes the entrance of a cave. You will need two days (and water for two days) to explore the area thoroughly.

Mount Longonot

Now a national park, with an entrance gate where fees must be paid, Mount Longonot is best approached from Longonot village on the old Nairobi-Naivasha road. This can be reached by bus, matatu or the train.

Camping is permitted at the park gate, but water is sometimes scarce (the rangers have a tank), but bring what you can with you.

To reach the gate from Longonot village, either take the path from near the level crossing on the southeast (Nairobi) side of the village, or from the police post on the main street, down to the railway station, cross the lines, then follow the track towards the mountain. Beware of 'guides' accompanying you part of the way, then aggressively demanding money. (Unfortunately, there have been a few cases of robbery in the area.) Guides are not necessary as a park ranger will accompany you on the walk.

Park fees are 540/- per day. There is no fee for the ranger, but a tip of 50-100/- would be suitable.

From the gate you can hike up to the rim of Mt Longonot (about 1-2

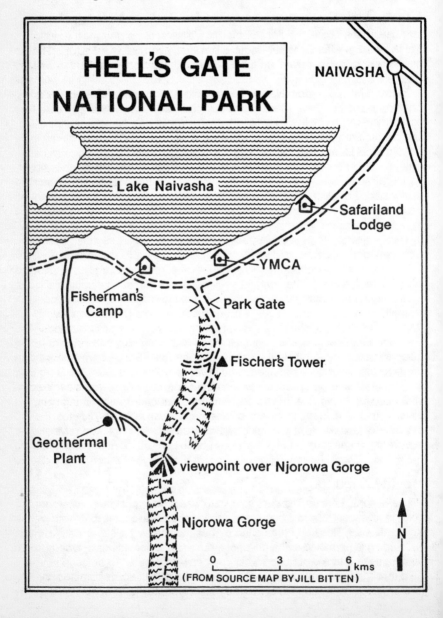

HELL'S GATE NATIONAL PARK

NAIVASHA

Lake Naivasha

Safariland Lodge

YMCA

Fisherman's Camp

Park Gate

Fischer's Tower

Geothermal Plant

viewpoint over Njorowa Gorge

Njorowa Gorge

N

0   3   6 kms

(FROM SOURCE MAP BY JILL BITTEN)

hours). The view from here is good, but for more excitement carry on round the crater to the summit, then continue round the crater to descend back to the gate. This is a long hike (about 6 hours in total – but that does not count stops for bird-watching, and gazing at the magnificent view). It gets very hot in the middle of the day.

There's an interesting secondary cone on the north flank of the volcano, and the rocks on the higher portion of the crater wall testify to the violence of the explosion that removed a major portion of the peak.

Hell's Gate National Park

This park is within walking distance of the south shore of Lake Naivasha, so one of the campsites there (the Y.M.C.A. is nearest, but Fisherman's Camp is a much more pleasant site) can serve as a base. If you continue west half a kilometre past the Y.M.C.A. you arrive at a left turn and a sign 'National Park'. 2km up this road is the park entrance where you must pay your fees (600/- per day, plus 150/- camping).

There are three campsites in the park. All are very basic and water must be carried from the gate, where there is usually a good supply.

Walking into the park from the gate, you'll soon come to Fischer's Tower, an impressive volcanic monolith at the apex of the road junction. The right fork leads towards the main wall and out of the gorge, the left curves round towards the grassland on the eastern side of the park, and straight on continues from Fischer's Tower down the main gorge itself.

At the end of the main track, near the far boundary of the park, on the left, is a ranger station and information centre. Camping (and sometimes water) is available here. About a half kilometre further on the track forks: the fork to the left leads to a spectacular viewpoint overlooking the lower gorge, the one to the right climbs steeply to the geothermal plant (outside the park boundary). It's a 2-3 hour walk from Fischer's Tower to the viewpoint.

'This track is accessible by vehicle, so much of it is a tourist walk. The surroundings vary from 500ft cliffs of vertical fluted columns, to idling grassland with gentle hills. A variety of large animals can be seen, including zebra, hartebeest, eland and giraffe. Nyanga swifts flit and swoop from their cliff face nests, and occasionally an Augur buzzard or Verreaux's eagle soars overhead. There have also been rumours of lammergeyers nesting here, but I have not seen them personally, nor met anyone who has.'(I.R.)

From the viewpoint a small steep path descends to the floor of the lower gorge. After heavy rain the gorge can be full of water, but at other times the stream is often no more than a trickle, or it may even be completely dry, so you can walk here.

Upstream you reach the area that gave the whole gorge its name. The early explorers saw it as the entrance to Hell itself. The main path follows a shelf to the right and a deepening cleft descends past sheer cliffs and further volcanic plugs. Eroded rock and ash formations and obsidian outcrops can be seen by the sharp-eyed. In earlier times it would have looked more imposing and sinister, but there is not so much steam to be seen here any more. Today the Geothermal Power Station harnesses this commodity.

Another tower, known as El Barta, rises from the floor of the valley as the

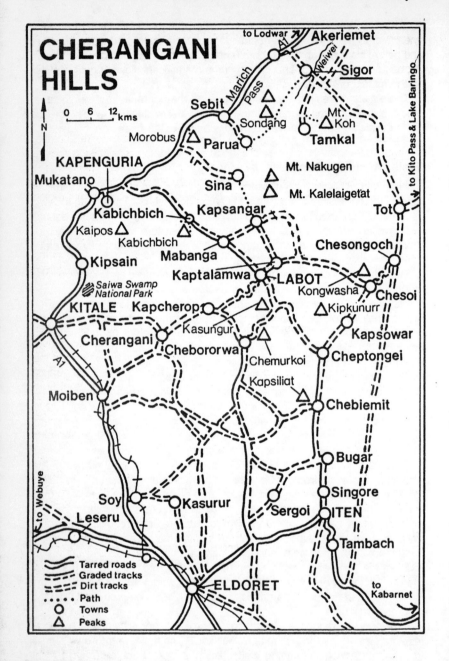

whistling thorns eventually give way to larger trees.

A tarred road leads from the plant back to Lake Naivasha passing to the west of Hell's Gate gorge. Transport runs along this road so it may be possible to hitch, making a circular route feasible, but it would be a shame to miss the return walk through the gorge.

The Cherangani Hills

Introduction   North of Kitale, and to the east of the road to Lake Turkana, are the Cherangani Hills. This is a good and seldom visited hiking region. There are many peaks here, the highest and most remote being in the northern area. In the southern part the lower hills make it good farming country and quite densely populated. Opportunities for hiking in this region are almost limitless.

Approaches   Hikers without a car will find it easier to approach from Kapenguria (on the main A1 road 30km north of Kitale) to the west of the Cheranganis, from Iten (on the Eldoret – Marigat road) to the south, or from Sigor (just off the main A1) to the north.

Accommodation   There are two excellent places to stay in the Cherangani region. North of the hills, near the town of Sigor, is Marich Pass Field Studies Centre. The centre provides residential and educational facilities for student groups but is also open to independent travellers. Guides for walking in the Cheranganis can be hired, and guards too, if you want to leave your vehicle or tent up in the hills while walking. To reach the centre continue north from Kitale, through Mukatano, and up the Marich Pass. Approximately 100km from Kitale, pass the junction to Sigor. After another 2km turn right on to a track, and follow signs to reach the centre after another 1km. Enquiries to Mr David Roden, PO Box 2454, Eldoret, or tel Nairobi 332067.

South of the Cheranganis is Sirikwa Safaris Guest House, on the main road between Kitale and Mukatano, about 5km north of the turn-off to Saiwa Swamp National Park. The guest house is an old settler farmhouse, with comfortable rooms, providing bed and breakfast. Camping is on the large lawn behind the house. Very knowledgeable bird-guides can be hired to take you round the nearby forest and farmland, or around Saiwa Swamp. If you've done the Cheranganis and are heading off to Mount Elgon (or the other way around), Sirikwa Safaris Guest House is an ideal place to rest up for a few days. Reservations are preferred. Enquiries to Mrs Barnley, PO Box 332, Kitale, or through Let's Go Travel, Nairobi.

Hiking routes

On the Cherangani Hills numerous narrow tracks and paths link the scattered villages. Some drivable tracks have been improved and are called 'Rural Access Roads'. The graded dirt road 'Cherangani Highway' is the area's main road joining Kapenguria and Iten via Kabichbich, Labot, Cheptongei, and Bugar. Matatus run irregularly along these roads and with a fair bit of luck you can ride them into the hills, hike for as long as you want, then catch a matatu back down.

Several hikers have sent us reports:

'We caught matatus from Eldoret to Iten, and from Iten to Labot. Labot itself is nothing more than a couple of shacks on the side of the road but because it's on a main crossroads it gets regular matatu traffic (about three times a week). From Labot we walked a few kilometres to Kaptalamwa and then another 8km to Kapsanger. This narrow track was drivable but no vehicles passed us that day. This is an interesting area because you pass from the lands of the Maraqwet people to those of the West Pokot. From Kapsangar it's 15km in a roughly northerly direction to Sina by the track, but we took a more direct route using footpaths. We met local people and were able to check our direction (some basic knowledge of Swahili would be useful here). We asked permission to camp the night at the dispensary at Sina, and the next day we caught a matatu to Mukatano, and from there another back to Kitale'. (Mary and Roger Thorn)

Note: Most public transport to Kapenguria (the main town in the area) goes only as far as Mukatano, a small town on the main A1 road a few kilometres from Kapenguria. Kapenguria itself is off the main road.

'To reach the northern peaks take any transport heading north on the A1 and get off at the junction a few kilometres past Akeriement. From here occasional matatus cover the 8km down to Sigor village. Nearby is Mount Koh, which we'd heard offered excellent views over this part of the Cheranganis.

'Sigor village has dukas and tea-shops, and a large market every Thursday, when many people come down out of the hills to buy and sell. Sigor has a couple of basic lodging houses, but we were allowed to camp at the Catholic mission. It may also be possible to camp at the District Officer's office with permission. (Some other travellers have suggested that it may be necessary to report to the D.O before going on to the hills.)

'To climb Mount Koh head southeast on the main track out of Sigor towards Tot. After 5km you pass an Italian aid project. Turn right over a small bridge onto a trail, walk for another 1-2km through the shambas, and after that all you need to do is basically head for the peak. There are many trails which can be confusing but if you keep heading up you shouldn't go wrong. The Pokot women here wear traditional dress: colourful beaded neck-rings and heavy bangles on their arms and legs.

'You can reach the peak in 3-4 hours so a day trip from Sigor is possible, and gear can be stored safely at the mission or the D.O.'s office. But it's far more pleasant to camp on the way. The best place is below the steepest section of the trail before the summit; this way you can save the 'final ascent' for the morning. There is water in the valleys but this is a long way down; the local people may show you springs higher up but it's worth carrying some water. Guides can be found in Sigor but are not really necessary.

'You can also hike on deeper into the Cherangani Hills, but once again you would need to be self-sufficient. A compass would be essential here'. (Sabine Tamm)

'Hitch or take a bus from Kitale to Sebit, from where a dirt track leads into the hills. Walk for three hours to Parua where the track ends. There is a school with friendly teachers (the local Pokot people are more reserved). Continue south east up the valley, keeping to to the left side on village paths. After several kilometres take one of the paths to the left, climbing up the left side of the valley to the village of Nyarakulian – and another school (ask local people for directions if necessary). This ascent takes another three hours. From here you can continue south on a good path to Kaibichbich (a day's hike) which is on a road that descends towards Kapenguria. The views are wide and impressive – Mt Elgon and the vast savannah.' (J. Noakes and C. Combrie)

'My start point was Chesoi, reached by matatu from Iten. The the last stretch from Kapsowar to Chesoi was very scenic hill farming country. I wouldn't have minded walking this stretch. Views out over the Kerio Valley from Chesoi were great.

'I stayed the night at the Roman Catholic church mission in Chesoi with very friendly church staff. The next day I followed an old, now disused, four wheel drive track west further into the hills.

'After an hour I reached forest – very pleasant strolling, and I saw quite a number of colobus monkeys. After 4-5 hours I came back out into farmland and continued on to Kapyego and camped in the church grounds – where I was guarded by an askari. From there I walked north up a good dirt road which gradually deteriorated, before heading up to a high point in the range. From there I followed the ridge on a disused vehicle track and stopped near the village of Kasinion to camp in a secluded spot (difficult to find). The following morning I continued on to Sondhang. For the last few kilometres there was no real track, so I just stuck to the western side of the ridge. Views to the west were quite spectacular. In the afternoon I followed the long spur down towards Ortum getting there in the early evening. This descent is a little tricky in a couple of spots if you have a full pack on, but is not technically difficult.

'After this walk, I stayed a night at the Marich Pass Field Studies Centre. From here you can do a three day walk to the top of Mt Sekerr which lies to the northwest; again, stunning views over the plains and back towards the Cheranganis. The study centre can provide a guide. I wanted to do Mt Koh, but on checking with the police they recommended that I didn't go up alone because of tribal troubles in the area.' (Scott Morgan)

'We started at Kaibichbich, and walked for four days through the villages on this side of the hills. Then we turned north into the wilder area of the High Cherangani. This is Pokot territory. There are no roads, schools or missionaries. The people speak only their own language, not even Swahili. We walked for six more days, crossing ridges and passing through patches of forest, to finally reach Kamalogon, the highest peak in the range. From there we continued east to the twin peaks of Chesugo, which had the most magnificent views over the Rift Valley, then descended to a village called Chesegon. From here we got a lift north to Sigor, but other vehicles were also heading south.

'The thing which helped us most were the 1:50,000 maps which we got in Nairobi after obtaining special permission from the Ministry of Land and the Defence Department.' (Javier Grinfeld, Liora Donskoy, Yoel Jurgeman, Israel)

Saiwa Swamp National Park

South of the Cherangani Hills, in between Mukatano and Kitale, is this small national park well worth visiting to see the remarkable sitatunga (aqueous antelope) and de Brazza monkeys. This park, which lies east of the A1, about 20km north of Kitale, can only be visited on foot (ideal for those without their own vehicle) and has a campsite.

Mount Elgon

By Ian Redmond, updated by David Else.

Note: Most of the introductory information in this section was written by Ian in 1980 shortly after his studies on the elephants of Mt Elgon. During the 1980s, sadly, there was very heavy poaching in this area and these unique, salt-mining elephants were all but exterminated. In the early 1990s, however, thanks to the activities of the Kenya Wildlife Services anti-poaching patrols, the slaughter was abated. In 1991 it was reported that elephants had returned to this part of Elgon and were once again visiting the caves. Obviously the herds are much reduced in numbers and the elephants themselves very wary of humans, so you would still be very fortunate to see elephants in the caves.

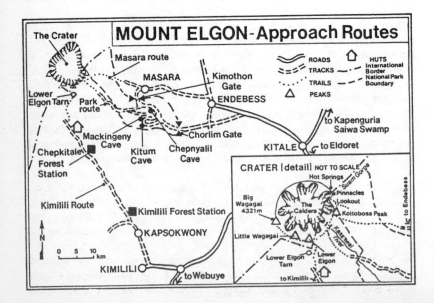

Introduction Mount Elgon is a huge, extinct volcano that sits astride the Kenya/Uganda border. On the Kenya side one section of the lower flanks of the volcano are National Park and may only be visited by vehicle, but other low sections plus the upper regions are outside the National Park and are open to visitors on foot. Here is some of the best, and least crowded, hiking in Kenya. Being lower than Mt Kenya, altitude sickness is less likely to be a problem, and there is the additional joy of hot springs.

Mt Elgon was formed some eight to ten million years ago, and though it hasn't erupted for the past three million years, hot springs are still to be found in the crater. The l00km wide base has led some to speculate that in its prime it might have towered above all other peaks in Africa, if not the world. Now it only ranks fourth in East Africa after Kilimanjaro, Kenya and the Ruwenzori range. It is a worn down shadow of its former self, with a circle of peaks around a 8km wide caldera. The highest peak, Wagagai, is now 4,321m and the floor of the crater around 3,600m. This is below the permanent snow line but hail and driving sleet are common on the high moorlands.

Flora and fauna The Elgon region offers a wealth of interest for the naturalist, with several unique features. The three main vegetation zones have representatives from 105 families of plants, with many species or subspecies peculiar to Elgon. From 2,000m to around 2,500m is tall, verdant mountain rain forest; huge *podocarpus* and *euphorbia* trees tower above the prickly-leaved barrier of blue-flowered *acanthus* bushes. This is the playground for innumerable troops of the spectacular black and white colobus monkeys, their long white 'shawls' flying as they run nimbly over the canopy and launch themselves on death-defying leaps to crash into the next treetop. Elephant, buffalo, giant forest hog, bushbuck and duiker can be glimpsed in the forest, and in clearings you may see small herds of defassa waterbuck, females and calves clustering around their male with his magnificent horns. On the more open areas an oribi or two can sometimes be seen.

Climbing above 2,700m takes you into the bamboo zone where dense stands of this amazing grass are the dominant growth, until you emerge onto the moorlands above 3,000m. Here the afro-alpine flowers are a delight to botanist and non-botanist alike, with perhaps a glimpse of a suni – an antelope not much bigger than a hare. Here too one can have that rare treat of looking down on birds of prey such as augur buzzard and crowned eagle soaring over the treetops below. Now we are in the land of giant groundsel or *senecio* – unearthly plants like cabbages on sticks (but with flowers almost identical to our common groundsel) and the long flowering spikes of the equally weird giant lobelias – great favourites with the sunbirds.

The Caves (Mt Elgon National Park) The most remarkable phenomenon to occur on Mt Elgon concerns the many caves that are hidden in the folds of its valleys. The elephants here, along with buffaloes, antelopes and monkeys, penetrate deep into the dark zone of the huge caverns that extend into the hillside. It is the only place in the world where such unlikely creatures go underground, and the reason for this peculiar behaviour is the animals' need for vital mineral salts which occur in the rock. They feel their way around rocks and crevasses to mine the rock in total darkness; in effect it is a subterranean salt lick. So much rock is removed in the stomachs of elephants that this mining is thought to be the major force in the formation of the caves.

Many of the caverns have been lived in by pastoral people of the El Kony tribe (Maasai-like people whose name – mispronounced – was given to the mountain) who also mined the rock to give to their stock. Some El Kony I met claimed to have been brought up in one of the caves, and there are one or two (outside of the park) that are still inhabited, They are roomy and quite comfy with fences to partition off the cattle and goats from the human living area. Most of the caves are cul-de-sacs up to 200m or so deep extending behind a cliff face at the head of a small valley and usually with a stream cascading over the cave mouth. Three such caves are now open to the public in Mount Elgon National Park. The largest, Makingeny, is easily the most spectacular with a slender 30.5m cascade falling over the vast entrance; one kilometre from Makingeny is a smaller cave but the one which is most frequented by elephants: this is Kitum. Before poaching took its toll, small herds of elephants used to arrive at dusk and spend up to five or more hours inside, their low rumblings of contentment being amplified as the sound reverberated around the cave; special permission must be sought from the park warden if you want to spend a night there in the hope of experiencing an elephant visit. The third cave, Chepnyalil, is a rather unusual 'double-decker' cave with signs of recent human habitation, including a peculiar rock painting.

Climbing Mt Elgon

Preparations The best (and only) map available is *Mount Elgon Map and Guide* by Andrew Wielochowski. You can buy this in Nairobi or from West Col Productions, Goring, Reading, UK.

Weather variations on Mt Elgon are not so much wet and dry, but wetter and drier. Though not as wet as the Ruwenzoris, it pays to carry warm and waterproof gear, even on the finest of days. Drier months are usually December to February, and wetter ones June to August.

Because of the adverse weather conditions, sleeping out on the upper slopes is not advisable – you need a tent. A compass is essential for hiking on the moors – cloud can drop in minutes to reduce visibility to a few feet. For this reason you should start hiking soon after sunrise, when the weather is usually clear.

Provisions may be bought in Kitale.

Warning Much of the ivory poaching that occurred on Elgon was blamed on Ugandan rebels and soldiers armed with machine guns and other war weapons. Although the civil war in Uganda is now over and the poaching reduced, the area is still sensitive. Unaccompanied walking and camping around the caldera is not encouraged. If you enter through the national park, you are supposed to take a park ranger to accompany you on the walk from the roadhead to the crater.

Approach Kitale is the access town for Mt Elgon. It is five or six hours' drive from Nairobi, and well served by buses and matatus. Your route from Kitale to the Mt Elgon crater depends on whether you have your own vehicle or are using public transport. You are not permitted to enter the National Park on foot, so unless fortunate enough to hitch a ride, backpackers must bypass the park and use either the Kimilili Route or the Masara Route, although the latter may be closed to walkers.

The Park Route   From Kitale take the road to Endebess. A dirt road runs south towards the park from the post office. Turn right at the first junction to the park entrance at Chorlim Gate. Another track to the park gate (signposted) turns left off the road between Kitale and Endebess. If hitching you must wait here for a lift (not recommended except during peak holiday periods – not enough traffic), although the walk through farmland to the park gate is very pleasant.

Park fees must be paid at the gate. These are 540/- per day and 180/- per night for camping.

Those without a vehicle will have to wait at the park gate for the chance of a lift. The first campsite inside the park is about 2km from the gate and the rangers might let you go there to camp and ask around for lifts.

For drivers, once inside the park follow signs to Koitoboss Peak. It is 30km to the roadhead. The track is muddy, rocky and steep in places, climbing through the forest and bamboo belts up to the moorland. 1km before the roadhead a spring provides the last water before the crater (in the dry season this may not be reliable). Driving takes three to five hours. If you manage to hitch into the park and then start walking it is more than a day's hike (and technically illegal).

To reach the crater from the roadhead get to the path (made by animals) near the top of the ridge on your left either by scrambling up the rocky section, or finding a way round it. Keep high – do not drop into the valley. It takes about three hours to hike to the col (pass) at the southern base of Koitoboss Peak (a large, squarish buttress of rock which forms one of the highest points on the Kenyan side of the crater) where there are flat places to pitch a tent. The area is windy, and there are frosts at night, but at least the sun hits the rim early in the morning to warm you up.

Koitoboss Peak and the hot springs   The summit of Koitoboss is gained by a steep scramble up on the northwest side of the peak. The path is indistinct and very steep in places, so this route should not be attempted in mist. It's about an hour's climb from the col to the summit and the same back.

The hot springs will probably be your first goal, however. They can be reached by skirting the base of Koitoboss Peak on its western side, which is easier than tussock-jumping across the crater floor. Head through the giant groundsel towards the rocky block in the centre of a small gap in the crater wall. From here you can look eastwards towards the hazy distant peaks of the Cheranganis. To the west, inside the crater, the path becomes well-defined, crossing a flat section before plunging down to curve left around impressive rock pinnacles to the head of Suam Gorge. On the way down the path veers to the right beneath the pinnacles. Cross the large stream to step illegally into Uganda and reach the springs. The hot spring water mixes with the cold stream so you can choose your bath temperature.

From the col to the hot springs takes two to three hours. Allow the same for the return journey.

The Kimilili Route Kimilili is a small town, with shops and a few cheap hotels, on the south of Mt Elgon which can be reached by bus or matatu. From Kimilili there are matatus to Kapsakwony, the access village for this route.

Kimilili Forest Station (now called Kaberua Forest Station) is 4.5km north of Kapsakwony on a dirt road towards the mountain. A forest ranger is usually stationed at the gate and visitors are required to enter their details in a book and pay a small fee. From Kimilili Forest Station to the disused Chepkitale Forest Station is 20km up the dirt road through dense forest, bamboo and open moorland. You can camp in one of the disused buildings, but water must be collected from the stream 3km before Chepkitale.

About 7km beyond Chepkitale Forest Station is a ruined hut (sometimes called 'Austrian Hut'). Although the hut is no longer usable (sad - it was only rebuilt by British and Austrian volunteers in 1985) there is excellent camping nearby, and water from the stream 5 minutes away. At night it is very cold, and often foggy. No wood is available nearby, so bring some from the forest further down.

From Kimilili/Kabuera Forest Station to Austrian Hut is a long day's walk (about 10 hours).

To reach Lower Elgon Tarn, a lake below the crater, continue up the track for about an hour. On the right an indistinct path (marked by a cairn) leaves the track and goes up to the left side of a craggy valley, passing a very large outcrop (marked on some maps as Sudek), and then drops to the lake which cannot be seen until almost reached. The path is marked with occasional white paint marks. From the hut to the lake takes 3-4 hours. There are a number of idyllic campsites beside the lake, and this makes an ideal base camp for excursions to other points on the southern side of the crater.

From the lake it is possible to reach Lower Elgon Peak, on the edge of the crater, in about an hour by following cairns and a steep gulley to the top.

You can go right (northeast) from Lower Elgon and reach the col below Koitoboss Peak, which is the top of the Park Route, in about four hours, although this is a tough hike (and the chance of getting lost in the frequent mist is high). From here you can reach the summit of Koitoboss, the hot springs, or descend on the Park Route.

You can also go northwest from Lower Elgon to reach Little Wagagai Peak on the crater rim in about two hours and Big Wagagai Peak, the highest point on Mt Elgon and in Ugandan territory. Allow four hours to reach Big Wagagai from the lake, and the same for your return. The easiest route is to go south of the lake, then west arriving at the rim between Little Wagagai and Lower Elgon Peak.

Both of these routes from Lower Elgon are rarely travelled and not at all easy – make sure you are especially well prepared with map, compass, food, water and protective clothing.

The Lakes

Introduction The geological upheavals of the Rift Valley have created a series of lakes, running in a line, roughly north to south, down the centre of the country. Of the Kenyan lakes, Turkana, Naivasha and Baringo are fresh water, but the others are 'soda lakes' with a high saline content. The alkaline water harbours a large quantity of algae and tiny crustaceans which are the main food for the millions of flamingos for which the lakes are famous. The deep pink ones are lesser flamingos (*Phoenicopterus minor*) and the whitish ones are greater flamingos (*P. ruber*).

Nakuru and Bogoria are national parks, so are not open to independent travellers without their own transport. Now hiking is no longer permitted in Bogoria (except in pre-arranged, organised groups) and most of the flamingos have left, it has been omitted from this section. Nakuru, however, is such a spectacular place it is worth describing for those who have their own (or a hired) vehicle, or can afford a taxi or safari.

Lake Naivasha

This is a bird-watcher's paradise and has many other attractions, not the least being its proximity to Nairobi (88km north) and the ease with which it can be reached by public transport. The lake lies to the southeast of Naivasha town, and the hotels and 'camps', offering cottages, bandas (huts) and camping, line its southern shore. These can all be reached via Lake Road South. From Naivasha town walk towards Nairobi along the old A104 road (the truck route). After 5km turn right at the Lake Road South junction (follow the signs to the hotels and camps). If you've come in on the old road, you'll reach the junction before you get to the town.

Occasional buses and matatus serve the small villages on this road, or you can walk or hitch. After passing the Sailing Club (private) and the Hotel (exclusive) you reach Safariland Lodge, 10km from the Lake Road South Junction. This is a slightly up-market, well organised, 'tourist village' with a campsite attached (for an extra fee campers can use the hotel facilities). A further 6km brings you to the Y.M.C.A. (also called the Youth Hostel), a very run down site with a few dilapidated bandas and limited water supplies, but with a cheap campsite. If you still have energy, 4km further still is Fisherman's Camp (also called a Youth Hostel), with reasonably priced self-catering cottages and a grassy campsite right next to the lake. Rowing boats can be borrowed free of charge, and fishing rods hired.

There are 350 species of bird in the area, including the ubiquitous lovebirds, which are not a native Naivasha species – they were released from local aviaries. This being a freshwater lake, the water birds are mostly different species from those found in the soda lakes. In fact the whole ecology is different. The Crescent Island Sanctuary, near the Sailing Club, is the best place for bird-watching.

Between the Y.M.C.A. and Fisherman's Camp is the entrance to Hell's Gate National Park (see *The Rift Valley* section).

Lake Nakuru

Between one and two million lesser flamingos feed around the shores of Lake Nakuru, providing one of the most beautiful and dramatic sights in all Africa. (Periodically the lake conditions change and they migrate to other soda lakes, so check the situation before going to the expense of hiring a vehicle.) The forested areas around the shores of the lake also shelter many species of animal not often seen in the savannah game parks – waterbuck, reedbuck, and vervet monkeys, as well as smaller mammals. A rhino sanctuary has also been established here.

Nakuru town is easily reached from Nairobi by public transport, and the entrance to the national park is only 5km from the town centre.

You are not allowed in without your own vehicle, so probably the best bet is to see the park by taxi: this can be arranged in the town or at the park gate itself, where a few taxis often wait for business. Prices start high though, so be patient and bargain hard. Expect to pay about $15 per hour. Jomima Tours, with an office in Nakuru near the post office, run safaris into the park. Check their prices; you may be able to join a group which would work out cheaper than a taxi.

Lake Baringo

This is a great place to relax – a fresh water lake with a campsite next to a luxury lodge with all the facilities you could wish for – a swimming pool, library, table tennis – open to non-residents for a daily fee of about $3. The campsite is Robert's Camp, and the lodge is the Lake Baringo Club. From the club you can go on bird-watching trips by boat or on foot. Highly recommended.

The camp and club are easily reached from the main B4 road; turn right off the B4 on the minor road towards the village of Kampi Ya Samaki. The campsite is off this road, between the junction and the village.

Towards the North

The Samburu Highlands

If you are heading for the eastern shores of Lake Turkana it's well worth stopping over at the town of Maralal. This lies at the southern end of the Samburu Highlands, a green and fertile range of hills rising above the surrounding plains. Mists are common here, and the temperatures often cool.

Maralal is the unofficial capital of the red-robed Samburu tribe, a semi-nomadic cattle-raising people related to the Maasai.

There is a hostel and campsite about 4km south of Maralal, run by Yare Safaris, which is well-equipped and very reasonably priced.

Information and maps of the Samburu Highlands are available, and guides for walks in the surrounding area can be arranged. Camping safaris by truck and camel run regularly from the hostel to Lake Turkana, Samburu National Park, the Mathews Range, and other places of interest in the surrounding area.

Buses from Nyahururu run daily to Maralal. The road is well graded but traffic infrequent, so hitching would take a long time. Yare Safaris also operate a bus service between Nairobi and the Maralal Hostel. Anyone can use this service, but it is free of charge to passengers booking a safari. Contact Yare Safaris, Africa Travel Centre, Union Towers, PO Box 63006, Nairobi.

Javier Grinfeld, Liora Donskoy and Yoel Jurgeman, from Israel, wrote: 'From Maralal, it's worth hitching or taking a matatu 20km north to Poror. From there it is possible to walk about 7km west to Lesiolo which gives a wonderful view of the Samburu Hills and Rift Valley. You can find a guide in Poror but the walk is very easy.'

INTERMEDIATE TECHNOLOGY IN KENYA

This charity's aims are to 'enable poor people in the Third World to develop and use technologies and methods which given them more control over their own lives and which contribute to the long-term development of their communities'.

IT has several projects in Kenya. One recent success has been in encouraging the government to change their planning and building regulations. These had been devised in colonial times, and required, among other things, that roofs could bear the weight of four inches of snow and that every plot had car-parking space. Houses that did not conform were deemed illegal so did not receive government services.

Rural projects range from 'harvesting' rain water, to the very successful Stoves and Household Energy Programme (SHE) which trains women potters to produce and market the fuel-efficient *upesi* stove. This uses less wood so protects the dwindling forests, saves the labour of carrying firewood or the expense of buying it, and produces less smoke.

The emphasis is always on using local ideas, local labour and local material. The *upesi* stove, for instance, can be made by women whose traditional craft is pottery.

Another project has helped the Maasai adapt to change. The Maasai's traditional nomadic lifestyle required houses which could quickly be dismantled. Their staple diet was blood and milk, needing no cooking, so smoke from cooking fires was seldom a problem. If the Maasai ate meat, the smoke seeped out through the roof; rain also seeped in.

Their way of life could not withstand outside influences indefinitely; first came a change of diet, introducing foods which needed more cooking and so produced more smoke. More smoke meant more respiratory disease. Then the government encouraged the Maasai to build permanent homes. These were constructed with better roofs which kept out the rain but kept in the smoke.

Under IT's guidance the women of Kajiado, near the Tanzanian border, made drawings of their ideal home. These included gutters to collect rain-water into a ferro-cement collecting jar, improved ventilation, and internal improvements like higher ceilings giving more room. Several have now been constructed and the ideas copied by neighbouring communities.

To learn more about the work of Intermediate Technology write to Myson House, Railway Terrace, Rugby, CV21 3HT. Tel: 0788 560631.

Mathews Range

The Mathews Range lies to the north of Samburu National Reserve, to the west of the Isiolo-Marsabit road. The hills are well watered and thickly forested supporting a great variety of wildlife. At the southern end of the range the Nyeng River flows through the Kitich Valley where there is an exclusive luxury tented camp, a public campsite and a rhino protection unit, but otherwise there are no facilities for hikers.

Occasional matatus run to Wamba, the nearest large settlement, but it's still at least 40km, on rough roads, to the Kitich Valley. Hikers without a vehicle will find it very difficult to get beyond Wamba. As yet there have been few trekkers here, but several operators have their eye on it now better-known mountains are becoming so popular.

It is possible to stay in Wamba, and walk for the day from there. Local boys will act as guides. If you get to the Kitich Valley, water is available at the public campsite but all supplies should be brought from Archers Post or Isiolo. The tented camp provides full accommodation. There are no marked trails in the area, so guides are recommended and can be arranged at the tented camp.

Gerhard Bronner, a biologist studying the vegetation in the area, sent an account (quoted from below) of a trip where the 'guide' he arranged in Wamba had never been on the mountain before, causing him to spend a waterless and thirsty night in the forest:

'We decided to climb Lpiwa on a different route. Before, when we'd climbed the mountain, we'd used buffalo paths... We walked along the river, always being wary of buffaloes that might hide in the bushes. Then we followed cattle tracks through dense scrub, often caught by thorny bushes and climbing plants.

'It was hard going and we were sweating... Gaining altitude, we left the bushland behind and entered the forest. In the hot, dry lowlands around Wamba it is hard to imagine that up the mountains there is real forest with tall trees, and in the upper regions even rain forest. In the rainy season this forest has a special atmosphere. The dense canopy and ground cover swallowed every sound, even birds. The trees were covered in mosses and lichens hanging down like curtains. Sometimes the hoarse cry of giant hornbills or the strange rolling-grunting noise of colobus monkeys could be heard. In the afternoon mist the forest took on an even stranger appearance, like the deep dangerous forest of fairy tales...'

The description becomes less lyrical after they got lost, but Gerhard leaves no doubt that this is potentially a marvellous backpacking area. As always though, if you do hike in this area be prepared with map, compass (or knowledgeable guide) and a good supply of water.

The Lake Turkana Region

By David Else and others

In the far northwest of the country, Lake Turkana is the largest of Kenya's Rift Valley lakes. Much of the northern half of Kenya is desert or semi-desert scrubland, and Lake Turkana is a long ribbon of blue cutting through the parched landscape. The level of water in the lake is constantly falling; the many years of drought in the area and in Ethiopia, source of the rivers feeding the lake, have caused this.

Compared to the other lakes and national parks in Kenya, Lake Turkana is very seldom visited, although a few up-market companies offer fly-in-fly-out weekend breaks at one of the two posh 'fishing lodges', and some of the camping safari outfits run overland epics for budget travellers up to the eastern shore.

Apart from those who choose to stay in the isolated luxury of the lodges, most of the tourists who visit the Turkana region come to experience the wild beauty of the place or to see the various interesting tribal groups which inhabit the area. Although some parts of Lake Turkana are now slightly touristy, there are other areas which offer almost endless walking possibilities for adventurous travellers.

There are very few boats across the lake, and to get from the west to the east side of Lake Turkana by road means returning to Kitale and from there to Eldoret (and probably even to Nakuru) before going north again through Nyahururu and Maralal. So you'd better decide early which section you want to see!

The West Side

The main town on the west side of the lake is Lodwar, joined to Kitale by 300km of tarred road (daily bus and hitching possible with patience). From Lodwar you can travel on to Eliye Springs (run-down lodge and campsite) or to Kalakol – marked Lokwa Kangole on some maps – (exclusive Lake Turkana Angling Lodge, camping possible on the beach nearby). Experienced and self-sufficient hikers could walk between these two sites, or for a couple of days (north or south) along the lake shore. Guides, and even pack camels, can be arranged if required.

It is not advisable that you go too far north from Kalakol as this is a sensitive border area. Neither should you go too far south of Eliye Springs: this is one of the hottest, driest and least populated parts of Kenya. Whichever way you go remember that crocodiles are a real danger along the water's edge.

We heard about a group of three walkers who had walked from Ferguson's Gulf to Eliye Springs, and further south before following a small four-wheel-drive track back to the sealed road to Lodwar. They took nine days, but had to walk a lot at night because of extreme heat during the day (over 40°C in the shade).

Let's Go

CAMPING Free information on two to twelve day camping safaris by road, camel or foot, to parks and off the beaten track. We also book 'tailor-made' exclusive camping safaris.

CAMP BOXES Hire of camp boxes containing two man tent, mosquito proofed, with sewn in ground sheet and fly sheet, single gas cooker, gas light, all crockery, cutlery and cooking utensils for two.

LOCAL Free Tariff sheets, Hotel and Lodge bookings, Regular departure tours, Camping safaris, Self-service bandas, Walking safaris, Camel safaris, Mountain treks, Balloon safaris, Flying excursions, Domestic flights, Train bookings.

CAR HIRE Self drive, Chauffeur driven, Daily rates, Weekly rates, Monthly rates, Unlimited mileage rates, Vehicles ranging from economical Suzukis to 4-wheel-drive.

Let's Go Travel

P.O. BOX 60342, Nairobi, Kenya. Tel: 340331, 213033
Fax: 254-2-336890.
Caxton House, Standard Street, Near Main GPO, Opposite Bruce House.

The East Side

The east side of Lake Turkana offers more hiking opportunities. The main settlement on this side of the lake is Loyangalani, but getting here is not always easy. Traffic to Maralal is reasonable but it gets pretty thin north towards Loyangalani. An infrequent matatu goes as far as Baragoi, but after that hitching is the only way to get there if you want to travel independently, and you might have to wait a couple of days between lifts.

But if you do make it this far on your own, the hiking is wild and remote. Areas we know people have hiked in this area include Mount Kulal, the Ng'iro Range and the Ndoto Range. Extracts from their letters are included here.

Mount Kulal The summit (actually two peaks about 8km apart) lies about 35km east of Loyangalani. Although the surrounding area is dry and barren the mountain is high enough to be damp and well-vegetated. In fact the whole mountain is of such scientific interest that it has been designated a biosphere reserve. Although the area seems remote, a number of small farming settlements have been long established on the mountain. The main settlement on the mountain is called Gatab, on the southern slopes. Gatab can only be approached by road from the south as a large canyon separates the mountain's two main peaks. Lifts to Gatab are easier to find in Marsabit than in Loyangalani as the mission in Gatab occasionally goes there for supplies.

Gatab and the southeastern slopes of Mount Kulal can be approached on foot from Loyangalani. But although the mountain seems near it takes at least two days to walk between Gatab and Loyangalani.

'We hitched a ride from Marsabit, across the Chalbi Desert, to Gatab. (Make sure you arrange a lift all the way to Gatab as some vehicles only go as far as Kargi.) We camped near the mission in Gatab after asking permission. In this area a surprising number of vegetables and crops are grown. The people also keep cattle and goats. There are lots of birds and animals; the rare greater kudu is sometimes seen up here, and we even heard stories of lions. We walked down towards Lake Turkana and eventually reached the track that runs along the lakeside. From there we walked to Loyangalani.' (Ady and Dudy, Israel)

Hikers walking this way should realise that they are crossing a desert. Water supplies on the route are unreliable so you need to carry all your needs. You may be able to arrange a guide in Loyangalani.

Ng'iro Range This is an area of high ground to the northwest of South Horr, forming the western side of the Horr Valley. Like Mount Kulal, the area is fertile and green, and able to support a population. The main settlement on the west side of the range is Tum on the western side of the range. Tum is reached via a track which branches west from the main Maralal to Loyangalani road halfway between Baragoi and South Horr. The highland area around Tum is interesting but beyond Tum, heading northwards towards Lake Turkana, is serious backpacking country, and hikers should be experienced and well-equipped.

'We got lifts on trucks from Maralal to South Horr and then to Tum, which is a larger town. There's a mission and some shops. We wanted to walk from

Tum to the southern tip of Lake Turkana, and from there to Loyangalani. We hired a guide in South Horr and he helped us arrange jerry-cans, donkeys and a handler in Tum. We walked via the small water hole of Parakati; not shown an any map we've seen. If it hadn't have been for the guide we would not have found it and might have found the walk impossible without extra water. It took us three days to reach the lakeshore near Teleki's Volcano. We were so happy to see the lake after walking in the heat on rationed water but we couldn't swim because a huge crocodile was sun-bathing on the shore nearby. The volcano is an impressive sight, seeming to be made out of one solid rock. We climbed up to the rim and the view was even better from the top. It was another two day's walk along the lake shore to Loyangalani. Our water was still low, but luckily it was cloudy so relatively cool. When we arrived in Loyangalani even the warm sodas were very welcome!

'Our guide's name was Benedict Boritiye (Ben) and he lived in South Horr. If he is still there we can recommend him.' (Arik Orbach and Limor Rozen, Israel)

We've since heard from a TV film company in Britain who also used Ben as a guide, and were able to confirm this recommendation.

We've also heard from some other intrepid Israeli hikers who walked from Baragoi to Tum, then went up into the Ng'iro Range with a guide for three days to reach the summit, called Mowo-Engo-Sawan, and descended to South Horr. This was reported to be a difficult walk, with 'lots of bush and thorns...but excellent views!'

GAME PARKS AND FOOT SAFARIS

As well as the mountain national parks described in this chapter (Mt Kenya, Mt Longonot, Mt Elgon), Kenya also has many national parks where wild animals in the open savannah are the main attraction. These are generally called 'game parks', even through the animals are no longer hunted for sport. National parks are run by the state (through Kenya Wildlife Services), where the wildlife and ecology of the area are completely protected, as far as possible, from human encroachment. Kenya also has many national reserves, which are similar to national parks, but they are run by local councils and some human access is allowed.

Most game parks are only accessible by vehicle, and these are well covered in other publications (see *Further reading*). Very briefly, however, I'd recommend **Samburu** and **Marsabit** for beauty and unusual species (Grevy's zebra and reticulated giraffe), **Maasai Mara** for huge herds of just about everything, and **Nairobi National Park** if you really can't afford a safari but want to see a park (it's surprisingly good, considering its proximity to Nairobi). **Amboseli** suffers from overuse and erosion, but it's conveniently located for Nairobi and has that incomparable backdrop of Kilimanjaro.

Park fees have increased considerably in Kenya over the last few years. They are currently (1993) 600/- per day (US$15), plus 180/- per night for camping. Reserves are still a very reasonable 80/- (around $3) per day, but are likely to catch up with the parks in the future.

A few game parks do allow visitors on foot, providing they are part of an organised group. This is a far more exciting and authentic way of seeing wildlife and highly recommended for those after a safari with a difference.

Kenyan tour operators offering walking safaris on the mountains and/or in the game parks include:

Tropical Ice, PO Box 57341, Nairobi (Tel: 23649). Escorted treks and climbs on Mt Kenya, and walking safaris along the Tsavo and Galana Rivers in Tsavo National Park.

Natural Action, PO Box 12516, Museum Hill Shopping Centre, Nairobi (Tel: 740214); also 16 Swyncombe Ave, London W5, UK (Tel: 081 758 9157). Specialists in climbs, hikes and treks on Mt Kenya and several other Kenyan mountains, plus Kilimanjaro and the Ruwenzoris.

Bushbuck Adventures, PO Box 67449, Gilfillan House, Kenyatta Ave, Nairobi (Tel: 212975); also 26 Newnham Green, Malden, Essex, UK (Tel: 0621 853172). A wide range of walking and vehicle game-viewing safaris on Mt Kenya, the Aberdares and many of the wildlife parks. Also have their own tented camps in several mountain areas which make good bush-walking bases.

Kenya Hiking & Cycling, PO Box 39439, Arrow House, Koinange Street, Nairobi (Tel: 218336). Adventurous walking and mountain biking safaris to Mt Kenya, the Rift Valley and the wildlife parks. Also using boats on Lake Turkana.

Gametrackers, PO Box 62042, Kenya Cinema Plaza, Moi Avenue, Nairobi (Tel: 338927). Wildlife safaris in the national parks and to Lake Turkana, plus backpacking in the Aberdares and camel-trekking in the Ndoto Hills.

Yare Safaris, Africa Travel Centre, PO Box 63006, Union Towers, Moi Ave,

Nairobi. (Tel: 214099). Wildlife safaris in the Kenyan national parks and gorilla safaris to Zaire and Rwanda, plus camel treks in the Maralal area.

Kentrak Safaris, PO Box 47964, Nairobi (Tel: 334863/29050); also at Special Camping Safaris, PO Box 51512, Gilfillan House, Kenyatta Ave, Nairobi (Tel: 338325). Adventurous bush-walking and backpacking safaris in the N'gong Hills and Rift Valley.

Let's Go Travel, PO Box 60342, Standard St (near the British High Commission), Nairobi (Tel: 340331) represents a wide range of operators: safaris for all budgets and tastes, including most of the safari companies above and the 'tree' hotels described in *Other places of interest*.

Companies in the UK and USA which arrange safaris in the mountains and game parks are listed in Chapter 5.

OTHER PLACES OF INTEREST

In a country as rich in interest as Kenya, I am only listing some personal favourites.

Gedi

On the coast, some 25km south of Malindi, this is a 13th Century Arab City which was smothered in jungle until it was excavated in 1948. Apart from its archaeological interest, the jungle – which still seems to have the upper hand – is one of the main reasons to visit the site. There are plenty of birds and monkeys, and naturalists will want to look for the golden-rumped elephant shrew, unique to the area.

Lamu

Almost everyone loves Lamu, even though it is now heavily visited. This car-free island on the northern part of Kenya's coast, has a strong Swahili culture, marvellous mangoes and yoghurt, cheap accommodation in private rooms, and an air of tranquillity that nothing can destroy (except, perhaps, the navy base being built on a neighbouring island).

Lamu is reached by ferry from the mainland town of Mokowe, reached by a long bus ride from Malindi.

The Ark and Treetops

In the Aberdare Mountains, in the area of Kenya once known as the White Highlands since the early colonists were attracted to the fertile land here, is Aberdare National Park. Two animal viewing centres, The Ark and Treetops, have been built where tourists can watch animals attracted to a saltlick. They are expensive and sound terribly touristy, but The Ark was the highlight of my posh safari when I visited three major game parks (of which Samburu was my favourite). What makes The Ark (and Treetops which I haven't visited) so special is the opportunity to watch animal *behaviour* rather than just look for photo opportunities. You arrive in the late afternoon and the serious game watching is done from a comfortable glass-enclosed lounge or open verandah. At dusk and during the night animals wander under the spotlights to enjoy the saltlick or drink from the lake. A bell in the rooms alerts visitors to the presence of unusual animals. In fact I stayed up until 3 am, unable to tear myself away from the elephants, bushbuck, giant forest hog, and the small nocturnal animals such as bush babies and genets. Well worth a splurge if you can afford it. (If you go, bring warm clothes. It can get very cold at night.) A single cabin at The Ark costs around $100 full board. Prices at Treetops are similar. You can book direct to The Ark, PO Box 101, Mweiga, or to Treetops, PO Box 23, Nyeri, or through any travel agent in Nairobi, which is easier and often cheaper.

Shimba

Another 'tree' hotel is the Shimba Lodge in the Shimba Hills National Park, two hours by bus from Mombasa. This hotel is also built on wooden poles overlooking a water hole which is visited at night by elephant, giant forest hog, and other animals. It costs around $60 (low season). Many of the coast hotels can arrange one or two night trips to Shimba.

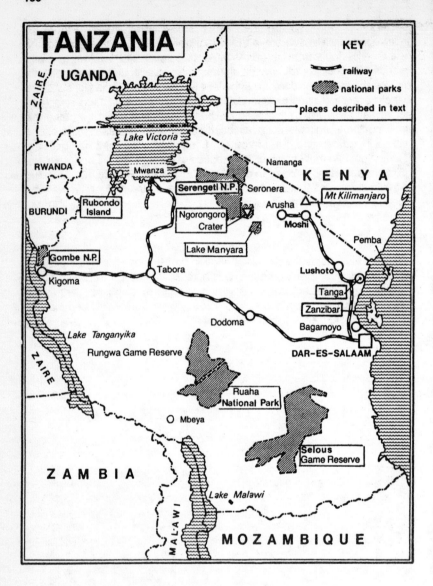

TANZANIA

ZAIRE

UGANDA

RWANDA

BURUNDI

Lake Victoria

Mwanza

Rubondo Island

Serengeti N.P.

Seronera

Ngorongoro Crater

Lake Manyara

Gombe N.P.

Kigoma

Tabora

Namanga

K E N Y A

Mt Kilimanjaro

Arusha

Moshi

Pemba

Lushoto

Tanga

Zanzibar

Bagamoyo

DAR-ES-SALAAM

Lake Tanganyika

Rungwa Game Reserve

ZAIRE

Dodoma

Ruaha National Park

Selous Game Reserve

Mbeya

Z A M B I A

MALAWI

Lake Malawi

M O Z A M B I Q U E

Banded mongoose

Chapter 10

Tanzania

Updated for this edition by Philip Briggs with further contributions by Patrick Frew, Lluis and Jaume Tort, Joan Masoliver and Diana Clement

FACTS AND FIGURES

Tanzania was never a British colony as such; up to the First World War it was a German possession, and subsequently named Tanganyika and governed by the British under a League of Nations mandate and then a United Nations trusteeship until independence in 1962. The union between Tanganyika and its offshore islands of Zanzibar and Pemba was formally established in 1964 when the name Tanzania was adopted.

From independence to 1985, the country was shaped by President Julius Nyerere, who followed a policy of socialism and self-reliance based on the *Ujamaa* (brotherhood) rural village cooperatives. In 1985 Nyerere stepped down in favour of Ali Hassan Mwinyi, but remained chairman of the CCM, Tanzania's sole political party. The government has now moved away from rigid socialism.

Tanzania is the largest country in East Africa, with a land area of 945,000 square kilometres. Most of the country is a plateau between 1,000 and 1,400 metres high, with mountains grouped in the north-eastern and south-eastern sectors. Mt Kilimanjaro (at 5,985m the highest peak in Africa) and Mt Meru make up the former, while the latter group includes the modest Mt Rungwe (3,100m).

Temperatures are governed by the altitude, with the coastal strip always hot and humid. The Long Rains fall between April and May and the Short Rains between November and December.

The main foreign currency earner is probably tourism.

People

Although there are about 120 tribes in Tanzania, none is dominant in political or business life and the government actively discourages any pursuit of tribal customs and encourages national (rather than tribal) unity. Although one third

of the Asian community has left the country since independence, a sizeable number remain.

Swahili is the official language, but English is widely spoken in main tourist centres; you'll need a bit of Swahili if you travel off the beaten track.

Only 20% of the population are Christian or Muslim. The rest follow their own beliefs.

TRAVEL

Impressions

Tanzania is in many respects the perfect East African country, with the best game parks and people who embody African elegance (some of the women's hairstyles are amazing). For many years Tanzania was a difficult country to travel in. It suffered from persistent fuel and food shortages, and there was a frustrating level of petty officialdom. This is no longer the case: Tanzania has a positive attitude to tourists and shortages are a thing of the past.

There is a well-developed tourist circuit in the north of the country, but few travellers have as yet explored beyond the more obvious attractions; there are many alluring off-the-beaten-track possibilities in the little-explored south and west.

Tanzania is remarkably free of the tribalism that plagues most of Africa – it is the only country I [Philip Briggs] have visited where people tell you which town they come from as opposed to their tribe. In other ways, however, Tanzanian society is deeply conservative, and a strong emphasis is placed on politeness, especially towards elders. For me, it was a pleasure to spend time in a country where the word you most often hear is *karibu* (welcome) as opposed to *mzungu* (white person), but many travellers – especially those who don't bother to learn even the most basic of Swahili greetings – mistake Tanzanian politeness for stand-offishness or even hostility. I agree wholeheartedly with the sentiments expressed by Jim Noakes and Claudine Combrie in the last edition: 'We liked the atmosphere and the mood of the people in Tanzania – very relaxed and egalitarian, no positive or negative discrimination towards us, just straight.'

Entry and exit

Members of Commonwealth countries do not need a visa, and can obtain a free visitor's pass valid for one month on entering Tanzania. The Tanzanian High Commission in London claims that British citizens must buy a visitor's pass in advance, but this is expensive and I've never heard of anyone being refused one at the border. Visitor's passes can be extended for up to three months at any immigration office. This is a straightforward procedure, but in large towns you may spend some time queuing.

Members of most non-Commonwealth countries must buy a visa in advance.

An airport departure tax of $20 must be paid in US dollars *cash*. If you leave Tanzania by ferry, you must pay a $5 port tax, also in hard currency.

It is forbidden to export more than around $10 in Tanzanian currency. Few people will feel an irresistible urge to infringe this law, and it no longer seems to be strictly enforced.

Border crossings

You're unlikely to encounter problems at Tanzania's northern border crossings. The southern border posts used to be infamous for corruption, and travellers who were suspected of having been in South Africa were refused entry. There are no longer restrictions on people who have visited South Africa and I have not heard of people being hassled at southern borders recently.

If arriving from Burundi by the Lake Tanganyika ferry via Gombe Stream, note that although there is a border post in Banda the customs office is in Kigoma.

Money

The Tanzania shilling (Tsh) was effectively floated in early 1992 and has stabilised at around US$1 - Tsh400 (Dec 1992). Money can be changed at a bank, but you get 25% more at a Bureau de Change. These can be found in Arusha, Mbeya, Dar es Salaam, Mwanza and Dodoma and at the Namanga border post. In Dar es Salaam, shop around before changing large sums.

There is no black market; anyone who approaches you in the street is trying to set you up.

Tourist hotels, air tickets and game reserve fees must be paid for in hard currency, preferably US dollars. To avoid receiving change in shillings, bring about $200 in $1, $5 and $10 bills.

What to buy

Makonde ebony carvings are distinctive and fascinating. The best place to buy them is Mwenge Market, about 5km from Dar es Salaam on the Bagamoyo Road. Buses to Mwenge leave from in front of the Post Office on Maktaba Street and take about 30 minutes. The market is five minutes' walk from the terminus.

Meershaum pipes are made in Arusha and can be bought directly from the factory. Since they're not bulky or heavy you can carry them in your luggage and avoid the hassle of forms and export licences which are needed when you mail parcels home.

For other curios, the shops around the clock tower in Arusha sell quality goods and are reasonably priced. Curio stalls in Dar es Salaam are much more expensive, as is the very touristy market in Mto wa Mbu near Lake Manyara.

Maps and guidebooks

A good range of inexpensive topographical maps is sold at the Department of Land and Surveys in Dar es Salaam (on Kivukoni front a few blocks past the Kilimanjaro Hotel). You no longer need authorisation to buy maps.

The best general map of Tanzania is the BP map, stocked by the book stall in the foyer of the New Africa Hotel in Dar es Salaam.

The *Guide to Tanzania* by Philip Briggs (Bradt) includes up-to-date information on all the main attractions, and covers dozens of off-the-beaten-track places for the first time.

Warnings

Tanzania has a reputation for muggings, but there is little apparent foundation for this; in four months I only heard of one such incident which occurred in an alley at night in Dar es Salaam. In my opinion, wandering down alleys at night in a large city is tempting fate. The only places where there is reason to believe mugging is a threat are Dar es Salaam, Kunduchi Beach, Bagamoyo and Zanzibar; nowhere is it as bad as in Kenya.

Casual theft is commonplace. It is not specifically aimed at tourists and can happen anywhere. The way to counter it not to carry valuables. Luggage is said to be tampered with on Tanzanian buses but nothing of the sort happened to me on 30-odd bus trips. Most of the incidents I heard of occurred on overnight buses, mainly the Dar es Salaam-Mbeya and Arusha-Dodoma routes. If you avoid overnight buses I think the risk is minimal.

It is expressly forbidden to take photographs of government installations such as bridges or railway lines, and you could also land in trouble if you take pictures of Tanzanians without their permission. Outside of recognised tourist areas, be careful where you point your camera; if in doubt, ask.

Tanzania is a conservative country with a large Muslim community. Dress modestly.

Accommodation

Tourist hotels are pricey and must be paid for in US dollars, but in most towns there are a couple of acceptable hotels that offer self-contained rooms for under $10, payable in local currency. Basic hotels, generally called guest houses, vary in standard, but if you look around you should find something decent for under $2. In areas that see little tourism, accommodation is very cheap.

Hoteli is Swahili for restaurant. If in doubt, ask for a guest house (*gesti*).

Except in the game reserves and around Arusha, there are few campsites. Beware of thieves if you camp in an unguarded area.

Eating

Tanzania has a large Asian population and some marvellous curries. Shortages of basic foods are a thing of the past.

Transport

Wherever possible, it is advisable to use trains or ferries in preference to buses. I used about 20 ferries and trains while I was in the country; in general they are reliable, prompt and as comfortable as you could reasonably expect.

TRADITIONAL HONEY HUNTING IN TANZANIA

By Claire Footitt

African honey bees, perhaps more renowned as 'killer bees' due to their ferocious nature, are playing a vital role as custodians of the natural tropical dry forest — the Miombo woodlands — which cover 48% of Tanzania's land area.

Traditional honey hunting is practised in many parts of Tanzania, and has been incorporated into a commercial activity in the Tabora region. Building on a long history of traditional beekeeping, a co-operative was established in the 1940s and today the Tabora Beekeepers' Association has about 1,000 members, producing 10,000 tonnes of honey a year.

The honey hunters hire a lorry and are driven into the forest where they have their hives. Camps may have over 50 hunters and last for several weeks, while new hives are made and honey cropped. Hives, which can be up to 250cm long, are made from hollowed out logs. The logs are cut in half lengthwise and fixed together with long wooden pegs or wire. They are then wedged horizontally in the fork of a tall tree, out of reach from the honey badger, or alternatively hung from a branch. The tree is chosen for its proximity to water and forage for the bees. Hives are baited with wax to attract a swarm, or sometimes a sweet scented plant is used. When gathering the honey, the bees are smoked, emulating the effect of a forest fire: the bees swarm to feed on honey, storing food for an expected flight, which renders them less likely to sting. As the bees become soporific, the hunter carefully removes most of the honeycombs, leaving behind some brood honey for the bees. Rarely wearing adequate protective clothing, the honey hunters appear to work in harmony with the bees, instinctively knowing the best time to crop honey, and to avoid being stung. Established beekeepers will have as many as 1,000 hives, which are normally cropped every couple of years.

On return from the honey camp, the majority of honey is used in brewing honey beer, which has in itself become a thriving small business. The beer is decanted into recycled Coca-Cola bottles and then sold locally. Honey also provides a valuable nutritional source, being used in ethnic cooking; it has medicinal properties and also features in traditional ceremonies. Excess honey is exported to the EEC, where the honey is accredited with an organically produced certificate due to its purity and lack of additives. The other by-product from honey is wax, and this too provides a valuable source of income, most of it being sold to local Afro-Indian traders for export.

Inevitably, Tanzania's forests are threatened by alternative land uses, such as tobacco, agriculture and the requirement for wood as the main source of cooking fuel for the rural population. But beekeeping provides a sustainable use of the forest, and generates an income to the local people, who help to defend the forest from adverse development. The Miombo woodlands are endangered, but maintaining traditional beekeeping will help to conserve the ecosystem and the bio-diversity of this natural dry tropical forest, as well as ensuring the continuity of cultural traditions associated with honey production.

If you would like more information, Bees for Development, Troy, Monmouth NP5 4AB, UK, is a charity concerned with promoting the use of beekeeping to conserve natural habitats throughout the developing world.

Ferry There are several useful ferry services, most of which are reliable, comfortable and easy to book onto at short notice.

There are a few ferries every day between Dar es Salaam and Zanzibar; these should have been extended to cover Tanga, Pemba and Mombasa by the time you read this. A separate fortnightly service runs between Dar es Salaam, Mafia and Mtwara. The booking kiosks for ferries from Dar es Salaam are near the passenger harbour on Sokoine Drive.

All lake ferries are run by Tanzania Railways. The weekly Lake Tanganyika ferry connecting Kigoma to Mpulungu (Zambia) and Bujumbura (Burundi) is an amazing ride: the lake is clear and serene, and there is plenty of activity as small fishing boats ferry passengers to and from lake shore villages. Of the many services on Lake Victoria, the most useful are the daily service between Mwanza and Bukoba and the weekly service between Mwanza and Port Bell in Uganda (this leaves Mwanza on Sunday and Port Bell on Monday). There are two ferries a week between Itungi and Mbamba Bay on Lake Nyasa (the Tanzanian name for Lake Malawi).

A port tax of $5 is levied on departing most ports. It must be paid in hard currency.

Train There are three trains a week in each direction on the northern line between Dar es Salaam, Tanga and Moshi, and four along the central line between Dar es Salaam, Kigoma and Mwanza.

There are two fast and three slow trains weekly on the Tazara Line between Dar es Salaam and Kapiri Mposhi (Zambia). Slow trains only go as far as the Zambian border and they pass through the Selous Game Reserve during daylight hours.

Compartments should be booked in advance. For some reason, it is easier to get last minute bookings on trains heading to Dar es Salaam than trains leaving from it. Northern and central line trains leave Dar es Salaam from the central station in Sokoine Road. The Tazara Station is 4km out of town on Pugu Road.

Road Road transport in Tanzania consists almost exclusively of buses. Regular and relatively speedy buses run the length of the well-maintained Arusha-Dar es Salaam-Mbeya road. There is a high risk of theft on overnight buses between Dar es Salaam and Mbeya; break the trip up at Iringa or, better, catch a train instead.

Roads in the rest of the country are variable, and buses are slow and overcrowded. On dirt roads, expect to cover no more than 20km in an hour.

TOWNS

Dar es Salaam

The name means 'Haven of Peace', and although this is hardly descriptive, the city has undergone a face-lift in recent years, and is no longer the down-at-heel place it was in the 1980s.

Accommodation is not particularly cheap and if you arrive late in the day your chances of finding a room in a budget hotel are slim. There are, however, several mid-range hotels which always have rooms available. Budget hotels are clustered near the Morogoro Road bus station. Two of the better are the Jambo Inn and Safari Hotel, both of which charge under $10 for a self-contained room. The YWCA on Maktaba Street near the post office is popular with couples and women.

There is no notable sightseeing around Dar. One option is to head out to Kunduchi Beach, 30km north of Dar, where the Rungwe Oceanic Hotel and adjacent Silversands have campsites (the one at Rungwe looks more secure), air-conditioned rooms for around $10, and good facilities including a restaurant. It's unlikely that either will be full. A shuttle bus which leaves from in front of the New Africa Hotel on Maktaba Street every two hours stops at both hotels.

Further afield, Bagamoyo was an important slave trading centre in the 19th Century and it was also briefly the German capital. The church at the mission 3km from Bagamoyo is the oldest in East Africa; the mission also houses an excellent museum. Bagamoyo is three hours from Dar by bus. You can stay at Badeco Beach Hotel on the beachfront. The road from Bagamoyo to the mission has a reputation for muggings; go there in a group or, better, arrange a guide at Badeco.

Kigoma

This is the exit point for those leaving Tanzania via Lake Tanganyika and the base for visiting the chimpanzee reserves of Gombe Stream and Mahale Mountains. The Lake View and Kigoma Hotels, opposite each other in the main road, are cheap and fine.

Ujiji, 10km from Kigoma, was a major 19th-Century Arab trading centre — it has a Swahili feel that is unusual in this part of the country — and is where Henry Stanley uttered the most famous words ever spoken in Africa: 'Doctor Livingstone, I presume'. A plaque marks the spot where the two men met. Regular buses run to Ujiji from Kigoma or you can walk via the village of Mwanga.

Arusha

In the heart of Tanzania's coffee-growing region and overlooked by Mount Meru, Arusha is one of the most attractive towns in Tanzania. It is also one of the most visited, as it is the gateway to the country's major game reserves: the Serengeti and Ngorongoro Crater.

Tanzania National Park's headquarters is in the International Conference Centre, as are dozens of safari companies.

Comfortable express buses from Dar es Salaam to Arusha take about ten hours. You can also get an overnight train from Dar es Salaam to Moshi, two hours from Arusha by bus. It takes about six hours to get between Arusha and Nairobi via the relaxed Namanga border post.

There is plenty of accommodation. Guest houses start at $3; try the Safari, Kilimanjaro Villa or Friend's Corner. The popular Naaz Hotel on Sokoine Street has self-contained rooms for $15.

There are a few campsites near Arusha. The most scenic, at Lake Duluti 15km out of town, is 20 minutes walk and signposted from the Moshi road. Maasai Campsite, run by Tropical Trails in the foyer of the New Equator Hotel, is 3km from Arusha on the old Moshi Road. It has showers and a restaurant and is well-guarded. The campsite at the Tanzanite Hotel near Usa River has similar facilities and is convenient if you want to head into Arusha National Park. All these campsites cost about $3 per person.

Mwanza

Mwanza on Lake Victoria is Tanzania's third-largest town and an important route focus, connected to Dar es Salaam by rail and to Port Bell (Uganda) by ferry.

There are plenty of cheap guest houses around the station. Good moderate hotels include the Delux and Lake. The Delux Hotel has a very pleasant restaurant.

Although the zoo on Saa Nane island, 3km from Mwanza, is uninspiring, the island naturally supports a diverse bird life and is crawling with lizards, notably the colourful rock agama and massive water monitor. Boats cross to the island every couple of hours from a jetty adjacent to the Tilapia Hotel (signposted from the town centre). There is a nominal entrance fee.

Further afield, there is a daily ferry to and from Nansio on Ukerewe Island. The trip takes about three hours and is a good way of seeing some of the lake. There is ethnic dancing every Saturday at the Sukoma Museum, about 20km from Mwanza near Kissesa on the Musoma road. You can camp at the museum but facilities are limited.

Mbeya

Mbeya, southern Tanzania's largest town, is passed through by travellers heading to Malawi. It has a lively atmosphere, lies in the centre of an important agricultural area, and is a good base for exploring the southern highlands.

The Moravian Youth Hostel 500m out of town is popular with travellers. There are several guest houses around the bus station and a few mid-range hotels in the town centre. The food at the Rift Valley Hotel is superb and reasonably priced. You can eat well for around $1 at Cathy's Cafe near the market.

The Tazara railway station is 5km from the town centre on the main road towards Zambia.

HIKING

Although Tanzania is opening up to hikers, they mostly restrict themselves to Mts Meru and Kilimanjaro, the latter being the goal for many East Africa bound travellers. Why anyone should want to pay $500 for the privilege of vomiting on the highest point in Africa is beyond me, but plenty do, so read on!

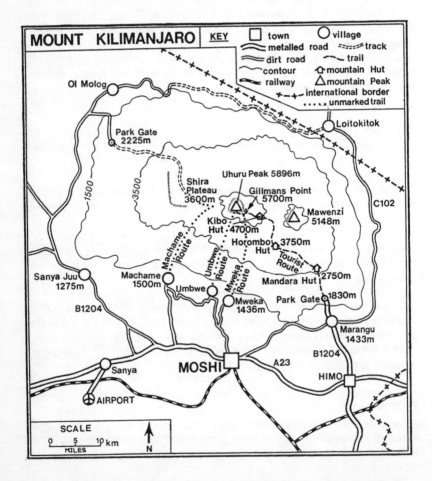

See advertisements on pages 177 for Kilimanjaro specialists.

Mount Kilimanjaro

Introduction This is not only the highest mountain in Africa (5,895m), but it is the only one of its size in the world that can be climbed by ordinary tourists with no technical mountaineering skills.

The volcano which is Kilimanjaro was born during the upheavals that created the Great Rift Valley some two million years ago. Eruptions created three peaks, one of which, Shira, was eventually smothered in lava from the other two, Kibo and Mawenzi. These continued to grow until about 100,000 years ago when a final eruption formed the cone of its rim. This is the highest peak and the highest point in Africa. The volcano, though dormant, is still active. Kibo was first climbed in 1889 by Hans Meyer and Ludwig Purtscheller. Kilimanjaro National Park was gazetted in 1977.

The first European to see Kilimanjaro described it as possessing 'imposing majesty and unapproachable grandeur'. On learning the cost of climbing the thing, some backpackers will choose to view it from the bottom. The total cost of climbing Mt Kilimanjaro starts at around $300 and can be as much as $600-800, and the time allowed for the ascent precludes adequate acclimatisation so many people suffer horribly from altitude sickness (that's where the vomiting comes in). That said, however, most people find the experience worthwhile for the scenery and changes in vegetation, as well as for the sense of achievement.

Mt Kilimanjaro is best not climbed in April and May, the wettest months. The driest periods are December to January and June to August.

Preparations To climb Kili with anything resembling enjoyment, you must be properly equipped. Although all the necessary gear *can* be hired in Moshi, it will be of very poor quality (although clothing will be OK). Night temperatures at the top hut can go as low as 0°F (-20°C), so a really warm sleeping bag, insulating mat, and thermal underwear are essential, as well as a warm jacket, gloves, wool hat, etc (see the equipment list in Chapter 3).

Unless you are climbing the Marangu Route you are advised to bring a tent and stove – in fact your full backpacking gear – since the huts on other routes are smaller and there may not be room, and many are now damaged and completely unusable.

All Kili climbs have to be arranged through a local tour company. Unless you arrange otherwise, food will be provided, but some people prefer to bring their own freeze-dried food to avoid diarrhoea. Bring a large water bottle or canteen, or better still, one of those folding plastic water containers that holds 4 or 5 litres; remember that dehydration aggravates mountain sickness.

Other essentials for any route are sun-glasses or snow goggles, sunscreen, chapstick, and first aid kit. Keep all valuables – and that includes chocolate! – in your own pack; although the majority of porters are completely honest, there's no point in putting temptation their way.

Porters and guides Guides are mandatory on all routes, and will be provided by the tour company organising your climb. Since you cannot hike alone anyway, you might as well take a porter or two and give yourself more chance of enjoying Kili unencumbered. The cost is relatively low.

Maps and guide books   On the Marangu route a map is useful but not essential; on other routes a map is needed. The *Walkers Guide and Map to Kilimanjaro* by Mark Savage is available from some shops in Nairobi and Arusha, and from good map shops (such as Stanfords in London) or direct from the publisher, West Col Productions, Reading, UK. The map's scale is 1:50,000 and it shows all routes up the mountain (although there are some inaccuracies) and has detailed information on routes and other aspects of Kili on the back. Equally recommended is the booklet *Kilimanjaro National Park* in the series put out by the National Parks department (see *Game Parks*). This gives a detailed account of the natural history as well as descriptions of the lesser known routes, along with maps which are the most accurate available. The book is only available in Tanzania, in Arusha and possibly in Moshi.

The *East Africa International Mountain Guide*, the *D.O.S map of Kilimanjaro*, 1:50,000, and *Stanfords map of Kilimanjaro*, 1:100,000, a corrected Landsat image, are all available from Stanfords Map Shop in London.

Cost   The main reason for the high cost of climbing Kili is that, at the time of writing, park fees in Tanzania are $15 a day, (payable in hard currency), plus rescue fee of $20 per trip. Hut fees on the Marangu route are $15 per night (whether or not you use them). Since you need a minimum of five days in the park, that's $155 for starters. Add to this the fee you pay the tour company for your food, your guide and porters (which include their park fees), plus the cost of getting to the start of the trail (the unwary have found themselves paying $100 for a taxi from the airport) and of course hiring extra clothing, porters' tips, etc.

Getting organised   The centre for climbing Kilimanjaro is Moshi, which can be reached by road, rail or air from Dar, or by road from Kenya. There are plenty of low-price hotels (two of the more popular places to stay are the Y.M.C.A and Hotel Newcastle – around $10 per night) and a number of tour companies organising Kilimanjaro climbs.

It is no longer possible to arrange your own climb on Kili. You must make arrangements through a tour company. The Y.M.C.A., Tropicana Tours and Kilimanjaro Travel Services are amongst the cheaper companies. Shah Tours are more expensive, but reported to be better quality. Several of the smarter hotels also organise climbs. These include the Keys Hotel in Moshi (around $25 a night), and the Marangu Hotel in Marangu village (about $40 per night) which runs very good quality trips, and is a delightful place to stay with fine food and atmosphere. The Kibo Hotel, also in Marangu, is equally good.

Warnings   A very high proportion of people suffer from altitude sickness on this climb, and quite a number literally die in the attempt. (I recently heard of a chap who had the misfortune to hear himself pronounced dead by a doctor; fortunately it was decided to carry the 'corpse' down to the next hut where he sat up and asked for a cup of tea!) Do *not* climb Kilimanjaro if you know you are susceptible to altitude sickness or if you are not in excellent physical shape, and do not push yourself to continue if you feel terrible. Read the section on altitude sickness in the *Health* chapter.

Routes

Apart from the Marangu Route, there are four other routes to the highest point on Kibo, Uhuru Peak, as well as the officially illegal Loitokitok approach from Kenya. Whatever route you use, your trip must be organised through a tour company.

Only the Marangu Route has good quality huts; on the other routes you rely on metal shelters, whose floors have been ripped up for firewood, or caves. On these, a tent is essential.

Whatever route is taken up, most people descend via the easy Marangu route, although the huts there are supposed to have been prebooked. This is no problem if you're camping anyway.

Only experienced hikers should use the other routes. Although a guide is required, there seems to be no guarantee that he will actually know the way, and above the tree line there is no worn path to follow. You should take the responsibility of having a good map, compass, etc; On all routes, apart from Marangu, there is a certain amount of scrambling on scree and snow-covered rocks.

Marangu Route

Scenically this is probably the least interesting, but it is the easiest climb and has the best huts: Mandara (2,750m), Horombo (3,720m) and Kibo (4,703m). The trip to Uhuru Peak or Gillman's Point (5,700m) at the lower end of the crater takes five days. For acclimatisation purposes six days would be far preferable, but the extra park and porter fees are a deterrent to most people.

Most organised climbs include transport to Marangu Gate. But if you want to save money, matatus and buses run to Marangu village. From here it's a pleasant two hour walk through the *shambas* which dot the south-eastern slopes up to the Marangu gate itself. Much of Tanzania's coffee comes from this area, along with bananas and sisal.

Above the gate cultivation is not allowed and the forest is dense and the path often muddy. It's a three hour walk from the gate to Mandara hut (2,750m) where you spend your first night. The hut is in fact a collection of buildings able to sleep 200 people, and a main eating hut. There are mattresses and kerosene lamps.

The distance hiked the next day is a little longer (five or six hours) with an altitude gain of 1,000m. Now there are periodic clearings offering great views of the neighbouring mountain of Mawenzi (5,148m) and Moshi far below. You'll see some of Kilimanjaro's 'everlasting flowers' and the weird afro-alpine plants, giant lobelia and giant groundsel, before reaching Horombo hut (3,720m). This can also sleep around 200, and is the best hut in which to stay two nights for acclimatisation. There are some rewarding day hikes in the area.

Leaving Horombo hut the next morning, you make your way through increasingly diminishing vegetation, open areas covered with grass and heather, to the beginning of bare scree. Before this point you'll reach the last water and should fill your canteens. The porters will fill their vessels for the night. Your night's destination, Kibo hut (4,703m), does not come into sight until you are almost upon it, but from the saddle there is a fine view of Kilimanjaro. Many people suffer the first pangs of altitude sickness on the third day, so you should walk very slowly, stopping to breathe deeply at intervals. This can help reduce the effects of the oxygen-thin air. Most groups arrive at Kibo in the mid afternoon and try to rest before the ascent early next morning. And I mean early: about 1 a.m.

Few people actually sleep. The night is bitterly cold and the lack of oxygen makes sleep difficult even if you're not suffering from the headache and nausea of altitude sickness.

No one enjoys the midnight start or the five hour slog up a ghastly scree slope in biting cold, stopping to gasp for breath every few steps. Gillman's Point may not be the highest point on Kilimanjaro, but at least it's on the caldera's edge; the two hour walk around the caldera to the snow and ice-covered Uhuru Peak may be an altitude gain of only 200 metres, but at this height it is gruelling. Some will find their arrival at the summit something of an anticlimax; there's a fair bit of litter, a plaque, and a visitor's book rubbing in that you are far from unique in having conquered Kilimanjaro. If you arrive in time for sunrise, however, the sense of achievement and fantastic views will make it all seem worthwhile. And if you are feeling more than half dead at this point, remember to take photos so you can enjoy the achievement and view when you get home!

If you're feeling OK, as a worthwhile alternative to returning to Gillman's Point the way you came, if the conditions are good ask your guide if you can descend the caldera and walk across the ice-field to the actual crater where there are steam vents. Gillman's Point is then reached via a different route.

After descending to Kibo hut and a rest, continue down to Horombo. You'll marvel at the ease of the descent after that hard slog up.

The last day is a very long one since you miss Mandara hut and continue to Marangu, where you'll be warmly congratulated and receive a nifty diploma.

Recent reports suggest the Marangu Route is becoming increasingly over-used. Lluis & Jaume Tort and Joan Masoliver made the following comment: 'Uninteresting landscape, too crowded, too touristic, too dirty, and too expensive'. They did say you could avoid the crowds on parts of the route: a narrow path from the Marangu Gate which joins the main track after 90 minutes; from Mandara Hut, take the trail towards Marundi Crater, then the left fork before the crater, which rejoins the main trail after 30 minutes; from Horombo hut, take the Upper Route which rejoins the main route left of the saddle.

Patrick Frew wrote with this advice: 'The going price for a cheap 5-day trip is $300. Whoever you go with, you get the same deal, same food, same mountain. If you are fit and acclimatised, I would advise leaving Kibo Hut at 2 a.m. We left at 1 a.m. and were at Gillman's at 4.30 a.m. It was dark and freezing cold. We were on Uhuru before sunrise and I though I would die from cold.'

Mweka Route

This is the most direct, so steepest route to Uhuru Peak. There are two huts offering basic shelter, the first at 2,900m and the second at 4,600m. Paul Hunt, describes the route: 'We took the Mweka route most of the way to the top, then cut around the South Kibo circuit to the main tourist route, then up to the Kibo Hut and Gillman's Point, and around the crater rim.

'Mweka village is only 12km north from the Y.M.C.A. From the Mweka Wildlife College the dirt road continues uphill through banana and coffee plantations. The trail is very overgrown in places. It is a steady climb up through the forest to the Mweka Huts, two metal shelters in the heather zone. The climb from Mweka village takes about seven hours. There is a nearby water supply at Mweka Huts and lots of heather wood.

'Next day, the trail is easier to follow through the heather zone and continues up to the South Kibo Circuit junction at about 4,000m. The climb to this point takes about nine hours. It is another two hour climb up a barren, rocky ridge to Barafu Huts – two metal shelters at about 4,600m. The route is marked by cairns. At Barafu there is no vegetation, and no water unless there is snow lying on the ground.

'Above Barafu the Mweka route becomes steeper and climbs a ridge between the Rebmann and Ratzel glaciers. It snowed while we stayed at Barafu Huts and the rocks were covered in snow and ice, so we decided not to continue up this route. We returned down to the South Kibo Circuit which runs at an elevation of just over 4,000m around the southern slopes of Kibo, and followed this trail to Horombo hut on the Marangu Route.

'From Kibo Hut we went up to Gillman's Point (where I watched the sunrise) then walked around the crater rim towards Uhuru Peak but the route was covered with fresh snow and ice and was treacherous without crampons, ice axe or snow goggles. We covered about half of the distance to Uhuru Peak and turned back after reaching the top of Ratzel Glacier. This was well worth it for the views into the crater and down the glaciated outer slopes of Kibo.

'We spent five days climbing up and one day down and suffered no ill effects from the altitude at all.'

Umbwe Route

More difficult but very spectacular, this route is becoming increasingly popular.

It begins at Umbwe village, which is some 16km from Moshi. From Umbwe head for Kifuni village and a track leading into the forest. This forks left and climbs through moss-covered cloud forest to become a ridge path between the Lonzo and Umbwe rivers. The first shelter (caves) and camping place is at 2,900m, about seven hours from Umbwe.

On the second day you leave the cloud forest and after about five hours reach a fork in the path. To the right is Barranco Hut (3,900m) where you will spend the night whichever route you take. From Barranco you can contour round the mountain to the east to join the Mweka route, scramble up to the moraine facing the southern glaciers, or double back to the fork and head up the western lateral moraine. Traverse left, crossing two streams, and climb the ridge to Lava Tower Hut (4,600m), damaged by rock falls and hardly usable. From here you climb steeply towards the site of Arrow Glacier Hut (4,800m). (The hut was also destroyed by a rock fall.) The route climbs steep scree then steep frozen scree and finally rotten rocks to a lava outcrop forming a natural staircase through a breach in the cliffs (the Western Breach) and further scrambling on rock and scree brings you onto the floor of the crater and Uhuru Peak.

Machame Route

West of the Umbwe Route, and considered to be the most scenic of the relatively easy routes, this starts at Machame village, north-west of Moshi. The path runs through shambas and then forest to reach Machame Hut (3,000m) at the treeline.

Next day, from Machame Hut you cross a small valley and then go along a ridge before climbing steeply to Shira Plateau and the Shira Hut on the Shira Route (see below).

Shira Route

The long approach across the Shira Plateau on Kilimanjaro's western flank means that this route is really only suitable for those with a four wheel drive vehicle. It is 55km from West Kilimanjaro/Londorossi to the top end of the drivable track.

Shira Hut, at 3,800m, is only about two hours from the road head. From here you continue east to join the Umbwe Route near Lava Tower Hut, and then on to Arrow Glacier and follow directions for the Umbwe Route (see above).

Mount Meru

Mt Meru, at 4,556m the fifth highest mountain in Africa, lies in the Arusha National Park between Arusha and Moshi. There's plenty of game in the park and the climb offers excellent views across to Kilimanjaro. Considering how accessible the mountain is, surprisingly few people climb it: all the more reason not to pass it up yourself. Lluis & Jaume Tort and Joan Masoliver climbed it immediately after Kilimanjaro, and wrote a really enthusiastic letter on which the following details are based.

Preparations and costs   The simplest way to get to the Arusha National Park from Arusha is to hire a taxi. It is possible to take a bus as far as the turnoff at Usa River and try to hitch the final 29km, but there isn't much traffic. There are camping facilities and a park guest house at Momela Gate, the start of the climb (and also the posh Momela Lodge nearby), but there is nothing preventing you starting up the mountain on the day you arrive. It's compulsory to hike with a ranger, as there are buffalo in the park. This can be organised at the gate. A variety of park fees must be paid, adding around $35 per person per day plus an extra $20 for the ranger. Most people climb Mt Meru over three days, but if you're not in a rush four days would be ideal.

The climb   The first day involves a fairly gentle three hour climb to Miriakamba Hut (2,600m). There's a good chance of seeing plains game such as buffalo and giraffe on this walk.

The second day is a steeper climb to Saddle Hut (3,600m), crossing a heather forest before you turn right into the saddle, the pass between the main peak and Little Meru. You'll pass through montane forests; look out for colobus monkeys. This is also a three hour walk. With a bit of luck, from Saddle Hut you can expect to see Kilimanjaro above the clouds! It is possible to leave your stuff at the hut and do the eight hour return hike to the top of Mt Meru on the second day, but most people leave it until the third.

On a three day hike, you're in for a long third day: from Saddle Hut to the top takes four to five hours, the descent to Saddle Hut a further three to four hours, then it's five hours back to the gate.

Scott Morgan adds: 'The lodge at Momela is run by Lions Safaris and serviced by a Land Rover. In the high season it might be possible to hitch. It is also possible to arrange an all-inclusive hike with some safari companies in Arusha for about $140. The Arusha National Park is worth visiting as well as Mt Meru: there is a little crater and a group of small lakes, where you can walk amongst the wildlife (with a ranger).'

Steven Bell wrote with the following information about a shorter walk on the foothills of Mt Meru, starting in Arusha: 'Opposite the Mt Meru Hotel a dirt track leads straight up the mountain. About three hours up this track you reach an area of new eucalyptus and pine plantation. Beyond that you can go into bamboo and can go all the way to the treeline. Alternatively you can scramble down a very steep trail to a stream. Follow this for less than an hour to reach a spectacular 200ft waterfall.'

Hiking off the beaten track

Tanzania's many intriguing hiking possibilities were rarely explored by travellers in the past, mainly due to the possibility of encountering excessive red tape. Tanzanian authorities have relaxed greatly in recent years; there is little reason to think you will hit problems of this nature now. That said, you should expect the worst if you break the law, for instance by trying to climb Meru or Kilimanjaro via an illegal route to avoid paying park fees, or if you are caught photographing a government installation such as a bridge or railway line.

The official position regarding permits seems to be that provided you stick to roads and footpaths no special permission is needed to hike anywhere in Tanzania. This is not as limiting as it might sound: roads through remote areas may go days on end without seeing a vehicle and provided there are people there will always be footpaths.

The areas listed below are on their way to becoming recognised hiking areas. Elsewhere you are entering the unknown; notify someone in authority of your plans (the district headquarters, police station or forestry office) and, if possible, try to get something in writing, at least until we've heard more reports from people who have attempted off-the-beaten-track hikes.

In all 'new' hiking areas you should be self-sufficient: carry food and camping equipment and take along topographical maps and a Swahili dictionary. If you pass through villages it is politic to exchange greetings with the village headman.

We were questioned a couple of times in remote areas, but it was all perfectly friendly and you would have had to have been pretty paranoid to read anything into it. If you are questioned, bear in mind that asking where you have come from (*natoka wapi*) and where you are going (*nakwenda wapi*) is the normal stuff of Swahili small talk – the chances are that the authority concerned is relishing an opportunity to practise his English and has used his official status to approach you. If you are polite and friendly, you are unlikely to hit problems; if you become aggressive and treat someone like a petty bureaucrat, you run the risk of aggravating him into behaving like one.

Usambara Mountains

This range west of Tanga is home to many localised and endemic plants and animals. The western Usambara is heavily settled but very scenic. The main town, Lushoto, can be reached by bus on a good tar road from Mombo on the Moshi-Tanga highway and has several guest houses. Irente viewpoint is a worthwhile goal for a day walk; if you have maps, the possibilities for longer hikes are boundless.

Natural history enthusiasts will be attracted to the eastern Usambara. Amani village, established as a botanical garden in 1902, has a genteel atmosphere that contrasts pleasantly with the surrounding jungle. From Amani you are likely to see black-and-white colobus and blue monkeys, and an abundance of birds and butterflies. There is a daily bus to Amani from Muheza on the Tanga-Moshi road. Once there, you can stay at the Amani Rest House or, if it's full, camp outside. If you plan on hiking using Amani as a base, buy maps in Dar es Salaam. The IUCN office 500m from Amani Rest House will be able to recommend routes.

Poroto Mountains

This scenic range east of Mbeya is notable for its crater lakes. Two of these, Ngozi and Masoko, can be reached as day trips from Tukuyu, the region's principal town. Longer hikes are possible on Mount Rungwe, which overlooks Tukuyu, and elsewhere in the region. The place to stay in Tukuyu is the attractively-situated Langiboss Hotel. The manager, who speaks English and knows the surrounding area well, is worth speaking to for up-to-date hiking information. Again, buy maps in Dar es Salaam.

Udzungwa Mountains

This is Tanzania's newest national park, opened to the public in October 1992. At that time facilities were limited to a short trail from the entrance gate, but there are plans to establish longer hikes. The Udzungwa, like the Usambara, is notable for its endemic-rich forests and because it borders the Selous there is a chance of seeing game animals such as elephant.

There is no accommodation in the national park, but it may be possible to camp at the entrance gate. The Twiga Hotel, 500m from the entrance gate, is inexpensive and pleasant.

Udzungwa lies between the towns of Ifakara and Kidatu, both of which have a selection of guest houses. All Tazara trains stop at Ifakara; you can get to Kidatu by bus from Morogoro or Mikumi village. Pick-up trucks run between Ifakara and Kidatu every morning and will drop you at the entrance gate.

For the latest information on hikes in the Udzungwa, contact the National Parks headquarters in Arusha.

THE NATIONAL PARKS

Tanzania is considered to have the finest game parks in Africa, most notably the Serengeti and Ngorongoro Crater in the north of the country.

Entrance to national parks costs $15 per 24-hour period and camping costs $10. Gombe Stream is $50 per 24-hour period plus $30 to camp.

Tanzania National Parks has published an excellent series of booklets to the national parks, containing maps and background information. These cost $2.50 at the National Park headquarters in Arusha but are more expensive elsewhere. There are booklets for Gombe Stream, Mikumi, Ruaha, Arusha, Kilimanjaro, Tarangire, Serengeti, Lake Manyara and the Ngorongoro Conservation Area.

The Northern reserves

Tanzania's most famous game parks, the Serengeti, Ngorongoro, Lake Manyara and Tarangire, are clustered in the north of the country and are normally visited from Arusha. The Serengeti and surrounding reserves are composed of volcanic ash soil spewed out during the activity that formed the rift valley and more recently Kilimanjaro (there is still an active volcano in the area, Ol Doinyo Lengai, the Maasai mountain of God). This soil does not hold water, but after rains the minerals produce a wonderful lushness. This seasonal variation between plenty and scarcity is the reason for annual wildebeest migration between the Serengeti and Kenya's Maasai Mara, where the soil is less porous.

The Serengeti is not on a main route and there is little non-safari-related traffic in the area. Hitching is risky; you may be lucky, but you may also get stuck in a national park for a few days and pay fees without seeing much game. If you are determined to hitch, a daily bus goes from Arusha via Mto wa Mbo (near Lake Manyara) to Karatu (between Manyara and Ngorongoro). Fig Tree Camp in Mto wa Mbo and Safari Junction Camp 1km from Karatu cost $3 per person camping. On-site tents at Safari Junction cost $10. There are guest houses in Mto wa Mbo.

Buses which go between Arusha and Mwanza via the Serengeti are your best bet for seeing the area cheaply, but you will still have to pay $30 in park fees on top of the bus fare. At least two buses cover this route every week.

Organising a safari

Most people explore the area on an organised tour or safari. There are hundreds of safari companies catering to all tastes and budgets in Arusha. Typical packages are a three-day trip to Manyara, Ngorongoro and Tarangire or a five-day trip to Manyara, Ngorongoro and the Serengeti. The Serengeti is at its best during the rainy season (November to May); during the dry months Tarangire provides better game-viewing. Some companies will suggest you squeeze all four parks into five days, but this means covering a lot of ground. You are better off exploring three parks at a more leisurely pace, or allocating six or seven days to do all four.

Safari packages generally include all park fees, food, transport, petrol and the services of a driver and cook. Prices are dependent on group size: the larger the group the cheaper the individual cost. Most companies can organise a safari on the spot (there are no fixed departures), but the onus is on you to get a group together. If you're looking for people to go on safari with, the restaurant at the Naaz Hotel and the Chinese restaurant on Sokoine Street are good places to start.

The lowest rate for a camping safari is around $40/day per person for four people, but don't expect too much for this sort of price. Vehicles are likely to be old and poorly-maintained and breakdowns are common. If you can, it's worth paying a bit more (around $60/day) to go with a more professional outfit: Roy Safaris and Hoopoe Tours (see addresses below) are recommended. If money isn't an issue, several reliable companies can arrange lodge-based or exclusive camping safaris for upwards of $100/day.

Most safari companies can arrange Kilimanjaro and Meru climbs, but it is probably better to arrange Kilimanjaro climbs in Moshi. It is possible to do walking safaris in the Ngorongoro area; Tropical Tours specialise in this sort of thing and have a good reputation.

The following companies are worth checking out:
Tropical Tours, PO Box 727 (office in India Street);
Tropical Trails, PO Box 6130 (office in the Equator Hotel);
Sengo Safaris, PO Box 207 (office in the International Conference Centre);
Jeff's Safaris, PO Box 1469 (office behind Coopers and Kearsley on the main street);
Roy Safaris, PO Box 50 (office off Sokoine Street opposite the Greenland Hotel);
Hoopoe Tours, PO Box 2047 (office on India Street).

Lake Manyara National Park

This park was popular in the early 1980s after Ian Douglas-Hamilton's marvellous book *Amongst the Elephants* created interest in these animals. In 1987, Douglas-Hamilton did an elephant count and discovered that numbers had halved in two years, the count of 181 animals being the lowest ever recorded. Most elephants over the age of 30 had been poached. Poaching is now under control, but the elephants that remain are very shy and you are unlikely to see any large tuskers. Despite the scarcity of elephant and elusiveness of its other rumoured attraction, tree-climbing lions, Lake Manyara is worth visiting. There are often large herds of animals on the lake shore and the scenery is fantastic. When conditions are right, large flocks of flamingo can be seen.

Guest houses and a campsite can be found at the village of Mto wa Mbo, about 4km from the park entrance gate. Mto wa Mbo means 'River of the Mosquito'; make sure you have mosquito netting. The curio market in the village is very overpriced.

Ngorongoro Conservation Area

If you only visit one park in East Africa, this is *the* place. The centrepiece is the Ngorongoro Crater, a 20km-wide forest-rimmed collapsed volcanic caldera, the floor of which is home to an unparalleled concentration and variety of animals. The view from the rim is breathtaking. The crater is the last place in East Africa where rhino sightings are virtually guaranteed, and it is not unusual to see at least four of the so-called big five in a half-day game drive.

There is a campsite on the crater rim. The only cheap rooms are at the Driver's Lodge, but tourists can not normally stay here. Food is usually available at the Crater Village. If you arrive independently, you could hire a park vehicle to take you into the crater, but this costs at least $200 per day.

Serengeti National Park

Africa's most famous game park never disappoints. The sparsely-wooded plains offer exceptional visibility and just about every East African animal is abundant. It is most famous for its annual wildebeest migration of about *four million* animals (including gazelle and zebra).

Camping safaris generally base themselves at Seronera in the south of the park. Wildebeest disperse into this area in about mid-November, when it is not unusual to see herds of a few thousand animals. The best months to visit the park are January and February when the main migration starts.

Serengeti is renowned for its predators, of which lion and spotted hyena are the most frequently seen. Leopard are surprisingly common in the Seronera valley where they can often be seen in flat-topped acacias; look out for the giveaway tail dangling from the canopy.

The Serengeti covers 14,763 square kilometres. Several days are needed to explore it thoroughly and it is worth spending as long as you can there. Bearing in mind that Seronera is a good half-day's drive from Ngorongoro, two nights is the minimum.

Apart from Seronera, there are few cheap options in the Serengeti: all other campsites are so-called special campsites and cost $40 per person. There are several tourist lodges.

Tarangire National Park

In the dry season (July to September) this park rivals the Serengeti for the concentrations of animals that can be seen along the Tarangire river. Elephant are particularly numerous, but the most characteristic feature of the park is its plentiful baobab trees.

Tarangire is two hours from Arusha on a good tar road. It is often tagged onto the end of a longer safari, but if your time is limited it can be visited as a day trip from Arusha. This means missing out on the early morning and late afternoon, the best game-viewing times, so an overnight trip is better. There is an attractive but expensive tented camp, or you can camp for the usual $10.

Meet-the-people tour

An enterprising Tanzanian, Joas Kahembe, has set himself up as a tour operator working specifically with backpackers and budget travellers to give them a taste of Tanzanian life as lived by ordinary people. Kahembe's Hotel is in Babati, some 70km from Tarangire. Joas writes: 'I am essentially aiming at low income tourists and the 40-60 age groups who would enjoy climbing small hills and mountains after visiting the national parks. I am also providing a chance for a tourist to learn something about the people and cultures, eat the local foods, exchange conversation and ask casual questions, take video pictures as souvenirs...' This locally-run sort of tourism is just what Tanzania needs, and deserves your support. Further information from Joas Kahembe, Kahembe's Hotel, P.O. Box 366, Babati, Tanzania.

Other national parks

Selous Game Reserve

Twice the size of Denmark, this is one of the last true wilderness areas of East Africa as well as its largest reserve. Because of its size and inaccessible location, Selous (usually pronounced *Seloo*) may only be visited with an organised safari company. The Impala Camp is the least expensive and encourages backpackers. You can take a bus to Mioka, about 25km from the Camp, and a vehicle will pick you up. Phone them in Dar es Salaam to make arrangements: (051) 25779.

The Southern Parks

In addition to Selous, southern Tanzania has other game parks that are less visited than those in the north, and where species not found in East Africa, such as the magnificent greater kudu, with it spiralling horns, can be seen. **Ruaha** and **Mikumi** National Parks may only be visited by vehicle, but look out for them on safari company brochures.

Rubondo Island

Rubondo Island, in Lake Victoria, has been a national park since 1977 and offers travellers an interesting change from the popular big game parks. Within its limited space, Rubondo has a great variety of habitats from savannah and open woodland to dense evergreen forests and papyrus swamps. Birds are particularly numerous. Animals you are sure to see include hippos, crocodiles, bushbuck and vervet monkeys, and you may catch a glimpse of the shyer forest species such as elephant, or chimpanzees. Rhino have been successfully introduced here. There are no large predators.

The park's attraction is the forest trails with tree hides provided for animal viewing. However, recent reports are that these have not been kept clear and rangers are not so keen on taking visitors around. Still, it's a lovely place to relax in, with palm-fringed sandy beaches and a campsite. Alternatively there are two self-catering huts which provide bedding and cooking utensils. No food or other supplies may be bought on the island.

Rubondo is not difficult to get to, but a round trip from Mwanza will take the best part of a week. You must first get a ferry from Mwanza to Nyamirembe Port, where there are a few guest houses and the Fisheries Office can help you organise a boat to the island. Technically speaking, accommodation (including camping space) and boats across must be organised in advance, but the park is so rarely visited that you are unlikely to hit problems if you arrive unannounced.

Gombe Stream National Park

I rate my stay at this chimpanzee reserve by the shores of Lake Tanganyika as one of the highlights of my wildlife viewing in Africa. Seeing some of the animals described by Jane Goodall in her books and television programmes was like meeting celebrities in the flesh. Even without the chimpanzees the boat ride on Lake Tanganyika and the hilly, luxuriant forest scenery of the park are well worth the trip. However, these days a visit is expensive: the park fee is $50 for 24 hours and accommodation a further $30. The prices go up regularly, so check the latest at the Railway Hotel in Kigoma.

Preparations   There are bandas to accommodate visitors, or you may camp. The kitchen is for communal use. There are no other facilities or shops so all food supplies should be taken along. A stove is useful too, since to use firewood means, ultimately, the destruction of trees and the chimpanzees' habitat.

Most basic supplies are available in the shops and market at Kigoma. Carry food inside your backpack, not in your hands; baboons are adept at snatching visitors' food en route to the kitchen from the bandas. If you keep fruit in your tent baboons may try to get inside.

The Tanzania National Parks department include Gombe Stream in their excellent series of booklets.

Getting there   The park is situated on Lake Tanganyika between the Burundi border and Kigoma, the nearest town which is about 16km away. From the beach near the railway tracks in Kigoma water taxis – wooden motor-powered boats – go north along the lake shore. The boats usually leave between 10.00 and 11.00 am every morning, and it takes about four hours to reach the National Park. These boats carry on to Banda, the border town with Burundi, so Gombe Stream can also be approached from that direction.

The boatman will drop you at Gombe Stream beach where the park warden will meet you and take you to the guest house just behind the beach. You will need to pay the fees for the park entrance and for accommodation. It is compulsory to take a guide into the forest. You must pay in foreign currency.

Trails From the guest house a trail leads up through the forest for about 2km to the chimpanzee research station, where park staff record the activities of the animals, and continues for another mile to a waterfall in Gombe Stream. If the chimpanzees are not at the research station, the guide will take you on smaller trails up the hills or track them through the forest.

Another interesting walk where you don't require a guide is northwards from the guest house along the lake shore. Here there are small fishing villages and wonderful scenery with the possibility of sighting baboons, chimps or other wildlife.

Boats return to Kigoma early in the morning, and it may be necessary to wave them to shore to pick you up.

Warning Chimps are susceptible to the same diseases as humans, their closest relatives. *Please* do not visit the reserve if you have a cold or other infectious illness. You will recover, the chimpanzee may not.

Mahale Mountains National Park

There is another chimpanzee reserve here which is a lot cheaper to visit, although the chimps are less easy to see. Here it costs an entry fee of $15 for 24 hours, and $10 for the bandas and campsite.

The Lake Tanganyika ferry stops at Mugambo, which is 15km from the park, after a 7 hour journey from Kigoma.

An alternative approach was recommended by Steven Bell: 'I went on the ship from Kigoma south to a point near the village of Mgongo, on the north side of the Mahale Mountains peninsula. From the ship I transferred to a water taxi (difficult in choppy water with a loaded pack!). From there it's about 15km walk through shambas to the park boundary at the foot of the mountains, which are always in sight, so you can't get lost. Be sure to exchange greetings with village headmen along the way, so your trip has the blessings of officialdom. Once you are in the park, get a guide, deal with the formalities and enjoy Mahale. The chimps require more effort to see than at Gombe, but in my opinion the walking and scenery are better at Mahale.'

Dick and Jen Byrne, primatologists, did some research at Mahale a few years ago. Their letter about the experience was so interesting I am reproducing some of it here: 'The day to day observations included a fantastic array of behaviours and incidents including hunting and eating monkeys, making and using tools to catch ants, an attempt to kill an infant chimp by five males, eating rotten wood and licking rocks, mobbing and displaying at two lions, and, most extraordinary of all, an attack on a female leopard and her cub. They caught, killed, but did not eat the cub and then displayed strange behaviour over its body – like grooming and play – for a long period.'

OTHER PLACES OF INTEREST

Zanzibar

Now that Zanzibar has decided positively to welcome tourists, rather than do everything it can to discourage them, this unspoiled island is becoming very popular with travellers who are not looking for sophisticated tourist facilities.

Zanzibar only became part of the African mainland at the time of its union with Tanganyika when the two countries formed Tanzania. Before that all influence and power came from Arabia. It was ruled by Sultans, and was once the largest slave-trading centre in East Africa.

Zanzibar and its offshore islands have been separated from the mainland long enough to have several unique species or sub-species of flora and fauna, including 13 mammals. Efforts are being made to have the home of many of these creatures, Jozani Forest, gazetted as a reserve.

Around the island are many palm-fringed beaches and coral reefs. The island's economy is dominated by cloves, and the villages also produce coconuts, mangoes, pineapples and other spices, fruits and vegetables.

Getting there   There are daily flights to Zanzibar from Dar es Salaam, but these are usually booked well in advance, and the service is chaotic. You can also fly from Mombasa, which is slightly more expensive but much more reliable (but remember that airport tax will be a lot more as this counts as an international flight).

The best way to travel between Dar and Zanzibar is by ship. There are at least three services each day, on modern efficient boats with one-way fares starting at $10. Tourists are no longer allowed to travel by dhow (traditional wooden sailing boat).

Other ports from where boats go to Zanzibar are Bagamoyo, Tanga, and even Mombasa, but long waits may be necessary.

Being there   Zanzibar is a separate state within the Union of Tanzania, and on arrival you must have your passport stamped. This is largely a Muslim island, and both men and women visitors should dress modestly.

All hotels and most services must be paid for in hard currency (US dollars preferred). Low-budget hotels start at around $5.   In Zanzibar Town, the Malindi Inn and the Pyramid Guest House are both popular with travellers; clean and cheap. Food can be bought with Tsh and is cheap.

For getting around, buses, pick-ups and minibuses specially for tourists run from Zanzibar town to various parts of the island. Bicycles and motor-scooters can be hired.

Apart from the museum, which is a must for its historical exhibits, there are many other places to see around the old town including the Anglican Cathedral on the site of the old slave market, the impressive 'House of Wonders' palace, the fishing harbour of dhow boats, narrow winding alleys and beautiful carved wooden doorways. Just outside Zanzibar Town are several old ruined palaces dating from the time of the sultans.

Around the island are idyllic beaches. Many of these have small guesthouses nearby where you can stay for as little as $5 a night. Cheap meals are available, or you can buy food from the market in Zanzibar Town and prepare your own.

Jack Clayton wrote:'I stayed at Paje, on the east coast, for a week. I bought lobster and squid from fishermen and fruit from farmers. Zanzibar's beaches were really magical places for me. Try walking on a beach at night with the warm trade winds blowing and watch the lanterns of the fishermen bobbing up and down in the tide, and you'll know what I mean...'

For complete information about the islands of Zanzibar and Pemba, including details on hotels, travel, beaches, palaces, history and wildlife, we highly recommend (of course) the *Guide to Zanzibar* by David Else (Bradt).

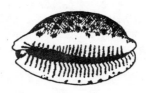

HYENA

Looking like a badly put together dog, hyenas in fact are more closely related to civets, in a family of their own which also includes the insectivorous aardwolf. There are three species of hyena, the largest and most frequently seen being the spotted hyena.

Spotted hyenas have several extraordinary features. The most surprising is that females appear to possess male genitals, leading to the understandable assumption, until recently, that the animal was hermaphrodite. The replica penis and scrotum, accurate in every way, are for appearances only, and no-one seems to know exactly why nature should go to this sort of trouble, although the fact that the females are dominant and have an unusually high amount of testerone no doubt has something to do with it. Cubs are dependent on their mother's milk for far longer than other African carnivores — for six to nine months they receive nothing else, and since their mother may be off hunting for three or four days at a time, childhood can be a hungry period. It is not surprising that when the females return, their cubs suckle for hours.

Spotted hyenas live in large clans, but make their sorties in smaller groups; they are more efficient hunters than lions, though equally accomplished scavengers and opportunists, with a reputation for enjoying car and small aeroplane tyres!

To hear a group of hyenas in conversation is an amazing experience. Their vocalisation varies from blood curdling whoops, to grunts, whines, chuckles and giggles. The Laughing Hyena is no myth; listen to a group giggling over a kill and it's hard to tell them from school girls.

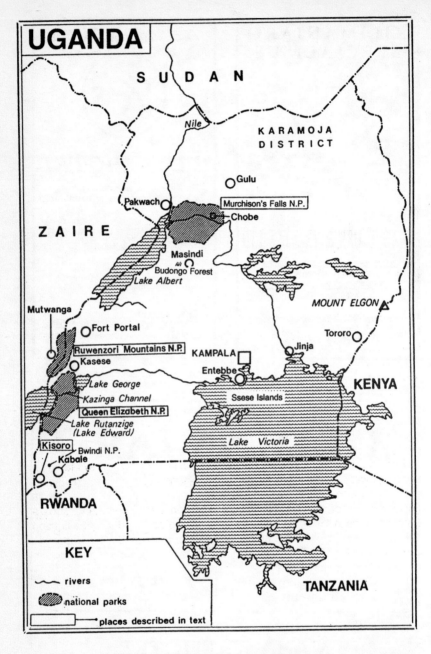

"Uganda is a fairytale. You climb up a railway instead of a bean-stalk and at the top there is a wonderful new world. The scenery is different, the climate is different, and most of all the people are different from anywhere else in Africa".

W. Churchill. 1908

Chapter 11

Uganda

Updated for this edition by Philip Briggs with Said Famao, Julius Lubega, Scott Morgan, Patrick Frew, Lluis Tort, Jaume Tort, Diana Clement, and Joan Masoliver.

FACTS AND FIGURES

Once the most prosperous country of the East African Community, Uganda is exceptionally fertile and well watered by the White Nile which passes through its boundaries. About twenty per cent of the country consists of papyrus swamps and open water.

Most of the country is a high plateau ranging between 1,000 and 2,000 metres, with the Ruwenzori mountains forming the western border. Temperatures are thus moderate, except in the north which is semidesert. Most of the rains fall in March and April, and in October and November.

Uganda is still the Commonwealth's biggest coffee producer, and this product accounts for almost all its foreign exchange earnings.

Uganda gained its independence from Britain in 1962, and in 1971 Idi Amin seized power. Amin's notoriously brutal regime reduced the country to economic chaos, until he was toppled by a united group of Ugandan exiles (including the forces of Milton Obote) assisted by a Tanzanian People's Defence Force in 1979. But Uganda continued to decline during the fighting that went on under the leadership of first Obote, then Okello. Under the current president, Yoweri Museveni, Uganda is now peaceful and anxious to develop its tourist industry.

People

There are 40 tribes in Uganda; the Baganda are the most numerous, comprising nearly 20 per cent.

Three main languages are spoken along with many different dialects, making English the most practical – as well as the official – language, although Swahili is spoken in the eastern part of the country, and to a lesser extent elsewhere.

Before Amin took power, the Asians in Uganda were estimated to number

250,000, and were prominent in all aspects of business. They were expelled in 1972 but many have now returned from exile.

When the white explorers and settlers arrived, Uganda had a medieval monarchy with the religious life centred around ancestor worship. The last king, Sir Edward Mutesa, was assassinated in London in 1969, and was buried in 1972 at Kasubi tombs.

Recently Museveni granted legal recognition to the old kingdoms of southern Uganda, and in July 1993 the British-educated son of Mutesa, Ronald Mutebi, returned to Uganda for his coronation as the new Kabaka (king). It is uncertain what role 'King Ronnie' (as the British press likes to call him) will play but there is no doubt about the popularity of this move. Likewise, Omukama Patrick Olimi has been returned to the throne of the Toro tribe.

The main religions are Christianity and Islam.

TRAVEL

Impressions

The recent bloody episode in Uganda's history was particularly tragic in a country which was once the showpiece of all Africa. Even during the Amin era we found Ugandans to be the most cultured and well-educated people we met in Africa, and apart from a brush with the army we experienced nothing but incredible goodwill and generosity.

Recent travellers' impressions are similar: 'The people are perhaps the friendliest I have encountered. Due to some of the interesting and striking things I saw, Uganda was my favourite country. The people remain optimistic yet slightly hardened. They are extremely good-hearted considering their troubles. Now with Aids (or 'Slim' as they call it) a new and perhaps more difficult war is being waged.' (Jack Clayton)

Warnings

Most parts of Uganda are now as safe as anywhere in Africa, but rebel groups are still fighting in the north, so it is best to avoid the Karamoja, Acholi, West Nile and Madi areas. Army road-blocks cause occasional hold-ups but they are increasingly rare.

Entry and exit

The visa situation is changeable and you are advised to check the latest requirements at the Ugandan Embassy or High Commission. At the time of writing only Irish and Scandinavian visitors do not require visas - most others, including Commonwealth, must have one.

On arrival at the airport or border, your vaccination certificate may be checked. Make sure it's up to date.

If you fly out there is a $20 exit tax.

Border crossings

Being a land-locked country, there are plenty of border crossings to choose from: into Kenya, Tanzania, Rwanda, and Zaïre (Sudan is not possible at present due to war in the south, and at present Rwanda and Zaïre borders are frequently closed because of unrest in those countries). Crossing from Kenya and Tanzania is straightforward by bus or lake ferry.

Money

The currency is the Ugandan shilling (Ush or /-). There is no black market and 'Forex' bureaux are now permitted to buy and sell currency at free market rates. Most banks also have a Forex desk. Daily rates are published in the 'New Vision' newspaper. The rate seems to be stabilising: in October 1993, US$1 = 1,150USh.

If you enter overland there may be no Forex bureau so you will need to change money with local people, or you may be able to exchange some with travellers coming the other way. Note that the largest denomination bill is currently 1,000/-.

Currency declaration forms are no longer required.

Maps

The Department of Lands and Surveys has a Map Sales Office on Parliament Avenue in Kampala, with a branch office in Entebbe near the post office. The large scale maps are excellent and ideal for hiking.

Accommodation

The old requirement to pay for hotels in the upper price range in hard currency has been abolished, although prices are still quoted in dollars. There is a good selection of cheap local-type hotels in most towns.

Eating

Kampala and most towns have street stalls offering cheap and freshly cooked meals. The long years of strife have made the people self-sufficient and dishes with a maize or plantain base are always available. Try the local version of a doughnut, *Mandazi*. Processed food in cans and packets from Kenya is also available.

Transport

Buses are the preferred means of travel in Uganda, being fast, safe, and reliable. There are also **matatus**. Fares are usually about $1 per 100km. Main roads are in very good condition, but some dirt roads are terrible, making progress very slow. **Hitchhiking** is possible, but there are few private vehicles on the roads.

Trains are cheap but very slow and unreliable. There are two lines: Tororo (border with Kenya) to Kasese, and Tororo to Pakwach (although the latter is not always functioning).

The Kampala-Kasese train takes anything from 20 to 40 hours and sleeper cars are no longer available. On all trains bring water and eating utensils. You can usually buy hot meals in the restaurant car or at stations along the way.

Air Uganda **planes** cover much of the country.

There is a weekly **ferry** between Port Bell and Mwanza in Tanzania. This leaves Mwanza on Sunday afternoons and Port Bell on Mondays.

TOWNS

Kampala

The ravages of war are still evident here, although some energetic rebuilding is taking place. There is a posh part of town, up on Nakasero Hill, with embassies and expensive hotels, and the lower town thronged with people and street stalls.

The very helpful tourist office is located on Parliament Avenue opposite the British High Commission.

For sightseeing, a visit to the Kabaka's palace and Kasubi tombs is fascinating. The National Museum is also worth while.

The GPO sells superb postcards of gorillas, and all proceeds are used in primate conservation.

Near the airport are the Entebbe Botanical gardens and zoo; well worth a visit, particularly for backpackers interested in the flora and fauna of the places they are hiking through.

At the Luwero triangle, just north of Kampala, is a grisly memorial to the attempted massacre of the Baganda people by Obote's troops. By the roadside are numerous bones, skulls, and some weapons.

Sleeping and eating

The very popular YMCA (camping or mattresses on the floor for about $2) on Bombo Road has recently been replaced in travellers' affections by the Natete Backpacker's Hostel, run by an energetic Australian, John Hunwick. The hostel is on the outskirts of Kampala – you need to take a minibus or taxi to Natete.

Budget hotels offer basic, dingy rooms for around $10; a (still basic) self-contained room costs upwards of $15. If you don't want to stay at the YMCA or Hostel, it's best to splash out (around $25) on a mid-range hotel; I recommend the Antler Inn on Bombo Road, the Lion Hotel near the bus station or Silver Springs Hotel on the Port Bell road.

A better option than any of these – provided you have a tent – is the Entebbe Resort campsite on Lake Victoria. Regular matatus between Kampala and Entebbe take 30 minutes.

Kasese

This small town in western Uganda is the base for trips to the Ruwenzori and Queen Elizabeth National Parks. Most travellers stay and eat at the Saad

Hotel ($14 for a self-contained double). The manager is friendly and a good source of up-to-date travel information (he helped update this chapter). There are several more basic lodgings.

Kabale

This town near the Rwanda border is a popular base for day walks to Lake Bunyoni and longer trips to the mountain gorilla reserves in Uganda and Zaïre. The Visitours and Skyblue Hotels, opposite each other near the bus station, are geared to travellers, with friendly staff, cheap rooms and excellent food. You can organise a guide to Lake Bunyoni at either hotel, and should also be able to pick up the latest news about mountain gorilla viewing.

HIKING

Uganda's altitude and varied topography make it an ideal country for hiking. Apart from the hikes described here there are plenty of other scenic areas where adventurous do-it-yourself trips can be planned.

The Ruwenzori Mountains

By Armand Hughes D'Aeth, updated by Philip Briggs, Patrick Frew, Scott Morgan, Lluis Tort, Jaume Tort, Joan Masoliver

Introduction   The Ruwenzori mountain range is an area of great geographical and historical interest straddling the border of Uganda and Zaïre. It is a land of high mountains rising to 5,000m, steep valleys thickly covered in vegetation, varied fauna and extensive areas of bogs and forests, with the whole region perpetually covered in mist. This is Rider Haggard's 'Land of Mist' and, it is widely believed, the true site of the legendary Mountains of the Moon. The views and astonishing vegetation make the Ruwenzoris a goal for many experienced hikers and climbers.

The range is roughly l20km long and 48km wide and lies just north of the equator along the western side of the Rift Valley. It is a massive uplifted block of rock arising from the movement of the earth's crust and not of volcanic origin as are some of the other mountains in the surrounding area. There are six ice-capped mountains with extensive glaciers and a number of rocky peaks separated by passes and deep valleys. They are Mt Stanley (5,l09m), Mt Speke (4,889m), Mt Baker (4,843m), Mt Gessi (4,797m), Mt Emin (4,79lm) and Mt Luigi di Savoia (4,626m). There is a permanent snowline at about 4,500m.

Since 1991 much of the higher ranges have been made a national park, called the Ruwenzori Mountain National Park. (The nearby Queen Elizabeth National Park – which was briefly called the Ruwenzori National Park – has now reverted to its former name.)

Flora and Fauna   One of the most interesting aspects of the Ruwenzoris is its vegetation which is astounding in its variety, richness and at times freakishness. As a result of going from a low altitude to a relatively high one within a short space of time, you can climb through a number of altitudinal zones each of which affects the vegetation. The difference in vegetation is not only caused by altitude but also by the variety of soil. It is unique because, as a result of some weird evolutionary pattern, common plants grow to gigantic proportions; the small common-or-garden lobelias weigh sixty kilos, groundsel plants tower above you and the familiar Scottish heather suddenly attains a height of some ten metres.   The zones are usually divided into:

a)   Grassy foothills (900-l,800m); areas of tall elephant grass and occasional red-flowered coral trees.

b)   Montane forest (l,800-2,500m); tangled vegetation, bracken, tree ferns and some beautiful orchids.

c)   Bamboo (2,500-3,000m); tree heather, bamboo and some giant lobelias where the ground is wet.

d)   Heather (3,000-3,800m); carex sedge tussocks in the valley bottom where it's boggy; heather forest on the ridges and rocks; mixed type of woodland of mostly small shrubby trees of the rhododendron family and tree groundsels on the slopes which are well drained.

e)   Alpine (3,800m to the snowline); giant groundsel, giant light blue coloured lobelias and sedge tussocks near the lakes and bogs.

According to earlier reports on the Ruwenzoris, the forest areas used to provide sanctuary for elephants and leopards but poaching has all but eliminated these. Animals most commonly seen are blue monkeys (and, if you're very lucky, chimpanzees) and hyraxes. There are also bushbucks, red forest duikers, hogs, buffaloes and servals.

Climate   The Ruwenzori has its own micro-climate and it must be one of the worst in Africa. The mountains are perpetually wreathed in mist and the rain lashes down turning the slopes into greasy slides. There are occasional patches of clear weather during the 'dry' months but hitting them is a matter of luck and it's almost impossible to plan ahead. The dry periods are supposedly from early June to July, and late December to January or early February. Locals report that the best time to go into the mountains is January and February as the air is clearer and the peaks can be seen. During my stay throughout June and July, I can only remember four consecutive days of clear weather. (However, Jim and Claudine, hiking in December, report: 'We had excellent weather – four hours of rain in two days on the mountain, but the vegetation is permanently wet so you still get soaked!')

People   The inhabitants of the lower slopes of the Ruwenzoris are mostly BaKonjo tribesmen who speak their own language, LuKonjo. They act as porters and guides but apart from the hunters, the BaKonjos do not usually go very high into the mountains, reportedly because they believe that is the realm of the gods. They are a short, tough and sturdy people, with heavy features and are normally very reliable and cheerful.

Hiking the Ruwenzori Circuit

The main entrance to the park is at Nyakalengija, near Ibanda, in the foothills of the mountains some 22km from Kasese. The most popular hike is a circuit that takes in the Bujuku and Mubuku valleys, crosses some high passes and offers great views of the main peaks and glaciers. You should note that the circuit hike described here takes at least six days, although it's easy to take up to ten days if you're not in a rush. The hike should not be undertaken lightly since the constant rain and cold temperatures, not to mention the bogs and heavy going, make it very arduous. Don't attempt it unless you are fit, well equipped and prepared. Your efforts will be well rewarded.

If you want to get up to any of the summits this means branching off the circuit and crossing one of the glaciers. This involves extra days, and you need to be familiar with ice-axe, rope and crampons.

Cost and logistics   Like Kilimanjaro, hiking in the Ruwenzoris is becoming a highly organised affair, complicated in 1993 by competition between the traditional holder of this privilege, the Ruwenzori Mountain Service (RMS), established long before the mountains became a national park, and a private tour operator. The RMS is a highly respected organisation which maintains the huts and trail and monitors the environmental impact of hikers. They charge high fees and channel the profits into self-help projects for the local communities. They also used to hold the monopoly for organised treks, and in 1993 they tripled their prices. In response, travellers started to arrange their own treks through the National Parks Headquarters in Ibanda, which was far cheaper. In October 1993 the government granted the RMS exclusive use of all the huts and the cleared areas around them. This challenge has been answered by Semliki Safaris, who have just opened a campsite near Ntandi, creating their own trail starting at Ntandi and meeting the circuit trail near John Mabe hut. They plan to set up alternative huts to those operated by the RMS. It is impossible to predict the outcome of this 'trail war' so make enquiries before setting out for the region. The RMS can be contacted at PO Box 33, Kasese; Tel: (0493) 4225, and the Natete Backpacker's Hostel in Kampala is likely to have the latest information.

The directions below assume you are doing the trip through the RMS. Unlike Kilimanjaro, you *can* go into the park on your own without guide and porters, and without the help of the RMS, but this is not advisable for a variety of reasons: the trails are indistinct and the chance of getting lost is high; porters are inexpensive, and by hiring them and using the RMS you are helping the local economy. Lone backpackers contribute nothing. That said, however, if you are short of time and money but want to have a taste of the mountains you could potter about the lower slopes on your own.

Preparations   The RMS is based at Nyakalengija, near Ibanda, right next to national park HQ. In the last few years RMS have built new huts in the mountains and renovated some of the old ones. They have also built new bridges and laid boards over some of the bogs.

It is usually a day's walk between one hut and the next. If you're fit it can be 4-5 hours, but most people take longer than this. Even though distances are short, the walking is very tiring.

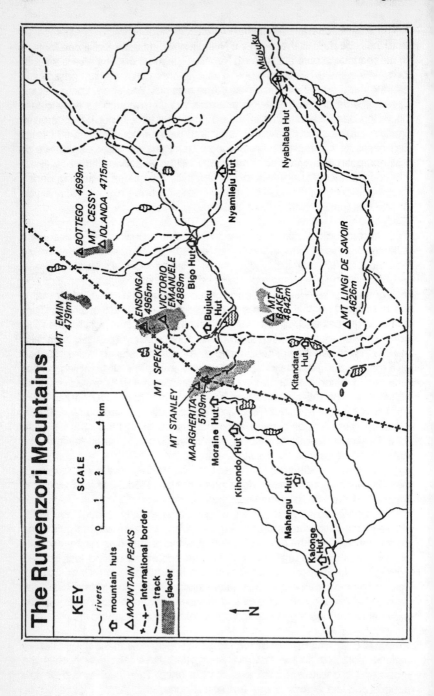

The Ruwenzori Mountains

KEY

∿ rivers
⌂ mountain huts
△ MOUNTAIN PEAKS
×–·+–· international border
–·+– track
▓ glacier

SCALE

0   1   2   3   4 km

N

MT EMIN
479m

BOTTEGO 4699m
MT CESSY
OLANDA 4715m

ENSONGA
4965m

VICTORIO
EMANUELE
4889m

Bigo Hut

Bujuku
Hut

Nyamileju Hut

MT SPEKE

MT STANLEY

MARGHERITA
5109m

Moraine Hut

Kihondo Hut

Mahangu Hut

Kalonge
Hut

MT BAKER
4842m

MT LINGI DE SAVOIR
4626m

Kitandara
Hut

Nyabitaba Hut

Mubuku

The Ruwenzoris are becoming increasingly popular and sometimes the huts can be full. It's well worth bringing a tent to give yourself more independence. You'll also need a stove, cooking gear and good sleeping bag.

RMS has an office in Kasese, at plot 33 Alexander Street, where arrangements can be made, or you can go to Nyakalengija. To get there, hitch or take a matatu towards Fort Portal for 10km, and take a left turnoff for Ibanda. Look for the RMS sign. You will probably have to walk the 12km to Nyakalengija, although there are occasional vehicles. RMS have a pick-up van going each way, at least once per day. If you book with them, they will also pick you up from your hotel. The RMS provides an excellent service: guides and porters can be arranged quickly and you can usually start walking the day after your arrival in Kasese. You have to provide cooking pots and blankets for the guides and porters, but RMS make all these arrangements. You can also pay your park entrance and hut fees to RMS and a small service charge to cover all the arrangements. The price is clearly broken down and explained to you: you hand over the money, and away you go!

The porters carry 22 kg each, 12 kg of which is for clients. Bags are weighed at the start of the trip. If you actually want to get up to one of the summits, which means crossing the glaciers and the use of ice gear, make sure you get a guide who is familiar with the routes. Not all of them are. Tips for guides and porters is usually an extra day's wages, and letting them keep the cooking pots and blankets.

The map of the circuit trail sold by the RMS is fine for ordinary hikers. If you plan to ascend the peaks you should get the Central Ruwenzoris one at scale 1:250,000, edition 2-U.S.D, or the 1:50,000 Margherita (65/11 series Y732, edition 3-U.S.D.) showing the main part of the range. These are available from the RMS office. *The Ruwenzori Map and Guide* by Andrew Wielochowski, available from West Col, UK, and from the Saad Hotel, Kasese, is also useful. You must also have a compass.

You'll also need to take your own supplies. 'A wide variety of foodstuffs is available in Kasese – fresh and processed. The dried fish keep well and make a nice change. As the weather is cold higher up, fresh food keeps fairly well.' (Scott Morgan)

(There are moves within the national park and RMS to prevent porters using wood fires on the higher parts of the range, in the interests of conservation. This is commendable and should be supported by visitors.)

'When we visited the Ruwenzoris it was the wet season. We found gum boots (available in Kasese) to be more useful than mountain boots and gaiters. Telescopic walking sticks were also very useful, or the guide can provide you with a bamboo pole cut from the forest.' (Lluis Tort)

Nyakalengija (1,615m) to Nyabitaba (2,651m)   The trail is clear going through a small coffee plantation and a meadow followed by elephant grass and then into the bush. Regardless of the temperature, you would be well advised to wear long trousers – the local species of nettle is plentiful and vicious. Keep the Mubuku river (full of trout) to your right. The ascent can be awkward in wet weather as the rotting vegetation and mud turns the trail into a steep slide (a walking stick is essential). There is a short but steep descent to the edge of the river and then a rise into the forest. Descend steeply, cross two streams, and continue on the level for several kilometres. Cross the Mahoma river and then follow a steep moraine ridge to Nyabitaba. In this area you may pass small grass and twig huts about 40 centimetres high with offerings of food inside. These are shrines erected by the BaKonjo hunters in order to pacify the gods who rule over the forest and to ensure successful hunting as well as the safe return of travellers from the inhospitable higher regions. At the top of the ridge you will pass a small rock shelter to the left of the path and just beyond this lies the clearing where the newly renovated hut (with a piped water supply) is situated. The porters have their own hut. Across the valley to the north are the rocky (and largely unclimbed) buttresses of the Portal Peaks.

Nyabitaba Hut to John Matte Hut (3,305m)   This is the most strenuous section of the trail and will take at least seven hours. Follow the ridge through the forest and be sure to take the right-hand fork that drops steeply to the new suspension bridge that crosses the Mubuku river. From the bridge there is a steep climb up the bank (difficult in wet weather) followed by several kilometres of good walking through bamboo and then a long and gruelling ascent. Numerous boulders obstruct the path. There is a rather inadequate rock shelter at roughly two thirds of the way. You reach Nyamiliju Hut (3,322m) in the region that the heather trees and groundsel make their first appearance; Nyamiliju means 'place of beards' from the lichen and Spanish moss festooning the trees. This hut is rarely used now: most of the floor has either rotted or been taken for firewood. It's about another hour on to the new John Matte Hut. Water is available from the Bujuku river, about 200m away.

John Matte Hut to Bujuku Hut (3,962m)   Expect to take about five hours for this section. Slide down to the river bank and follow the path up the side of the river. You pass through heather forest (note the brilliantly-coloured mosses). Carry on through an open area and up two steepish moraines to Lower Bigo Bog. Cross the river. At this point the trail virtually ceases to exist. Work your way to the left-hand edge of the valley, keeping the bog to your right and follow around its edge. This section can be quite fatiguing, whether you choose to leap with agility from one tussock of carex sedge to the next, or wade through thigh-deep mud.

Bigo Hut is in relatively good condition, but not used much these days as it is half way between John Matte and Bajuku Hut. If you do stay in the hut, as usual the porters will opt for the rock shelter just above it.

At this point you are at the junction of several routes, and must choose whether to go northwards to the Roccati Pass between Mts Emin and Gessi (whose summits can be seen due north), north east to the Bukurungu Pass between Gessi and the Portal Peaks, or southwest to Lake Bujuku and the main circuit trail. We describe only the Bujuku route; if you want to do any of the others make sure you bring a guide who knows the way.

From Bigo Hut the path veers southwest following the southern bank of the river. The route is obvious as it leads in between the spurs jutting out from Mt Speke and Mt Baker. There is a steep rise at first but this soon levels off as you round the southern spur with the Grauer rock towering above. Soon the

Kibatsi (Upper Bigo) bog is reached. Wooden boards have been laid across some of the bog by RMS.

At the end of the bog you come to a steep rise. The last section isn't too bad as the going is much drier through patches of groundsel. Pass Lake Bujuku (magnificent views!) on its east side and continue beside the stream to reach Cooking Pot Cave, from where two tracks lead off; the southern one goes to the Scott-Elliot Pass and the other goes northwest to the Bujuku Hut which is clearly visible.

Bujuku Hut is in a majestic setting, backed by Mt Baker's scree slopes with views of Mts Speke and Stanley. Mt Speke is hidden by its colourful moss-strewn lower cliff base, over which flows a stream from the Speke glacier issuing out of a fantastic ice cave. Glacier-ribbed Mt Stanley is awe inspiring.

Bujuku Hut to Kitandara Hut (4,023m) Retrace your steps to Cooking Pot Cave and take the right fork which climbs steeply up towards Scott-Elliot Pass. At the steepest section, a steel ladder has been erected. You'll pass through plenty of giant groundsel and below a cliff before coming to boulders and scree. At the head of this scree slope you'll see a rock buttress, and the pass is on its right; turn left through a cleft in the rocks and begin your descent beneath the vertical cliffs of Mt Baker. Keep to the left side of the valley until you climb a rise and then drop down to Lake Kitandara, an idyllic spot and only half a day's walk from Bujuku. There are two lakes here and the hut is by the lower one.

When crossing between Bujuku and Kitandara you can detour to the small Elena Hut (4,541m), high on Mt Stanley. Water is from snow or rock pools and there is no fire wood. Do not stray on to the glacier unroped, even if there are footprints leading up. 'We found the glacier quite crevassed – two people fell in!' (P.F.)

Kitandara Hut to Guy Yeoman Hut (3,505m) Begin with the very steep strenuous ascent to Freshfield Pass to the east, then drop down to Bujongolo, a cliff overhang providing good shelter. Kabamba, with its more generous overhang and beautiful waterfall, is a short way further down. It's another hour on to the new Guy Yeoman Hut. This is normally a five hour day.

'We climbed Mt Baker. One can do this from Kitandara or from the Freshfield Pass. Most of the climb is on easy rock, there is a cairned route which the guide will know, but there are two short sections of glacier to cross – crevassed and steep – so ice-axe and rope are essential.' (P.F.)

Guy Yeoman Hut to Nyabitaba Hut (2,651m) Another five hour walk. The descent continues to Kichuchu where there is another rock shelter, and you continue down through bamboo forests and bog to the Mubuku river which must be forded. The path then follows a ridge and drops down to the Nyabitaba hut. It is then simply a matter of retracing your early steps to Nyakalengija.

Feasting Round off your hike with a meal at the highly recommended Mubuka Valley Restaurant in Ibanda. Meals must be ordered in advance.

Mount Elgon

Mount Elgon straddles the Kenya/Uganda border. Until recently it was normally climbed from the Kenyan side, but the highest peak, Wagagai (4,321m) is in Uganda and there are now good facilities on the Ugandan side.

The base for climbing Elgon is Budadiri, where you can stay at the Wagagai Hotel ($5 per room or camping free). This is the home of the Mount Elgon Club, which will organise a four-day climb for about $50. You need a tent, warm clothes and sleeping bag; the hotel organises guides, porters and food. You should bring water-purifying tablets. The first day brings you from Budadiri, which lies at 2,300m, to a campsite by the river Ssasa (3,000m). From here you ascend to a site just below Jackson's Summit, from where, on the third day, you climb Wagagai peak (4,322m). Another day is needed if you want to circle the caldera.

The best months to climb Elgon are from December to March, and June and July.

To reach Budadiri from Kampala, you must first get to the regional centre of Mbale, a five-hour trip by minibus. Mbale is a pleasantly provincial place with several affordable hotels. A few matatus leave daily for Budadiri, taking about two hours.

In the Mbale region Scott Morgan recommends Sipi Falls as a pleasant place to stay. 'The guesthouse here is an old colonial governor's residence, and you can camp in the grounds. To climb Mt Elgon it is possible to hire forest rangers as guides from the next town, Kapchorwa (north of Budadiri)'.

This whole area provides good hiking possibilities. Julius Lubega, the librarian at Mbale Library, writes: 'the scenery at Wanale (Nkokonjeru Hill), on the outskirts of Mbale, is very pleasant with flowing rivers and refreshing breezes.'

The Kigeza region

In the far southwestern corner of Uganda is Kigeza, a beautiful region of green hills and lakes which the locals call 'The Switzerland of Africa'. This is the main tea growing part of the country, and the land is intensively farmed and terraced. It is ideal hiking country.

When the border with Rwanda is open, many travellers enter or leave Uganda through the region on their way to that country. Kabale, the main town of Kigeza, is also the highest town in Uganda (2,000m) so be prepared for some chilly nights.

Kisoro and the Mgahinga National Park

The Mgahinga National Park protects Uganda's portion of the Virunga volanoes (also called Mfumbiro volcanoes). Most people go here for gorilla viewing, but there is some excellent hiking in the park. Guided trips to the peaks of Gahinga (3,473m) and Muhavura (4,127m) take you through Afro-alpine vegetation of the type found in the Ruwenzoris, but with less effort and expense (but you should be of above-average fitness – these are strenuous and long day trips). Park fees of $20 will have to be paid, and $15 to hike up to the peaks ($5 for half-day walks). There is also a $10 fee for the services of a ranger (compulsory) but this is divided between the number of people in your group. Porters are also available.

Kisoro is the access town to Mgahinga, and the park headquarters are here. Kisoro is a two-hour matatu ride from Kabale. There are a few hotels in Kisoro; the Traveller's Rest ($6/double) is the best place to get up-to-date information on Mgahinga.

Kabale to Kisoro via Lake Bunyonyi   Jack Clayton decided to do the 85km journey between the two towns on foot: 'From Kabale there is a road to Lake Bunyonyi. From there you head around the lake to the north. At the north end of the lake a road joins the path that eventually goes to Kisoro, although many short cuts are available – people are always glad to assist. The walk took me two days but three would have been better.'

OTHER PLACES OF INTEREST

The National Parks and reserves

During the years of economic chaos and war, many of the animals in Uganda's game parks were killed for meat. Elephants were poached for their ivory and rhino were completely wiped out. Animal populations are now recovering, however, and the game parks can offer you an experience not far below that of the neighbouring countries of East Africa and without the tourist hordes; for many people the launch trips are more exciting than being cooped up in a vehicle. The relatively low park fee of $20 *per stay* (not per day) and the fact that there is often no need to have your own vehicle is an added attraction for backpackers.

The National Parks office in Kampala is at 31 Kanjoka Street, (tel: 256534)

GORILLAS

The eastern lowland gorilla (Gorilla gorilla graueri)

At present these are found in scattered pockets of surviving forest in Eastern Zaïre, including the reserves of Kahuzi-Biega and Maiko. No detailed information exists on the numbers of animals within these areas, but it is estimated that in Kahuzi Biega there are about 300 gorillas in 18 family groups, and several solitary males. Group sizes range from two to 37 animals. An average group consists of one 'silverback' dominant male, seven adult females, five juveniles, and three infants. The family is headed by the silverback, and roam freely according to changing food preferences.

This sub-species may attain a height of 175cm, and weigh approximately 160kg. They are herbivorous and diurnal. Sexual maturity is reached in 7-8 and 10-12 years in females and males respectively. Pregnancy occurs every four years, and the gestation period is 8½-9 months. Young are weaned at around two and a half years. A gorilla's life span is approximately 40-50 years.

The mountain gorilla (Gorilla gorilla beringei)

Half of the world's remaining mountain gorillas are confined to the Virunga Volcanoes, a region of relatively recent volcanic activity on the floor of the western split of the Great Rift Valley. This small area lies at the meeting point of Uganda, Zaïre, and Rwanda and is shared by the three nations. Strenuous conservation efforts over the last few years have helped the countries concerned to appreciate the value of keeping this region in its natural state, but political strife jeopardises the safety of the gorillas. Uganda's Bwindi Forest is home to the other half of the world's population of mountain gorillas.

The mountain gorilla only lives at altitudes of between 2,500m and 4,000m. They have longer hair and are slightly larger than lowland gorillas, with full-grown males reaching a weight of 180kg or more. They live in very dense vegetation of which an adult can consume up to 15kg a day! The favourite food plants are bamboo shoots, wild celery, nettles, bedstraw and thistles. The range of a family group is between 10 and 30 square kilometres, and groups will often overlap each other's home range. The families generally avoid one another, however. Gorillas build sleeping nests on the ground or in trees. There are only about 650 of these animals left in the wild.

Gorillas may be seen in their natural habitat in Rwanda, Uganda and Zaïre. Gorilla tourism began in Uganda in the 1950s, but Zaïre was the first country to realise the financial potential of tourists visiting habituated animals; the gorillas of Kahusi-Biega have been 'at home' to tourists since the early 1970s but economics have sometimes been put ahead of the animals' welfare. Rwanda and Uganda, however, put conservation first and tourism second.

The book and film Gorillas in the Mist have raised awareness and interest in these magnificent animals, and those who manage to see gorillas in the wild will not be disappointed. It is one of the most memorable wildlife experiences in the world. See the relevant chapters for information.

The Dian Fossey Gorilla Fund is concerned with the protection of mountain gorillas in the Virungas. With poaching increased ten-fold during the recent civil war in Uganda, anti-poaching measures are the present priority. Contact the DFGF at 110 Gloucester Ave, Primrose Hill, London NW1 8JA. Tel: 071-483 2681.

and can give you the latest information on the seven national parks that fall under their jurisdiction. Forest reserves come under a different ministry, the Department of Forestry on Springs Road on the outskirts of Kampala.

In recent years Uganda has become the focus for gorilla and chimpanzee viewing. Local tour operators, including Hot Ice (P.O. Box 151, Kampala; tel: 242733) can arrange trips for you.

Queen Elizabeth National Park

This park was briefly renamed Ruwenzori National Park, but it has now reverted to its former name. The park is near Kasese by the lakes that are once again known by their colonial names of Edward and George.

This park used to be famous for its 4,000-strong herds of elephant; these were reduced to no more than 400 in the late 1980s but protection is now effective and numbers are increasing. There are launch trips (well worth it) along the Kazinga Channel which links the two lakes and you'll see plenty of hippos and crocodiles (which have been introduced). The many fish in the channel attract a great variety of waterbirds. The launch costs $60 for up to 20 people.

Mweya Safari Lodge provides very good accommodation at a reasonable price ($35 double), the Institute of Ecology Hostel is $10 and there's a Student Camp (indoors) and campsite ($5, but the latter is overrun with hippos, which doesn't make for relaxing nights).

It is relatively easy to arrange a game drive before being dropped off at Mweya to do a launch trip the following morning. Check around in Kasese for drivers who will take you into the park, or get a group together and hire a taxi. You can usually hitch out from Mweya.

Murchison Falls National Park

Murchison Falls is a mighty cascade on the River Nile flowing between Lake Kyoga and Lake Albert. The park (briefly known as Kabalega National Park and labelled thus on some maps) has always been one of East Africa's most rewarding parks, with the superb boat ride to Murchinson Falls and the upper Nile being a highlight.

It is not an easy park to get to on your own, but worth the effort. There are regular minibuses from Kampala to Masindi, the nearest large town, then one bus a day on to Wanseko, on the shore of Lake Albert. Get off the bus at Bulisa, about 5km before Wanseko. There's a guesthouse here, where you'll have to stay the night.

Next day, you can arrange to hire a bike from the guesthouse ($5 a day) and ride to Paraa, the park headquarters, which is about 33km and takes 2-3 hours. The lodge at Paraa is being rebuilt and should be operational in late 1994, but there's a basic rest camp on the opposite side of the river where you can camp for $5 per night or rent a comfortable banda with mosquito nets for $15.

From Paraa you can arrange a ride in a boat to the base of the falls. This costs $80 for the whole boat.

There's a huge hippo population, and if the crocodiles are also there in profusion you're in for a treat. For bird-watchers this is the best chance in Africa of seeing the shoebill.

The boat operators have been encouraged by tourists to get too close to the hippos and rev the engines to make the frightened animals flee from the water. However photo-oportunistic this may be, please do not encourage it.

Budongo Forest

This will eventually become a chimpanzee viewing area, but until the infrastructure for this is set up the reserve offers some excellent walking and bird-watching.

The forest is about 30km west of Masindi on the Butiaba road. Rooms and camping are available at Nyabyeya Forestry College guest house. Bring food with you.

Mountain gorillas and chimpanzees

Two of Uganda's national parks, Mgahinga and Bwindi, have been proclaimed with the primary intention of conserving the rare and localised mountain gorilla. Two mountain gorilla populations are left in the wild, one in the Virunga Mountains, shared by Uganda, Rwanda and Zaïre, and the other in Bwindi Forest in Uganda. Together they number fewer than 650 animals.

The future of the Virunga gorillas is far from secure. The recent civil war in Rwanda has affected the Ugandan and Rwandan populations, and reports suggest there are inadequate controls over the heavily-visited gorillas in Zaïre. The Bwindi population lives within a single country, one with sound conservation policies; its short term future looks reasonably secure.

There are three semi-habituated groups of chimpanzees in Chambura Gorge, Budongo Forest and Kibale Forest.

Gorilla viewing

Mgahinga National Park   This is the Ugandan section of the Virunga volcanoes where troops of mountain gorillas range between three countries. While neighbouring Rwanda was having its political problems, Mgahinga was closed but it re-opened in September 1993. However, gorilla trips have yet to be restarted. This situation may well have changed by the time you read this, and the uncertainty works to the advantage of independent travellers since the gorilla visits will not be booked months in advance by tour operators.

There is plenty to do in the area while you wait to see gorillas, including walks and climbs in the national park (see *Hiking*).

Kisoro is on the Zaïrean border and is currently the base favoured by travellers visiting the Zaïrean gorillas.

Crossing the Zaïre border to Djomba   The hut from which the gorillas are visited is a two-hour walk (via a short cut) from the border. Gorilla-viewing costs $120 per person. You can either buy a Zaïrian visa in advance ($80 or more) or negotiate a price at the border (up to $50). If you are prepared to leave your passport at the border, you can negotiate a cheaper rate.   This sounds risky but it is now established practice and no-one has reported any problems.

If all goes well, you can visit the Zaïrean gorillas as a three-day round trip from Kabale. A limited number of people are allowed to see the gorillas every day, so if a couple of overland trucks have arrived it may take longer.

Crossing the Rwandan border to the Parc des Volcans   Rwanda's gorillas are once again being visited by tourists, but the political upheaval in Burundi makes the future uncertain. Again, independent travellers will reap the benefits since this is the best organised of all gorilla viewing places and in peaceful times is booked up a year ahead.

You will probably have to walk the 10km to the border, but there are matatus from there to Ruhengeri. You will need a visa, which you should get in Kampala. For full information on gorilla visiting, see the Rwanda chapter.

Bwindi National Park   Bwindi, alternatively and more alluringly known as the Impenetrable Forest, was made a national park in 1991. It only opened to tourists in April 1993. Three gorilla troops have been habituated, but only one may be visited by tourists. A maximum of six visitors are allowed per day, and the current cost is $80 per day plus $20 park entrance. The price will soon rise to $120.

It is easiest to visit Bwindi on an organised tour from Kampala, but you can get there on your own. From Kabale take a matatu (Tuesday, Friday and Sunday) to Bututoga (basic accommodation) then make your way the 17km to the park headquarters at Butoma. At Butoma there is a campsite and a lodge, and tasty food. Even if you can't get to see the gorillas (they will be booked months ahead) it is well worth going there for guided nature walks and the hopes of a cancellation.

Chimpanzee viewing

Chambura Gorge is part of Queen Elizabeth National Park. The chimps here are best visited with the safari company Hot Ice who currently give a 70% chance of seeing the animals. Budongo Forest has a chimpanzee population which are being studied by scientists so tourist visits are not encouraged. This situation may change in 1994 so check at the Department of Forestry in Kampala.

The most promising place to see chimps is in Kibale Forest, which is outstanding in its number of primate species (eleven), so even if you don't see chimps you should have a wonderful time wandering the many paths with binoculars at the ready.

Kanyunchi is the base for guided chimp-viewing walks, and you can camp here. It is near the village of Bigodi, where there is a guest house, on the Fort Portal to Kamwenge road.

Ssese Islands

These forested islands on Lake Victoria are an ideal place to spend a few days relaxing and doing day walks or cycling trips from the town of Kalangala on Buggala, the largest island. The island is marvellously scenic and there is plenty of wildlife around, most visibly monkeys, birds and butterflies. The Andronica Lodge in Kalangala is very traveller orientated; maps of the island are sold here and there are bicycles for hire. Nearby is the new Church of Uganda Hostel, where camping costs less than $1 and rooms less than $2.

A ferry runs twice-weekly between Port Bell and Kalangala. On Mondays, Wednesdays and Fridays a bus leaves Kampala at 10am, passes through Masaka at around 2pm, then crosses by ferry to Buggala, arriving at Kalengala anywhere between dusk and midnight. The bus returns to Kampala the next day.

WEAVER BIRDS

Belonging to a large family of birds that includes sparrows and whydahs, *Ploceidae*, weavers are delightful birds to observe because of their talent in nest making. The beautiful tear-drop structures hang from the branches of numerous African trees, and there are ample opportunities to watch them being built. It only takes a few days of frenzied activity by the male to complete a nest, but the apparent skill with which strips of reed or grass are woven together is fascinating. When the nest is complete, the bird makes an equally frenzied attempt to attract a mate, fluttering and twittering at the entrance of their potential home. If a female deigns to come down for a closer look, he almost explodes from excitement. And if she doesn't like it, he may even rip it apart and start again.

The nests are perfectly designed to protect eggs and nestlings from predators, having a false upper chamber and being suspended from thin branches that would not support a heavy animal (although snakes often manage to gain entrance).

In southwest Africa the weaver bird nests look like a giant haystack wedged in a tree. The sociable weaver builds a communal nest that may house 150 birds at a time. Within the one huge nest are numerous chambers for individual pairs, but nest building is a group effort and they are so well-made that they may last 100 years. The insulated nest is necessary protection against the extremes of heat and cold (this being desert or semi-desert land) as well as against predators. The black-necked cobra is the birds' worst enemy; a snake may enter the nest and move from chamber to chamber devouring eggs and nestlings. Telegraph poles are becoming increasingly popular sites for nests, possibly because snakes cannot climb the smooth pole.

EAST-CENTRAL AFRICA

Rwanda
Burundi
Eastern Zaïre

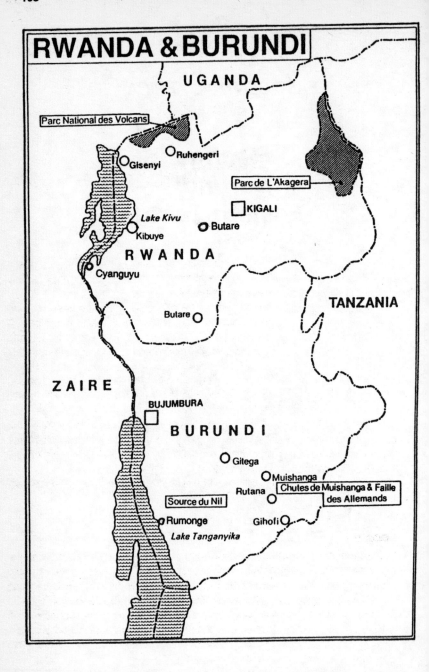

RWANDA & BURUNDI

Chapter 12

Rwanda

1993 revision by Casper Hoebeek

FACTS AND FIGURES

This land-locked country is smaller than Belgium or Vermont, but has a population of over eight million, giving it the highest population density of any country in Africa: 306 people per square kilometre.

The whole of the country lies just south of the equator, and is sometimes referred to as 'The land of a thousand hills' (one can also add that it has 28 lakes). Its altitude varies between 1,200m and 4,500m with the Virunga volcano range dominating on the north-western border. The scenery owes its lushness to the high rainfall; l,550mm annually in the mountains and l,000mm on the plateau. The short rains last from mid-September to mid-December, and the long rains are from March to the end of May. There is a higher rainfall on the Zaïre-Nile Crest and the Virunga volcanoes.

Due to population pressure Rwanda is heavily cultivated, mostly around the shores of Lake Kivu, the Rusizi river area, and around the Virunga volcanoes. The entire centre of the country is under cultivation. Coffee is the main export, followed by tea, cotton and pyrethrum.

The dry season is from June to September with December and January fairly rain-free.

People

The majority of the population are from the stocky Hutu tribe (88%) with the tall Tutsi (11%) forming the minority. The Twa, pygmies, make up the remaining 1%. Due to intermarriage there is little visible difference between these groups but social differences and historical hatreds keep them apart. In October 1993 thousands of refugees flooded into the country from neighbouring Burundi, exacerbating the tribal tensions and overcrowding.

Many expatriates work in Rwanda with gorilla conservation and various aid programmes. Most people are Catholics.

The official language is Kinyarwanda. French is the second language and widely understood. English is spoken only in tourist areas. Swahili is seldom spoken except near the Tanzanian border.

Vocabulary

English	French	Kinyarwanda (phonetic)
hello	bonjour	muraho/jambo
good morning	bonjour	mwaramutse
good afternoon	bonjour	mwiriwe
good evening	bonsoir	mwiriwe
how are you?	ça va?	amakuru?/wites?
fine, thank you	ça va bien, merci	mweza/amakuru/ego
yes	oui	ego/yego
no	non	oya
thank you	merci	murakose
how much?	combien?	ngahe?
when?	quand?	iyo?/ryali?
today	aujourd'hui	none
tomorrow	demain	ejo (hazaza)
day after tomorrow	après demain	ejo bundi (hazaza)
this week	cette semaine	iki cyumweru
next week	semaine prochaine	igyumweru gitaha
where?	où?	hehe?
on the right	à droit	ibulyo
on the left	à gauche	ibumoso
straight ahead	continuer	imbere
north	nord	amajyaruguru
south	sud	amajyepfu
west	ouest	iburengerazuba
east	est	iburasirazuba
hill	mont	umusozi
lake	lac	ikiyaga
river	rivière	umugezi
spring/waterfall	source/chute	iliba/isoko
town	ville	umudugudu
village	village	akadugudu
restaurant	restaurant	restaurant
drinks	boissons	ibingobwa
goodbye (day)	au revoir	mulirirwe
goodbye (evening)	au revoir	muramukeho
goodbye (farewell)	au revoir	murabeho

In Rwandan pronunciation, the "r" and "l" sounds are freely being exchanged, and the "v" in Zaïrean names is often being replaced by a "b" in the Rwandan version. This might cause some minor problems with understanding the people.

Recent history and politics

To understand the politics of Rwanda it is necessary to know something of its history.

According to oral tradition, Rwanda was a highly developed country from the late 14th Century. Isolated geographically by high mountains and bodies of water, and by the people's fierce reputation, Rwanda escaped invasion from neighbouring tribes. The Tutsi minority ruled the country through its powerful kings (*mwamis*) and maintained a strict overlord-peasant relationship with the Hutu majority. In 1989 their isolation was penetrated first by German colonists, then by the Belgians in 1916. The new white overlords found this feudal system much to their liking and simply added a supervisory tier to the existing structure.

In 1957 there was a long-due Hutu uprising. The Tutsi response was to kill the Hutu intellectual elite. Two years later the Hutu had their revenge with a wholescale massacre of the Tutsi. Thousands of Tutsi, including the king, fled to neighbouring countries. Rwanda gained its independence in 1962, with the Hutus in power. They have retained that power ever since. President Juvénal Habyarimana took power in a bloodless coup in 1973 and has been re-elected (unopposed) in 1988. The president has skilfully maintained relationships with the West and the Church as well as calming tribal tensions.

Meanwhile a disaffected population of Tutsi refugees in Uganda formed a rebel force (the FPR) and invaded northern Rwanda in 1990. With the help of French, Belgian and Zaïrean troops the government agreed on a cease-fire, but fighting flared up again in December and continued until an effective cease-fire was signed in August 1992 leading to the signing of a peace agreement in 1993 when repatriation of refugees was agreed on. This has held until the time of writing (October 1993) but must be put under severe strain by massacres of both Tutsis and Hutus in neighbouring Burundi and a new influx of refugees.

These recent developments may affect President Habyarimana's commitment to a multi-party system. The country is also suffering from severe economic problems (their main foreign-currency earner, the mountain gorillas of the Virunga volcanoes, were unvisited during the fighting, and both the gorillas and the economy suffered).

TRAVEL

Impressions

Casper Hoebeek, who travelled to every corner of Rwanda to update this chapter writes:

'For such a small country, Rwanda offers some excellent attractions to travellers, ranging from volcanoes to gorillas and from dense mountain rainforests to savannahs, but just travelling through the country is already worth the trip. The main roads give magnificent views over a varied countryside composed of lush farmlands which seem to cover every hillside, which are sometimes terraced. Other interesting points are the shores of Lake Kivu, the swampy lakes in eastern Rwanda, and the numerous hot springs and waterfalls which can be found anywhere in Rwanda.

'The people are generally very friendly to foreigners, but remember that tourists are very rare in this part of Africa [most just go to see the gorillas]. The attention that backpackers receive can become very tiring, even annoying, as do the constant yells of "Muzungu!" and "Donnez-moi de l'argent!" from the children. Because of the density of the population, people are everywhere and their rural way of life is very interesting. Try to learn some Kinyarwanda which will open many doors to you. If you speak French you will have the opportunity to converse with students and young people in a language they understand well.

'Generally from the traveller's point of view Rwanda appears rather quiet and prosperous, but remember that the ethnic, political and economic tensions will sooner or later become a problem in this overpopulated country.'

Warnings

Rwanda is an expensive country. Luxury items are readily available but are *very* costly. Accommodation even in mission hostels is expensive. Casper suggests a budget of $15-20 per day.

Be very careful over what or whom you photograph: border areas, the army, the national guard, the police and their vehicles, and the buildings they protect. Workmen dressed in pink will be prisoners, so do not photograph them. Always ask before taking a photograph; even a beautiful landscape can conceal something of military significance.

Don't discuss politics in public, particularly the Hutu-Tutsi situation. While emotions are inflamed it's best not to use those words at all. On the other hand, money is a completely acceptable subject of conversation and male Rwandans will be very keen to hear your views on such matters!

Entry and exit

Everyone needs a visa except Germans. The cost varies from country to country (outside East Africa expect to pay from $10 to $30). Regulations also vary, but usually require an exact date of entry, a yellow fever vaccination card, a return ticket, and two photos. It's best to get your visa in a neighbouring country: Burundi (Ave de Zaïre, Bujumbura), Uganda (Baumann House, Parliament Ave, Kampala), Tanzania (Upanga Rd) or Kenya (Mama Ngina St). It is sometimes, but not always, possible to get a visa at the border. If entering from Zaïre visas are usually issued by border officials (for $45!). Visas can be renewed (expensively) at the immigration office in Kigali (Rue de Commerce).

Land crossings present no problem if the border is open – try to find out from other travellers. The difficulty will be in finding on-going transport. Minibuses only run from Butare to the Akanyaru crossing (to Kayanza/Bujumbura) on Sunday, Tuesday, and Friday mornings. The best day to get from Kibungo via Kirehe/Rusumo to the Tanzanian border is Wednesday (in Kibungo get a minibus to Kirehe and hitch from there to Rusumo and the border post).

Money

The monetary unit is the Rwandan franc (franc Rwandais, FRw). The mid 1992 exchange rate was US$1 = FRw136. There is a black-market. Remember that national park fees must be paid in hard currency.

What to buy

There are some beautiful woven baskets with pointed lids, clay statuettes of native life, masks, charms, etc. An unusual purchase would be one of the local pangas, *umuhurus*, which have a blade shaped like a question mark.

Accommodation

The only cheap places to stay in Rwanda are the missions or *Centres de Accueil*. Officially these are for missionaries on leave from their rural areas, so do not take it as your right to stay there, and try to dress and behave with some decorum.

African hotels are called *Hotel* or *Logement* and are usually very low quality.

Camping is officially forbidden except in established campsites: in Kinigi, the national parks, and Nyungwe Forest.

Transport

There are green modern **buses** from Japan (infrequent and slow), and **minibuses** (faster, and a bit more expensive) which run between the main towns on surprisingly good roads. Otherwise you must take the **minivans** which hurtle along the damp, winding roads. They don't leave until they are full – and that means 19-21 people! The bus station (*gare routière*) is always located in the centre of town.

In some areas there are **motorbike taxis** (*taxi-moto*).

With a large expatriate population, **hitchhiking** is fairly easy.

There is a **ferry** service on Lake Kivu between Cyangugu, Kirambo, Kibuye and Gisenyi. It leaves Cyangugu on Mondays and Thursdays at about 7am and returns from Gisenyi on Wednesdays and Saturdays. The full journey takes about 9½ hours and costs FRw780.

If you want to visit the Akagera National Park a car is essential. Car rental is expensive; the cheapest seems to be the Hotel des Milles Collines in Kigali, at FRw6,000 per day.

PUBLIC HOLIDAYS

Since everything shuts on a public holiday this list will be useful in planning your trip.

All Catholic holidays including Ascension Day and All Saints Day
Democracy Day – January 28
Labour Day – May 1

National Holiday / Independence Day – July 1
National Peace and Unity Day (anniversary of 1973 coup) – July 5
Umuganura Day/Harvest Festival – August 1
Culture Day – September 8
Kamarampaka Day (anniversary of 1961 referendum) – September 25
Armed Forces Day / Government Holiday – October 26
Justices' Holiday – November 24

TOWNS

Kigali

An unusually attractive capital (for Africa), Kigali has a lovely climate, some fine buildings and flower-filled gardens. The population is some 180,000. There is nothing in the way of sightseeing, but just strolling around is very pleasant.

The tourist office, Office Rwandais du Tourisme et des Parcs Nationaux (ORTPN), where bookings to see the gorillas are made, is at Place de L'Indépendence at the junction of Blvd de la Revolution and Avenue de l'Armée. For details on how to book gorilla visits see page 208. The office has a number of brochures and information sheets, some of which are in English.

The American Cultural Center, next to the American Embassy on Ave de la Revolution, entrance on Ave des Grands Lacs, provides welcome respite in the form of newspapers and magazines.

Sleeping and eating   The cheapest place seems to be the Logement au Bon Accueil on the Rue du Travail. The Town Hotel Restaurant, on Avenue du Commerce, is popular with travellers. Mission hotels offer more comfortable accommodation for a similar price: Auberge d'Accueil de Kigali (FRw300-600) at 2, Rue Député Kayuku is popular, but there are several others.

These places do not generally serve meals. If you are staying at the Auberge try the restaurant Umaganura on nearby Blvd de l'OUA: good and inexpensive local food.

Butare

This is the second largest town and the cultural centre of Rwanda. it is the home of the National Museum, the National University, and the National Institute of Scientific Research. The museum is well worth a visit (although the exhibits are only labelled in French and Kinyarwanda); open Tuesday to Sunday, 9.00-12.00, 14.00-17.00. Butare also has an arboretum.

Small, cheap places to stay can be found around the market and on Avenue du Commerce. Recommended are the Hotel Chez Nous, Hotel Weekend, and the rather more expensive International Hotel (FRw1,000 double, with private bathroom and hot water). The best mission guest house is the Procure d'Accueil de Butare, which is almost opposite the cathedral.

Kibuye

A wonderful place to relax on the beautiful and scenic shores of Lake Kivu.

The place to stay (probably the best accommodation bargain in Rwanda) is the Home St. Jean. Try to stay in one of the upstairs rooms which are more expensive but worth it for the view. If this place is full try the EPR Centre Béthanie. Both guest houses are well-signposted. Food at both is very good.

Cyangugu and Kamembe

These are two small towns close to one another at the southern tip of Lake Kivu. Kamembe is worth visiting for its large market on Tuesdays and Fridays. It is the country's main tea centre.

Cyangugu is the point of departure for Zaïre.

The cheapest place to stay in Kamembe is Hotel Inyelyeli, and in Cyangugu the best bet is the friendly Home St François. If you are catching the 7am ferry the expensive Hotel du Lac is convenient.

Gisenyi

This is an excellent place to spend a few days. It is beautifully located on the northern shores of Lake Kivu, where there is safe swimming, and offers a reasonable selection of moderately priced accommodation and the lake ferry.

There are cheap hotels but your best bet are the three mission guest houses: Centre d'Accueil St Francois-Xavier (FRw200 for a dormitory room); Centre d'Accueil et de Formation Gisenyi, on the Rue du Marché in the centre of town (you may camp here); Centre d'Accueil d'Eglise Méthodiste Libre au Rwanda, which has a beautiful garden for camping by the lake but is some way from the centre of town (though well sign-posted).

Ruhengeri

This is the access town for the Parc National des Volcans and for visiting the mountain gorillas. It is also a pretty area for relaxing and hiking. Its altitude of 1,860m ensures a pleasant day-time temperature and the views of the volcanoes are magnificent. The National University is here, and also an army training centre (so be very careful about photography).

The Centre de Accueil on Ave de la Nutrition is very popular with travellers. If this is full try the Home d'Accueil on Ave du 5 Juillet. Both are quite near the bus station.

HIKING

This is a lovely country for wandering on foot and seeing the rural way of life. The Rwandais are an agricultural people, with 95% of the population living outside the cities and dependent on subsistence farming. You can walk almost anywhere along local paths and will see every aspect of the working life of the average Hutu peasant, from beermaking to brickmaking, and from agriculture to forestry.

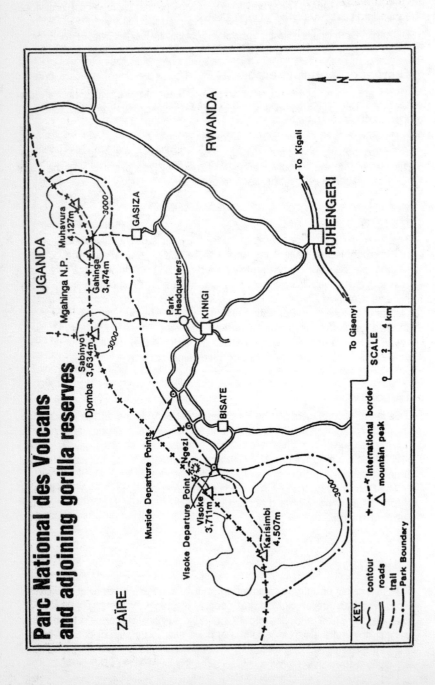

Parc National des Volcans and adjoining gorilla reserves

The Mabanza area (Ndaba Falls and river hike)

This area east of Kibuye is very scenic and this hike makes a pleasant day trip if you are staying at Kibuye. The Ndaba river runs into Musogoro river and then into Lake Kivu. The Ndaba Falls are 40 metres high, and have been declared a national monument. Buses running towards Kigali pass Ndaba, which is 30km (about an hour) from Kibuye, just past the roadside village of Rubengera. Ask the driver to tell you when to get off. You will see the waterfall a few metres downriver from a small bridge. The falls are on three levels, and with a bit of scrambling you can reach all of them. At the last waterfall you will see a small path running along the stream. You can follow this path, which is used frequently by the locals, through farmlands and banana groves, and past small settlements, which gives an excellent view of rural life in Rwanda.

The path has many steep sections. You cannot get lost providing you always take the path that stays closest to the river. After about four hours you will reach a dirt road (it runs between Mabanza and Birambo). Turn right and after about 3km another road joins it on the right. You are now on the Kigali-Kibuye road where you can flag down a minibus.

NATIONAL PARKS

The Virunga Volcanoes: Parc National des Volcans

The park covers 120 square kilometres, and offers hiking through remarkable scenery and mountain gorillas. The Virunga chain of extinct volcanoes forms the boundary between Rwanda, Zaïre and Uganda, and is covered with dense forest. This acts as a sponge, storing water in the wet season which provides irrigation for the surrounding agricultural land during the dry months. Ecologists are trying to persuade the local people that further encroachment on the park for agricultural purposes, as happened in the late 1960s when the park area was halved, is in the long run detrimental for the farmers.

Gorilla viewing

The Fauna and Flora Preservation Society established the Mountain Gorilla Project in 1978 and a consortium was formed with other conservation bodies, including the WWF and and the African Wildlife Foundation. This has turned out to be one of the most successful conservation projects in Africa. Great progress has been made, not only in protecting the gorillas, but in improving tourist facilities in the park.

Gorilla viewing is expensive everywhere and Rwanda is no longer much more costly than the neighbouring countries (although the cost of living/travelling generally is higher). Because of the perceived instability of Rwanda, this may be the best chance of seeing the animals since the trips are not heavily booked by organised groups. The current (1993) price is $120, which includes your entry fee and entitles you to spend three days in the park, one of which is spent gorilla-tracking. Only eight people may visit each gorilla group once a day, and may spend up to one hour with the gorillas. Since Rwanda has had the longest experience in taking tourists to see gorillas, you can be sure that the trip will be well-organised and your guide competent.

Gorillas and guerillas don't mix, and during the rebel activity in this region in the early 1990s there was much anxiety over the safety of the animals, especially after the park headquarters were attacked in February 1992 and two park employees were killed. The research centre had to be abandoned, which left the gorillas vulnerable to poachers, and wild rumours abounded. To the relief of conservationists the damage was less than feared. There was considerable disturbance from the fighting and an upsurge in the number of snares set for antelope; one gorilla was shot, and a few more died as a result of the disruption.

The peak months for gorilla viewing are in the 'dry' seasons of mid June to the end of September, and December to March. During normal times it will be virtually impossible to get a place in a gorilla-viewing group during this period. Below is what you do to ensure a place.

First go to the tourist office (ORTPN) in Kigali. They will tell you when there is next a space in a group visiting the gorillas. Often all groups are fully booked by tour operators but are not yet paid for. Since you are at the office, money in hand, you will be able to take one of these places. You may need to remind the desk officer that this is possible – and indeed sensible. You will have to pay in hard currency (cash or travellers cheque). If all groups are full the best possibility is to go to the park headquarters near Kinigi (two hours' bus ride from Ruhengeri) before 8am and try for a 'no show'.

Camping is permitted at designated campsites near the park headquarters in Kinigi (officially only for those with a firm booking) and there are also chalets where your possessions will be safe.

Looking for gorillas is hard work. Locating a group may take several hours during which time you will be scrambling up mud-slicked banks and fighting nettles and other hostile plants. Tough trousers should be worn (not shorts) and leather gloves are helpful. Whatever the weather when you set out, bring waterproofs. Water and trail snacks will add to your enjoyment.

Hiking

There is some excellent hiking in the park, and since your ticket is valid for three days, you should have two days in hand after seeing the gorillas. A park ticket without seeing the gorillas costs $16 but is valid for three days.

Trails lead to the summits or craters of five volcanoes, taking the hiker through various vegetation zones: bamboo, hagenia-hypericum forest, giant lobelia and giant senecio, and finally, alpine meadows. A guide is mandatory for all hikes, and porters optional, but recommended. If you are planning to camp out rather than use a hut, you must make sure the porters have some sort of cover. There are designated campsites.

The volcanoes and other destinations in the park are: Karisimbi (4,507m) the highest volcano in the range and the most strenuous hike requiring two days from the Visoke departure point; Visoke (3,711m), an easier climb to a beautiful crater lake at the top; Ngezi Lake (3,000m), a crater lake which involves a three or four hour round trip from the Visoke departure point; Sabinyo (3,634m), a ridge walk with dramatic drops on either side, and convenient for those without a car since the trail starts from the Kinigi headquarters; Gahinga (3,474m), starting point to the east of Kinigi; Muhavura (4,127m), a volcano involving a two day hike beyond Gahinga.

Akagera National Park

This is essentially an open grassland area to the west of the Akagera river which forms the border with Tanzania. It contains six lakes, some wooded valleys and papyrus swamp. The variety of habitat in this park makes it very rich in wildlife; amongst the renowned birdlife to be found here (over 500 species) is the whale-headed stork or shoebill. The rare sititunga swamp-dwelling antelope may also be seen here.

You can only enter the park in a vehicle, but for those looking for a relatively un-touristed game park this may well be worth the expense. Once there, you can take boat trips on Lake Ihema. There are several designated campsites (but are said not to be very safe); Hippo Beach is recommended for its views of hippos and crocs. This is a popular picnic area (there are tables, etc.) so at the weekend you may be able to get a lift here. An excellent booklet on the park is available from ORTPN in Kigali.

Forêt de Nyungwe

This lush forest in south-west Rwanda is the habitat of a rare sub-species of colobus monkey and 13 other species of monkey, and a wealth of other forest-dwelling animals. There are over 275 species of birds and, in the rainy season, over 100 species of orchid. The altitude is 1,600m to 2,950m giving it a very agreeable climate. It is well-worth a visit, especially for bird-watchers.

The park headquarters are at Winka, 55km from Cyangugu/Kamembe and 90km from Butare, so are easy to reach on public transport. The entry fee is FRw300. Inside the park you'll find well-maintained and sign-posted paths, huts, viewpoints, and several designated campsites for FRw500 per person (no facilities). A guided tour costs FRw1,000. There are plenty of streams to provide water but this should be purified. Maps and brochures (some in English) are available at the park headquarters.

Casper Hoebeek has written a comprehensive guide to Rwanda. In it he gives detailed information on all the towns and eight other hikes. This will not be published until the political situation stabilises, but if you are interested in a pre-publication copy please contact Bradt Publications.

MUSICAL INSTRUMENTS

To most people, African music is synonymous with drums, but although these certainly play a major part in music making, there are many other popular instruments that backpackers, with their opportunities for reaching remote areas, should see and hear.

The *sansa*, or thumb piano, is a simple linguaphone consisting of a small box with flexible bamboo or metal tongues attached. These are twanged with the thumbs, the resulting music being harmonious and pleasant.

Of the several stringed isntruments, the lyre is the most beautiful, and is still played in Ethiopia and East Africa. Two arms support a cross stick where the strings are attached.

Another popular and intriguing stringed instrument is the *massinqo*, a one-stringed fiddle. The diamond-shaped sound-box is covered front and back with cow-hide or parchment, there is a tuning peg, and a single string of horsehair. The arc-shaped bow is also strung with horsehair. The massinqo is quite melodious and you'll often see men fiddling away on it in various parts of Central and East Africa.

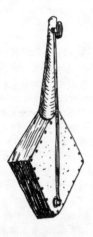

Those with a particular interest in African music will find a huge selection at Stern's African Record Centre, 116 Whitfield St, London W1.

Chapter 13

Burundi

1993 revision by Casper Hoebeek

FACTS AND FIGURES

Burundi is Rwanda's twin in size, geography, climate, population density, and tribal mix. Its history of intertribal fighting and massacres is even grimmer than Rwanda's – indeed, it is the worst in Africa – and at the time of writing the country is once again embroiled in conflict.

Burundi is a little larger than Rwanda with a smaller population (about six million) so the pressure on the land is not as intense. Only about 2% of the population lives in towns, the rest are scattered in the countryside which has a central plateau averaging 2,000 metres with mountains up to 2,600 metres, and lowlands along Lake Tanganyika. There is a short rainy season in October and November, then the long rains from February to the end of May.

People

Over 80% of the population is made up of the short and stocky Hutu who maintain their traditional rural occupations of farming and fishing. The tall and aristocratic-looking Tutsi form only about 14% of the population but are still very much in charge of commerce and administration. The two groups have kept their identity far more than in Rwanda, with few intermarriages, so the racial difference is very clear.

Music and dance are a strong component of the Tutsi culture. Drums and unique musical instruments (which, however, resemble the western violin and flute) play an important part in festivities and the Intore dancers have a reputation beyond the borders of Burundi.

Kirundi is the tribal language, with Swahili widely spoken. French is still the official language. The majority of people are Roman Catholics.

Recent history and politics

The early history of Burundi is the same as Rwanda, with the original inhabitants, the Pygmies (Twa) becoming dominated by the Bantu Hutu around the end of the 10th Century. The Nilotic Tutsis arrived from the north in the 15th Century and soon developed an overlord-peasant relationship with the people they conquered. A loosely organised aristocracy of 17 Tutsi kings (*mwamis*) developed, each with his own powerful army, ruling different parts of the country whose borders have not changed in centuries. The kings fought each other from time to time, but the Hutu led relatively peaceful, if oppressed, lives. German colonists arrived in 1892, and in 1899 made Burundi part of German East Africa, but lost the region to Belgium in the First World War. Under a League of Nations mandate, Belgium ruled Ruanda-Urundi (as the region was then called) until independence in 1962.

As in Rwanda, the whites found the existing feudal system much to their liking and made no effort to change it. Education and government jobs went naturally to the Tutsi and the peasant Hutu were given no chance to better themselves. The perception that the Tutsi were naturally more able and intelligent was reinforced, and only they were trained to take over power when independence was granted.

The murders and massacres that mark Burundi's post-independence history started two weeks after the first elections (held under UN supervision) in 1961 when the Prime Minister, Louis Rwagasore, was assassinated. Tension between the Hutus and Tutsis escalated in 1965 when it became obvious to the Hutus that independence was not going to bring majority rule.

A Hutu uprising in October 1965 resulted in an almost-successful attempt at genocide by the Tutsi. An estimated 100,000 Hutus were killed on a systematic basis which including all the most educated Hutus and the political elite. Death squads visited schools to select the brightest students for elimination, and the very act of wearing glasses became a death sentence. A further 20,000 died under similar circumstances in 1973 after another unsuccessful revolt. Thus the Hutu's attempt to become part of the political process was crushed until the late 1980s.

In 1987 a bloodless coup deposed President Bagaza. The new president, Pierre Buyoya, made cautious moves to improve the strained relations with the Catholic Church and some political prisoners were released. He also appointed four Hutu to the 20-member Council of Ministers. Sadly, a Hutu massacre of several hundred Tutsis in the north of the country nipped this progress in the bud: retaliation killed 20,000 Hutus and a further 60,000 fled to Rwanda. In 1988 President Buyoya continued his reforms. He brought more Hutus into the Council of Ministers until they formed the majority, and appointed a Hutu Prime Minister, Sibomana. A Council of National Unity was set up to investigate the 1988 massacres and promises were made to end discrimination in education, employment and – most significantly – in the armed-forces, over 99% of whom were Tutsis. Despite these moves, tribal killings and counter-killings continued unabated. Nevertheless, the first official opposition party was established in 1992 and elections were successfully held in July, 1993 after which President Ndadaye, a Hutu, took office.

The transition to democracy appeared to be going smoothly until October 21 1993 when an uprising led by Colonel Jean Bikomagu, the army chief of staff, and Jean-Baptiste Bagaza, the former president, brought about the death of the president and six ministers (one third of the cabinet). At the time of writing the surviving members of the government still hold power, but the Hutu revenge has been terrible. The government estimate that 150,000 have been butchered, mainly Tutsi, since the coup, and the UN figure for the number who have fled to neighbouring countries is 700,000.

TRAVEL

Impressions

Burundi has always been one of the least-visited countries in Africa. With no major sights nor distinctive wildlife, it retains its character untroubled by the demands of tourists. This gives it appeal for adventurous travellers, and although all should be appalled by its human rights record, Burundi is well worth a visit. Casper Hoebeek, who spent a couple of months travelling in Burundi, notes its advantages: 'Important brochures covering the national parks and reserves are being printed, an excellent and detailed map exists, new national parks and reserves are being established and existing ones improved, and services in Bujumbura are good. This lively town is a good place to collect visas for neighbouring countries. Budget travellers claim that Burundi is quite cheap, especially if staying in a tent, and above all the people are open and friendly, with none of the begging and trickery found in more touristed countries. The country is a paradise for hikers.

'In the countryside white people are such a rarity that children touch your skin wonderingly, and you will often be called *patron* by the older people.'

Warnings

Try to find out the current situation concerning intertribal fighting before going to Burundi.

Although it may seem alarming to go to a country where murder is commonplace, there is very little antagonism towards whites (or other foreigners) and providing you behave sensibly you will be perfectly safe.

It should go without saying that politics and tribal problems should not be discussed. Do not allow yourself to be drawn to expressing an opinion. The most acceptable and popular topic of conversation is money; your interrogators will be particularly interested in the purchase price of all your visible possessions and it will further international relationships if you suppress your own cultural taboos and tell them!

In theory the rules against photography have been relaxed; in practice you should be very careful.

Entry and exit

Everyone needs a visa and this should be acquired before your arrival at the border. It is simpler and cheaper to get your visa from the Burundi Embassy in a neighbouring country: Tanzania (Plot 1007, Lugala Rd, Dar es Salaam; next to the Italian Embassy at the back of the Palm Beach Hotel. Or in Kigoma at the Consulate by the Kigoma Hotel); Rwanda (Rue de Ntaruka, Kigali; near the Hotel des Milles Collines); Uganda (2 Katego Rd, Kampala; near the museum); Kenya (14th Floor, Development House, Moi Ave, Nairobi).

Border crossings

Most people come in from Tanzania, using the Lake Tanganyika steamer from Kigoma or Banda (near Gombe Stream chimpanzee reserve), but you can also enter from Zaïre (Uvira) and Rwanda. Border formalities are usually relaxed and easy.

Tickets for the ferry are purchased in Kigoma at the railway station. In Bujumbura contact the shipping office, SONACO, Rue des Usines.

Money

The currency is Burundi francs (FBu). U.S. dollars are easier to change than travellers cheques.

What to buy

Baskets are a good buy; these are often sold by the roadside in weekend resorts such as Kisosi. Otherwise the crafts are similar to those in Rwanda.

Maps

A Road Map of Burundi, published by Burundi's Geographical Institute in conjunction with the French IGN, is available from Stanfords and in Burundi. Scale 1:250,000, contoured, with index of place names and inset plan of Bujumbura. Pricey, but worth it if you plan an extended stay in the country.

Accommodation

There are few cheap hotels in Burundi so away from the largest towns you should ask for the nearest mission. The type of accommodation available is similar to Rwanda, but prices are a little lower.

Camping is permitted anywhere (except in National Parks where you must camp in designated campsites) and is generally safe. The relentless attention of the locals can be tiresome, so it's best to ask permission to camp in a Mission or to find a place well away from habitation.

Eating

International restaurants are plentiful and tempting in Bujumbura. Otherwise food is unexciting but acceptable.

Transport

The public transport system is quite good. As in Rwanda, there are green modern **buses** from Japan, and **minibuses** (faster, a bit more expensive, called *matatus* in other countries) which run between the main towns. Near the Rwanda borders there are **motorbike taxis** (*taxi-moto*). **Hitchhiking** is fairly easy, but if picked up by a local person expect to pay double the minibus rate.

Roadblocks are common but normally handled courteously.

TOWNS

Bujumbura

The capital is an attractive, lively city with the elegant boulevards laid out by the Belgians adding a graciousness that is rare in this part of Africa.

The Tourist Office is at 2, Ave des Euphorbes, near the cathedral. More useful is the Tourist Office Shop at 7, Blvd de l'Uprona, in the town centre near the Novotel Hotel, which has a good supply of tourist literature, handicrafts, postcards, etc.

Homesick Americans (and other English-speakers) will enjoy a visit to the Reading Room of the American Cultural Center on Chaussee Prince Louis Rwagasore, Tel: 223312.

There is quite a bit to do in Bujumbura, including the interesting ethnological Musée Vivant, and the Parc du Reptiles next door. A new attraction is the group of chimpanzees at the Jane Goodall Institute. These animals have been saved from illegal pet-trading and are rehabilitated before being released into a national park. The Centre is located on the Blvd 1 de Novembre, opposite the Garage daSilva. For an appointment to visit the American-run Centre phone 228430. Entrance is free, but be sure to make a donation towards this valuable work.

If you fancy a swim, the pool at the Novotel is open to non-residents and Americans may use the pool at the Embassy on Monday afternoons.

Sleeping and eating   Accommodation in the mid-price range in the centre of town includes Hotel Burundi Palace (2, Blvd de l'Uprona, opposite the Novotel) and Le Doyen (Ave. du Stade, near the expensive Hotel Source du Nil). For budget accommodation try the Bwiza district (the northern section of town). There are several hotels along Bwiza's 5th Avenue.

You can camp at the Yacht Club (Cercle Nautique) on the corner of Ave de la Plage and Ave 13 Octobre. Tel: 232059. Friendly and secure. But the most popular place is Johnson's Mission Kigobe/Kamenge, at the end of Blvd 28 Novembre (take a minibus towards Kamenge and get off at the petrol stations. Turn right onto R.N.1, then right again at a fork, then ask for directions). The Mission is about 6km from the centre of town, and the phone no. is 232059. Camping here is free, thanks to the hospitality of the (Protestant) Johnson family. They allow you to use the sanitation facilities and even provide a free breakfast. It goes without saying that this hospitality should not be abused. A donation should be paid at the end of your stay. In addition there are likely to be some household chores you can help with.

If you want to splash out with eating, try Cercle Nautique, on the lake. The best places to eat inexpensively are at the numerous patisseries. There are cheap restaurants in the Mbuiza district.

Gitega

This is the second largest town in Burundi, a very pleasant place with a cool climate and some interesting walks in the area.

The National Museum is here (but is barely worth the visit), and the headquarters of the National Parks (INECN). The office is located on the left side of the Gitega-Bujumbura road, and here you will find all the information you need on the National Parks.

The Catholic Mission, next to the cathedral, has a guest house about 2km south of Gitega, in Mushasha. Clean rooms are available at a reasonable price and good meals are served. The Sisters prefer clean and tidy visitors! A centrally-located alternative is the Hotel Restaurant Songa which is on the Gitega-Bujumbura road. More expensive than the mission, but very convenient and with an excellent restaurant.

Rumonge

This small town on the shores of Lake Tanganyika makes a good base for exploring the region. For accommodation there are four rooms available at the 'Restaurant' and two new hotels are being built.

Rutana

This is the base for Burundi's best hiking areas. There are two hotels along the road leading from the Catholic church, the one called 'Guesthouse' being excellent value.

HIKING AND NATIONAL PARKS/RESERVES

Burundi is the perfect country for people-orientated walking. Being so densely populated, there is a network of paths linking village to village through the beautiful small-scale landscape, and the opportunities for seeing people going about their day to day business are endless.

Gitega and Kisosi are good bases for this type of hiking. Casper Hoebeek has researched all the best hikes, some of which are described here. For the full text of Casper's very detailed Burundi chapter please write to Bradt Publications.

Day hikes and backpacking trips

Source du Nil (Source of the Nile) and hot springs (sources chaudes)

Although this can be made into a two day backpacking trip by camping at the hot springs it can easily be done as a day hike. The southernmost source of the Nile is located about 6km south of Rutovu, where there is accommodation (FBu2,000) at the Catholic Mission.

Take the main road out of town and look for a path to the right at the point where the road swings left to circle a pretty, cultivated valley. Several small paths run down into the valley (a steep descent – difficult after rain) to join the road that leads to the small pyramid marking the source.

From the pyramid look down into the valley and you will see some green vegetation backed by a range of mountains. These trees mark your next destination, the hot springs, an easy 2 hours away. The springs themselves are somewhat disappointing, being much used by the locals for washing their clothes! To return to Rutovu it is best to follow the dirt road around the valley.

Chutes de Muyshanga (Karera Falls) and Faille des Allemands (German Gorge)

This two or three day trip combines Burundi's two Natural Monuments. The Karera Falls (also known as Muyshanga) are four beautiful waterfalls, one 60m high, just south of the small village of Shanga or Muyshanga. German Gorge, at the village of Nyakazu, was the scene of the last battle between the Belgians and Germans during the First World War.

The trip starts at Rutana (see *Towns*). Take a minibus to the Shanga turn-off, about 19km on the road toward Gitega. Shanga is 11km along a pleasant track (you may be able to hitch a lift but plan to walk the whole way) which will take about 3½ hours. When you reach the park entrance you will be charged a small fee, then it's a further 2km to the falls. You can camp here, and there are some huts for shelter.

To hike to the gorge from the falls takes about 5 hours. To the right of the first waterfall you will see a small path. Follow this uphill, then through hilly country with many banana groves for about 12km to the village of Kivoga. Here you will join the main Kayero-Nyakazu road which you follow to the sign announcing "INECN Failles de Nyakazu". If you have retained your ticket to the Karera Falls you will not have to pay another park fee. It is best to take a guide to show you around all the gorges. Plan to camp near the gorges – it is a long walk to your next destination.

From the third gorge you should head for Gihovi, a town near the Tanzanian border, and the centre for sugar production. Although the way is all downhill, it will take about 4 hours to descend parallel to the gorge to the flat valley below, and a further 3-4 hours to Gihovi. For comfortable accommodation continue for a further hour to the sugar factory (*sucrerie*) where there is a 'Guesthouse'. The cost, for a lovely room with hot water and use of a swimming pool, is FBu2,000 (about $10). There is transport back to Rutana from the factory or from Gihovi.

The National Parks

For such a small country Burundi has an impressive number of nine protected areas. At the time of writing these provide good backpacking and wildlife viewing opportunities for a very low cost, but plans are in force to raise the park fees to a more realistic level to provide an income for improved protection. Before heading for the parks and reserves you should check the fees at the tourist office in Bujumbura or the INECN office in Gitega.

Casper Hoebeek has visited and described all of the protected areas but I have room for only three. For Casper's complete text write to Bradt Publications.

Parc National de la Kibira

This park comprises the entire Zaïre-Nile Crest and its mountains which are covered with high-altitude tropical rainforest. There are ten species of primate and about 200 bird species.

There are well-maintained hiking trails in the park, and many walks can be done as day hikes without a guide. The best short trails are in the Teza area. The strenuous Zaïre-Nile Crest trail should only be attempted with a guide and porters. It takes 2 to 3 days.

Park offices are located at the north end of the park, in Mabayi, in the central part, Rwegura (there is excellent accommodation here), and at Teza in the south where there is a good campsite and restaurant. The friendly staff at these offices should be able to give you the information you need. There are huts in the park but these tend to be locked so you are safer to bring a tent. Campsites are designated but have no facilities.

Réserve Naturelle de la Rusizi

Burundi's national park protecting a river habitat (and an estimated thousand hippos), Ruvubu, is too undeveloped for easy visiting. The small reserve surrounding the delta of the Rusizi River, described here, is more suitable since there are observation towers from which you can watch the wildlife.

There is nowhere to stay in this reserve which must be visited as a day trip. It is easily accessible from Bujumbura; take a minibus to Gatumba, a village near the reserve entrance. The park offices are located at Nyabisinda (on the Muyinga side of the river) and at Muremera (on the Cankuzo side). Bring snacks, water and your binoculars.

Réserve Naturelle du Lac Rwihinda

This is the place for bird-watchers, with over 300 species recorded. Boat trips are available at reasonable cost, and there is a campsite (no water, no facilities) by the lake. The nearest town with accommodation is Kirundo, from where you can hire a moto-taxi to take you to the reserve entrance about 5km away. Keen birders will camp the night in order to make a dawn boat trip for optimum bird watching.

Réserve Naturelle Forestière de Bururi

This large forest reserve is ideal for hiking, with well-maintained trails and plentiful wildlife including several species of monkey. It can also be linked with a hiking trip to the hot springs near Kiremba (see *Hiking*).

Access is via the one entrance just west of the town of Bururi which is 7km from Kiremba which has good accommodation at the Pentecostal Mission (*Mission Pentecôte*).

LIONS AND OTHER CATS

The King of the Beasts, one of the most sought after animals on safari, is actually one of the most boring unless you catch it in a rare moment of activity. Adult lions spend about 18 hours a day sleeping or resting! However, the social life of these animals is fascinating and worth knowing something about.

Lions are territorial, spray-marking the vegetation with urine, and both sexes defend their territory against invaders. A pride of lions is composed of related females and their cubs, along with one or more resident males. Young males leave the pride when they are around three years old and become nomadic, usually in sibling groups, until they have reached the stage of maturity to secure their own territory and females. They sometimes form male coalitions to achieve this, with very little rivalry between them. The new males in a pride will kill the younger cubs to establish their own genes in the next generation (the female being receptive to mating almost immediately after the death of her cubs). While a new male or males are becoming established in a pride the females come on heat frequently for five or so months without conceiving; this probably strengthens the bond. Mating is a casual affair, with little competition among males since a female on heat may mate around 150 times in the space of a few days. Births within the pride are usually synchronised, with mothers willing to suckle the cubs of others off on hunting excursions.

Social behaviour is highly developed, with the animals greeting each other in the familiar cat way of rubbing their heads and bodies against the other animal, and licking each other.

Alone in the cat family, males are strikingly different from females. This gives them advantages when fighting for, and dominating a pride, but they are too slow and heavy to hunt effectively so this is generally left to the females. Only about 20% of hunts end in a kill and there is fierce competition for the meat. Greater success comes when the pride hunts co-operatively, allowing them to surround and bring down large animals such as buffalo, which are killed by strangulation.

Unlike other cats, **cheetah** cannot retract their claws. This animal is built for speed. Their small heads, long legs, and extremely flexible spines enable them to reach 112 kph (70 mph) making them the fastest of all land mammals. In the evolution towards speed, strength was lost, and cheetahs cannot kill an animal larger than a gazelle (and they usually hunt only young, small animals) and they cannot maintain their fabulous burst of speed for longer than a short distance so depend on stalking their prey. They kill by suffocation, compressing the animal's windpipe until it is dead. Cheetahs are unable to defend their kill against other predators, and lose at least 10% of their kills.

Cheetahs are less social than lions, living in small family groups or alone. They are largely diurnal, habitually doing most of their hunting during the early part of the morning. In the popular game parks, however, there is evidence that tourist pressure is changing this behaviour. To avoid being harassed by convoys of vehicles, some cheetahs have learned to hunt during the lunch hour(s) when tourists are safely in the lodges!

The **leopard** is the most versatile of the big cats; remains of one have been found in the Kilimanjaro icecap, and they have adapted to urban life where they prey on dogs and other domestic animals. Their diet includes invertebrates such as beetles. The leopard depends on stealth to surprise its prey, and does not give chase like other cats. It then uses its great strength to pull its prey, usually gazelle, into trees where it is stored to be eaten at leisure. Leopards avoid confrontation and will relinquish their meal to a smaller predator.

Leopards are nocturnal and solitary, so not often seen on safari except near lodges where bait is put out at night, under spotlights.

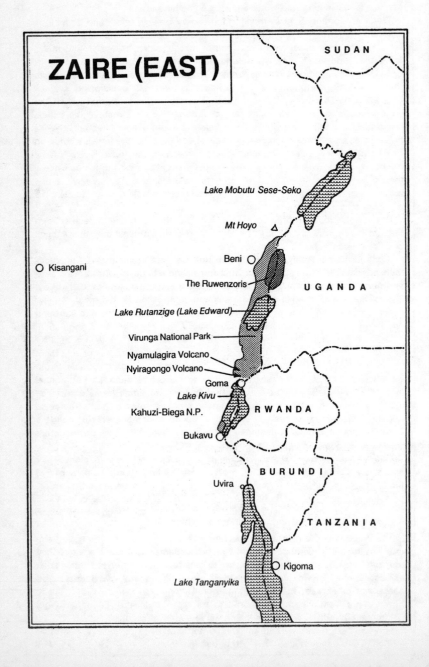

ZAIRE (EAST)

SUDAN

Lake Mobutu Sese-Seko

Mt Hoyo △

Beni ○

The Ruwenzoris

UGANDA

Lake Rutanzige (Lake Edward)

Virunga National Park

Nyamulagira Volcano
Nyiragongo Volcano

Goma

Lake Kivu

Kahuzi-Biega N.P.

Bukavu

RWANDA

BURUNDI

Uvira

TANZANIA

Kigoma ○

Lake Tanganyika

○ Kisangani

Chapter 14

Eastern Zaïre

Updated by Allard Blom

FACTS AND FIGURES

The former Belgian Congo was granted independence in l960 and resumed its historic name. The name 'Zaïre' is a corruption of the Kikongo words 'nzere' and 'nzadi', meaning 'the river that swallows all rivers'. The first European to discover the Congo River estuary, a Portuguese sea captain named Diego Cao, could not pronounce the words used by the local Bakongo people.

This is a huge country (2,345,409 square kilometres and the third largest in Africa) but sparsely populated (just under thirty million). 55% of the land is low lying, hot and forested, but the eastern part described here (Kivu) is mountainous. (For information on the rest of Zaïre see *Zaïre (Africa Handbook)* from Bradt.)

Kivu is mainly agricultural, with large plantations of coffee, tea, tobacco, quinine, bananas and pyrethrum. Zaïre's main exports are copper ('shaba' in Swahili and mined in the region of the same name in southern Zaïre), cobalt, diamonds, coffee and palm oil.

The driest months are from December to March, and July to September.

People

There are dozens of different tribal groups with over 300 languages and dialects, and many different physical types ranging from Pygmies (Wambute) to the tall Tutsi.

After President Mobutu decreed a national authenticity campaign the Zaïois abandoned their Christian names in favour of traditional African ones, and adopted African clothes and hairstyles which they wear with grace and elegance.

The official languages are French and Lingala, with Swahili spoken in the east.

Catholicism is Zaïre's most important organised religion. There are also a number of Protestant missions, mainly run by English and American Baptists.

TRAVEL

Impressions

Travellers have always found Zaïre to be one of the most challenging countries in Africa. No other country in this book can compete in hassles, chaos, and frustrations, but the combination of superb wildlife viewing (gorillas) and outstanding scenery makes it (sometimes) seem worthwhile. To get around you need a good command of French and Swahili.

Bribery is a way of life here, particularly where government officials are concerned (border posts, check points and so on). They are rarely paid so this may be their only source of income. Since Zaïre specialises in hassles, it also specialises in 'fixers' who are well worth their tip if you need to organise a complicated trip. But don't trust everyone who offers to fix something for you.

Warnings

Zaïre is currently going through a politically turbulent phase while efforts are made to oust President Mobuto. The country is indulging in its own version of 'ethnic cleansing', and in Kivu an estimated 6,000 people of Rwandan tribes have been killed. A coup or attempted coup is probable.

Entry and exit

All nationalities require a visa, and these are sometimes frustratingly hard to get. The Zaïre embassies in Kampala and Nairobi are favoured, but you may prefer to apply in your own country. Visitors popping over the border from Uganda to see the gorillas have no problem (see Chapter 11).

Border crossings

The most popular crossing points are Gisenyi (Rwanda) to Goma, and Mpondwe (Uganda) to Kasindi. The former is the easiest, since there is a reasonable amount of through traffic. The latter is fine for hikers.

Make sure your documents are in order and that you are in a benevolent frame of mind before you approach the border.

Money

The basic unit is the zaïre, divided into 100 makutas. Recently, due to massive devaluation, new banknotes have been issued. Travellers cheques are hard to cash; you are safer to bring well-hidden dollars.

What to buy

Wooden carvings are the best bet. Poached ivory often finds its way into Zaïre; don't buy it. Zaïre does not enforce the international ban on trading in live animals or animal products. Please do all you can to discourage this activity.

Maps

Maps are usually unobtainable in this part of the country. In London, Stanfords has a series of Zaïre reference maps, scale 1:2,500,000 (published in Moscow, 1987). These are primarily aeronautical charts, but they do provide good topographic reference even if all place names are not included.

Accommodation

Hotels are scarce and expensive. Mission hostels, *Centre d'Acceuil*, are often cheap and excellent. Camping is safe and permitted in most areas, if you don't mind 24 hour surveillance by dozens of curious Zaïreans.

Eating

The lush countryside with its many lakes provides good subsistence living: there are always fish, chicken, eggs, etc., even at out-of-the-way places. Zaïre is a great country for beer drinkers! Try the local banana beer too – it can pack quite a punch.

Transport

What transport? 'You'd better be into walking! Normal public transport is non-existent. Beside coffee trucks (between Goma and Beni) there are also mid-sized Dihatzu trucks that travel the eastern routes. Remember all these are dirt roads.' (J. Clayton)

If a vehicle does stop, always fix the price before you get on and bargain strenuously. Most roads are impassable in the rainy season.

Hitchhiking is very difficult because of the scarcity of traffic.

There is (was?) a steamer on Lake Tanganyika running between Uvira, Bujumbura, Kigoma and Kalemi, and also a boat between Bukavu and Goma on Lake Kivu. Check locally whether these are still running.

With all the problems of land transport, you sometimes have to resort to flying. Although Air Zaïre has a comprehensive and regular network of flights all over the country, most planes take off 24 hours or more behind schedule and are hopelessly overbooked. Each departure resembles a rugby scrummage and the restrained European often gets left behind.

Private air companies are much more reliable and often no more expensive. Scibe Zaïre has been recommended. To get around Kivu you may have to use one of the four-seater private planes that go from Goma south to Bukavu and north to Rwindi, Beni and Mt Hoyo. If there are four of you this is not impossibly expensive.

"The use of travel is to regulate imagination by reality, and instead of thinking how things may be, to see them as they are".

Samuel Johnson

TOWNS

Goma

For most travellers this is their first town in Zaïre, and a very agreeable place
it is too. Set by the north end of Lake Kivu, Goma is the unofficial capital of
Eastern Zaïre, and a resort town with some rather grand houses as well as
the usual African shacks.

Goma is the administrative centre for Virunga National Park which includes
the two nearby volcanoes Nyiragongo (3,470m) and Nyamulagira (3,055m).
The National Parks Office (IZCN) is located next to the Banque Commerciale.
Here you can buy a seven day permit for all the local parks. It is here that
you should arrange your gorilla viewing trip.

Bukavu

A large and attractive town on the shores of Lake Kivu. Low priced hotels are
found along Ave des Martyrs de la Revolution which starts near the dock –
the further you get from the lake, the cheaper the hotel. The market is also
here. The posh street is Ave President Mobuto, where the National Parks
Office (IZCN) is found.

An airport provides service to parts of eastern Zaïre if you're tired of waiting
for road transport, and boats to Goma (may) run three times a week.

HIKING AND THE NATIONAL PARKS

Eastern Zaïre offers some excellent walking and climbing, and if you are not
carrying much extra stuff in your pack, you can treat Kivu's roads as
marvellous hiking trails where you won't get lost and will meet plenty of
friendly Zaïreans. Several of the national parks are specifically for hikers.

A complication is the park fee system. To keep up with inflation, fees are
usually doubled twice a year. Since the rates of exchange (official and
unofficial) will change proportionately, this makes less difference than you
might think; the way to cash in on the situation is to try to visit the parks in
June or December, just before the prices rise in July and January, although
it takes a while for official word to filter through to the less-visited parks even
after the prices go up. Gorilla visits must be paid for in hard currency. Check
the travellers' grape vine for the latest prices.

Within all national parks it is obligatory to be accompanied by a guide. The
services of a guide are supposed to be free, but you are expected to tip
generously at the end.

Even the most die-hard backpackers are likely to succumb to porters on
these climbs; indeed, they *should* succumb since these men have no other
means of support. The rules (or traditions) are the same in all parks: visitors
pay for food (which the guide and porters purchase themselves) before the
trip and pay the wage/tip afterwards. Gifts of cigarettes are almost mandatory.

The following descriptions of the parks and their wildlife are by John Elwell,
written for the last edition (1990). They should still be correct.

Parc National des Virunga

800,000 hectares, and divided into three sections – Parc du Nord, Parc Central, Parc du Sud – each with its own headquarters. The entrance fees are variable. The northern section incorporates Mt Hoyo and the Ruwenzori Mountains. The central section includes all of the lowland plains area to the north, west, and south of Lake Edward (Queen Elizabeth National Park in Uganda covers all of the eastern side of the lake, thus it is surrounded by national parks). The southern section of Virunga administers the area of the Nyiragongo and Nyamulagira volcanoes, and some areas of the Virunga Volcanoes – home of the mountain gorilla.

Parc du Nord and Parc du Sud are described under *Hiking and gorillas*.

Parc Central – Rwindi

The majority of this section incorporates Lake Edward and its surrounding open grasslands, at an altitude of around 950m. To the west the area is bordered by a range of high hills (rising up to 2,800m) which are the remnants of a very old Rift Valley escarpment. To the east are Uganda's rolling hills, to the south are the Virunga Volcanoes, and to the north the Ruwenzori Mountains rising to snow-capped peaks at 5,100m. There can be only a few places in the world where so many diverse geographical features occur in such close proximity to one another. Many rivers flow into Lake Edward, but only one flows out – the Semliki. It is a large fast-flowing river that runs a short way north into the southern end of Lake Albert, from whence the Nile flows north.

This area also has some swamp, and small amounts of forest – mostly in the foothills to the west of the lake. Lake Edward is believed to contain the highest concentration of hippo in the world (30,000). The aquatic bird population around the lake is also an outstanding feature of this park.

There is one (fairly expensive) lodge in the park, and camping and walking are not permitted.

Parc National de Kahuzi-Biega

A relatively small park (70,000 hectares) situated at the south-western end of Lake Kivu, and known primarily as home to some habituated eastern lowland gorillas (see *Gorilla viewing*).

The highest point in the park is Mt Kahuzi (3,308 m), which can be climbed from Kahuzi.

Wildlife

Between them, these parks shelter an abundance of flora and fauna the diversity of which is unlikely to occur in any one area in the whole of the rest of the world. To list all these would be impractical here, but to give some idea of what you might see, the animals include: forest elephant, plains elephant, forest buffalo, cape buffalo, giant forest hog, warthog, lion, leopard, hyena, thousands of hippo, most of Africa's better-known antelope including dik-dik, duiker, topi, reedbuck and bongo. Among the smaller animals are civet, serval and genet cats, mongoose, etc., etc.

In the mountain forests are an assortment of primates: chimpanzee, baboon, mountain gorilla, and eastern lowland gorilla.

Birdlife includes a whole host of storks — marabou, woolly-necked, yellow-billed, saddle-billed, open-billed; also crested crane, secretary bird, and assorted eagles: martial, bateleur, crested and fish eagle. Also frequently seen are glossy and sacred ibis, egrets, plovers, stilts, ducks, heron, Nile geese, kingfishers, bee-eaters, partridge, superb starling, parrots, turacos, weavers, hornbills...

Some wildlife species found only in Zaïre are: okapi, eastern lowland gorilla, and Zaïre peacock. Species with a wider African distribution, but having Zaïre as their stronghold, are: mountain gorilla, chimpanzee, forest elephant, northern white rhinoceros, and giant forest hog.

[The description above makes recent reports of widescale poaching all the more disturbing.]

HIKING AND GORILLAS

Virunga (Parc du Sud): the volcanoes

Nyiragongo

Even when dormant, as at present, Nyiragongo dominates the skyline from Goma, and when active its orange fires light the sky at night.

Kibati (l,900m), the starting point for the ascent, is only l3km north of Goma and has a small restaurant and camping area. The chief guide here can issue a permit if you don't already have one, and arrange for a guide and porters. Although you can do the trip in a day you are recommended to spend the night in the hut below the crater (or, better, camp in your own tent, although camping space is very limited near the hut), and this is essential if the volcano is erupting so you can see its fireworks display in the dark.

Bring enough food for the trip, sleeping bag, stove, water bottle (large) warm clothes, a torch (flashlight) and spare batteries.

It takes about five hours to reach the top hut, up a well maintained and scenic trail. It's another half hour beyond the hut up to the crater rim. There is no water in the immediate vicinity of the hut (it's five minutes below) so fill up during the climb.

The next morning, as the sun rises, is the time to climb to the crater, if you are spending the night on the mountain, since the weather is usually clear then.

Nyamulagira

The climb up Nyamulagira provides a real African Safari experience, and of the two volcanoes, this is at present the most interesting hike. You must take a gun-toting guide and porters — a necessary requirement given the rugged terrain, indistinct trail, and presence of wild animals. The trip takes three days, two nights being spent at a hut near the treeline.

Preparations   You'll need a ticket/permit which is purchased in Goma (if you climbed Nyiragongo you should be able to do Nyamulagira within the seven days allowed on the permit).

All your food supplies should be bought in Goma (there's a limited selection of tinned food). It'll be cold on the summit, especially at night, and may rain at any time so bring suitable clothing.

The climb   Nyamulagira's base camp is 60km north of Goma, a singularly beautiful journey. You'll eventually hitch a lift there but it's no hardship to hike through this splendid scenery.

The first day's six hour hike is extraordinarily varied. You cross lava flows ranging in age from 30 years to ancient, and the growth they support varies with their age. The newest support very little, while dense, upland jungles flourish on the old flows. Smooth lava pools make ideal bath tubs, and very hazardous walking if at all damp. The view across the valley into Rwanda, through the fringe of volcanoes along the border, is spectacular. Buck, chimpanzee, forest elephant, buffalo and lots of bird life may be seen along the trail if you're lucky. We saw two species of forest deer and heard a troop of chimps. The guides are expert game scouts.

An enormous, rambling house is your camp for the night. The guide and porter(s) make themselves useful and cook their own food. They appreciate a pack of cigarettes at this point.

The trail gets a little wetter beyond here, and the vegetation changes suddenly. The tree line is only an hour after leaving the camp, then it's up across new lava and past recent cones. After another hour the crater's rim is reached. Looking down into the steaming, tormented landscape is an eerie experience, and you should allow a full day to explore the crater. There are steaming fissures in the lava, yellow sulphurous deposits, weird rock formations, and fascinating vegetation.

Another night is spent in the hut before the descent the next day.

Virunga (Parc du Nord): the Ruwenzori Mountains

This mountain range is these days more normally climbed from the Uganda side. However, some may prefer the probably cheaper option of climbing from Zaïre.

The headquarters of the park is Mutsora, a village now more or less engulfed by the rapidly-expanding community of Mutwanga, home of all the mountain porters. They are all mostly from the one tribe, Wanande, and are very hard-working, industrious people. The main business of the region is coffee.

The western valleys leading up to the mountains are very steep and densely covered in vegetation, and, apart from the one established route, the going is almost impossible because the carpet of rotting matter, fallen trees, prickly bushes and nettles sometimes gives way so that the unwary sinks waist deep or finds himself in a subterranean maze. However, the Butawu route described here is not too difficult (though strenuous) and can be done in five days. For information on what to bring, a map, flora and fauna, etc., read the Ruwenzori section in the Uganda chapter.

Preparations   You need a permit (available in Mutsora or Goma) and it is obligatory to hire a guide and porter(s).

Food for the five day trip is best purchased in Beni, the nearest large town, which has a number of shops. There is a good market twice a week in Mutwanga where fresh vegetables and dried fish are in good supply, but pre-packed food is difficult to obtain.

Of all the Zaïre parks, this is the one most used to organised groups so expectations of guides and porters may be higher than elsewhere. Come to an amicable agreement on prices, etc. There is little joy in hiking for five days in a state of mutual hostility. The same applies to cigarettes; porters and guides expect these as a perk and will fill the huts with smoke. There is not much that you can do about it. It would be helpful to provide porters with a strong plastic bag in which to carry food and other equipment; their bags will be anything but waterproof. Most backpackers prefer to carry their own sleeping bag and clothes – for safety in the case of sudden bad weather as much as to save money on extra porters, whose loads must not weigh more than 20kg.

It is very cold at night and firewood is virtually unobtainable. Bring a stove. Basic equipment, including sleeping bags and warm clothing can be hired in Mutsora. They also rent out good quality climbing gear (recently donated by the EEC).

There are four huts which had been recently renovated in 1992 but may have since deteriorated. If they are still in good condition it is not necessary to have a tent, although this gives you more freedom and is insurance against the huts being full. There is no charge for using the huts. A separate hut is provided for porters near hut 2, but everyone crams in the other huts together.

Weather   January and February are the best months as it is relatively dry. June and July are usually reasonably fine, but remember this is an area of very heavy rainfall. Proper clothing is absolutely essential.

Approach   From Beni take the road west towards the Uganda border. You will see the turn-off to the left, well after crossing the Semliki river. This road leads to the park headquarters at Mutsora where you can camp and arrange for guide and porters. There is no restaurant.

From Beni it is sometimes possible to hitch a ride with vehicles going to the border and to get off at the Mutwanga junction, 35km from Beni. From the junction it is 12km to Mutwanga along a level muddy track. Mutsora is 3km further on.

The ascent   The trail starts from the centre of Mutwanga and passes into the national park just above the town at 1,700m. For the first few hours you walk through monotonous plantations, so try to leave early to avoid the heat of the sun. After the guard post you enter the forest. Ferns proliferate, including the balsamine with its orchid-like flowers whose spurs often grow to a length of 15 metres. Begonias and huge wild banana trees (the fruit of which contains only seeds) are common sights. Monkeys are frequently seen, and lots of birds. The average temperature is 16°C here with very high humidity.

Kalonge hut (2,138m) is reached in five or six hours. On the second day there are giant nettles with ferocious stings to contend with, before you reach the bamboo zone. The young shoots grow at an incredible 30 - 50cm a day to reach their maximum height of around 30m in two or three months.

The bamboos end at around 2,600m and moss becomes the prevailing vegetation. It covers the ground, growing over roots, trunks and fallen trees like a spongy carpet. It is easy to put your foot on what appears to be a solid piece of moss only to fall through the tangle of roots and find yourself in a deep hollow. This is the hardest section of trail, climbing between steep moss-covered banks where the tramp of numerous boots has exposed a network of tree roots which provide both hazard and foothold in the mud. Ascend slowly to avoid altitude sickness.

Orchids, bilberries and heather also grow at this altitude, the bilberries as large bushes and the heather as trees six to nine metres tall. There is almost continuous cloud and fog, and the atmosphere is saturated with water, although it actually rains less than lower down the slopes.

The second night is spent at Mahanga (3,310m), just above the treeline which is reached in five to six hours. The worst stretch is the first one to two hours.

On the third day you head for Kiondo hut (4,200m) which again takes five or six hours. This building is made of stone, and only six people could sleep here in relative comfort.

The path begins with the familiar moss-lined root-tripping tunnel, then lichens become dominant and hang in grey-green festoons from the branches of hagenia trees. At about 3,800m you reach the treeline and the magnificent giant plant species for which the Ruwenzoris are famous come into view – giant lobelia and giant groundsel. There is clean water available from streams, and often the mist clears for some wonderful views.

This is the alpine region, extending to an altitude of 4,700m, well above the moraine. The daytime temperature does not rise above 2°C, and at night drops below freezing. There is constant humidity and the vegetation grows apace all year round.

At about 4,000m heather and sphagnum finally disappear and between here and 4,700m you see many deep rush-covered marshes and small lakes with names such as Grey, Green, Black and White. Dense low vegetation covers the uneven ground, with lobelias rising above it, the upper part of their long stalks (three to five metres high) covered with tight blue flowers. The giant groundsels, growing to a height of six to eight metres, would not look out of place in an alien science fiction landscape.

As you climb, the plants get smaller and less abundant, and between 4,500m and 4,700m only lichen survives, covering the rocks and often growing beneath the snow. Beyond this are only glaciers and eternal snows.

From Kiondo hut an hour's walk leads to Wasuwameso, a 4,450m peak commanding an excellent view of Mt Stanley's west face. This is the end of the normal 'tourist' route.

The final hut is Moraine Hut (4,350m) and is only used by experienced climbers. Stefano Ardito writes: 'The trail towards the hut is not difficult. It crosses the steep south side of Wasuwameso, with two exposed but easy passages equipped with fixed ropes. Then you descend to Green Lake (very beautiful) in one hour, plus a further 45 minutes to Grey Lake (around 4,300m), an excellent area to camp. Moraine hut is another hour away, but much worse than the lower ones – only a shack in a windy position.

'One day camping and exploration around Grey Lake is highly recommended. Porters and guide will go back to sleep at Kiondo and will come back next day to pick you up (make sure they understand before you start that this will be the arrangement and pay them accordingly). Fit hikers can go from Mahangu Hut to Lake Grey in one stretch.

'The normal route to Mt Stanley is within the capabilities of most trained and equipped mountaineers. However, the ascent to Stanley Plateau is less straightforward than most guidebooks suggest: the glacier has retreated and the first part can be a steep ice-pitch. There is also considerable stonefall from the south face of Alexandra.

'To do this 'mountaineer's route' up the Ruwenzori you should allow six or seven days (as against four or five days for the 'tourist route'). An extra day is recommended to give you more chance of seeing the peaks free of clouds.' (S.Ardito)

See page 186 for a map of the Ruwenzoris, including the Zaïre side.

Gorilla viewing

Zaïre has both eastern lowland and mountain gorillas (see page 192). At the time of writing the cost of visiting these animals is about the same as in neighbouring Rwanda and Uganda: $120.

Gorilla viewing is highly organised (as it should be) and you are more or less guaranteed to see the animals. Family groups have been habituated (ie, slowly accustomed to the presence of man) and you can get to within a few yards of the animals. This is a magical moment, and too many visitors spoil the impact by fumbling with their cameras. Try looking first and photographing later! (For good photography you will need very fast film; the light is poor.)

Gorillas are gentle animals, but like any species they can be dangerous if they feel threatened. Your guide will indicate how you should behave, but this usually involves adopting submissive gorilla-like behaviour, lowering your eyes, crouching down, and, of course, keeping quiet. (Although I must admit that in Kahuzi Biega I forgot all this when we were the target of a mock-charge by a young gorilla. I found myself with my arms in a strangle-hold round the guide's neck.)

In your quest for gorillas you will use the services of a guide and team of bushcutters. If you don't see gorillas on your first day, the fee entitles you to return until you succeed. This is no easy trip. Kahuzi-Biega covers a vast area of mountainous terrain covered with dense upland jungle. Djomba and Rumangabo in the Virunga National Park are a little easier and this is now the preferred gorilla viewing park. In each case the strategy for finding gorillas is the same: plunge into the jungle where the guide will look for recent traces of the animals. This is not difficult as they make large sleeping nests and browse slowly during the day leaving a well trodden path of destruction behind them. It can take up to five hours to locate a gorilla group (although the average is two) and this is five hours of steep climbing through the dense vegetation. Underfoot it's often very slippery, and you may have to wade through streams and swamps. Many of the plants have thorns or stings, so tough leather gloves are very helpful – you will often have to pull yourself up using handy vegetation. Bring a waterproof (whatever the weather when you set out) and some snacks.

Parc National de Kahuzi Biega

This is the habitat of the eastern lowland gorilla. The heavily forested park lies some 35km north-west of Bukavu near the southern end of Lake Kivu.

Unlike the Karisimbi area, Kahuzi Biega has not had a history of careful scientific work, and only one group of gorillas is properly habituated. Some reports indicate that this family are getting fed up with human visitors and sometimes show uncharacteristic (for gorillas) aggression. Mock charges are not uncommon.

It's advisable, but not essential, to book a gorilla trip at the park office (Institut Zaïrois pour la Conservation de la Nature) in Bukavu (185 Ave President Mobuto). Alternatively you can turn up at the park station, Tshivanga, on the day. It would be sensible to camp there, since you must check in by 8am.

Getting to the park can be a bit of a problem. There are occasional buses from Bukavu that pass the park turn-off at Miti. It's a 7km walk from here. Alternatively you may be able to get a lift with one of the wardens; enquire at the Bukavu office.

Virunga (Parc du Sud)

This is in a region of outstanding beauty with many volcanoes, the highest being Karisimbi, rising to a height of 4,507m (in Rwanda). The valleys and lower regions are fertile agricultural land, but above 2,500m there is only high altitude rain forest. This is the home of the mountain gorilla.

The gorilla sanctuary is run by the Institut Zaïrois pour la Conservation de la Nature (IZCN), along with the WWF. The gorilla groups are approached from two centres, Djomba, where 12 people a day are allowed to visit the two gorilla groups, and Rumangabo, where six may visit one group.

Djomba is 100km from Goma, the access town being Rutshuru (70km) which can be reached by bus from Goma. The turn-off for Djomba is about 4km before Rutshuru, and from there it is 30 km to the park headquarters beyond Djomba. If you don't take the fancy tour you will probably have to walk in and camp at the headquarters. You must be at the headquarters by 9.00 on the morning of your visit.

Backpackers will do better at Rumangabo. The trek starts with a beautiful three or four hour hike, through small villages and plantations, to the ranger's hut where you spend the night. It is in a lovely location, on the edge of the park, and even without the gorillas this would be an enjoyable trip. As always, you cannot predict how long it will take to find the gorilla group, but one or two hours seems to be average. For full details check at Goma.

OTHER PLACES OF INTEREST

By John Elwell

Mount Hoyo

Mount Hoyo is situated some 105km north of Beni along one of Zaïre's main arterial roads. This route frequently becomes impassable during the wet seasons, and is slow and bumpy at any time.

Mount Hoyo itself is actually not very high (1,450m), and is situated in forested hill country that stretches all the way up to the Sudan frontier, although the dense rain- and cloud forests give way to scrub and then savannah as you approach Sudan. In colonial times it was perhaps best known for the mining of bat guano in its vast (25km) labyrinth of limestone caves.

The area has, for many years, been home to Pygmies of the Wambute tribe. These people are quite familiar with the ways of foreign visitors, and will go to a lot of trouble to ensure that they are given a thoroughly comprehensive 'Pygmy experience'.

Most of the Pygmies speak Swahili as well as their own language, and some know a few words of French.

Traditionally, Pygmies are nomadic, only staying in one place long enough to 'hunt-and-gather' in localized areas of forest until supplies become low. The Wambute of Mount Hoyo, however, no longer practise this habit. Although they live in tiny stick-framed dwellings made entirely from foliage, they seldom move out of the area. They still 'hunt-and-gather' to some extent, but are now largely dependent upon trade with the local Bantu tribe of Walese, who provide them with some basic requirements in exchange for money (from tourists) and occasional work.

The Pygmies will take visitors on long walks through the forest and an insight into their way of life. They may also lead the way into the afore-mentioned cave system (home to millions of bats), or take people to see their villages.

Wildlife in this region is reasonably abundant although not easily seen. It must be remembered that whilst visibility on the plains may be 20km and more, in the forest one can only see a few metres ahead into the undergrowth. As well as the usual tropical forest dwellers, there are tree hyrax (whose nocturnal shrieks will make the hair stand on the most hardened traveller's neck), parrots, giant rat, various smaller antelope, and okapi. Forest buffalo, forest elephant, and gorillas have long-since been hunted out, but there are assorted primates in residence including chimpanzee. There is no shortage of snakes either.

At Mount Hoyo there is a substantial lodge with some very comfortable chalet-style rooms offering fantastic views over the Great Ituri Forest. You may also camp in the grounds or nearby.

A short walk into the forest from the lodge will lead you to the 'Staircase of Venus', a beautiful cascade of water falling from the forest above over a series of steps, and illuminated by shafts of sunlight filtering through the canopy of foliage high overhead. A swim in the pool below is delightful. It should be noted that the river that supplies this waterfall is dependent upon seasonal rains.

The Loya River

15km from Mount Hoyo, back on the main road, a bridge crosses the Loya River. It is possible to coax local boatmen into taking you for a ride in a dug-out canoe. The canoes are able to carry two seated passengers and two boatmen. They will punt the craft downstream to the point where the Loya flows into the Ituri River, and back again. On the way they sometimes stop off to visit a small group of Pygmies that have taken up residence on the bank of the River.

Parc National de Ituri and Okapi Wildlife Reserve

This new national park was planned in 1992 to protect Zaïre's national emblem, the okapi, along with 50 other species of large mammal and 329 bird species. Recent upheavals may have halted progress, however.

If all has gone to plan there will be accommodation in huts, a campsite, nature trails and a chimpanzee island. The nearest village is Epulu, where the park headquarters are/will be located.

Parc National de la Garamba

This new national park was established with the help of the WWF in happier times. Whether it has fulfilled its promises is not known. The plan was to have elephant rides (yes, trained African elephants) as part of the tourist experience, and nice rondavels had been constructed for accommodation. There are also campsites, and walking safaris.

This is savannah habitat with the usual savannah animals to be seen with the addition of the very rare northern white rhino (in 1991 there were 27 animals). There are 5,000 elephant, 30,000 buffalo, hippos, numerous antelope and their predators.

A branch of the IZCN should be able to give you more information.

Ishango

Ishango is a tiny settlement of national park personnel, situated at the north end of Lake Edward in the Virunga National Park, and set with a background of open grassland rolling down to the lakeside. Normally it comprises two houses built for the national parks, and three rest-houses for visitors, which overlook from a height of 15m the Semliki River as it emerges from the lake. In 1992, however, these were ransacked by guerillas and may not have been rebuilt. The description below should still apply.

'Sitting on the ridge above this river and lake in the evening is an experience that could not be bettered anywhere in Africa. To your left the lake vanishes over the horizon like some enormous mirror. Ahead of you in the distance a huge range of rolling hills stretches beyond view to left and right, beyond which lie the towns of Beni and Butembo, and behind which the sun sets in a spectacular blaze of fire and light. There are few places that can evoke such a feeling of vastness.

Closer by, in the immediate foreground, the river becomes alive with hundreds of hippo, and every kind of wild animal comes down to drink at the water's edge. The birdlife, too, is just fantastic.' (J.E.)

Suitable campsites are plentiful, so even if the huts have not been repaired, and despite poaching having depleted the wildlife, it is worth your effort to go there. The standard park fee will be charged.

WILDEBEEST

Wildebeest, or gnu, are the clowns of the plains. Seemingly badly designed in every respect (the mortality rate during the Great Migration is one in six) they exist in huge numbers so the Creator obviously got something right!

As always, the most interesting time to observe wildebeest is during the early morning or evening, when they are at their most active. Being territorial animals, they have to make sure they are not attacked when passing through another's area to reach water or grazing. By keeping the head low, they are demonstrating a submissive posture. Assertive behaviour, with high head and stiff tail, is used to herd females and to challenge other males. Most territorial dispute are in keeping with the wildebeest's comical reputation: there's a minimum of actual horn bashing, and a maximum of pretending to graze and think of something else, or showing off by gouging the ground with one horn. These "displacement activities" are actually a very sensible way of avoiding physical damage and similar ones are widely used by our own species.

CENTRAL-SOUTHERN AFRICA

Malawi
Zambia
Zimbabwe

THE ROUTE THROUGH MOZAMBIQUE

By David Else.

Following the 1992 peace accord Mozambique is opening up for tourism and travellers are now able to go the length of the country by public transport. This gives a fascinating alternative to the conventional overlander's route through Malawi, Zambia and Zimbabwe.

You will need a visa (there are embassies in Tanzania, Zambia, Malawi, Zimbabwe and Swaziland) and a lot of time and endurance since the public transport is still erratic and hotels few and rundown. This is changing, however.

From the north you can reportedly enter the country from Tanzania (though in December 1993 I had no first-hand information), and from the south there is a twice-a-week bus service to Maputo from Mbabane, Swaziland. The safest road is from Zimbabwe (Mutare) through Tete province to Beira. This Tete Run is protected by UN troops.

If you are travelling south, your best bet is probably to enter from Tanzania and make your way down the coast to Beira, then take the bus or train to Mutare. The route can be reversed for those heading north. This gives you a look at the marvellous beaches, off-shore islands and snorkelling of northern Mozambique. You miss Maputo, but that's no great loss.

The *Guide to Mozambique* (Bradt Publications) gives detailed information for travellers.

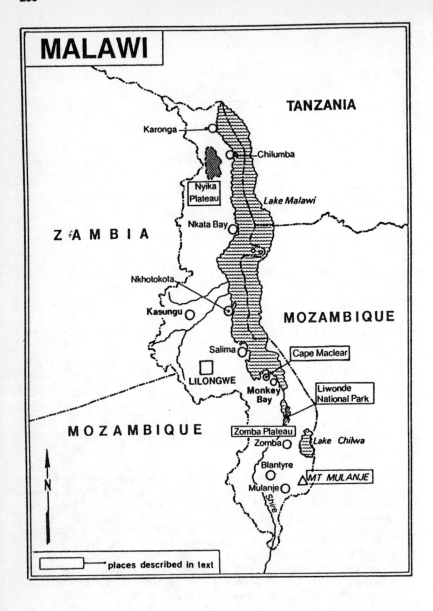

MALAWI

TANZANIA

Karonga

Chilumba

Nyika
Plateau

Lake Malawi

Z A M B I A

Nkata Bay

Nkhotokota

MOZAMBIQUE

Kasungu

Salima

Cape Maclear

LILONGWE

Monkey
Bay

Liwonde
National Park

MOZAMBIQUE

Zomba Plateau

Zomba

Lake Chilwa

N

Blantyre

△ *MT MULANJE*

Mulanje

Shire

□ **places described in text**

Chapter 15

Malawi

1993 updates by David Burden, Deborah Shaw and Philip Briggs

FACTS AND FIGURES

The name Malawi is derived from the word 'Maravi' meaning 'reflected light or bright haze' referring to the beautiful sunsets and sunrises over Lake Malawi. One fifth of Malawi's area is covered by Lake Malawi (formerly Lake Nyasa). The remaining land area covers 94,000 square kilometres and supports a population of almost nine million.

Designated national parks cover an impressive 21 per cent of the country's land area.

The capital city is now Lilongwe, but the former capital Blantyre is still the commercial centre.

In the wet season rainfall is moderate from November to April in the south, but the northern highlands experience up to 2,000mm of rain annually.

Malawi's chief exports are tea, tobacco and sugar. The country is more or less self sufficient in food, although poor distribution results in occasional local shortages.

People

Malawi is inhabited by several tribes, the largest being the Chewa of the central and southern regions, the Lomwe and Yoa of the south, the Ngoni in the central and northern regions and the Tonga, Nkhonde and Tumbuka tribes in the far north.

The official languages are Chichewa and English.

Half of the country's people practise traditional religions, 45 per cent are Christians and 12 per cent Muslims. About 95 per cent of the population live in rural areas and are subsistence farmers.

Business concerns still tend to be managed by expatriates. Gradually this is changing, and a few of the major hotels and tourist facilities are now run by Malawians. A large proportion of doctors are European/American: the government welcomes this form of aid.

Education is strongly promoted and although the school fees and required school uniform are a strain on many families, most manage to send their children to school.

TRAVEL

Impressions

Like most visitors, I loved Malawi, although those expecting exotic tribal people and abundant wildlife would be disappointed. It is the scenery, compactness, and relative ease and safety of travel which attracts.

In the previous edition Adge Last wrote: 'Friendliness and law and order are my main impressions... It is expected that visitors will be shown respect. I enjoyed the interesting, varied countryside – the lake, dry game parks and cool mountains all in a relatively small area.'

At the time of writing Malawi is coming to the end of an era. The president, Dr Hastings Banda, is said to be in his 90s. There will be changes before long.

Entry and exit

British Commonwealth citizens, Americans, South Africans and most western Europeans do not need a visa. The exceptions are Austria, France, Italy, Spain and Switzerland. You may have to complete a currency declaration form.

At the time of writing there is a strict dress and morality code in Malawi. By law men must have short hair and be conservatively dressed, and women may not wear slacks; their skirts must cover their knees. However, once embarked on a 'sporting activity' (e.g. hiking) the normal clothes for that sport may be worn.

You may not import any material considered by the government to be pornographic or subversive.

If you comply with these regulations, have an onward ticket or sufficient funds, a vaccination document for yellow fever (if arriving from endemic areas) and are not a journalist, you will have no trouble at the border or airport.

If you are leaving Malawi by air, departure tax is $20.

Money

In Malawi you'll spend kwacha which are divided into 100 tambala. Banks in the bigger towns will change travellers cheques, and some larger hotels will change money, if they haven't run out of cash. In the smaller towns and remote areas changing money is harder: in remote regions travelling banks pass through small towns and villages about once a month. Alternatively, travellers cheques may be cashed at the treasury cashier's section of the local District Commissioner's office every day but Sunday. British visitors may find sterling easier to change than US dollars.

At certain major banks – the Commercial Bank, for example – cash may be obtained with a Visa card.

The punishment for dealing on the black market may be severe.

Visitors may not import or export Malawi currency in excess of K20.00.

What to buy

Malawi has some very nice ebony wood carvings. The local craftsmen make weird collapsible chairs with intricately carved backs. Mulanje cedar wood chests are a popular item, as are ebony carvings from Mua where you can watch the carvers at work.

The handicapped workshops in Lilongwe and Blantyre produce good tie-dyed fabrics.

The country is land-locked, so surface mail overseas is slow (up to six months) and a bit unreliable; if you're flying or driving out of Malawi it's better to carry your purchases with you and ship them from another country.

Maps

The Department of Lands and Surveys on Victoria Ave in Blantyre sells excellent maps of Mt Mulanje and other hiking areas. There is also a government relief map of the country, scale 1:1,000,000. The latter is available in Stanfords Map Shop in London, and best bought before you get to Malawi.

Warnings

Malawi is not a land of law and order by chance. Visitors must comply with the laws and show respect for the President, and symbols of the Presidency, at all times. If you go to the cinema, be prepared to stand to attention, not only for the National Anthem but for the photo of President Banda that precedes the main feature. Do not discuss politics in public.

Observe the dress laws. Although you may wear appropriate sporting clothes *during* sports participation, you must still be correctly dressed when leaving the hotel. A long skirt over hiking boots looks rather chic!

At the time of writing (December 1993) there have been riots in Blantyre and clashes between the supporters and opponents of the present government. Things are changing in Malawi so follow current events when planning your trip.

Official AIDS figures are very low but Malawi is perhaps one of the worst affected countries. Blood for transfusions is screened for the HIV virus.

CHAMELEONS

Contrary to popular myth, chameleons don't dramatically change colour to match their background but to express emotion. Most of the numerous African species are green, a convenient camouflage colour for creatures that spend much of their time on leafy branches. Put on another background, such as a dusty road, they will change to a sandier shade of green but that's all. A chameleon in a rage, however, lives up to its reputation. If confronted by another of its kind, these territorial creatures change colour dramatically. A normally leaf-green chameleon becomes darker and spotted and striped, or it may change its colour completely. Then there is a the change of shape; when threatened or threatening, a chameleon will puff itself up, inflate its throat pouch (which is garishly striped with colour), open its mouth wide, and give a very passable imitation of a mini dragon.

Chameleons are fascinating creatures, and unlike most other members of the lizard family, they are very slow moving and easy to catch. It's most interesting to keep a chameleon captive for a day or so to study it. You'll see some of their colour change abilities when you catch one, but your first shock will come when you see your chameleon after dark. It will have turned almost white. For this reason dedicated chameleon fanciers do their hunting after dark with a torch when the reptile's light colour stands out in the dark foliage. A chameleon's skin reacts automatically to light, or lack of it. In bright sun it will turn much darker and you can "write" your initials on its side using a paper cut-out; the area protected from the sun stays light-coloured.

Watching chameleons eating insects is a constant source of enjoyment. Normally their eyes swivel around independently of each other, but once a chameleon has spotted a fly both eyes point forward to give the necessary binocular vision for a perfect aim. The tongue protrudes a little way, then zap, the fly is trapped on the stickly suction cup end. Chameleons can shoot their tongues out to a distance the equivalent of the length of their body.

Chameleons are not only found in the countryside. We visited Nairobi's City Park with the express purpose of capturing a three-horned Jackson's chameleon. It only took about ten minutes to find one, and we bore it triumphantly home in the bus, to the horror of our fellow passengers. Most Africans have a superstitious fear of chameleons, so don't expect any black friends to share your delight.

Jackson's chameleon

Accommodation

Large hotels, though relatively expensive, are good value. For budget travellers the local lodging houses are basic, but the government runs a chain of excellent value rest houses. Some, depending on their class and location, cost more than others but they're always reasonable. All come with camping sites attached, and usually a restaurant nearby. Forestry rest houses and campsites are particularly recommended.

Most rest houses will let you store your luggage while you go hiking.

Eating

'Malawian supermarkets are well stocked, and you can buy many things even in small roadside shops. However, we were struck by the near total absence of citrus fruits and the rarity and expense of other fruits like bananas.' (David Burden and Deborah Shaw)

Transport

Most roads are very good, and those in the north of the country are in the process of being upgraded. Express buses run between major cities; they are reliable and not too crowded. Local buses run everywhere; they are cheap, crowded and unreliable. A luxury coach links Lilongwe, Blantyre and Mzuzu – the cost and comfort is comparable with Europe, and seats can be booked in advance.

Hitchhiking proved both good and bad. Generally it's easier on the main routes. There is no collective taxi system, so pick-up trucks get used as transport, with fixed fares between destinations.

Provided you have a valid UK or international licence, cars can be hired at the airport, Lilongwe, or Blantyre, at similar rates to the UK.

Malawi Railways have services inside the country but they are very slow and cost more than the bus.

Malawi's main transport is on the lake. Two lake steamers, the *Ilala* and the *Mtendere*, carry both passengers and cargo between Monkey Bay and Karonga on a regular schedule. The route, the same for both ships, covers 1,200km and twelve ports. Each round trip takes six days. The ships are operated by Malawi Railways.

There are three classes. Third class should not be taken lightly: you'll be sitting upright on wooden benches for the entire trip. Second class at least has softer seats and even tables, but sleeping space is at a premium. We found it easier to sleep on top of the cargo under a table. First class is expensive but worth it, and is booked up well in advance. Good meals are served to first class passengers. For enquiries and bookings, contact the Chief Traffic Manager, Malawi Railways Ltd, PO Box 5500, Limbe, Malawi. Tel: 640844.

For second and third class there is no advance booking. Just buy your ticket like everyone else at the entrance to the shipyard. Food may be purchased on board (including freshly grilled fish, the remains of which are discarded with gay abandon all over the boat) but it's advisable to bring at least some of your own food for relief.

TOWNS

Blantyre

Blantyre is a rather bland city, 'the only place we saw where the market was more expensive than the supermarket!'

The Blantyre rest house is between the railway station and the long distance bus depot, about one kilometre from the centre of town. We found the campsite quieter than the main building. You can also buy temporary membership of the Blantyre Sports Club and camp there as well as using the facilities.

The Central Bookshop has a large selection of books and maps.

If you have a tent and want to escape the city's blandness, the Michuru Mountain Conservation Area, about 2km from the city centre, looks an attractive option. The mountain is criss-crossed with trails, and chances of spotting wildlife – including hyena and leopard – are good. Camping is permitted, as is hiking at night, when a number of more unusual animals may be spotted. Details and maps are available from the Michuru Mountain Club (PO Box 619, Blantyre).

While you're hiking for the day, you can store luggage cheaply and safely at the train depot.

Lilongwe

This is the new capital of Malawi, and as you would expect, a characterless place. This is where the embassies are if you need visas for neighbouring countries, and the National Parks and Wildlife Office.

Lilongwe Nature Sanctuary, which protects an area of acacia woodland between the new and old towns, is easy to get to and well worth a visit: there are a couple of day trails in the reserve, and a good variety of mammals and birds are present. Brochures are available from the education centre near the entrance.

Zomba

Once the capital of Malawi, and a more traditionally African town than Blantyre. 'The best market (very compact) and rest house (the government one, not the Local District one near the bus station) in Malawi!'(A.L.)

Livingstonia

A beautiful town with a good climate and superb views, Livingstonia is ideal for relaxing. There's a good cheap rest house with a campsite. There is plenty to see here: a museum, old buildings, craft shop, and the spectacular Machewe Falls about 5km from the town, where you can also camp. The 20km road dropping 1000m from Livingstonia to the Lake Shore is a good hike, especially if you stop at Machewe.

HIKING

The Mulanje massif provides some of the best hiking described in this book and its system of huts is perhaps the best in Africa. The very active Mountain Club of Malawi (run mainly by British expatriates) is another plus. And when you consider that after your efforts you can spend a few days relaxing on the beach by Lake Malawi, it's hard to beat! In addition to Mulanje there is another hiking area, the Zomba Plateau. This can't really compete with Mulanje, however, being rather civilised with a road up there and hotels on the top. However, there are plenty of trails and campsites and visitors short of time will probably find Zomba more rewarding than a hurried visit to Mulanje. 'In just a morning's hike on Zomba we saw almost as many butterflies and flowers as we did in five days on Mulanje' (D.B., D.S.) There is also Mt Michuru and several other smaller mountains for day walks in the Blantyre area.

One of the rewards of hiking in this country is the abundance of flowers and birds. On Mulanje there are 17 species of everlasting flowers giving permanent colour to the mountains, and 600 bird species have been recorded in Malawi. The tourist office in Blantyre produces a checklist.

The postal address of the Mountain Club of Malawi is PO Box 240, Blantyre, Malawi.

Mulanje Plateau

Introduction   Seen from the plains surrounding its base in southeast Malawi, the dominating granite walls of the Mulanje Plateau are awesome. This massif covers about 363 square kilometres, and abruptly rises to heights just over 3,000m from a flat cultivated plain at 610m above sea level. Whoever named Mulanje a plateau evidently hadn't done much walking over it, for the terrain is rolling and rugged.

The massif is well known for its unique Mulanje cedar trees, which grow to great heights in damp and mossy gorges. Wild flowers grow profusely on Mulanje especially amongst the boulder-strewn grasslands. In the forested ravines tall tree ferns and aloe plants with flaming red flowers edge the small mountain streams and cold swimming holes.

The area is a forest reserve and most hikers come across the woodsmen at work; ragged barefoot men turning hundred foot cedar trees into planks using only a crosscut saw.

Wildlife you're likely to see includes rock hyrax (dassie), and sometimes klipspringer and blue monkey. There is a profusion of birds, including the spectacular Knysna Loerie whose brilliant green and red plumage is easily seen against the dark pines. White-necked ravens are numerous and always seemed to appear whenever we rested, alighting very close and evidently expecting a hand-out.

About 30 plant species and several animal species are endemic especially among invertebrates, fishes, reptiles and amphibians. Because of this biodiversity IUCN (the World Conservation Union) believe Mulanje could qualify for World Heritage Status. A recent proposal to upgrade the Forest Reserve to a Biosphere Reserve is a step in the right direction.

September to April is the fishing season and trout can be hooked from streams on the Chambe and Lichenya plateaux of the mountain. Unfortunately it was out of season when we passed through but I did hear some fishy tales of the big ones that didn't get away.

The best months for backpacking on Mulanje are from mid-April to late September during the drier season, although haze from lowland bush fires obscures long distance views in the last two months. Hiking during the rainy season from December to March/April is possible and photography is at its best but the trails can be wet and slippery. You are advised to carry 30m of rope in this season because the streams you cross become raging torrents. (But unless you're familiar with river-crossing techniques, it's better not to try this. You're unlikely to have this much rope in your rucksack anyway!)

During the dry season, a thick, wet, cold mist known as *chiperone* can make conditions dangerous due to poor visibility and then it's advisable to stay put. It can last up to five days.

Seven Department of Forestry huts are located on top of Mulanje for backpackers to use for a low fee. Well marked hiking trails lace the mountain and from the huts day trips can be taken to climb numerous peaks where you can see some of the best views in Africa. The huts are spacious and built of cedar with a watchman living nearby. He will bring firewood and water, and wash your dishes for a small fee. Locked away at the huts are beds, lanterns and cooking utensils for Mountain Club members only, so if you're not accompanied by a MCM member bring all your requirements.

Porters can be found at all trail-heads by asking around and they will carry your things up the mountain at a set and economical fee. If you plan to retain them overnight or for several days you must provide food and blankets. It is more usual, though, to pay an extra fee and the porters will provide their own blankets and food. For backpackers, probably the best plan is to hire porters to take your stuff up to the first hut and show you the way, and to start early enough to give them time to descend to their villages that evening.

'I had a fantastic week of walking and

Knysna loerie

scrambling in the mountains. During that time I did not meet any other tourists for five out of the seven days. This solitude and the beautiful atmosphere, views and flowers made it a memorable experience' (A.L.)

'On Mulanje we were rewarded with some of the best hiking we have ever done. Compared with the hassle, expense and tourist mentality of Kilimanjaro, the simplicity, order and solitude of Mulanje was heaven. The size and scope of the place we didn't fully comprehend until we were faced with enough peaks and ridges to keep a mountain club busy for a year'. (D.B., D.S.)

Preparations   All the information you need about huts, fees, trails, porters and so on is available at the Likhubula Forest Station (Box 50, Mulanje. Tel: 465218) near Mulanje town. The Chief Forest Officer is also responsible for fishing permits.

You must purchase your food supplies either in Blantyre or Limbe, where there is everything you'll need, or in Mulanje town, where you can also find most things. Bring candles and cards for those lazy nights in the huts. You'll also need cooking utensils, warm sleeping bag, a pad or air mattress (you'll be sleeping on the hut floors) and small change to pay the hut watchmen and porters.

An excellent and informative 1:30,000 map called Mulanje Mountain Forest Reserve made by the D.O.S. may be bought from the Department of Surveys in Blantyre or Lilongwe; it is highly advisable to buy a copy, although all the huts have maps and route information hanging on the walls. This map is accurate and its walking times reliable. The Forest Department also produces a useful leaflet for hikers. In Blantyre bookshops you can also buy the *Guide to Mulanje Massif* by Frank Eastwood, which contains a good deal of information for walkers and rock climbers.

Directions   Mulanje town is easily reached from Blantyre or Limbe; buses leave several times a day but are slow and crowded. In Mulanje town you can stay at the Mulanje Motel, or at the tea-planters' Mulanje Club just outside the town, where you can also camp. You might meet somebody here who can help you with a lift before or after your hike.

Although you can walk or hitch to any of the trail-heads, you're supposed to go first to Likhubula forestry depot which is about 7km northwest of Mulanje town. This is where you pay hut fees, and the only place where porters can easily be found. To reach Likhubula, take the early morning bus that runs along the dirt road that branches off the main Blantyre-Mulanje road, although the road is sometimes impassable in the rainy season. Anyway, it's not a bad walk. There are three economically priced chalets at Likhubula, so you can spend the night there and be fresh for your climb up the mountain the following day. Nearby are some beautiful pools for swimming and trout fishing in season.

Routes

The Lichenya hut is five to six hours walk from Likhubula, with an altitude gain of over 1,000m. The trail is not steep, however, and passes through pleasant forests and meadows and across two streams. The hut is in excellent condition and situated on the edge of the Lichenya plateau. From Lichenya you can head for Chambe or continue your hike to Thuchila, five or six hours away. This trail goes through rolling country, rocky grasslands and wooded ravines. The views are splendid. En route you'll pass the turnoff to Sapitwa, central Africa's highest peak (3,003m). The name means 'don't go there' so we didn't. There's a small metal shelter near here. From Thuchila hut the Minunu trail continues to climb towards a pass studded with large lichen-covered boulders. You'll see signs here to Chinzama hut. There is a difficult but exciting route down from here, following the largest and wildest gorge in Mulanje, the Big Ruo. The woods here are magnificent and you'll pass the Minunu logging camp, and the new Minunu hut. Past here the trail is very steep and shouldn't be attempted in the rainy season. You'll reach Lujeri tea estate some five hours after starting your descent. It's 10km from the estate to the main road, but you may be lucky and get a lift.

David Burden and Deborah Shaw sent us a description of their hike on Mulanje: ' We took the Chapaluka Stream path up from Likhubula to Chambe Hut. This is a good alternative to the standard 'Skyline Path': much of the climbing is done in the shade of the woods beside the stream. Once over the crest of the plateau, it's a gentle walk through the forest to Chambe Hut. We got there about 3 pm, giving our porters time to head back down. The view of Chambe Peak from the hut is superb.

'Next day we did Sapitwa. The walk started with 7km and a 300m height gain to reach the metal shelter at the junction at the start of the 'Red Route' (the way to the summit is marked with red arrows painted on the rocks). Fill your bottle at the stream near the shelter – this is the last water. The bushes gradually give way to long and steep rock slabs. At about 2,500m the fun really begins: although you can see the main peak, the route to it leads round the back of another peak, through a miniature rain forest in a small valley, through a boulder-field that feels more like caving than hiking, and finally around a huge rock overhang before the final scramble to the summit. The views are superb and the elation we felt at having completed such a bizarre route was tremendous. We then retraced our route back to Chambe Hut, getting there as darkness fell after 12 hours of hard hiking. A wonderful, if exhausting, day.

'From Chambe we walked to Thuchila Hut, and then to Chinzama and down the Big Ruo to Lujeri. In all, five days of excellent hiking in what must be one of the best walking areas in the world.'

Zomba Plateau

'I enjoyed two days walking here and covered most of the plateau. There is a well-provided campsite near a hotel (and source of beer!) on the plateau. The views from the skyline ridge are excellent, extending to Mulanje 60km away, and to the rift valley and Lake Chilwa. Contrasting nicely with the plains are the ordered forestry plantations and occasional indigenous woodland thickets, and a pleasant stream and trout farm. Overall I would say that Zomba is worth a day or two – the altitude and resultant pleasant climate alone justify a visit – but it is tame in comparison with Mulanje.' (A. Last)

OTHER PLACES OF INTEREST

Lake Malawi

This huge lake dominates Malawi and influences all aspects of life in the country. Commerce is dependent on the cargo/passenger boats that ply the lake, and no visitor should leave Malawi without sampling Chambo fish. The lake contains over 240 species of fish and many of the colourful ones are exported for aquaria. This is perhaps the best place in the world for fresh-water snorkelling – a new experience for those more used to looking at coral reefs. Underwater viewing will be much more rewarding with *A Guide to the Fishes of Malawi National Park*, an outstanding book with numerous colour photos.

Lake Malawi is almost the only lake in Africa free from Bilharzia, so the beach resorts are deservedly popular. The dress code is relaxed at these resorts and you may wear shorts or swimsuits.

Getting There   The main port is Monkey Bay, which is well served by buses. There is a rest house near the bus stop. From there you must pick up local transport. If you are staying at one of the resorts below, you may be able to arrange transport with the manager.

Cape Maclear

The Golden Sands Holiday Camp, on the edge of Cape Maclear village, is the most popular place to stay on the lake with bungalows, cheap camping and a lovely setting. Snorkelling here is great, with lots of colourful tropical fish, and you can take a dug-out canoe ride. At the camp there are rocks to dive from and cold beer to cool you off.

If you don't want to camp, an excellent base is Mr Stevens's Rest House in the main village along the beach from Golden Sands. His phone number is Monkey Bay 01301.

It's best to bring your own food from Monkey Bay, although some basic staples are available in the village. There is a short but nice walk from the camp to Otter Point and another trail directly behind the camp which leads you to a remote fishing village about two hours away. Have a local person show you this trail. He can also show you the hippo pond not far from Monkey Bay. I saw fourteen hippos there.

Salima

North and inland of Cape Maclear is Salima. About 21km away, on the shores of the lake, is the Livingstonia Beach Hotel and campsite. The hotel has recently been restored and now has a swimming pool. Rooms are not cheap, but the campsite is very good value. There is a small market of sorts about one kilometre up the tarred road from the hotel. The local fishermen haul their nets in right in front of the camp and will sell you fish. We cooked ours on hot coals next to the beach, then a local boy took us on a two hour walk to a hippo pond and a fish eagle nesting tree. You can also take a boat ride out to the guano-covered Lizard Island where you can see fish eagles, hammerkops, and 4ft long monitor lizards.

Liwonde National Park

This National Park borders the Shire River, which flows from Lake Malombe, the southern extension of Lake Malawi, on its way to join the Zambezi. By East African standards it is not spectacular, but nevertheless is a nice little park for those unable to visit the more famous reserves of Kenya and Tanzania. It has the best concentrations of game in Malawi: mammals include elephant, hippo, warthog, and a variety of antelope including the impressive kudu and sable. This is also an excellent place for bird-watching.

You need your own transport to tour the park, or you can join a short safari organised in Lilongwe. You may also be able to hitch to the main camp, from where boat trips are available (which are anyway the best way of seeing game) and you can hire a scout for early morning guided walks.

The accommodation (self catering only) is very pleasant.

More information from the Department of National Parks and Wildlife or from a travel agency (see *Useful Addresses*).

USEFUL ADRESSES

Safaris, transport bookings, car hire, etc can be arranged through Soche Tours and Travel Ltd, PO Box 2225, Soche Hotel, Blantyre (Tel: 620777) or The Central Africa Travel Shop, PO Box 489, Lilongwe (Tel: 723527).

For maps, contact the Survey Department, PO Box 120, Lilongwe. (Tel: 720355), or visit the office on Victoria Avenue in Blantyre.

For enquiries and accommodation reservations in national parks: Department of National Parks and Wildlife, PO Box 30131, Lilongwe 3. (Tel: 731322/730944).

For general information: Malawi Department of Tourism: Delamere House, Box 402, Blantyre (Tel: 620300); The Wildlife Society of Malawi, PO Box 1429, Blantyre (Tel: 643428).

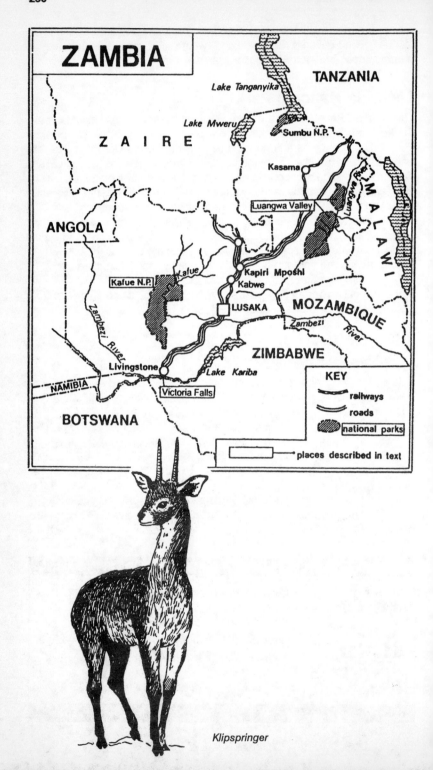

Klipspringer

Chapter 16

Zambia

Updated by David Burden, Deborah Shaw, Luc Lebeau and Philip Briggs

Note: *Zambia does not have much in the way of set hiking routes and trails, and (with the exception of the Lungwa Valley National Park, and the Zambian side of the Victoria Falls) the country has little in the way of tourist attractions. Consequently, most overland travellers pass through the country rather quickly, using it as a bridge between Malawi and Zimbabwe. Some basic travel information is included here to help you cross 'the bridge'.*

FACTS AND FIGURES

Landlocked Zambia covers about 753,000 square kilometres (three times the size of Great Britain), but is sparsely populated by five million people. Formerly Northern Rhodesia, the country gained independence in 1964, taking its name from the Zambezi river.

Copper is virtually the only export, and the low price of this mineral in recent years has severely affected the country's economy.

The dry season is from April through October.

In the Luangwa Valley, Zambia has one of Africa's best – and least visited – game parks. Until recently this was the last stronghold of the black rhino, but heavy poaching has drastically reduced the numbers.

People

There are four main tribes, the Lozi, Tonga, Bemba and Ngoni, who speak their own languages with over 70 dialects. English remains the official language and is widely spoken. Christianity is the predominant religion.

TRAVEL

Impressions

Budget travellers rarely stay long in Zambia, but it is a popular gateway country with access to Burundi, Tanzania, Zaïre, Malawi, Botswana, and

Zimbabwe (as well as Mozambique and Angola). With so many border options it is a shame that many travellers report problems with Zambian officials, although in the last edition Jim Noakes and Claudine Combrie wrote: 'We had no problems whatsoever in Zambia, with immigration, police, or people generally. We did not attempt a single photo and kept our camera hidden from view. It seems that most problems are caused by photographs. We found the people lively and the fastest to get on and off buses in Africa! (No touring around town looking for more passengers.) Good roads and well developed cities (Ndola is amazing).'

Jim and Claudine went on to say that they found the scenery boring, but perhaps they should have looked further. Peter Moss wrote: 'Zambia has an extremely pleasant climate. It is a land of wild rivers, lakes, waterfalls, forests, and spectacular animals (over 200 species of mammals, 720 species of birds) and has 18 national parks, including Luangwa Valley, which is one of Africa's best.'

Philip Briggs adds a few more thoughts on this subject:

'When I was in Zambia in 1989, I enjoyed myself, had no problems, and everyone I met who had spent some time in the country liked it. I suspect the negative attitude most travellers have towards Zambia is slightly self-perpetuating; everyone rushes through because of what they've heard, and consequently don't have the time to form much of an impression. That said, in 1989 cameras were best kept at the bottom of your pack, and anything vaguely suspicious or unusual (computer discs and scuba diving tanks are two I've heard of) would be likely to invite questions.

'In the past, the main reason for apparent suspicion of whites in Zambia has been that they might be South African spies. This is understandable: the ANC were based in Lusaka, and it was undoubtedly a target for South African Intelligence. Relations between Zambia and South Africa are vastly improved now; combined with the newly and democratically elected Zambian government this suggests that attitudes to travellers could well have improved.' I've had no recent letters to confirm or refute this, but if you are approaching Zambia from any of its neighbouring countries you should get an up-to-date picture from travellers you meet. Zambia sees few tourists yet has tremendous potential for backpacking and game-viewing: assuming things have improved, it should definitely be approached with an open mind.

Entry and exit

Visas are required by all but British, Irish and Commonwealth visitors. To avoid border hassles it is advisable to get your visa before arriving in Zambia.

Zambia Airways has an unusually good regional and international network of flights, including direct flights from New York and Frankfurt, Germany.

An onward ticket is often requested by immigration authorities.

Border crossings

Be particularly careful that your papers are in order before approaching a Zambian land border. The most popular routes into adjacent countries are on Lake Tanganyika (an interesting way to get to Burundi or Tanzania), by

TAZARA train (see *Transport*), by direct bus from Lusaka to Lilongwe (Malawi), and – most popular – to Zimbabwe or Botswana via the Victoria Falls.

Money

The currency is the Zambian kwacha, divided into 100 ngwee. Change only small quantities at a time since it's hard to get rid of kwachas once you leave the country. The black market offers twice the bank rate for dollars, but penalties for changing illegally are very high.

You are not permitted to take more than 10 kwacha out of the country.

What to buy

Zambian handicrafts are not particularly exciting but attractive copper goods can be found, particularly in Livingstone and the main hotels. The Lozi tribe are noted for its wood carvings.

Maps

The Department of Lands and Surveys is in Malungushi House, Independence Ave and sells a range of maps. The only maps available in London are air navigation charts (1:1,000,000) which show topographical features, but not all place names.

Accommodation

Government rest houses are moderately priced and found in most towns; otherwise hotels tend to be expensive.

Transport

The famous Chinese built TanZam Freedom Railway (now called the TAZARA) carries mainly freight (copper) between Kapiri Mposhi in Zambia's Central Province 150 kilometres north of Lusaka (the nearest town is Kabwe) and Dar es Salaam. It takes 48 hours for the full journey.

The train is inexpensive and goes twice a week. Schedule information from the booking office in Lusaka, on Cairo Rd, near the post office. Zambia Railways runs a daily service between Kitwe and Livingstone via Lusaka; it is this train that brings you into Lusaka from Kapiri Mposhi.

There are numerous buses running on unreliable schedules. Hitchhiking is fairly easy.

Warning

There are reports that robbery and mugging are common in large towns, especially in Lusaka, and I have also received a letter saying the the main road between Lusaka and the Malawi border at Chitapa was dangerous due to 'infiltrations' by Mozambique bandits, and that there were newspaper reports of villages in the area being attacked and rumours of a bus on this route being shot up. Vehicles using the road were forced to travel under army escort for protection. It would be sensible to make enquiries locally before using this route.

TOWNS

Lusaka

There is nothing special to see or do in Zambia's capital, although the National Botanic Gardens at Nunda Wanga are well worth a visit. For accommodation the Salvation Army hostel along Cairo Rd is recommended. There's a campsite 7km south of Lusaka on the Livingstone road, and a number of cheaper hotels on the city outskirts.

Livingstone

The access town for the Victoria Falls, this is a pleasant enough place with a good rest house. Most travellers, however, make for the camp site at Rainbow Lodge, on the banks of the Zambezi, just upstream from the Victoria Falls. The lodge restaurant is good value if you fancy a splurge. You can also take a boat ride in the evening. Nearby is the much more expensive Inter-Continental Hotel.

In the town itself, the National Museum and Maramba Cultural Centre, full of David Livingstone memorabilia, is worth seeing.

Mpulungu

You may well spend a few days at this small town on the south of Lake Tanganyika if you are waiting for the ferry. There are the usual lodgings in town, more attractive though to camp or rent a chalet in the garden of a very friendly person, Denish, about 1km out of town – ask around for directions.

HIKING

There are few wilderness areas accessible to unguided hikers in Zambia, and at present you must get permission from the local District Governor. The situation might well change, however, and expatriates working in Zambia claim there are plenty of good hiking areas. The main difficulty is that you need your own vehicle. Readers would do better to consider the foot safaris in Luangwa Valley National Park. These are probably the best of all foot safaris offered in Africa.

NATIONAL PARKS

Luangwa Valley

This national park lies along the Luangwa River, a tributary of the Zambezi, and supports more than a hundred species of mammal and four times as many birds. It is a beautiful area, with shady woodlands, lagoons and expanses of savannah.

Luangwa Valley National Park is 575km east of Lusaka, so the most practical way of getting there is to fly from the capital (people have tried hitching, but lifts are few and far between). Foot safaris, or wilderness trails, are organised by the Safari Lodges, and may be done from a base camp, or progress through the bush from camp to camp for up to a week. The months for a foot safari are June to October when the short grasses enable visitors to have a clear view of the animals (June is the coolest month, October the hottest).

These safaris are heavily booked so you are advised to apply well in advance to your nearest Zambian Tourist Board. In Britain the address is 2, Palace Gate, London W8 5NG; Tel: 071 589 6343.

If you are travelling through Malawi, it is also possible to arrange safaris to Luangwa from Lilongwe (it's much nearer than Lusaka!). Companies to contact are: Land and Lake Safaris, P.O. Box 2140, Lilongwe, Tel 723459; Central African Wilderness Safaris, PO Box 489, Lilongwe, Tel 723527.

Kafue National Park

Noted for its scenery, large range of habitats (the park is the size of Wales), huge herds of buffalo (up to 3,000 animals), and 420 species of birds, Kafue is also the place to see the less familiar southern species of antelope, such as the greater kudu and the lechwe (among many others). An artificially formed lake, Itezhitezhi (the result of a hydro reservoir) provides boating and fishing, as well as bird watching.

OTHER PLACES OF INTEREST

Victoria Falls

One of the greatest sights in the world, the Vic Falls should not be missed by anyone in this part of Africa. Even if you are planning to cross over to Zimbabwe, it's worth spending a day or two on the Zambian side first: it's far less touristy. Luc Lebeau wrote: 'We preferred the Zambian side of the Vic Falls. It was very calm and peaceful, more natural, less organised, no fees, with nice views of the river's meanderings'.

A day visit to the Zimbabwean side involves no border hassle (but remember not to take more than 10 kwacha with you). From the bridge between the two countries you can see the full majesty of the Zambezi River, a mile wide above the falls, dropping 100 metres into a narrow gorge.

You can view the falls from every angle, including above: on the Zimbabwe side a small plane takes you on a 'Flight of the Angels'. There are also white water rafting trips below the falls (1 to 7 days) as well as river cruises, canoe trips and more mundane walks along the banks.

Mbala and Kalambo Falls

The Mbala area by Lake Tanganyika is very pretty and the Kalambo Falls, 220 metres high (720 feet), well worth a visit.

Kariba

Here, by the huge man-made lake that was formed when the Zambezi was dammed, you'll find a kind of coastal resort with hotels, campsites, boating and fishing – and a popular gateway to Zimbabwe.

GIRAFFE

Herd structures are loose, and giraffes display little interesting social behaviour, apart from "necking" when sparring males bang heads and horns with resounding thuds. The horns of the male are much thicker than those of females (which have elegant little black-tipped horns) for this purpose. In addition a male has a horn in the middle of his forehead and four smaller bumps.

It is always fascinating to watch giraffes feeding: a full sized animal can eat foliage six metres (20 feet) above the ground, his 45cm (18 inch) purple prehensile tongue giving him the extra reach and dexterity. The giraffe's appealingly long eyelashes are probably a protection against thorns when browsing their favourite acacia trees. Watch how carefully they avoid damaging their tongues on thorns, and how skilfully they pull off the leaves by wrapping their prehensile tongues around them and jerking their heads back so the twigs are cut off by the lower incisors. Like a cow, giraffes must regurgitate their food and chew the cud. You can see the boluses travelling up and down the long neck.

Giraffes are unusual in that they "pace" rather than "trot": the fore and hind leg of each side are moved forward together.

MEASUREMENTS AND CONVERSIONS

Most of Africa uses metric measurements, and so have we throughout this book. I know that many people (myself included) still think the old way, so here are some helpful formulae and tables. Many peopl will want to convert metres to the more familiar feet. If you remember that 3 metres is 9.84 feet or just under 10 feet you can do an approximate conversion quickly; to convert heights shown in metres to feet, divide by 3 and add a zero, eg 6,000 metres = 20,000 feet.

Conversion formulae

To convert	Multiply by
Inches to centimetres	2.540
Centimetres to inches	0.3937
Feet to metres	0.3048
Metres to feet	3.281
Yards to metres	0.9144
Metres to yards	1.094
Miles to kilometres	1.609
Kilometres to miles	0.6214
Acres to hectares	0.4047
Hectares to acres	2.471
Gallons to litres	4.546
Litres to gallons	0.22
Ounces to grams	28.35
Grams on ounces	0.03527
Pounds to grams	453.6
Grams to pounds	0.002205
Pounds to kilograms	0.4536
Kilograms to pounds	2.205

Temperature conversion tables

The bold figures in the central column can be read as either centrigrade or fahrenheit.

Centrigrade		Fahrenheit
-18	**0**	32
-15	**5**	41
-12	**10**	50
-9	**15**	59
-7	**20**	68
-4	**25**	77
-1	**30**	86
2	**35**	95
4	**40**	100
7	**45**	113
10	**50**	122
13	**55**	131
16	**60**	140
18	**65**	149
21	**70**	158
24	**75**	167
27	**80**	176
32	**90**	194
38	**100**	212
40	**104**	

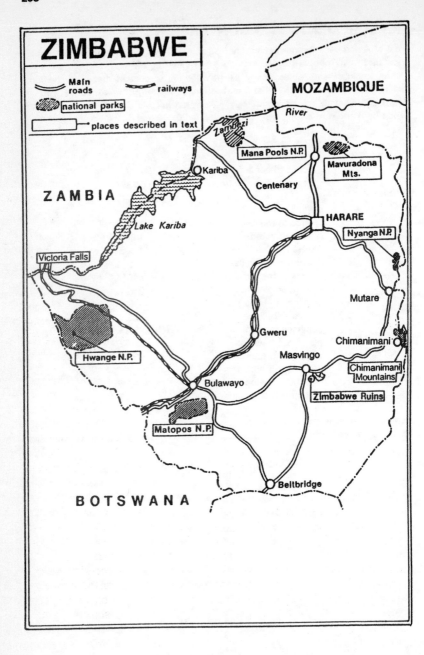

Chapter 17

Zimbabwe

By Simon Atkins

FACTS AND FIGURES

Land-locked Zimbabwe, with a total land area of 390,000 square kilometres, is slightly larger than Great Britain and sits on a high plateau between the Zambezi and Limpopo rivers, with a range of mountains rising to 2,592 metres forming its eastern border with Mozambique. Geographically the country is normally divided into three regions based on altitude: the lowveld (300m to 900m); the middleveld (900m to 1,200m); and the highveld (1,200m to 2,000m). The main towns and centres are all in the middle to highveld, which are cooler than the semi-tropical lowlands.

Being south of the equator, the cold season is from May to September, characterised by warm sunny days and cool nights. The hot season is from October to March, with storms and rain from December until mid-March. Day temperatures in summer generally range from 25°C in the highveld to 35°C in the Zambezi valley and lowveld, and from 10°C to 20°C in winter, when frost is common in the mountains.

Most of the country is covered with small trees and bush, punctuated by striking domed granite outcrops (*kopjes* or *koppies*) particularly in the east and in Matopos National Park. Agriculture and mining are the country's most important industries, with tobacco the largest foreign currency earning export. The economy is, however, diversified, largely as a result of the trade sanctions which were imposed on Rhodesia before independence forcing the country to become largely self-sufficient in all essential goods.

Zimbabwe became independent in 1980 after fifteen years of guerrilla warfare, with Robert Mugabe becoming the new country's first Prime Minister. During the mid 1980s clashes erupted between the two dominant political wings – ZANU led by Mugabe, and ZAPU led by Joshua N'komo – representing the two main ethnic groups of the Shona and Ndebele peoples. Following constitutional changes at the end of 1987, the Unity Agreement merged ZANU and ZAPU to make ZANU PF with Mugabe as president and N'komo vice-president. This put a halt to the 'dissident activity'. The 1990s have seen disenchantment as Zimbabweans face price increases for basic commodities, spiralling youth unemployment and increasing foreign debt.

People

The population of Zimbabwe is about ten million, but growing rapidly with one of the highest birth rates in Africa. The two main ethnic groups are the Shona (70%) and the Ndebele (20%), the latter being concentrated in Matebeleland around Bulawayo. Most of the black population is rurally based, or in low-waged urban jobs, although there are an increasing number taking well-paid jobs in the public and private sectors. There are about 100,000 white Zimbabweans, mainly commercial farmers and business owners, who together with the Tonga people on the shores of Lake Kariba, Asian Zimbabweans and immigrant workers make up the remainder of the population.

TRAVEL

Impressions

After living, working, and travelling in Zimbabwe, I still think it is a marvellous country to spend time in. Excellent roads and infrastructure make travelling a pleasure, though they conceal the striking contrasts between 'first world' towns and 'third world' rural areas.

Zimbabwe offers a real opportunity for the backpacker to get right off the beaten track with the minimum of hassle; much of the finest scenery and trekking is easily accessible through several well established national parks. Tourism and the number of travellers is, however, on the increase, and Harare has become the de facto traveller's capital of southern Africa.

Warnings

Zimbabwe is politically stable and one of the safest countries in Africa. Following the peace agreements in neighbouring Mozambique between rebel RENAMO (MNR) forces and the government army (FRELIMO) there is no terrorist activity in Zimbabwe even on the previously troubled Mozambique border.

In the main centres and tourist destinations, however, theft is increasingly common and all travellers should take great care of professional *tsotsies* or thieves who work in highly organised teams and will employ all manner of tricks to relieve you of your belongings! Be particularly careful in Harare. Violent crime, by contrast, is thankfully rare.

Entry and exit

A visa isn't necessary for citizens of Commonwealth or EC countries, Scandinavia, Switzerland or the USA. Onward air tickets and 'sufficient funds' to cover one's stay are occasionally insisted upon. There is a US$10 airport departure tax if you fly out.

Money

On arrival you will be given a currency declaration form on which you should record all your foreign cash and travellers cheques, and keep a record of all money changed into Zimbabwe dollars. The more expensive hotels and safaris will often require you to pay them directly in hard currency (foreign exchange).

Following the recent liberalisation of the economy, there is little black market demand for hard currency, and dealing on the streets is illegal and risky. Avoid at all costs the street money changers in Harare.

Border crossings

Most of Zimbabwe's border posts with Zambia, South Africa, Botswana and Mozambique are open daily from 6am to 6pm. There are through trains and buses across the borders to all of the region's capitals and some major towns.

Maps

Excellent, cheap maps are available of the whole country, including the national parks, in a wide range of useful scales. They can be bought from the Surveyor General in Harare at Electra House, Samora Machel Ave. (just west of Moffat St.). Street plans and full city maps of Harare and Bulawayo can also be bought here. Map buying is a *must* while you're in Harare, as most are unavailable elsewhere. Note that the office shuts at 4pm and at weekends.

Accommodation

Aside from the expensive and often luxurious hotels in the cities and main tourist centres, all the main towns have basic hotels with doubles starting at around Z$100 (£10) per night. The Youth hostels in Harare and Bulawayo are much cheaper but rather run down.

The best value accommodation is undoubtedly provided by the national parks. Self-catering chalets and lodges in the heart of national parks start at Z$30 (£3) per person. These are best booked in advance during weekends and school holidays. In Harare go to the National Parks Central Booking Office, 93B Jason Moyo Avenue, open Monday to Friday 8am to 4.15 pm.

Having a tent not only gives a lot of freedom but also saves money. All the main towns, game parks and other centres of interest have well-maintained campsites which are usually excellent value for money. They often have hot water, and always have toilet and shower facilities.

Eating

All the big towns have at least one supermarket and for hiking good supplies of cheese, packet soups, powdered milk and other lightweight foods are readily available.

Transport

Harare is well served by international flights, and is also the centre for a reliable internal service.

Zimbabwe National Railways offer services to all the major towns, and connections to Zambia, Botswana, and South Africa. The trains are slow, stylish and colonial – overnight 2nd Class being a particular favourite, especially from Bulawayo to Victoria Falls. Beware of your valuables if you dare to sleep in Economy (3rd Class), pickpockets abound. Book at least a few days in advance if you can, especially for sleepers.

For those on a tight schedule, **express coaches** run well-maintained, fast coaches between the major cities, usually stopping at the main hotel along the way. Ajays and Express Motorways are the main operators.

A multitude of **private bus companies** run cheap services across the whole country, using old and often dilapidated buses. These are usually still referred to as 'African' buses by the local whites. They operate from township bus stations a few kilometres from the town centres.

The country remains a good and safe place to **hitchhike**. It's usual to offer payment to the driver, about the same as the equivalent bus fare. Sometimes getting out of a town to a suitable hitching spot can be a problem, in which case find an **emergency taxi** (ET) going in the right direction to take you out of town a little way. ETs are invariably old stripped out Peugeot 504 estate cars, in desperate need of repair, which operate on fixed routes for around Z$1 per person.

What to buy

Zimbabwe cotton is among the finest you will find anywhere. Cheap and interesting cotton clothes and fabrics are well worth looking out for in Harare's main street shops and indeed in stalls along the roadsides.

Zimbabwean stone sculpture has become world famous in recent years, and has spawned a big stone carving and craft industry. It won't take long before you'll be introduced to some stone carvings in Harare's main shopping mall by the many street hawkers. Take your time and look around – there are big variations in price and quality.

TOWNS

Harare

Harare is a clean, modern capital city and a very useful base from which to plan your travels into wilder parts. The well laid out centre and spacious green suburbs lack the pollution and hassle that is so characteristic of other capitals, and give the city its laid back, almost provincial, feel.

The Tourist Office is near the corner of Jason Moyo Avenue and Fourth Street for general information on Zimbabwe, whilst the Information Centre in Unity Square has all the information that could be wished for on Harare itself.

The National Art Gallery near the large Monomatapa Hotel at the north end of Julius Nyerere Way, has some excellent displays of traditional and modern Zimbabwean art, including a large collection of fine Shona stone sculpture.

By Harare's main bus station in Mbare township, just south of the centre, is the country's largest market. Selling everything from fruit and vegetables to edible insects and baobab fruits, it's a fascinating place to spend a few hours.

For a swim in an open air Olympic size pool, try the Les Brown swimming pool, a few hundred metres along Park Lane from the Monomatapa and next to the beautiful and relaxing City Gardens.

If you're a climber and have a rope with you, there's an interesting disused granite quarry about 10km from the centre on the Mutare road. It's used by the Mountain Club of Zimbabwe on Wednesday afternoons. To get there, stop by the first turn-off on the left immediately past Daneko School, just past the drive-in which is on the right. It's a few minutes' walk up the track.

Sleeping and eating The cheapest place to stay is the City Campsite, offering the usual excellent facilities. To get there take the Mutare Road or Samora Machel Avenue eastwards toward Mutare for 6km to Coronation Park.

For those without a tent or wanting somewhere more central, the Youth Hostel at 6 Montagu Avenue (near Prince Edward Street) is cheap and popular with travellers despite being crowded and run down. It's open between 5pm and 10pm in the evening – you're kicked out in the morning!

Cheapest of the hotels proper, is the Selous Hotel on the corner of Selous Ave. and Sixth St. Doubles including breakfast are Z$120 (£12). The Russell Hotel and adjoining City Limits Apartels, on Baines Avenue between Third and Fourth street is your next cheapest recommended option.

For places to eat: Guido's in Montagu Shopping Centre near the youth hostel for inexpensive Italian food; the Bombay Duck on Central Ave. near Second Street for cheap Indian food and take-outs; the Vumba Restaurant at the Holiday Inn is surprisingly good value. For a more expensive but memorable night out, try Spagos Italian Restaurant in the Russell Hotel; Shezan Pakistani Restaurant at 88 Robert Mugabe Road; or Homegrown Vegetarian Restaurant on the corner of Speke Avenue and Leopold Takawira Street. The Harare Sheraton and the Monomotapa Hotel both do excellent all-you-can-eat monster breakfasts – good value if you don't eat for the rest of the day!

Transport The overland bus terminal is located 3km south from the centre at Mbare township by the market. To get there take an emergency taxi (ET) from the corner of Victoria Street and Speke Avenue, or walk. Long distance buses often leave very early in the morning.

The railway station is on Kenneth Kaunda Avenue, at the bottom end of Orr Street. There are nightly sleeper services to Mutare, Bulawayo and Francistown (Botswana). 1st and 2nd class should be reserved the day before, tickets for Economy (cheaper than the bus) on the day.

Bulawayo

Bulawayo is a very pleasant, spacious city, with exceptionally wide streets and some beautiful old colonial buildings. It is the cultural centre of Matebeleland as well as being one of the oldest white settlements in southern Africa.

The Tourist Information Bureau, in the City Hall on Leopold Takawira Avenue, is helpful for maps and general information.

Places to visit: the Natural History Museum in Centenary Park on Leopold Takawira Avenue 10 minutes walk east of the town centre is the most impressive in Zimbabwe. As well as imaginative displays of the flora, fauna and geology of Zimbabwe, there's an interesting appraisal of the contrasts between 'African' and 'colonial/European' cultures. For train buffs, the Railway Museum is near the station.

The Khami Ruins are second only to the Great Zimbabwe Ruins in size and importance. To get there, leave Bulawayo on Khami road (a continuation of 11th Avenue), travel about 20km west, and turn off onto a small road that leads to the village of Soluksi.

Sleeping and eating If you have a tent then undoubtedly the best place to stay is the Municipal Campsite, situated in Centenary Park 15 minutes walk east from the town centre near the Natural History Museum on Leopold Takawira Avenue – follow the signs for the Caravan Park. It is of a very high standard with 24 hour security guards, hot showers and firewood. There is a short cut past the swimming pool, and over a little bridge at the bottom of Ninth Avenue.

Next best is the Youth Hostel, on Third Street and Townsend Road out in the suburbs not far from the Bulawayo Inn at the eastern end of Twelfth Avenue. Reasonably priced hotels include the Palace Hotel and the Grand Hotel, both on Jason Moyo Street between Tenth and Eleventh Avenues. More expensive is Grey's Inn on Robert Mugabe Way and Jason Moyo Avenue.

For snacks and sandwiches, the Grass Hut near the corner of Fife Street and Eighth Avenue can be recommended. It's open all day and is a popular meeting place. For more substantial meals, Buffalo Bill's next to the Selbourne Hotel in Leopold Takawira Avenue serves enormous portions and is a great place for steak. Jade Moon, opposite the Sun Hotel on Josiah Tongogara Street and Tenth Avenue serves excellent chinese meals.

HIKING

Zimbabwe's climate, varied topography and well organised national parks system make it an excellent country for hiking. Although the best time of year is in the dry season (March to October) when you can expect cool dry weather, it's possible to camp and hike comfortably all year round. The main hiking area is in the Eastern Highlands, on the border with Mozambique, where there are several ranges of mountains and valleys with cool clear streams. For a completely different experience, Matopos National park offers rockier and rougher hiking in interesting bush country, and the Mavuradona Wilderness Area on the Zambezi escarpment has mountains, woodlands and waterfalls.

The areas and hikes described are largely in National Parks, and therefore mostly unpopulated. There are, however, many good hiking areas off some of the main roads, which offer original self-planned hikes away from the main trails. These areas are usually populated or privately owned, and permission to camp and hike should therefore be sought from whoever seems in charge.

Since no food can be bought in the Parks, buy all your supplies before you start. The Eastern Highlands are relatively well endowed with rivers and streams, but in Matopos and other areas expect to hunt around for water, or bring your own. Bear in mind that there is always good water available at any of the official campsites.

Nyanga National Park

Introduction   Nyanga is one of the main holiday resorts for Zimbabweans, only three hours drive from Harare. The mountains here are composed of granite, which gives the area a gentler and more rounded appearance than Chimanimani further south, but nevertheless provides some very impressive scenery. Clear streams, waterfalls and lakes are common, with forestry areas on the lower slopes and open moorland higher up, where there are numerous remains of stone forts, pits and ancient terracing.

Hiking in the mountains presents few difficulties, and Inyangani, Zimbabwe's highest peak (2,593m), is accessible to anyone of average fitness. Ordinary walking shoes or trainers are adequate, though don't forget waterproofs and warm clothing; it can rain here at any time of year, and does get quite cold especially at night.

Accommodation and transport   The best place to base yourself is the Inyangombe Campsite, on the road to Nyanga village and just past the turn-off to the park headquarters. Buses run to Nyanga from Mutare quite frequently, and hitching is good despite the small amount of traffic. Camping, with full facilities, costs Z$25 per site per night. Camping is only officially allowed at the campsites.

Alternative accommodation is provided by numerous lodges on Rhodes, Mare and Udu Dams, which cost Z$70 for two per night and should be booked at the tourist office in Mutare or Harare. They are often fully booked at weekends and holiday periods, but you may be lucky mid-week, and pick up a lodge at the Park Headquarters on Rhodes Dam.

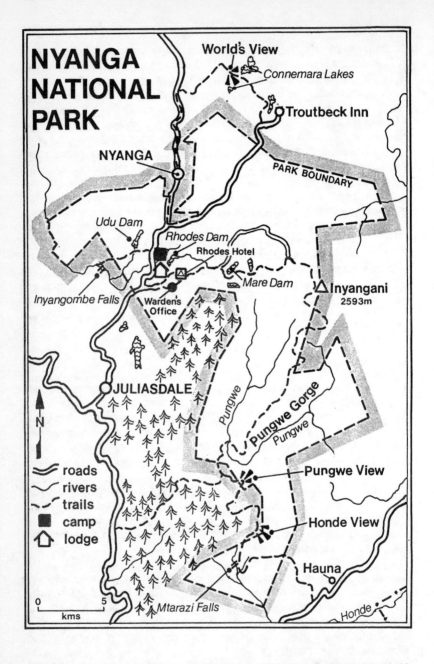

There are small stores in Nyanga, Troutbeck and Juliasdale, though it's best to bring most of your food in with you. If your camp cooking is getting you down you can nip over to the Rhodes Inyanga Hotel, 2km from the campsite, for a reasonably priced five-course dinner! There's also a small museum there full of Rhodes memorabilia.

The walks and hikes described here all start from the Inyangombe campsite.

Inyangombe Falls   Only 9km round trip from the campsite, this is really only a half-day walk along a well-used and not too exciting path going past Udu Dam. However the falls themselves are beautiful and well worth the walk. To get there cross the road opposite the campsite, and head west towards Udu Dam. About one kilometre beyond the dam you'll meet an old fence and prohibited entry sign (also old), which you should ignore and continue the extra one kilometre to the falls themselves. As a variation on the return, you can head north from the falls, and then trek cross country east to the campsite skirting the top of Udu Dam.

Troutbeck to Nyanga village via World's View   This excellent 16km hike can be completed in one day from Inyangombe campsite if you're lucky with buses and lifts. The difficulty is principally in getting to Troutbeck early enough in the morning from the campsite – there are occasional buses, and hitching is possible, though neither can be relied on. Equally it's not worth relying on transport for the 8km return trip out of Nyanga – you may have to walk this as well.

From Troutbeck head up the road about 1km before the village and hotel, coming from the campsite. Having crossed the golf course, continue uphill and straight on for 6km, avoiding the right turn up Joan McIlwaine Drive, and eventually taking the rough track that passes between the two Connemara Lakes rather than round them. The spectacular World's View is best pondered on the higher ground either side of the car park, away from the car-bound day trippers. Directly down from the car park is a steep, narrow trail which you should follow for 4km to the prominent dirt road which will take you into Nyanga village itself – another 6km.

The Inyangani Mountain – Mtarazi Falls – Honde Valley Trail   60km, 3 to 4 days. This ranks as one of the best walks in Zimbabwe, and takes in Inyangani, Zimbabwe's highest mountain; the Mtarazi Falls, the third highest in Africa; and the beautifully unspoilt Honde Valley. The trail follows small tracks or dirt roads for most of its length, so is quite easy going except for a few steep gradients, and a bit of bush bashing. Bring a compass – the descent from Inyangani can be difficult in bad weather. The finishing point is taken as the Honde Valley, from where you should be able to get a bus or hitch to Mutare with ease (as long as you are on the road by midday). You could cut the trail short by a day and stay in the area by taking the forestry track from Pungwe to the main Nyanga-Mutare road, but this does miss out some of the best hiking. Likewise, with a few lifts, the ascent up Inyangani makes a rewarding day hike.

Inyangombe Campsite to Inyangani   (18km) At 2,593m, this long flat-topped mountain is the highest point in Zimbabwe, and looks out over the park from its eastern border. It also holds considerable religious significance for the Shona peoples – a number of chiefs are buried here, and the mountain is reputed to 'eat people'. The belief certainly holds some truth;

some ill-prepared hikers have got lost in bad weather and not returned. Consequently the park wardens encourage everyone to register at the headquarters, which is fine if you're coming back the same day, but otherwise keep a low profile.

Walk or get a lift along the road to Mare Dam, and continue past it to the car park below the mountain. Take some time to look at the many small ruins in the area – small stone forts, pit structures, and terracing on the hillsides. From here, there is a clear path which ascends through rocky and lushly vegetated ground, then levels off and becomes boggy until the summit is reached, along with a trig. point. The views into the Pungwe Gorge and Honde Valley are superb.

The ascent takes 2 to 3 hours. To get to the nearest possible camping place, you can descend the mountain heading down one of the gullies in a south-westerly direction, but avoiding the cliffs to the south. The descent is steep and quite difficult, so take care in bad weather. Alternatively, go down the mountain the same way you came up and then walk round. Make your own way through the scrub for about 1½km until the ground levels off, and you cross a motorable track. There are several streams coming off the mountain, so hunt about for a place to camp here.

Inyangani to Pungwe Falls   (18km) The track continues in a south-westerly direction all the way to the Pungwe Falls, and is easy to follow as it skirts the edge of the magnificent Pungwe Gorge, through some beautiful remote country. We saw no one else during this stage of the hike. By the head of the gorge, the track turns south to give a full view of the gorge and cliffs, before turning sharply to the north-west up to some cottages and a ford across the river. You should look around here for a place to camp – we found a spot by the river downstream, on an old sand bar.

Pungwe Falls to Mtarazi Falls   (15km) A winding dirt road continues the trail, bringing you to Pungwe View where there is a small lay-by, and some *braii* stands. About a kilometre before this is the turn off for the track leading back to the main Nyanga to Mutare road through forestry land. Honde View, and the first sight of the trail's objective, is a further 8km along gently undulating forest and private land, and is yet another excellent viewpoint. You may even come across some adventurous motorists trying to make their way to the Mtarazi Falls.

The falls – back in the national park – are narrow but very high, plunging over the edge of the cliffs through incredibly lush montane forest, and into the Honde Valley 1,000m below. Again it's possible to camp here, just up from the falls by the river.

Mtarazi Falls to Honde Valley   (9km) To find the trail into the Honde Valley, backtrack ½km until you find the narrow and quite overgrown track heading off to the east. It's not as bad as it seems, and soon opens out to give a relaxing walk down to the main road. You'll pass through numerous small villages and settlements on the way. There's some small stores at Hauna village, about one kilometre north on the main road from where the track joins it, where you can while away the hours (waiting for the next bus to Mutare...).

The Chimanimani Mountains

Introduction   Also in the Eastern Highlands, the Chimanimani Mountains are geologically different to the Nyanga Mountains to the north, being composed of highly deformed, medium-grade metamorphic rocks, mostly quartzite. The scenery is consequently quite different here, with the large number of unusual rock formations giving the area an other-world, prehistoric appearance.

The national park offers perhaps the finest, and certainly the most rugged and remote, hiking in the country, with the added bonus that you can freely camp anywhere. There are basically two ranges of mountains running north-south for about 50km, with the Bundi Valley between them. The highest peak, Binga (2,440m), towers over the range and lies on the border with Mozambique, which stretches along the eastern watershed. Some time ago the area was used by traders crossing between Zimbabwe and Mozambique, and several trails still cross over the border, notably at the Saddle. Crossing the border is however strongly discouraged by the Zimbabwean authorities.

If you're intending to do anything other than the simpler hikes described here, then you should come fully equipped with all the food you will need, walking boots, compass, wet weather and camping gear. Having said that it's quite possible to make a quick visit with the minimum of equipment, stay in the mountain hut, or one of the many caves, and make day hikes from there.

Accommodation and transport   The nearest town to the park is the town of Chimanimani itself, which is best approached by bus or hitching from Mutare, though there is a road also from Chipinge and Birchenough Bridge to the south. Buses leave daily from Mutare township bus terminus in the early morning (around 7am), and sometimes also in the afternoon. The journey takes four hours.

The Chimanimani Hotel in the middle of town offers luxurious accommodation for Z$160 B&B (£16) for two. Staying here is an unforgettable experience; the interior decor, music and staff cannot have changed since the 1950s. You may also camp in the hotel grounds for Z$20 per person with full use of all the facilities, including hot baths and the swimming pool! The best value for those without a tent is the Traveller's Pot-Pourri. Similar to a youth hostel, there's a small dormitory (bring your own bedding) and a kitchen and bathroom. Ask at the hotel for directions.

The village has a post office, market, and several stores with most basic foods to stock up on for the mountains. There is little in the way of lightweight camping supplies though, which are best bought beforehand. Although not in the mountains proper, there are some worthwhile short hikes that can be made from the village.

Short walks in the area

Bridal Veil Falls (8km return). A picturesque waterfall, up a dirt road heading north west from Chimanimani, just before the hotel is reached.

Nyamzure (Pork Pie) Mountain (6km return). At the end of the village a dirt road, and then trail, leads to the north and up the 1,990m mountain. The panoramic view over the Chimanimani Range – and the wonderful sunsets

and sunrises – make the climb well worth while. An eland sanctuary has recently been set up on the slopes of Nyamzure, so you may see some zebra, bushbuck or baboons as well as eland on your hike. There are no restrictions to walking in the sanctuary.

Hiking in the Chimanimani National Park

Approach   Transport to the foot of the mountains and into the park is a problem without your own vehicle. There are no buses, and hitchable traffic is rare (try asking guests at the hotel if they're going into the park). It's usually either a 18km walk, or coming up with the money to hire a local to take you in their private car. We assembled a group of five, so it worked out at a reasonable price and conserved energy for the climb into the mountains later.

Near the mountains the road forks: the left fork goes to the Outward Bound School and Tessa's Pool, whilst the right leads to the National Park headquarters and official base camp at Mutekeswane. The wardens at the Park Office are very helpful, and can offer useful advice on walks, places to camp in the mountains, and the whereabouts of the caves. If you're doing any serious hiking make sure you have a 1:50,000 topographical map, obtainable from the Park Office, Harare. You are required to register here before you head off into the mountains, and also to de-register when you leave (the office closes at 5pm). You should also pay your park entry fee here. The official campsite is of the usual high standard, with showers and toilets.

Accommodation in the national park   The usual place to base yourself is at the mountain hut which occupies a superb setting in the Bundi Valley, with views towards Binga and the surrounding peaks. It has recently been refurbished and has excellent facilities including a shower, flush-loos and gas cookers. It costs a few dollars to stay here and is run by a warden who lives in a hut nearby. Bring candles.

Alternatively, if the intention is to avoid people altogether, there are plenty of suitable places to camp nearby, in addition to a number of cave shelters. These caves are kept clean by the wardens and have wonderful settings, though (obviously) offer no facilities. There are caves throughout the Park and a few of the most prominent are mentioned in the text. Ask at the Park Office for locations of further caves if you plan to be dependent on these.

The hut is usually reached by taking the steep path immediately behind the Park Office and base camp. The path is a little indistinct in places, and takes about 2 hours (more with a heavy pack) levelling off near the hut (4km). The hut can also be reached from the Outward Bound School. A number of good day walks can be made from the hut, though if camping or using caves, there is nothing stopping you from combining them together into longer hikes.

Binga Mountain   (10km return) This is Chimanimani's highest peak at 2,440m. Take the obvious path from the hut to the east, and toward the mountain. This is a very steep climb and takes 3-4 hours to the summit and 2-3 hours for the return. Bring plenty of water! The views into Mozambique are very impressive from the top.

A more satisfying but harder circuit is to climb directly up from the Bundi valley to the summit of Dombe (2 hours, no path) and then scramble along the rough ridge overlooking Skeleton Pass to join the main path up Binga.

Skeleton Pass   (6km return) This is an easy walk across the Bundi Valley and up to a col in the range known as Skeleton Pass, from where there are excellent views of Dombe Peak, and into the valleys below. A sign warns you that it is the Mozambique border.

For those with the time and necessary scrambling ability, there is a difficult direct route to the top of Dombe, from where easier scrambling takes you to Binga and the main trail back down. This circuit makes a satisfying full day's hike, but should not be undertaken lightly or by the inexperienced.

Peza (Ben Nevis)   (10km return) This is a much gentler climb than Binga, taking the path that goes north from the hut up the Bundi Valley. The mountain is so named for its clear resemblance to the original in Scotland!

At the end of the valley, as you start to ascend the mountain, you'll see a large cave (North Cave) just above a prominent waterfall. Another large cave (Red Cave) lies ten minutes' climb further up. Both make excellent overnight camps.

The Southern Lakes   9km south of the hut in the Bundi Valley the river widens at some sharp meanders to form two deep pools or 'lakes'. The combination of excellent swimming and some great camping make the lakes a very worthwhile excursion. They can be reached by a highly scenic trail that follows the west side of the Bundi river starting at the hut, the walk taking about 4 hours.

After about half an hour down from the hut, you'll pass a picturesque waterfall and a small rock overhang (Digby's Cave). Further on still is Peterhouse Cave adjacent to the path. Terry's Cave, just over halfway to the lakes, is remarkably well established and luxurious, but hard to get to. Try to find an indistinct path after crossing the river and climb up 15 minutes or so into rocky terrain.

A pleasant way to leave the lakes and head out of the park, is to take the direct 9km trail to base camp. Head up the ridge north of the lakes to find the start of the path, which works its way to the north west, dropping down into thick vegetation before joining the main track back to the camp. Leave about 3-4 hours for the walk – it's not that well used and so can be hard to follow at times.

Dragon's Tooth and the south   The area of the park south of the Southern Lakes is the most remote and least visited. The terrain becomes harder and the few paths indistinct. The Mozambique border strikes an arbitrary line through the range, cutting across the watershed and the more obvious routes south. The route south to Dragon's Tooth Rock and beyond – that keeps within Zimbabwe and the national park – traverses across the rough western slopes of the mountains and overlooks the spectacular deep gorges of the Bundi and Haroni rivers.

To get to The Saddle and a view of the Ragon Falls, cross the Bundi river just upstream of the Southern Lakes (difficult in the rainy season) and scramble up the steep river embankment to gain a clear path heading towards the Saddle (1 hour). The camping in the Saddle area is superb, with wonderful views, and you can easily spend a day exploring the peaks to the north and south of the Saddle, or the various views down to Ragon Falls.

The distinctive spike of Dragons Tooth Rock lies a further 10km south, on the edge of another area of flattish ground and good camping. The route is very indistinct, with the occasional cairn marking the way. Use your instincts and keep a mental record of the route for the way back.

Tessa's Pool   Near the Outward Bound School, this is a large pool at the foot of a marvellous waterfall, perfect for cooling off after coming down from the mountains if you've any time spare. To use it you must first get permission from the Outward Bound School (they sometimes use it in their courses) and make a small donation.

Matopos National Park

Introduction   Matopos National Park (also known as the Matobo Hills) is situated about 50km south of Bulawayo in the south west of Zimbabwe. The name – derived from the Matebele word for 'bald-headed' – describes the many hundreds of rounded granite hills or *whalebacks* that cover the area.

Some of these are covered by heaps of wind eroded boulders, often balancing precariously on top of each other, forming *castle kopjes*. The scenery and atmosphere is exhilarating and quite unlike anything you're likely to find in other parts of the world. The hiking is superb.

Another fascinating aspect of the area is the number, and quality, of the *Bushman* paintings to be found. Before the national park was formed in 1962, and the local people 'resettled', the area had been continuously inhabited for thousands of years. The paintings are thought to date from the late Stone Age, and may be as old as 10,000 years.

The park is divided into a number of areas with the western side set aside as a separate game park where white rhino, giraffe, buffalo and eland can be viewed – though you either need to have your own vehicle, or be on an organised tour to do this.

No special equipment is needed for hiking in the park. Camping is only allowed in the official campsites, where there is always a supply of water and washing facilities. Even outside the game reserve, there are still a significant amount of animals around, so be prepared to be lulled to sleep by a cacophony of unidentifiable noises!

Accommodation and transport   The main campsite – and a good place to base yourself for a few days – is at Maleme Dam, situated roughly in the centre of the park. There is at least one early morning and one afternoon bus leaving Bulawayo for Kezi each day, which can drop you off at the game park entrance about 9km from Maleme. Occasionally you may find buses going into the park itself, but the easiest way is to hitch, particularly at weekends and holiday periods, when people from Bulawayo come out for the day. From Bulawayo, take Robert Mugabe Way (Grey Street) to the south, and then fork right onto Matopos Road. Within the park, hitching is the only way to get between the main areas of interest apart from walking. There are no shops or supplies in the park – bring everything you'll need.

Camping sites at Maleme Dam are charged per site, so it pays to share. National parks chalets for two, with cooking facilities, cost only Z$30.00 per night – an excellent bargain. Beware the local troop of baboons which have become highly practised at stealing campers' food!

Hiking

The National Park Office, at the top of the hill just before descending to Maleme Dam, is open from 7am to 12 noon, and from 2pm to 5pm every day. Apart from useful advice, good 1:50,000 maps can be bought, and pony trails booked. These start at 8am and 2.30pm, for a maximum of two hours, and assume no previous riding experience. From Maleme there are several excellent day, and half day hikes within reach.

Pomongwe Cave   (From Maleme 9km by road, 3km scramble, round trip) The largest of the 'subspheroid' caves in Matopos, and occupied over 50,000 years ago. Unfortunately some of the paintings were destroyed by over-zealous attempts to preserve them, but there remain outlines of elephant, antelope, and a few human figures. Either take the tarred road past the Park

Office to a turn to the left, or climb up the Pomongwe whaleback itself from near the Park Office, where there is a trail marked by arrows.

Nswatugi Cave   (From Maleme 20km by road, 10km trail, round trip). One of the best examples of *Bushman* painting in Zimbabwe, and even southern Africa. From the campsite, cross the dam wall, taking the right fork when the road splits after about 3km. After a further 2km there's a wide plain on the right, and an unmarked trail on the left which is only about 500m from the cave. It is usually possible to follow the tracks made by the warden's bike, keeping to your right over areas of bare rock. If you take the road, continue for another 3½km, until just past Madingazulu Dam where a good road leads to the cave on the left. The cave site has a good information display, and a small museum.

World's View and Rhodes' Grave   (From Maleme 22km by road, 20km trail, round trip) One of the highest points in the park with some very impressive rounded boulders. Reached by a short access road that turns off from the main Bulawayo to Maleme road by some curio stalls. Note that the stirrups and reins on the Shangani Memorial are the originals.

It is also possible to hike to World's View by following the trail that leads north from the campsite along the right hand side of the Dam, and then heading over the whalebacks. About half way, there's a large cross on a hill to the right, which makes an excellent diversion and gives wonderful views over the Maleme valley.

A few kilometres past the World's View turnoff is White Rhino Shelter. This houses a number of fine Bushman paintings done in outline rather than the more usual coloured designs.

Toghwe Wilderness Area   A remote, mostly undeveloped and very beautiful part of the park, with some excellent cave paintings, accessed by a 20km gravel road which branches off the main tarred road to the east. There are two campsites at Toghwana and Mtsheleli Dams, each with an access road. Hitching from the main road is difficult so be prepared to walk. Once at the campsites, rough but rewarding hiking is the only way to explore the area further.

From Toghwana Dam, Nanke Cave with its excellent paintings can be reached in two hours or so along the 7km marked trail. The fairly steep hike makes its way up a large whaleback hill, and is marked by green arrows on the rock or small rock cairns (take care, it's not that clear!). The paintings rival those at Nswatugi, and the views are superb.

If you're planning any adventurous hiking into the area, bear in mind that the vegetation is most manageable during the dry season (May to October). There will, however, be little ground water apart from the main rivers and you should plan to take most with you. All water should be purified.

Mavuradona Wilderness Area

Introduction   Perched on the edge of the precipitous Zambezi Escarpment, the Mavuradona mountains hide secluded valleys with permanent streams, waterfalls and peaceful woodland. Wild and remote, this is Zimbabwe's newest conservation area. Originally the home to plentiful game, Mavuradona has now become largely hunted out, though there are plans to restock the area with selected animal species.

The scheme for the wilderness area is also notable for attempting to integrate the local people into the management by involving them in decision-making on a local level and using park funds to help develop facilities in the adjacent communal areas.

At present, there are no facilities in the wilderness area, so you have to come fully prepared with a tent and food. Finding water is not a problem, even in the dry season.

Accommodation and transport   The area lies north of the town of Centenary on the Zambezi Escarpment. Buses leave each day for Centenary from Harare, 130km away, a three to four hour journey. From Centenary, hitch or walk up the road towards the escarpment, then strike off into the hills wherever your fancy takes you! Make sure you've got a good selection of maps from the Surveyor General's office in Harare.

For more information on the area, and an update on the plans to build a basic bush chalet, contact: C.K.Pohl, Mavuradona Farm, P.O. Box 30, Centenary, Zimbabwe, or Safari Interlink Ltd., Trustee House, 55 Samora Machel Avenue (PO Box 5920), Harare. Tel: 720527 or 700911/2. This company runs a good selection of adventure safaris.

OTHER PLACES OF INTEREST

Bvumba Mountains

Bvumba (or Vumba) – literally 'mist' – is an area of montane rainforest and plantation about 30km south east of Mutare in the Eastern Highlands. The area, as its name implies, has a very high rainfall and is totally different from the rest of Zimbabwe in atmosphere and vegetation. The formal and very beautiful botanical gardens, contrast well with the adjacent botanical reserve – a part of the rainforest – with a number of marked paths. The views into the Mozambique valleys, especially in the early morning when the clouds are still well bellow the gardens, are truly spectacular, and matched only by the views in the opposite direction from Leopard Rock, 8km from the campsite and signposted.

There are some holiday cottages for let just outside the gardens (book in Mutare at the Publicity Association), and there is a good campsite within the gardens themselves, with hot showers.

There is no public transport into the Bvumba, though hitching is relatively easy from Mutare, especially over the weekend and holiday periods.

Great Zimbabwe Ruins

The word *zimbabwe* means 'venerated house' in Shona, and it was the ruins and what they represented that gave the name to the country rather than vice-versa. Built around 900 to 1,000 AD, these great walls and enclosures form the largest pre-colonial structure south of the Sahara, and were built without the use of any cement or mortar. They are an impressive and unique place to visit, housing also a museum in which are found the legendary stone 'Zimbabwe Birds', as featured on the national flag and currency.

The one hotel at the ruins – the Great Zimbabwe Hotel – is plush but expensive. Try it for a meal or a handsome breakfast. Otherwise, there is a campsite next to the ruins themselves with toilets and washing facilities.

The ruins, 30km south-east of Masvingo, can be reached by hitching or taking one of the local buses (two or three a day).

Victoria Falls

The Victoria Falls are one of the world's most beautiful and impressive great waterfalls, formed where the mile-wide Zambezi river drops 100 metres into a long, narrow gorge. The perpetual spray is enough to sustain a small patch of rainforest in the immediate area, as well as to ensure that any visit is a wet one. The African name *Mosi O Tunya* translates as 'the smoke that thunders'. The rainbows formed by the mist are very unusual – especially the double (and sometimes even triple) rainbows seen in the early morning from Danger Point, and the ethereal lunar rainbow, best a few hours after moonrise.

Whilst there is no charge to visit the falls themselves, there are plenty of other ways to spend your money. Daily air tours over the falls (*Flight of the Angels*) are available, lasting 15 minutes or 75 minutes (including a game flight). The most exciting trip is probably white water rafting on the Zambezi river just below the falls themselves. Neither of these trips is cheap, but if you've the money to spare they're well worth it.

There are two campsites, one in the town itself, and the other on the banks of the Zambezi 5km upstream from the falls, both administered by the office for the town site. For those without a tent, there are dormitories and chalets in the town site.

Eating can be another bargain at the Victoria Falls; the stylish Victoria Falls Hotel does a superb breakfast, buffet lunch and an extensive evening *braai* for prices less than the equivalent in Harare. These are 'all you can eat' and open to non residents.

Hwange National Park

This is Zimbabwe's premier game park and consists of 9,000 square kilometres of wild bush, varying from the semi-desert scrub on the Kalahari's fringes in the south of the park, to granite hills set amid valleys of *mopane* woodland in the north.

A car is really needed to tour Hwange, but guides can be hired for bush walks (maximum 6 people) from any of the National Parks camps, and Main Camp does organise regular 2 hour walks both in the early morning and at night (provided there's a full moon). To reach Main Camp take the train to Dete, or hitch/bus to Safari Cross, and hitch the remaining 20km or so into camp.

Mana Pools

Open from 1st May to 31st October only, this ranks as one of Africa's most exciting game parks. It's the only game park in Zimbabwe in which you are permitted to walk around freely, and so does not require you to have your own vehicle. In practice you need a vehicle to get into the park, but if you can't afford to hire one it's possible to hitch in from the turn-off on the main Harare to Chirundu road. You will need to get a park entry permit from the National Parks Office at the village of Marongora, just before the turn-off, and check here about campsites.

Alternatively, you can join an organised foot safari or backpacking trail. These are both run by Chipembere Safaris (PO Box 9, Kariba, Tel: 2946, or through a travel agent in Harare) from Chitake private camp, an idyllic spot at the base of the Zambezi Escarpment.

The foot safari includes bush walking and some game viewing by vehicle. To take full advantage of the wildlife activity in this area safaris are timed to coincide with the full moon each month. The Backpacking Trail does not follow a set route, but is led by an experienced guide through the wilderness area in the eastern part of the park, camping each night near water holes, with a good chance of seeing wildlife.

At US$500 per person for four days, these safaris may be beyond the budget of some travellers, but they are all-inclusive, and so very good value, and highly recommended for exciting game viewing. You can self-cater on the Backpacking Trail and reduce the cost to $400 per person.

Chipembere also do canoeing safaris on the Zambezi, and you can do a bush-walking and boating combination.

WARTHOG

Contrary to popular belief, warthogs do not always use their burrows when escaping from predators. An adult warthog can outrun its main enemy, lion, reaching a speed of 34 mph. When they do make a dive for their burrows, the adults always reverse before going in so their formidable tusks can be used in defence.

As well as being used as a sanctuary from predators, burrows serve as protection from the cold. Warthogs are the only members of the pig family to be able to live without drinking water for long periods of time; this adaptability to a dry climate is managed by sacrificing efficient thermoregulation which requires a high water intake. Warthog body temperature range is therefore unusually high for a mammal.

The Rhinoceros

There are two species of African rhino, the white and the black, but they differ in form and temperament, rather than colour. The white, or square-lipped, rhino gets its name from its 'wide' muzzle (*weit* in Afrikaans) which enables it to graze. It can also be distinguished by its very large head and a hump of muscle at the base of the neck. The white rhino has a generally placid nature and can be safely approached in those game parks which allow foot safaris.

The black rhino, on the other hand, can be thoroughly bad tempered and dangerous. It has a smaller head than the white, a dip back and no hump. Its upper lip is shaped like a parrot's beak and is prehensile so that it can browse on shrubs and plants.

Both sexes of both species carry the double horn of compressed hair that in the East is so valued as an aphrodisiac: a value that is bringing the African rhino to the brink of extinction. Today rhinoceros horn is literally worth its weight in gold. It's hardly surprising that poachers will risk everything to gain one of these prizes, and their efforts in East Africa have reduced the black rhino by 90% in the last few years. The white rhino has fared better. Having been on the verge of extinction 80 years ago, careful conservation in South Africa has saved it as a species. Although the poaching problem is not as severe in South Africa as in the huge game parks of East Africa, the white rhino is still not safe.

There is a small population of the extremely rare northern white rhino (a subspecies) in the Garamba National Park in Zaïre.

SOUTHERN AFRICA

South Africa
Swaziland
Lesotho
Namibia

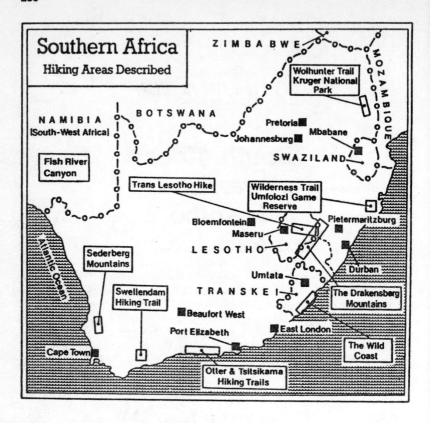

Southern Africa
Hiking Areas Described

Z I M B A B W E

MOZAMBIQUE

Wolhunter Trail
Kruger National
Park

N A M I B I A
(South-West Africa)

B O T S W A N A

Pretoria

Johannesburg

Mbabane

S W A Z I L A N D

Fish River
Canyon

Trans Lesotho Hike

Wilderness Trail
Umfolozi Game
Reserve

Pietermaritzburg

Bloemfontein

Maseru

L E S O T H O

Atlantic Ocean

Sederberg
Mountains

Durban

Umtata

T R A N S K E I

Swellendam
Hiking Trail

The Drakensberg
Mountains

Beaufort West

Port Elizabeth

East London

Cape Town

The Wild
Coast

Otter & Tsitsikama
Hiking Trails

*In South Africa, place names can be signposted in English or Afrikaans.
Know both names for the place you're heading for or it's easy to become
confused.*

Chapter 18

South Africa

Updated by Philip Briggs and Hilary Bradt

FACTS AND FIGURES

South Africa is basically a 1,200m high plateau edged by a narrow fertile belt along the Indian Ocean. The escarpment sweeps up from the ocean to approximately 340m, and inland lie the two vast desert areas of the Karoo at about 500m. The highveld (pronounced highfelt) extends up to 1,700m.

Temperatures throughout the Republic are moderate, but along the northeast coast summer heat combines with high humidity to make the climate quite uncomfortable for a few weeks. Cape Town's climate is kept temperate by the Atlantic's currents, while Johannesburg's elevation (I,820m) keeps it cool. In Cape Town most of the rain falls in the winter while this is the dry season in the north. Rainfall decreases as you move west. The east coast receives I,600mm annually, while the central plateau and highveld get I00mm on average, and the desert areas receive less than 300mm annually.

In 1962 the South African government started its policy of creating self-governing Homelands, four of which were granted 'independence': Transkei, Bophuthatswana, Venda and Ciskei. Their independent status was not recognised outside South Africa, nor are they likely to survive long into a post-apartheid constitution.

Exports are very diverse with gold heading the list. Wool, minerals, fruits, hides, wine and machinery all play an important part in the economy.

People

South Africa's population (an artificial figure because it excludes the 'homelands') numbers approximately 30 million. Thankfully apartheid has now been officially abolished, but the former divisions are useful for understanding this multi-ethnic country. The black population (over 22 million) can be divided into four main cultural and linguistic groups, all part of the larger Bantu language block, and within which a number of related languages are spoken. These are Nguni (Zulu, Swazi, Xhosa), Sotho (Tswana, Bapedi, South Sotho), and the less numerically significant Venda and Shengaan-Tsonga.

In the latter part of the 19th Century large numbers of Indians arrived to work the sugar plantations in Natal Province, while many Malays settled in

Cape Town. The first Coloured South African was born some nine months after the arrival of the first Dutch settlers early in the 17th Century.

Whites number about 5 million. A cultural and political gulf separates English stock from Afrikaners and the two groups keep their heritage separate.

The official languages are English and Afrikaans.

TRAVEL

Impressions

In the last edition of this book I wrote: 'The year I spent working in South Africa will always be remembered for Cape Town's incredible beauty, the friends I made, the profound injustices of apartheid, and the dilemmas I saw etched into everyone's life'. Revisiting 17 years later, in the year that Mandela and De Klerk won the Nobel Peace Prize, everything had changed yet nothing had changed. No one can visit South Africa and remain indifferent to that country's problems. Nor indifferent to its incredible beauty. I spent Boxing Day in one of the most idyllic hiking locations imaginable: the sound of falling water, the brilliant greens against a blue sky, the scatter of red gladioli against the dark cliffs of the 'kloof' (gulley), and the sensuality of swimming in the cold, crystal clear water is something I will never forget.

This is still an ideal country for backpackers: travel conditions are easy, accommodation and campsites are cheap and of a high standard, and there are hundreds of trails and reserves to choose from. The strict quota system ensures that none is overcrowded.

Entry and exit

British, Irish and Swiss citizens are the only ones who don't need a visa. Other nationalities should get theirs in advance. To enter South Africa you must have a ticket out of the country and have 'sufficient means'. Land border officials are said to be more lenient than those at the airports. If you leave South Africa and want to return on the same visa (when visiting Swaziland and Lesotho, for instance) you must get a re-entry permit.

It is still illegal to import literature considered by the authorities to be subversive or pornographic. However, these days your books would have to be *very* red or blue to be confiscated!

Money

The South African rand (pronounced ront by Afrikaans speakers) is a fairly stable currency, although it has slipped against hard currencies in recent years, making South Africa a cheap country to visit.

What to buy

Because there are many ethnic groups within South Africa tourists will find a large variety of interesting, high quality and beautiful items from all over the Republic, and imported from the neighbouring countries.

Sending your purchases home is no problem at all. Your parcels will be safe, and the sea links to other ports of the world are efficient.

Maps and guides

South Africa's tourist departments and various parks boards produce a wide range of good maps and informative brochures, and these are often free. A large range of Survey maps can be seen at Stanfords Map Shop in London.

Guide to South Africa by Philip Briggs (Bradt) covers over 100 National Parks and reserves, accommodation in towns and coastal resorts, and has suggested itineraries. It includes a general overview and booking address for most hiking trails in the country, though no detailed trail descriptions.

An excellent range of field guides and specific-interest guides are produced locally. Until recently it was difficult to get hold of these outside of the country, but quite a few shops in London now stock a reasonable range, including Stanfords. Russel Friedman Books do a natural history mail order service; see Chapter 5.

A good selection of hiking and climbing guides are available from Camp and Climb, which has several branches in Cape Town as well as in Johannesburg, Pretoria, and Port Elizabeth.

Accommodation

Hotels are well run and very comfortable, and are now open to all races. (Some hotel owners may still use the 'right of admission reserved' rule to exclude blacks, but this is illegal). With the depreciation of the rand, hotel prices are reasonable by European or American standards. In most towns you'll get a comfortable double for around $25.

Furnished self-catering accommodation is offered in most game reserves, municipal campsites, and many private resorts. This is normally paid for by the unit, not per person. Prices vary according to place and season, but you should normally be able to find something for about $15, often significantly cheaper.

There are many youth hostels, both official (requiring membership of the YHA) and unofficial. These are excellent places for meeting other backpackers and learning about hiking possibilities.

Best of all, bring a tent: there is at least one campsite in virtually every town and reserve. Not only are they scenic, but they're fully equipped and inexpensive.

The South African Tourism Board (SATOUR) publishes brochures on accommodation. The one on caravan parks (campsites) is particularly useful as it includes sketch maps.

Rest camps in National Parks and other popular accommodation may be considerably more expensive and fully booked-up during school holidays. Generally speaking the holiday seasons are two weeks over Easter, then mid

June to late July, the last two weeks in September, and mid December to mid January. If you are travelling during that time you are advised to make your reservations in advance.

Eating and drinking

You can eat extremely well and at relatively low cost in South Africa. Around Cape Town, Malay dishes are a speciality, and in Durban there's a good selection of curries.

If you're cooking for yourself, supermarkets in even the smallest towns are well-stocked (mind-bogglingly so if you've arrived from elsewhere in Africa) and local produce such as meat and vegetables is good value. Wine is up to Californian or French standards, and inexpensive.

The traditional South African party takes the form of a *braai* or barbeque outdoors.

One South African speciality particularly popular with hikers is biltong. This dried meat (including ostrich) is the equivalent of the North American 'jerky'.

Transport

Tourists come from all over the world just to goggle at and ride on South Africa's trains (a good steam train ride is the Outeniqua Choo-Tjoe between Knysna and George). Trains are a good way of travelling between major centres, though often they are quite slow (apart from the prestigious Blue Train between Pretoria and Cape Town), and they don't run on minor routes. Before booking on long-distance trains, check on the cost of flying: there are many bargains to be had, including 'mid-night' flights at half price. Alternatively, Intercity buses are reliable, quick, and slightly cheaper than second-class rail.

Most South Africans consider hitchhiking too dangerous these days. They are probably right, which is a pity: it's an excellent way of meeting South Africans and may be the only way to reach out-of-the-way places. If you hitch, get local advice on which areas to avoid.

Car Rental is an option worth considering, especially for groups. Cars are generally well serviced and provided you rent for a week you should be able to get one for around US$200 with no surcharge for kilometres driven. I'd recommend Tempest Car Hire (Tel: (011) 975 0026) in Johannesburg, although you will find cheaper deals if you shop around. Tempest also have offices in Cape Town, Durban, Port Elizabeth, and East London.

Warning

South Africa is a violent country, with Johannesburg having one of the world's highest homicide rates. Tourists are advised to keep well away from known trouble spots, and to avoid wandering about in cities after dark. Hikers on designated trails will be as safe here as anywhere in the world, however.

TOWNS

Johannesburg

Few people will want to linger long in Jo'burg, but the largest city in South Africa is likely to be first stop for anyone arriving by air. For information on Johannesburg, visit the Tourist Office on the corner of Kruis and Market St. Tel: (011) 29 4961. For information further afield, visit SATOUR in the Carlton Centre on Commissioner St. Tel: (011) 331 5241.

For accommodation the best bet is the Backpacker's Ritz hostel. This costs R25 per person ($8), and has excellent facilities including a swimming pool. They will pick up travellers free from anywhere in Jo'burg (Tel: 839-2068). Travellers should be careful in Jo'burg city centre especially after dark: muggings are commonplace. The worst area is Joubert Park, but nowhere in the city is safe. If you arrive in Jo'burg after dark, get a taxi (or ring the Ritz).

Cape Town

This is one of the most beautiful cities in the world, with Table Mountain providing an incomparable (and climbable) backdrop. The sights are too numerous to mention here, but try to make it to Groot Constantia, a lovely old building in typical Cape architecture; take a cable car ride up to the top of Table Mountain, wander around the Waterfront, and visit the South African Museum for its excellent natural history and ethnological exhibits.

For cheap accommodation, catch one of the regular trains from the city centre to Muizenberg. A youth hostel (Tel: (021) 788 4283) and Zandvlei Caravan Park (Tel: (021) 210 2507), which offers camping and cheap self-catering, are both a short walk from Muizenberg station (and near a good beach). Another excellent hostel is also a short train ride away from the city centre in Observatory. Rolling Stones Youth Hostel is very friendly and inexpensive and organises hiking trips and other excursions; Tel: (021) 448 1124. In the city itself, there is a very pleasant privately-run hostel called The Backpacker (Tel: (021) 23 4530), as well as a Y.M. and Y.W.C.A. If all the above are full, the CAPTOUR office in the Golden Acre Building next to the Central Station should be able to help you find a room. Tel: (021) 21 6274.

Durban

South Africa's largest port has a very popular beach and a pleasant atmosphere. The high Asian population gives the city an unusual flavour, and the Indian market is well worth visiting. Durban is probably best avoided during school holidays, but at other times of the year there's plenty of cheap accommodation on and around Gillespie St, only a few paces from the beachfront. A new Youth Hostel on Smith Street is said to be excellent (R18 or $6pp).

There is a good tourist office on the beachfront and on Church St. in the city centre (Tel: (031) 304 4934).

HIKING

South Africa is a thrillingly beautiful country, with very varied scenery, marvellous flora and fauna, and more organised hiking trails and more enthusiastic hikers than any other country in Africa. There are now well over 100 hiking trails in the country covering a huge variety of habitats, and ranging from relatively straightforward overnight rambles to arduous eight-day mountain hikes. I can only describe a few of the more popular trails which I have hiked myself or have received first-hand reports. Most trails operate on a quota system to prevent overuse and environmental damage. The most popular get booked up for months in advance so find out about the less-known trails: they are unlikely to disappoint and easier to get booked on at short notice.

Trail fees are negligible (about $3 per night) and normally include a trail map and/or brochure. Most trails have huts with bunks and mattresses; some allow camping in designated places. The number allowed on each trail at one time varies but is usually between 8 and 30 people a day. On many trails a minimum of two or three people per party is enforced.

Different trails are booked through a variety of authorities: those in mountain areas generally through the regional forestry department, those in reserves through the relevant parks board or local council, and there are some privately run trails.

Conventional backpacking trips (where a tent must be carried, and where you can camp freely) are also available in eight Wilderness Areas. These have no huts, the charge is nominal, and it is a less regimented experience. The rules state that the minimum group size is three.

As well as overnight trails, most reserves have day trails (the Royal Natal Park in the Drakensberg, for instance, has 20 such trails, ranging from 2km to 22km in length). You don't need to book day trails, and they are a good option if you're not kitted out for backpacking or have time restrictions.

Further information Brief descriptions and booking addresses for most trails are included in *Follow the Footprints*, a free booklet available from the South African Tourism Board (SATOUR). For a description of virtually every trail in South Africa and its neighbouring countries, buy Jaynee Levy's *The Complete Guide to Walks and Trails in Southern Africa* or the more recent *Discover Southern Africa on Foot* (Southern Books).

You can also write direct to: The National Hiking Way Board, Private Bag X447, Pretoria 0001. Tel: (012) 299 2632. They publish an excellent map/brochure on each established hiking trail.

The Otter and Tsitsikamma Trails

Introduction The road between Cape Town and Port Elizabeth on the Indian Ocean is known as the Garden Route and has always been popular with tourists. But whereas the motorist only gets occasional glimpses of the cliffs, beaches, rivers and forest that make the area so special, the hiker is right there. The two trails form a loop between the Storms River Mouth Rest Camp and Groot River Campsite at Nature's Valley, both of which are in the Tsitsikamma Coastal National Park. The Otter Trail runs along the coast protected by the national park, while the Tsitsikamma Trail follows an inland route through the Tsitsikama Mountains. The loop takes ten days, but of course either trail can be hiked separately or you can rest at the half way point of Nature's Valley. With the diversity of scenery and plantlife these are arguably the most rewarding of all South Africa's organised trails.

The best time to visit the area, especially the Tsitsikamma Mountains is between October and December when the flowers are blooming.

The Otter Hiking Trail

During the four and a half days it takes you to complete this walk you will pass swelling surf, sandy beaches and rocky shores with inviting tide pools. You'll climb steep cliffs and walk along erica-covered headlands and pass through luxuriant forests where the Knysna loerie flashes its green and red feathers. An altogether unforgettable hike.

There are four well constructed huts supplied with bunks and foam mattresses and you are required to sleep in them and not to camp.

The area is great for tide-pooling and fishing, although the latter is only permitted between Goudgate and Waterval. Animals, birds and flowers abound, and we even saw a clawless otter, for which the trail is named.

Preparations You need a permit and a reservation from The Chief Director, National Parks Board, PO Box 787, Pretoria 0001. Tel: (012) 44 1191. 12 hikers are allowed in per day. The Otter trail is often booked up a year in advance but you may get a last-minute cancellation.

Bring the usual backpacking equipment, but you won't need a mattress or tent. Do bring a water bottle (you'll have to carry water on some stretches), water purifying tablets, a stove, and, if possible, an air-mattress in preference to a foam one for floating your gear across rivers. Large plastic bags (garbage bags) are needed to keep it dry. You'll need a swimsuit, and a mask and snorkel are recommended.

Perhaps the most important and unusual item is a tide table – needed to plan your hiking. Rangers usually give them out free with each party beginning the hike. There are three major rivers to ford, all affected by the tide since you'll be crossing them within a short distance from the ocean.

There are ticks along this route and they are dangerous, tick bite fever being relatively common. Protect your legs with clothing or repellent.

Approach The walk begins at Storms River Mouth at a complex of buildings: hotel, restaurant, nature trail and park headquarters (it must begin here – you are not allowed to do the hike from west to east). It's about 12km from main road to coast, mostly downhill in case you have to walk. There's no public transport but you can usually hitch in.

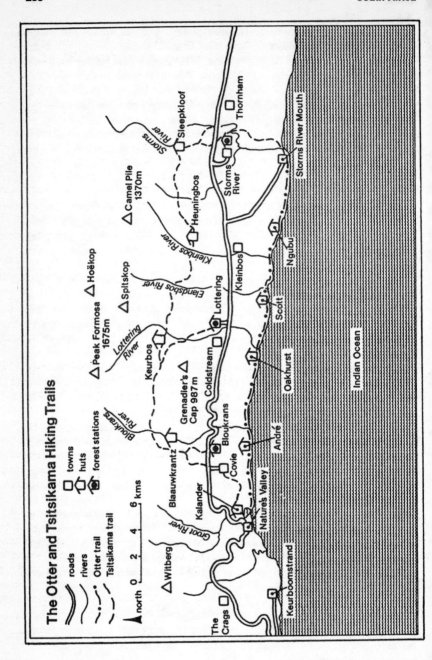

The Otter and Tsitsikama Hiking Trails

The trail The path starts down the beach directly in front of the shack by the main gate. You'll be walking through the camping area, and eventually you'll see a sign with a picture of an otter on it. That's the beginning of the trail. It's wise to begin the hike as the tide is going out, since the first couple of miles of walking only barely skirts the waves. There are arrows and otters painted onto the rocks for your guidance.

The only serious challenge along the trail comes when fording the rivers, and only one of these, the Bloukrans River, need trouble you. We crossed at low tide, but even so we waded through chest-high water. Packs are carried native style, on your head, or towed behind you on an air mattress. An unusual backpacking experience, so don't attempt the fording on anything but a low tide. The Elandsbos should also be crossed at low tide.

When you reach your destination, Nature's Valley, you are on the Garden Route so leaving the area is no problem if you don't want to hike the Tsitsikama Trail.

The Tsitsikamma Hiking Trail

Tsitsikamma means 'clear waters' in the Hottentot language and you will cross many streams during the five days it takes to wander the 72 kilometres back to Storms River Mouth. You'll pass through indigenous sub-tropical forests, flowering scrub-forests and veld, and pine tree plantations.

There are huts with bunks and mattresses at the starting point (for the use of hikers only) and on the trail. 30 hikers are allowed on the trail at one time. Bookings can be made by contacting The Regional Director, Tsitsikamma Forest Region, Private Bag X537, Humansdorp 6300. (Tel: 04231 5 1180), but are not normally necessary.

Groot River Campsite, where the Tsitsikamma Trail starts, is not far short of perfection, and worth visiting in its own right. Set in a magnificent strand of yellowwood forest, some 60km of day trails radiate from the campsite, passing through sub-tropical forest and a variety of coastal habitats.

Other trails If you can't get on the Otter Trail or are short of time, the nearby two-day 22km Harkerville and 9km Kranshoek trails cover similar terrain. Both start at a picnic site 10km off the N2 between Knysna and Plettenberg Bay. Contact Southern Cape Forestry Branch for details (Tel: 0445 23037).

Good accommodation is available at Knysna at the Hiker's Home (Tel: 0445 24362).

A worthwhile diversion from the Garden Route area is to Oudtshoorn, famous for its ostrich farms. Two are open to the public: touristy but fascinating places where you can ride an ostrich and learn all there is to know about the world's largest bird.

Swellendam Hiking Trail

Swellendam, the third oldest town in South Africa, lies 200km east of Cape Town, just below the southern side of the Langeberg mountain range. In the town there is an interesting museum which gives you a look into the area's history, and a pretty municipal campsite with chalets in the Cape-Dutch style at reasonable rates. There is a bus service between Swellendam and Cape Town (the railway carries only freight).

The Swellendam Hiking Trail is a 50km long circular route which takes five days. The trail criss-crosses the Langeberg range in an area called Marloth Nature Reserve. It is well marked and has a series of well-kept huts, each accommodating 16 people and having outside running water and padded bunks. The lower ones have fire pits with wood. There are two homemade showers and tubs for washing clothes at Wolfkloof, the last hut.

The trails go through fields of pinkish heath and past a variety of colourful wild flowers. Protea Valley is dominated by l,7l0m Misty Point, and is one of the best areas for seeing wild flowers such as the king protea. On a clear day you can see the Indian Ocean from the south side of the Langebergs.

To get a booking on the Swellendam Hiking Trail write to The Regional Director, Western Cape Forest Region, Private Bag 9005, Cape Town 8000 (Tel: 021 45 1224) or book personally at the offices of the Regional Director, Customs House, Table Bay Blvd. 7-9, Cape Town. If you arrive at the forest station outside Swellendam the forester in charge can issue you a permit if there are openings, which is quite likely.

The Cedarberg Mountains

This Wilderness Area lies some l80km north of Cape Town. It specialises in weird rock formations, the most notable of which, the giant 'Maltese Cross' recently succumbed to the forces of gravity so is a memory only. It is also very beautiful in a gently rugged way and one mountain, Sneeuberg, supports that rarest of proteas, the snow protea.

At the southern end of the Wilderness Area is the very dramatic Wolfberg Arch. This is a naturally carved stone arch, half a day's walk from the privately run camping area at Sanddrif. The Wolfberg Cracks are crevices in a rock hill, which is actually outside the Wilderness Area but you can get permission to visit them. There are rock paintings nearby, too. There are huts in the Cedarberg, but you may prefer to camp, which is permissible anywhere.

The centre for backpacking is Algeria; the turnoff is to the east between Citrusdal and Clanwilliam. Here permits are obtainable, and trail maps may be bought, but only on week-days before 5pm. Otherwise you must get your permit from The State Forester, Cedarberg State Forest, Private Bag X1, Citrusdal 7340 (Tel: 02682 3440).

Algeria itself has a lovely campsite, and the Sneeuberg hut lies a day's walk away. Permission to stay there is also obtainable at Algeria. There is a fireplace and firewood is available locally, with plenty of water nearby. The nights are brilliantly clear, and you may have the honour of a visit from an elephant shrew. It whiffled its long nose at our supper, then disappeared into the darkness.

The Drakensberg

This lofty escarpment divides the Natal province from Lesotho. It is South Africa's most popular mountain area and provides some of the finest views in the country. The Drakensberg offers unlimited opportunities for backpacking and rambling: get hold of David Bristow's *Drakensberg Walks* which provides route outlines and sketch maps for over 100 hikes and walks in the region.

There are two major reserves: Royal Natal Park and and Giant's Castle. As a rough guide, you will experience the most majestic views but the toughest conditions in the Royal Natal. Giant's Castle is gentler in nature, and protects a fair amount of game as well as easy-to-get-to bushman paintings. Both reserves have rest camps and campsites, and stock good hiking maps. Hutted accommodation is booked through the Natal Parks Board, PO Box 662, Pietermaritzburg, 3200, Tel: 0331 51514; camping at the individual park office. Royal Natal Tel: 03642 381803, Giant's Castle Tel: 0361 24434. Booking is advisable.

Between the two reserves lies the popular Cathedral Peak area. There's plenty of privately-run accommodation here, including upmarket hotels, self-catering, and camping. Worth a special mention is Inkosana Lodge: not particularly cheap at $20 per person including meals, but the people who run it know the mountains, and it should be a good place to meet other hikers.

Immediately south of Giant's Castle the Mkhomani and Mzimkulu Wilderness Areas provide totally unspoilt hiking terrain 60km long and an average of 20km wide. You'll need a good map and ideally a copy of *Drakensberg Walks* if you want to explore this area. For permits and further details contact The State Forester, Mkhomani Wilderness Area, PO Himeville, 4585 (Tel: dial 033312 ask for 1902); The State Forester, Cobham, PO Himeville, 4585 (Tel: 03392 ask for 1831).

There is one formal five-day hiking trail in the range, Giant's Cup, which runs from Sani Pass (the end of the trans-Lesotho hike) to Silver Streams at Bushman's Nek, and has huts equipped with bunks and mattresses. Reservations and information from The Regional Director, Natal Forest Region, Private Bag X9029, Pietermaritzburg 3200. Tel: 0331 2 8101.

No time of year is ideal for a visit to the 'Berg', and hikers should be aware that weather conditions are notoriously fickle. In the warm summer months it's likely to pour with rain every afternoon and in winter it'll be crisp and clear but very cold. It frequently snows. Spring or autumn seem best. Whichever time of year you select you must bring appropriate clothes. In the summer the most practical rain-wear is your bare skin. As the clouds build up, strip down to your underwear (or, more modestly, your swimsuit), make sure your pack is well covered, and enjoy a cool shower!

There is no public transport to the Drakensberg, so the backpacker without a vehicle must either hire one or rely on hitchhiking. Royal Natal and the Cathedral Peak area are easy hitches; other reserves might take a while to get to.

NATIONAL PARKS AND GAME RESERVES

As well as 18 National Parks, there are about 200 game and nature reserves run by various provincial, homeland, and municipal authorities. More than half of these have rest camps and/or campsites.

The larger game reserves rival those of East Africa for the quantity and variety of wildlife; however, because many of them are covered with scrub vegetation, it is easier for the shyer animals to hide, especially in the wet summer season when the grass is long.

The reserves described below are just the tip of the iceberg. It's worth trying to get to some of the smaller reserves. Many protect unusual habitats and are little visited – ideal places to pitch a tent in peaceful surroundings and ramble at leisure.

Kruger National Park

This is South Africa's largest reserve – about the size of Wales – and more mammal species have been recorded in it than any other on the continent, including elephant, lion, cheetah, leopard, rhino, hunting dog, hyena, hippo, giraffe and a large variety of antelope. There are 10 rest camps, most of which have huts, campsites with fireplaces, and shops selling everything you could possibly need. There are over 1,000km of roads in the reserve. To explore it thoroughly, at least a week is required.

The park can be visited in any saloon car, and consequently a self-drive safari (far more pleasant than a tour) is relatively simple and inexpensive. Two people spending a week in the reserve could expect to spend about $250 each (including petrol, fees, food etc) by hiring a car in Jo'burg, camping, and cooking for themselves. Hitching within the park is forbidden, but it is possible to hitch from outside the park to Skakuza Camp, where you can rent an Avis car for about $40/day (no surcharge). The southern gates are a four to five hour drive, or a day's hitch away from Jo'burg.

Although the Kruger Park isn't touristy in the way many East African reserves are, it does carry a much larger volume of traffic. Tar roads in the south of the park can get uncomfortably busy, particularly around the largest camp Skakuza where day visitors congregate. You'll have a more pleasant trip if you use dirt roads as much as possible or, even better, aim to spend a few days in the part of the park north of the Olifants River: few visitors do and it's far more peaceful as a consequence.

Kalahari Gemsbok National Park

This wonderfully remote park in the Kalahari desert abuts Botswana and Namibia and offers some of the most bleak and haunting scenery in South Africa. 'On three separate days I saw lion, cheetah *and* leopard, and a wonderful diversity of raptorial birds.' (Brian Rogers) Other animals include bat-eared fox and hyena, and their prey: blue wildebeest, springbok, eland, gemsbok (naturally), red hartebeest, and the delightful meerkats and ground squirrels which are common along the roadside.

Put aside a week if you plan to visit this reserve. It's a two-day drive (the second day on dust roads) from either Cape Town or Jo'burg: not worth it unless you spend a few days there. You can visit the reserve in any sturdy saloon car. The park is approached from Upington or Kuruman. Vehicle hire in both towns is expensive. Hitching up would be slow at best, but not completely out of the question. There are three camps.

The park is best visited in the winter – it is too hot in the summer. Bring warm clothes; it often drops below freezing at night.

The Zululand Reserves

There are a cluster of good reserves in the northern Natal province, an area often referred to as Zululand. The two best-known of these are Umfolozi and Hluhluwe (pronounced 'Shlu-shluy'), both of which protect all of the so-called big five and have the densest rhino populations in Africa. Rhino are also common in Mkuzi, a reserve particularly of interest to birdwatchers. There are rest camps in all three reserves, and there's a campsite at Mkuzi's entrance gate which you can stay at without a vehicle.

An interesting and easily visited part of Zululand is the 350 square kilometre St Lucia Estuary, the entire perimeter of which is a sanctuary. A good base is St Lucia village on the south of the estuary, which has four campsites, plenty of cheap self-catering, and good beaches. There are day trails and large mammals in the adjoining St Lucia Game Reserve. The Natal Parks Board office in the village can radio through bookings to other camps and hiking trails around the estuary.

Foot safaris

Several South African game parks have Wilderness Trails for people on foot. Kruger National Park has five (each lasting two days and three nights, and leaving on Mondays and Fridays), Umfolozi two, and Mkuzi, Pilanesburg and Itala one each.

These safaris are ideal for those not wanting to hire a car to visit the parks, since access to the meeting point by hitchhiking is not difficult. Wilderness Trails are very popular and, being limited to about eight people, are booked solid up to a year in advance. Avoid school or public holidays and you have more chance of getting a place. The safaris last three or four days.

Some National Parks have hutted backpacking trails: The Mountain Zebra Hiking Trail (three days) and Springbok Hiking Trail, Karoo National Park, (three days), both in Cape Province, are two of them. Bookings from the National Parks Board.

Further Information and bookings

The Kruger, Kalahari and other national Parks are run by the National Parks Board: PO Box 787, Pretoria, 0001; Tel: (012) 343 1991. The Zululand reserves are run by the Natal Parks Board: PO Box 662, Pietermaritzburg, 3200; Tel: (0331) 51514. A useful booklet *Our World of Wildlife* is available free from tourist offices.

A few tour operators do organised tours to the Kruger Park. Drifters in Johannesburg have an excellent reputation and offer a three day camping trip for under $200 per person all-inclusive. They do a number of other packages including an eight day Zululand tour for around $400 per person. Their address is PO Box 48434, Roosevelt Park, 2129. Tel: (011) 673 7012.

Transkei: the Wild Coast

The Transkei was the first 'independent homeland' and during the days of apartheid it provided welcome relief from government-imposed racial segregation, a glimpse at the culture of the Xhosa people, and perhaps the most beautiful coastal hike in the country, the Wild Coast. At the time of writing, however, the Transkei is considered a highly dangerous area. There have been many reports of shootings and stonings, so until the tension has eased it would be better to avoid it.

A helpful organisation which will be able to give you up-to-the-minute advice is the Transkei Development Corporation. Write to Daphne Lehradt at P/Bag X5028, Umtata, Transkei. Tel: 2-6881; Fax: 23548.

For information about the trail, reservations, maps (scale 1:50,000) and brochures, write to the Secretary General, Department of Agriculture and Forestry, P/Bag X5002, Umtata, Transkei 5100; Tel: (0471) 24322/249309.

OTHER PLACES OF INTEREST

South Africa's attractions are so many I just list my personal favourites.

Stellenbosch

This is South Africa's second oldest town, and it bristles with character. There are numerous old buildings and museums in the town, particularly on Dorp St. Stellenbosch is in the centre of South Africa's winemaking area and there are established Wine Routes on which you can visit a few wine farms and sample the produce. The 16km Vineyard Trail starts in the town. Details from the the Tourist office on Plain St, who are extremely helpful and can help you find accommodation. Tel: (02231) 3568. There are regular trains between Cape Town and Stellenbosch.

Namaqualand

This semi-desert part of the Cape Province erupts into bloom in spring when the rains fall. If you are in the country at that time of year (September) it's a spectacle which shouldn't be missed. Namaqualand's main town is Springbok, which has camping facilities and a few mid-range hotels.

Lamberts Bay

On the west coast, about 275km north of Cape Town, this fishing village has two attractions: in the spring the region is a mass of wild flowers, and at any time Bird Island is a mass of marine birds. Over 150 species have been counted – most spectacular are the Cape gannets, cormorants, and jackass penguins.

Eastern Transvaal

This mountainous area can easily be explored travelling between Jo'burg and the Kruger Park. A highlight is the Blyde River Canyon seen from the Three Rondawels viewpoint. The five-day Blyderivierspoort Trail runs through the canyon.

A good base for exploring the eastern Transvaal is the attractively situated town of Sabie, which has an abundance of cheap self-catering and camping. The 15km Loerie Trail on the slopes of Mt Anderson starts and ends in Sabie. For details of this, Blyderivierspoort, and other trails in the area, visit the Forestry Office in Sabie. Tel: (0131512) 307.

Kimberley

The Duggan-Cronin Bantu Gallery is the best museum of black African culture in South Africa. There are old photographs, paintings and objects used in everyday life, all beautifully displayed.

GLOSSARY OF SOUTH AFRICAN WORDS

Hikers (and readers of this book) often come across words – usually Afrikaans – which have entered the vocabulary of English-speaking South Africans. Here are some which will help you find your way around the countryside.

Donga	small ravine
Kloof	ravine
Koppie/kopje	rocky hill
Kraal	cattle enclosure or African huts
Mielie	corn, maize
Rondavel	round African hut
Veld	grassland

Your travels generally will be less confusing if you know these words ...

Bakkie	pick-up truck
Bioscope	cinema
Boerewors	sausage
Braaivleis/braai	barbeque
Mieliepap	corn porridge
Robot	traffic lights
Tackies	sneakers

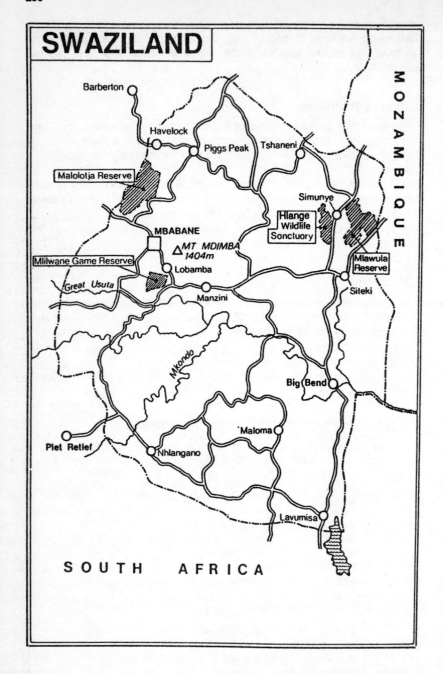

Chapter 19

Swaziland

FACTS AND FIGURES

This tiny kingdom is surrounded on three sides by South Africa on which it is largely dependent. It is a prosperous country which retains its traditional beliefs and ceremonies (King Sobhuza II was the world's longest reigning monarch at the time of his death in 1982), and is one of the most stable countries in Africa.

The altitude ranges from 2,000m to less than 100m, the country being divided into Highveld, Middleveld and Lowveld, according to the altitude. The Lubombo mountains run from west to east.

People

The population is in the region of three and a half million, the majority of whom are Swazis.

Languages are English and siSwati; Christianity is the main religion.

The dry season coincides with the southern hemisphere winter – April to October.

TRAVEL

Impressions

Swaziland makes an agreeable change from the efficiency and tensions of South Africa, and while South Africans were restricted in their travel destinations many visited this little country.

The nature reserves of Malolotja, with its excellent system of trails, make an ideal introduction to hiking or backpacking in Southern Africa, and are strongly recommended as an alternative to South Africa's splendid hiking areas.

Entry and exit

Commonwealth, American, and Scandinavian visitors do not need visas. Most others do; in the absence of a Swazi consulate these can be obtained at the British Embassy in neighbouring countries.

Remember you'll need a re-entry permit for South Africa if you're returning that way.

Money

The most widely used currency is the South African Rand, but Swaziland has its own money, the lilangeni, which has the same value.

What to buy

There are a number of handicraft centres producing a large variety of very good work. Batiks are popular, but the standard is uneven, and this 'traditional craft' was only introduced into the country around 30 years ago. Better are the soapstone carvings, basketware and wooden bowls. Recently Swazi candles in a variety of wonderful colours and patterns have become a popular item.

Maps

The DOS does an excellent relief map of the country, scale 1:250,000. Available from Stanfords.

Accommodation

Since the tourist industry is geared to the visiting South African, hotels tend to be upmarket and relatively expensive. There are two campsites on the Mbabane-Manzini road, Timbali Caravan Park and Paradise Caravan Park. Nature reserves also have camping facilities.

Transport

There is a regular bus service to all towns in the country. Hitchhiking is easy.

Mbabane

Swaziland's capital was one of the places South Africans came to get away from the restrictions of their own country, so there is an abundance of pornography and casinos.

The best budget accommodation is the Mennonite Guest House (Thokoza Church Centre) which has both dormitory accommodation and rooms. It is located on Mhlanhla Rd, across the river in the eastern part of town.

For information on the country write to Swaziland Tourist Department, PO Box 451, Mbabane, Swaziland.

HIKING AND NATURE RESERVES

This is an excellent country for backpacking, with a friendly, hospitable population and numerous paths linking village to village. Try the Usutu River and Piggs Peak areas. But the best backpacking is probably in Malolotja Reserve.

Malolotja Nature Reserve

Situated only about 30km from Mbabane, this park is well administered (and inexpensive to visit), has some beautiful mountain scenery, good trails and campsites, and wonderful flowers. Over 230 bird species have been recorded and there is also a good selection of animals – mainly antelope (wildebeest, hartebeest, blesbok, reedbuck, impala, oribi, klipspringer, duiker), although warthogs and even leopards occur. A network of backpacking trails allows trips from one to seven days; there are campsites near water, but no other facilities. Even if you don't want to backpack, there is a pleasant campsite near the entrance with a large choice of day hikes, or you can stay in comfortable log cabins (sleeping bag needed).

Try to avoid the park during South African school holidays, or public holidays, when it will be crowded.

Bookings for backpacking should be made in advance to: Swaziland National Trust Commission, Malolotja Nature Reserve, P.O. Box 1797, Mbabane, Swaziland, or in person at 5, Lansdown House, Post St, Mbabane.

You should bring food, a stove (no fires are permitted), rain gear (weather conditions change suddenly) and a compass. Maps and permits are obtained from the office near the park entrance.

Mlawula Nature Reserve

Not yet as well developed as Malolotja, this reserve also offers hiking trails as well as opportunities to see larger game animals including rhino. In the eastern part of Swaziland, abutting the Mozambique border, the landscape is a mixture of savannah and well watered mountains (the Lubombo Mountains).

More information from the National Trust address above, or from the Senior Warden, Mlawula Nature Reserve, P.O. Box 312, Simunye, Swaziland.

Hlange Wildlife Sanctuary

A small but interesting game reserve close to Mlawula, with camping facilities. Even without a car, quite a lot of game can be seen.

Mlilwane Game Sanctuary

South of Mbabane is Swaziland's first game reserve. More heavily visited than Hlange, Mlilwane has a good selection of animals for its size, and campsites. A shortish walk from the cabins and campsite are some bushman paintings.

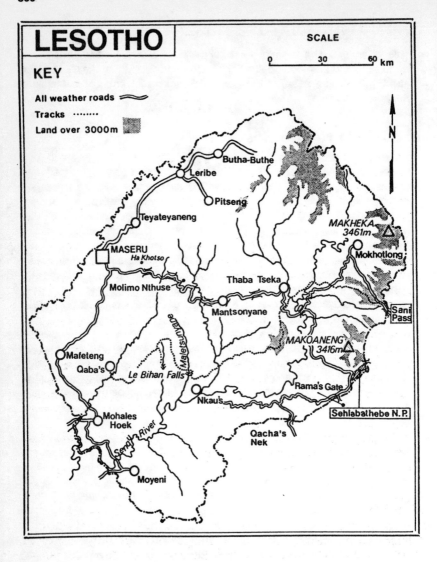

LESOTHO

SCALE

0   30   60 km

KEY

All weather roads

Tracks ········

Land over 3000m

N

Butha-Buthe

Leribe

Pitseng

Teyateyaneng

MASERU
Ha Khotso

MAKHEKA
3461m

Mokhotlong

Molimo Nthuse

Thaba Tseka

Mantsonyane

Sani
Pass

MAKOANENG
3416m

Mafeteng

Qaba's

Le Bihan Falls

Maletsunyane

Rama's Gate

Nkau's

Sehlabathebe N.P.

Mohales
Hoek

Qacha's
Nek

Senqu River

Moyeni

Chapter 20

Lesotho

Updated by Michael Nidd

FACTS AND FIGURES

Lesotho, formerly Basutoland, officially received its independence from Britain in 1966, but it has a long history of independence starting from the mid-18th Century when the first king repelled the invader Shaka Zulu. King Moshoeshoe II was deposed in 1990 while the country was under military rule. In March 1993 a civilian government took over. Clashes between rival army factions threaten democracy.

Lesotho (pronounced Lesutu) is a tiny country (the size of Belgium) completely surrounded by South Africa. It is the only country in the world that is entirely above 1,000 metres and the rugged terrain and scant natural resources make it a nation largely dependent on the rest of the world for aid. Its chief export is men; half the male population works in the South African gold mines.

The dry months are in winter (when there are nightly frosts) between May and September; During the rainy summer season many of the roads are impassable.

People

A million Basotho tribesmen live in Lesotho. There are many clans within this huge tribe, but the nation presents a homogeneous aspect when compared with almost any other country in Africa. Basothos wrap themselves in warm, colourfully patterned blankets, and the distinctive Basotho hat is the emblem of the country.

The official language is English, but Sesotho remains the local language.

TRAVEL

Impressions

Lesotho is a jewel of a country, especially in the spring. The people are hospitable, genial and polite, and the rugged countryside is perfect for backpacking. I shall always have a special affection for the place.

From his 1992 experiences driving around the country, Michael Nidds adds these impressions: 'We noted some stark contrasts. In Maseru in particular, there are plenty of locally-owned BMWs, Mercedes, even the occasional Jaguar (there are also plenty of vehicles whose continuing mobility owes more to divine intervention than to mechanical integrity). Elsewhere there are fewer signs of wealth, and infrastructure expenditure seemed lower. Lesotho is a poor country, with few indigenous industries and little mineral wealth (there is a diamond mine operational at Letseng-na-Terae. The principal rural activity is managing the herds of sheep and angora goats: a challenging task since there is a cultural taboo against fences and most families' wealth is measured by its livestock. We understand that, from infancy to the minimum age for a mineworker, every rural male becomes a full-time herd-boy. There is an ambitious Highlands Water Scheme in progress, involving the building of (eventually) three large dams: Katse, Mashai and Tsoelike, with accompanying hydro-electric and leisure developments. Apart from the economic benefits, there should be long-term benefits to the vegetation through effective water management. The highlands are almost entirely volcanic rock (basalt lavas) with very thin soils; most of the rain runs off, often flash-flooding, carrying the thin soil with it.

'In Maseru we experienced both extremes of politeness: the "high" resulted from asking an immaculately-uniformed traffic warden for directions to the Victoria Hotel; he jumped onto the dusty platform of our pick-up and navigated us through town in the fashion of a harbour pilot. The "low" was achieved by the staff of that hotel (the 3rd most expensive in town). Other highs included the gracious politeness of the rural folk to whom we'd given lifts, even after enduring (in one case) 150km of bone-jarring in the back of the pick-up, and the high standard of service provided by the proprietor and staff of that tiny Mountain Side Hotel in Quthing.'

Entry and exit

If you do not wish to go to South Africa, Lesotho can be reached by plane from Harare (Zimbabwe), Gabarone (Botswana), and Manzini (Swaziland).

In theory, visas are no longer required for a stay of less than 30 days. Overland travellers will need a re-entry permit for South Africa.

Finding your way

Michael Nidd, driving a hired 4-wheel drive vehicle (essential in the interior of the country) reports on the maps available: 'We already had the useful, and inexpensive, Road Atlas of South Africa, published by Map Studio, which covers the country at scales varying from 1:250,000 to 1:1,000,000, with Lesotho laid before us at 1:1,250,000: not sufficient detail. Stanfords of Covent Garden had the answer: Lesotho on two 1:250,000 contour sheets. Our third chart was a free single sheet, courtesy of BP petrol, at a scale of 1:860,000.

'And what fun we had on the road with these three maps! We found that they contradicted one another as to place names *and* locations, to the extent that we'd be desperately looking out for a village at a crucial road junction, not find it, and proceed with ever-increasing doubt, only to find that the village in truth lies 5km away from the road, the other side of a mountain. The best advice we can give is "if in doubt, ask: learn a few words of Sesotho, brush up your sign language and don't be afraid to flag down a lorry and ask the driver".'

Money

Although Lesotho has its own currency, the loti (plural maloti) divided into 100 lisente, this is tied to the South African rand which is accepted everywhere. The only facilities for money-changing are in Maseru.

What to buy

Unfortunately the characteristic Lesotho blanket is made abroad, usually in the United Kingdom, and imported by the Basothos. Basket making has reached high levels in the kingdom, as have pottery and jewellery, but by far the best buy is mohair. Mohair goats do well in the country's rugged terrain and climate. Several cottage industries buy the wool, process it and then produce beautiful rugs, tapestries, shawls and other apparel. The tourist office near the Holiday Inn in Maseru will tell you where these interesting places are located.

At the entrance to the Holiday Inn visitors will see a tourist shop in the shape of an enormous Basotho hat selling typical tourist items from all corners of Lesotho.

Posting your purchases home is fast and safe.

Accommodation

There are numerous rest houses, lodges, inns and hotels scattered throughout the country. Many have campsites, and camping wild is safe and very enjoyable.

Michael Nidd adds this summary of the hotels they stayed at:

'Maseru's Victoria Hotel is poor value for money, but the restaurant provided friendly, efficient, good-value service. The New Oxbow Lodge provides good-value rondavel-style rooms with all the tired traveller needs and a sustaining table-d'hôte menu. It is owned and managed by a genial Greek guy named Costas, who was a fund of useful and interesting information. At Quthing the Orange River Hotel was full so we followed a signpost up a dirt road to the small Mountain Side Hotel. Locally-owned and run, only the proprietor spoke any English and it was a super experience. Everything was clean, everything worked, and the food was excellent: dinner, bed and breakfast and morning tea on a tray cost us the equivalent of £20 for two! Qacha's Nek has the good-value Nthatuoa Hotel on the outskirts of town.

'If you prefer self-catering there is a chalet at the top of the Sani Pass owned by the Himeville Hotel (which is also recommended and better value than Sani Pass Hotel). The chalet has 8 rooms, some with 2 beds and some with 4 bunks: 26 beds in all. Take your own food, do your own cooking. Gas burners, utensils, crockery and cutlery, bedclothes, towels and soap are provided; there's a diesel generator for lighting, and usually hot water in the showers. You could use the chalet as a base for hiking and, depending on season and rainfall, there are plenty of opportunities to see and photograph wildlife and vegetation as well as the mountain scenery. Bookings may be made by writing to P.O. Himeville 4585, or phone 33722 and ask the operator for no 5.'

Transport

Roads are gradually being improved, but tarred roads are still scarce. They mainly run round the western perimeter of the country. With a few exceptions (see map) the interior of the country is served only by dirt roads requiring 4-wheel drive vehicles. This lack of roads is why Lesotho is such a paradise for backpackers. You do have to get to the start of the trail, however, and for this purpose there are occasional buses and minibuses. The latter go everywhere, radiating out from Maseru, especially along the tarred roads. The buses are slower, not as frequent, but cheaper and less crowded. All buses leave from the bus station near the market in Maseru.

Trucks and Land Rovers are frequently used on the rough roads into the interior, and will usually take passengers.

If you are in a hurry, internal flights are reliable and cheap. Although Lesotho has 29 landing strips, flying is limited by the weather.

Horses are probably the most efficient means of transport around the countryside. The Basotho pony is well known for its surefooted ride over long distances (see below).

Pony-trekking

Lesotho is the best country in Africa for riding – horses are the favoured transport of the Basothos, and the country is net-worked with bridlepaths.

The centre for riding and pony-trekking is the Basotho Pony Project at Molimo Nthuse Pass, 60 km from Maseru on the Mountain Road. From here you can ride for an hour or so, or join a four day trek which takes in Lesotho's most spectacular mountain scenery and waterfalls. Write to PO Box 1027, Maseru, for more information. The Malealea Lodge, run by Dick and Di Jones, arrange both pony-trekking and organised hiking trips in the Maluti Mountains. They can be contacted at PO Box 119, Wepener 9944, South Africa, Tel: 09266 785336; Fax: 785326, or by writing to P.O. Makhakhe, 922 Lesotho.

More information from The Lesotho Tourist Board, PO Box 1378, Maseru 100.

Maseru

This small capital (population around 60,000) used to cater to South Africans looking for the sort of Fun they couldn't get at home. Whether it will achieve a new focus or slide further into shabbiness remains to be seen. Most visitors stay here long enough to make arrangements, then leave for the countryside.

The Tourist Office, by the Basotho Hat crafts centre, is helpful.

Phomolong Youth Hostel (Lancer's Gap), off the Tayatayaneng road four kilometres north of Maseru, is your best bet if you're stuck in the capital. Meals are available. You can catch a bus here from the central depot. Alternatively you may be able to stay at the German or Swedish volunteer hostels.

HIKING

As you will have gathered by now, Lesotho offers outstanding hiking and backpacking opportunities. There are so many tracks and paths used by the Basothos, you can walk safely and enjoyably in any direction providing you have a compass and, if possible, a map. You will need to ask directions from the Basothos (school teachers should be sought out as most likely to speak English) but be warned that because they think (quite correctly) that Europeans are not as sturdy as they, they'll send you along vehicle tracks rather than paths. These are often indirect and sometimes cross rivers at dangerous points for walkers. Even if you're not asking directions you should greet everyone you meet in Sesotho.

There is no unsuitable time of year for hiking in Lesotho, but my choice would be between September and November, the spring months. Winter (May to September) is usually clear and sunny but there are heavy frosts at night. In the summer you have to contend with regular afternoon downpours and the roads are sometimes impassable. In the spring you'll have rain, but not excessively, and the hillsides will be covered in flowers. If you do hike in the summer, beware of having to cross rivers in full flood. Basically all rivers in Lesotho run north to south so impede walkers going from east to west. The locals know the best fording places. Don't take risks; if there has been heavy rain you must wait for the waters to subside. We waited three days for the Senqu River to be fordable.

The hikes below are just suggestions. With a good map of the country and the spirit of adventure, you can plan your own cross-country route, taking in some of the places described in *Other places of interest*. For a trans-Lesotho trek, remember that you can only cross into South Africa at recognised border points. On the eastern side of the country these are: Qachas Nek (taking you into Transkei); Rama's Gate (Transkei); Sani Pass (Natal).

One route to Sani Pass

Introduction This is a four or five day hike, plus an extra one or two to get from Maseru to the Senqu (Orange) River. It is not particularly rugged although you are seldom walking along a level trail, and the scenery, village life and wild flowers seen along the way are marvellous.

Frequently we didn't have the vaguest idea of where we were and it didn't matter. Everyone helped us along. One village chief, a former Member of Parliament, staged a dance for us and then insisted his niece carry my backpack on her head the next day. A woman invited us into her house for refreshments, then gave us eggs and guided us up over a pass. And finally a school master recessed classes for the day instructing his pupils to help us ford the Linakeng River and write an essay about it. They very nearly carried us across along with all our baggage. Rarely, in all of Africa, did we meet so many warm, friendly people eager to help.

Preparations   Provisions for five or so days should be purchased in Maseru although if you have any unusual culinary whims do your shopping in South Africa which sells special backpacking food. You will probably be able to buy eggs in the villages and trout from local fishermen. If you're a skilful angler yourself you should be able to catch plenty of fresh fish.

Be prepared for the wet of summer or cold of winter. The weather can change very fast in mountain areas. Fog is common so a compass is essential.   If you are making this traverse across Lesotho as part of an Africa overland trip, you won't want to carry the unnecessary luggage. Send it by rail from Bloemfontein (the South African town nearest to Maseru) to Pietermaritzburg where it will be waiting for you when you arrive from Sani Pass.

Approach   The Mountain Road carries traffic right to Sani Pass, but the condition of the 'road' means that it is very lightly travelled. It is up to you how much of the trek you do by vehicle and how much by foot. Perhaps the best is to get across the Senqu river on four wheels and start walking the other side.

Trails   The first leg of your journey is to get as far as possible up the Mountain Road. Buses leave Maseru for Mantsonyane every day, and there may be one to Thaba-tseka, or beyond. If you find transport to Makhotlong, take the opportunity of varying your route by starting to hike the other side of the Denakeng River. The scenery on this stretch between Mantsonyane and the Senqu River is spectacular, so it's no hardship to ride on an open truck where you get the best view. At Makhotlong you can stay at the Agricultural Training College.

You can start walking any time after you've crossed the Senqu River. It's impossible to describe accurately any particular trail. There are many paths connecting villages, and providing you walk due east you will come to Sani Pass (often known as Sani Top). It's best to remain south of the Linakeng River until you reach an easy fording place. You'll know when you're getting near your destination when locals react with matter-of-fact helpfulness rather than amazement when you ask 'Sani Top?' and point east.

On the fifth day you should reach the road linking Makhotlong with Sani Top, and can follow it to the Himeville Hotel or its self-catering chalet (see *Accommodation*). If you arrive at Sani Top on a Sunday, then you'll have little problem hitching a lift to Pietermaritzburg since many South Africans come up for the weekend.

Across the border on the South African side, the Sani Pass Hostel costs R20 per person or you can camp for R10. There is a bus to Durban twice a week (the Smith Street Youth Hostel has details).

By doing the walk in reverse (ie from Durban to Sani to Makhotlong) you might eliminate a lot of the way-finding problems.

Sehbathebe National Park

This is Lesotho's first National Park, established in 1969 to protect indigenous plants and animals. The park covers 65 square kilometres on the south-west side of the Drakensburg escarpment, with an altitude of about 3,000 metres.

The scenery is spectacular; dominating the park are three peaks, Baroa-ba-Bararo meaning The Three Bushmen. There are many sandstone caves and formations which have been eroded by wind into fantastic shapes, arches, and bowls, the latter providing lovely pools. There is plenty of interesting birdlife here, including the rare Lammergeyer.

For accommodation there's a luxury lodge as well as a hostel, and, of course, camping. Because this park is not easily reached by the average visitor, backpackers may well find they have the place to themselves. From South Africa you approach from Bushman's Nek, near Underberg which is 160 km from Pietermaritzburg. The hike up from Bushman's Nek takes five or six hours.

When you have finished touring the park you can either hike south-west to Qacha's Nek via Ramatseliso's Gate along quite a good track, or go north to Sani Pass, or head northwest to pick up the Mountain Road.

Lebihan (Maletsunyane River) Falls

The popular name for these falls, Semonkong, means 'the place of smoke'. This l90 metre waterfall is Lesotho's most spectacular sight and, being in a very isolated place, the ideal destination for a backpacking trip. The falls are situated in central Lesotho, the nearest town being Ramabanta's, which is as close as you can get by public transport. A dirt road now runs from Ramabanta's to Semonkong, which is also quite an important village, but is passable for vehicles only in the dry season. You ford the deep Makhalend River and go over the Terateng and Baboon's passes.

An alternative access is by a good trail running from Malealea and also Qaba's (Fraser Holiday Lodge), both due west of Semonkong. If you take this trail, when you reach the river beyond the first pass, walk south along its west bank for about five kilometres to come to the Ketane Falls.

Semonkong has a post office, stores and tourist accommodation, and anyone will direct you to the falls, about half an hour's walk away. You can see it from various view points above, or climb down a very steep path to the foot of the waterfall. The altitude loss is 350 metres so don't start out if you're tired.

When you're ready to leave Semonkong there are various possibilities. A good trail leaves the village to run southeast between the peaks of Thaba-Ntso and Thabana-li-Phofu.

It would be nice to continue in this direction, but the Senqunyane River would block your progress. Unless you could find a safe fording place (unlikely in the summer) you'd have to follow its west bank north to Cheche's Pass on the Mountain Road (Trans-Lesotho Highway) or turn south immediately after the pass to reach the village of Nkau's.

There's also a scheduled air service.

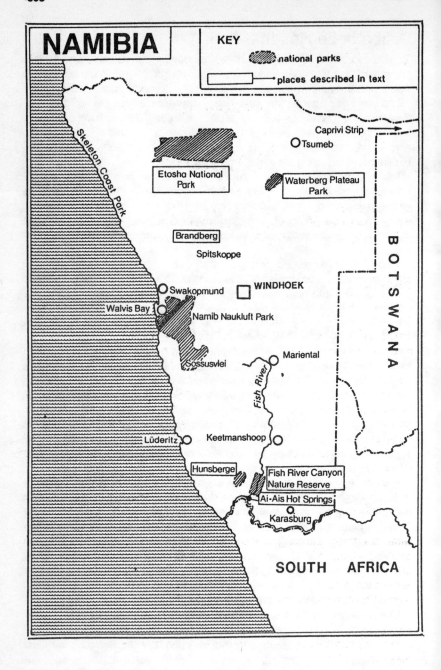

NAMIBIA

KEY

national parks

places described in text

Skeleton Coast Park

Caprivi Strip →

○ Tsumeb

Etosha National Park

Waterberg Plateau Park

B O T S W A N A

Brandberg

Spitskoppe

○ Swakopmund

WINDHOEK

Walvis Bay ○

Namib Naukluft Park

Sossusvlei

○ Mariental

Fish River

○ Lüderitz

Keetmanshoop ○

Hunsberge

Fish River Canyon Nature Reserve

Ai-Ais Hot Springs
○ Karasburg

SOUTH   AFRICA

Chapter 21

Namibia

By David Else.
With original contributions from Krieger Conradt, Alex Radway, Brian Rogers,
Gordon and Merlin Munday, Robin and Jannice Heath

FACTS AND FIGURES

Namibia is a large, arid and sparsely populated country, having borders with
Angola to the north, Botswana to the east, and South Africa to the south. The
west coast is bounded by the Atlantic Ocean. The country is roughly wedge-
shaped, wider in the north, with an area of some 823,000 square kilometres
(nearly four times the size of Britain). From the northeast corner a land
corridor called the Caprivi Strip links Namibia to Zambia and Zimbabwe.

Namibia was called German South West Africa until its surrender during the
First World War to British and South African forces. In 1929 the League of
Nations mandated the territory to South Africa, and this administration
continued for 60 years. After a period of peaceful transition, Namibia gained
independence on March 21 1990, and became a member of the
Commonwealth.

Namibia is a country of vast landscapes and far horizons, of great diversity
in its geology, topography, flora and fauna, with negligible rainfall and little
permanent running water. It can be divided into four main regions: the Namib
Desert, a band of inhospitable sand dunes and gravel between 80 and 140km
wide, stretching the length of the coastline; a central mountainous area
covering about half of the country, where vegetation comprises scrub
savannah in the south and thorn savannah in the north; the Kalahari Desert
to the east, a land of savannah grassland, trees and bush; and a northern
plain of bush and patches of vegetated riverine forest.

This is an ancient land, with a complex of delicately balanced and fragile
ecosystems. To protect these, in the interests of both conservation and
recreation, over 12% of the country has been set aside as national parks and
reserves.

The best time to visit Namibia is during the winter months of April/May to
August. Temperatures are usually comfortably warm (20 to 25°C), and good
for hiking, although the cloudless nights can be chilly. In summer, October
to April, temperatures are very hot (30 to 40°C) and nights warm. Rainy times
are October and November (the small rains) and January to April (the big

rains).

Namibia's chief exports are diamonds (mined from restricted areas along the coast), uranium and copper. Fishing, cattle farming, and the breeding of Karakul sheep also contribute to the country's economy. Tourism is also an important currency earner. About 70% of the population depends directly, or indirectly, on agriculture.

People

Namibia has a scattered population of only 1.3 million and is one of the most thinly populated countries in Africa, although the population is growing rapidly.

Eleven ethnic groups make up Namibia's population: Ovambos, Kavangos, Hereros, Damaras, Whites, Namas or Khoi, Coloured, Caprivians, San or Bushmen, Basters and Tswanas. Half the population are Ovambos. (Particularly noticeable in the main cities are the Herero women in their 'missionary' dresses of voluminous frocks and petticoats.)

Each group has its own language and dialect. Since independence English has been the official language, although this is spoken as a first language by a very small minority. Afrikaans is still the country's common tongue and German is also widely spoken and understood.

Christianity is the main religion.

TRAVEL

Impressions

Travel in Namibia was a real pleasure: everything is well-organised, campsites and national parks are properly maintained, the restcamps and guest-farms are comfortable, and the people (of all races) are friendly and hospitable. And on top of that you've got stunning landscapes and some of the best hiking areas in Africa.

Entry and exit

Entry regulations are straightforward. Visas are not required by citizens of most European countries and the USA. Tourists are allowed to stay for 60 days, but this can easily be extended.

Money

After independence Namibia's currency continued to be the South African rand (R), divided into 100 cents. In early 1993 £1 = R5. The new Namibian dollar, which will be tied to the rand, is planned for late 1993.

What to buy

Semi-precious stones are probably the best buy: there are several dealers in Windhoek. (Note that it is a criminal offence to be in possession of uncut diamonds.) Locally made leather goods and sheepskin clothes are also available. There are several shops and stalls in Windhoek selling traditional carvings, paintings, etc.

Maps and guidebooks

Maps and guidebooks are of quite a high standard. A good general map of the country, showing national parks and tourist sites is published by the Ministry of Wildlife, Conservation and Tourism (usually called, more simply, the Ministry of Tourism). This map is fine for all but the most adventurous off-road driving, and is available free from the tourist office in Windhoek (and usually from tourist offices in other countries – see below for addresses).

For more detail, 1:50,000 maps of most parts of the country (including the main hiking areas) are available from the Office of the Surveyor-General, part of the Ministry of Lands, Resettlement and Rehabilitation, in the Justicia Building, next to the main post office in Windhoek.

There are several general guides to Namibia, including *Guide to Namibia and Botswana* (Bradt) aimed at independent travellers, and the *Spectrum Guide to Namibia* (Camerapix) and the *Insight Guide to Namibia* (Apa) with more background information and colour pictures. *The Visitor's Guide to Namibia* and *A Guide to Namibian Game Parks*, both written by the knowledgeable team of Willie and Sandra Olivier, are also easy to buy in Windhoek bookshops.

Tourist Information

The Tourist Office in Windhoek is on Independence Avenue, near the Continental Hotel. The staff are very helpful and there's a good range of maps and leaflets available.

Namibia also has tourist offices in South Africa and Europe: Carlton Centre, PO Box 11405, Johannesburg 2000, tel: 011 3317055; Shell House, PO Box 739, Cape Town 8000, tel: 021 4193190; Postfach 2041, W-6380, Bad Homburg 3, Germany, tel: 06172 406650; 1 Approach Rd, Raynes Park, London SW20 8BA, UK, tel: 081 5432122.

Accommodation

There are hotels in all the cities and towns. Most have good facilities, and prices are reasonable by European standards although not cheap for travellers on a tight budget. Many towns and tourist centres also have a campsite or municipal restcamp (with bungalows) which are cheaper.

In rural areas you can stay at private guest-farms, which offer comfortable full-board accommodation, or restcamps, which may be more simple and have self-catering facilities.

Most national parks have restcamps with self-catering rooms, bungalows and campsites which are very good value, with toilets, shower blocks, fireplaces, shops and many other facilities.

For campsites and accommodation in national parks, the whole system is geared towards people travelling on fixed itineraries making prior reservations. Ideally, you should make your reservations for national park accommodation in advance by writing to the Reservations Office, Ministry of Tourism, PO Box 13267, Windhoek. To help plan your trip get a copy of the *Namibia Accommodation Guide for Tourists*, published annually by the Ministry of Tourism. Write to your nearest tourist office (addresses above) – for a copy. This booklet lists all hotels, guest farms, restcamps, campsites and national park camps, with details of prices, facilities and so on.

This system can make things difficult (but not impossible) for tourists coming to Namibia at fairly short notice. If you cannot reserve national park accommodation before you arrive, you can still do it in Windhoek by visiting the Reservations Office, on the corner of Independence Avenue and John Meinert Street. Make a rough plan of where you want to go, but be prepared to make a few changes to the plan. The system is normally very efficient.

For private accommodation (eg hotels or guest-farms), the easiest way to make a reservation is by mail in advance, or by telephone from Windhoek. All numbers and addresses are listed in the *Accommodation Guide* and the post and phone systems in Namibia are efficient.

Namibia is popular with visitors from South Africa, and during school holidays demand for accommodation is high. The holiday seasons are two weeks over Easter, mid June to late July, the last two weeks in September, and mid December to mid January.

Transport

Namibia does not have a good public transport system. Buses are rare or non-existent, even on main routes, and the rail network is limited, and trains very slow. To get around, local people either drive or hitchhike.

Car hire   For visitors, a car makes things easy and is the only way to reach many of the national parks and hiking areas. There are car rental firms in Windhoek and some other towns. Most places described in this chapter can be reached by saloon (sedan) car. Four-wheel-drive (4WD) vehicles are necessary only for remote areas. Prices for a saloon car are around R200 ($70 or £40) per day including insurance and unlimited distance. Cars with 4WD cost twice this.

Travellers on a limited budget may see this as expensive, but car hire costs should be weighed against cheap national park accommodation and entrance fees. Split between four people, the cost of a week's driving and hiking tour of Namibia compare favourably with a trek on Kilimanjaro or a walking safari in Zimbabwe.

Driving conditions   The main roads in Namibia are tarred, well-maintained and have very light traffic. Additionally, the country has a large network of gravel roads with good all-weather surfaces which are normally fine for saloon cars.

When driving on gravel roads you should remember that road surfaces can vary: be prepared for sudden dips and patches of soft sand, especially on corners. Inexperienced drivers can easily get into a slide and roll off the road. Quite apart from the risk of injury a long way from possible help, your hire car insurance does not cover this type of accident and you'll be liable for all costs. A speed of less than 100 kph is highly recommended on gravel roads. Also, watch out for wild animals and livestock, particularly at night. After heavy rains, look out for no road at all!

Most gravel roads are used by less than 20 vehicles per day so mechanical and medical assistance is limited. When hiring a car, make sure it has good tyres (including the spare), plus a basic tool kit (for changing it). Carry plenty of water and some emergency food, plus a sleeping bag or blanket in the car (night temperatures can be very cold) in case of breakdown.

Petrol is available in towns (large and small) and at most national parks. Off the main routes some farms also sell petrol. Generally, if you can reach a place easily in a saloon car, you can normally find petrol along the way. Even so, supplies are sometimes unreliable, so fill up whenever you get the chance. In areas where you need 4WD, petrol supplies are usually limited so you'll need jerry cans. Your car hire company will advise you.

Hitchhiking   If you decide to try hitching, the light traffic makes it very slow on all but the main tarred roads. It is not uncommon to wait more than day for a lift. It is normally impossible to hitch into the national parks where large animals are present, as you have to arrive and leave in the same vehicle. Also, most cars are so loaded up, they are unlikely to give lifts anyway. (Some hiking areas which can be reached without a car are described in the main *Hiking* section.)

Air   Air Namibia flies from Windhoek's Eros Airport (on the edge of the city) to Swakopmund, Keetmanshoop, Etosha and several other destinations. From the International Airport (about 40km outside Windhoek) Air Namibia also flies to Cape Town and Jo'burg (South Africa), Harare and Victoria Falls (Zimbabwe), Lusaka (Zambia) and Maun (Botswana). Air Namibia also operate regular flights between Windhoek and London (UK) and Frankfurt (Germany) which makes Windhoek an easy place to reach and an ideal centre for touring southern Africa (see Chapter 1, *Getting There* for more details).

DESERT ECOLOGY

Every living thing that inhabits the desert is uniquely adapted to withstand high temperatures and little or no water. In Namibia the coastal dunes are frequently bathed in fog, and it is this moisture that sustains life. Even in regions completely devoid of vegetation, the wind brings vegetable matter to feed the many insects, particularly beetles (over 200 species), that are at the bottom of the food chain. These provide food for reptiles and rodents. All have their ways of avoiding being burnt to a cinder in the sun in an environment where the temperature might reach 70°C: they burrow into the sand where air circulates around the sand grains. Even the golden mole finds enough oxygen at a considerable depth. Evaporation is reduced by burrowing, but some water is necessary to sustain life. Sea fogs provide it. A small flightless beetle, *Onymacris unquicularis*, does a headstand and lets the moisture trickle down its back and into its mouth.

Locomotion on hot sand is a problem. The *toktokkie* beetle "swims" across the sand, the sidewinder snake, *Bitis peringuey*, goes sideways, and the dancing white spider becomes a ball and rolls down the dunes (and dances a jig at the bottom). The gecko *Palmatogecko rangeyi* has broad feet which function as snow shoes, and other lizards are careful not to keep their feet on the hot sand for too long, lifting them alternately to prevent burning.

Vegetation, where it exists, is specially adapted to the environment. Rain promotes immediate rapid growth of grasses, but there are several plants that survive all year round. They store water in their bulbous stems or trunks. Many are unique to the region. The most famous is the long-lived Welwitschia dwarf tree, with its tattered leaves, and the kokerboom, or quiver tree, which is the symbol of Namibia. This vegetation nourishes the larger game animals, all of which are adapted to the conditions in some way. For example, the eland and gemsbok have an unusual system of blood circulation around the neck and nose that minimises heat absorption, and other desert-dwelling herbivores rely on water-storing desert plants to provide much of their needed moisture.

TOWNS

Windhoek

Namibia's modern capital still retains something of its colonial past, with old German-style buildings and German dishes on the menus, but there's little in the way of sightseeing, although the museum is good, particularly for the natural history exhibits.

Accommodation ranges from the top-class Kalahari Sands Hotel (around R500 (£100/$150) a double), through a selection of tourist-class hotels (eg The Continental with singles/doubles from R100/R250, or the Pension Handke at R150 a double) to the the Backpacker's Lodge (where a bed in the dormitory costs about R20). Camping is available at the Safari Hotel Caravan Park, about 5km from the city centre (there's a bus for hotel guests).

Swakopmund

Swakopmund was once Namibia's main port and is now its main holiday resort, and *the* place to go in the summer, when Windhoek gets too hot. At any time of year the town is worth visiting for its excellent museum, fine restaurants and good beaches. The town is linked to Windhoek by train and bus, and you can also hitch.

Swakopmund has several good hotels, and a municipal restcamp with reasonably priced bungalows. There is also a large caravan park 6km to the north of the town.

In the evening, a colourful sight is the return of thousands of flamingos and other waders to the salt pans north of Swakopmund. Also, watch out for pelicans on the lamp-posts around the town.

Walvis Bay

Walvis Bay is a South African enclave, completely surrounded by Namibian territory. In 1993 border controls were abolished, and visitors can pass through the town (travelling between Swakopmund and the Namib-Naukluft Park) without formalities. There is very little here of interest to tourists.

Lüderitz

Lüderitz is an old German colonial port of considerable charm (it was the first German settlement in Namibia), and warrants a few days' stay. Accessible by train or tarred road, the town is now a resort more than a working port: the seafood (especially lobster) and local recreational facilities are excellent.

Apart from eating, things to do in the area include a visit by boat to the nearby fur seal colony, birdwatching, plant hunting (there are several Namibian species to be found round here) and relaxing on the many beaches. The ghost diamond mining town of Kolmanskop is nearby.

HIKING

Perhaps surprisingly, Namibia has a good range of walking trails, mostly in national parks and protected areas. Following the South African style, trails are well-organised and well-defined: Hiking Trails follow a specific route and are clearly way-marked, with basic accommodation provided on trails more than one day long; Backpacking Trails usually follow a specific route, but are not way-marked (which means you may need a map and compass) and no accommodation is provided (so you need a tent or you sleep under the stars); Wilderness Trails do not follow a specific route, and are led by a professional guide. Accommodation may or may not be provided.

Trails of longer than one day are usually open to only one group at a time, and the number of groups may be restricted to around four per month, to avoid environmental damage. You usually have to reserve a date for doing the trail. This makes things difficult for visitors who come to Namibia at short notice, but slots sometimes become available as other people cancel. Bookings for trails are all handled by the Ministry of Tourism Reservations Office (see *Accommodation* above), so you can arrange your hiking and places to stay at the same time. A trail fee is usually charged, payable with your national park fees.

There are also several areas where one-day hiking trails are available, where reservations and trail fees are not required. For visitors with limited time a tour of several parks, doing a selection of one-day hikes, is an good way to see the country.

Equipment and clothing   You will need to carry a tent if you are backpacking during the rainy months, although for the rest of the year a sleeping bag and mat (and maybe a lightweight mosquito net) will be fine. Fires are not permitted on most trails, so you also need a stove and cooking gear. To avoid dehydration you need to start each day's walk carrying at least two litres of water, so extra bottles are required.

Even in the winter, the sun is very strong and you must have a sun hat, lipsalve and sun cream. Long-sleeved cotton shirts with collars are preferable to T-shirts. The choice between long trousers and shorts is usually down to personal preference, although some people swear by the extra protection offered by trousers in the rare event of a snake bite. Warm clothing should be taken for evenings as temperatures can fall rapidly, often close to freezing, as soon as the sun sets. Fleece or down-filled jackets are ideal as they are light and compact.

The Fish River Canyon

Introduction   The Fish River is the longest river in Namibia, rising near the centre of the country and flowing over 760km southwards to meet the Orange River on the South African border. It is one of few rivers in the country which continues to flow in the dry season. In the south the Fish River flows through a deep and dramatic canyon which, at 550m deep and over 160km long, is second in size only to the Grand Canyon of America.

The Fish River Canyon has been declared a national park, and a backpacking trail follows its most spectacular section, running along the floor of the canyon for 85 to 90km (depending on short cuts), taking about five days to complete. This is one of Africa's classic trails, although it remains virtually unknown outside the region.

Preparations   The trail is very popular with hikers from South Africa, and reservations must be made well in advance. Only one group (of minimum three and maximum 40 people) can start the hike each day, although some hikers have been allowed to join a group already booked with a spare space. The canyon can only be hiked from May to August. Other times are too hot.

When you make your reservation you are given a certificate for a doctor to complete (less than 40 days before you start), stating that you are suitably fit. Then your trail permit is issued. Visitors from overseas can get a letter from their own doctor, which may be accepted by the reservation authorities (although it may need to be verified by a local doctor).

An excellent leaflet describing the trail and many of its features, including the geology, history and wildlife of the area, has been produced by Willie and Sandra Olivier (authors of *Discover Southern Africa on Foot*) and is usually available from the Tourist Office in Windhoek. (Some extracts from the leaflet are reproduced here, with permission.)

Approach   The trail can only be followed north to south. It starts near Hobas Camp, which is 12km to the east of the canyon, on the northern boundary of the park. It is virtually impossible to reach the start, and do the trail, without the help of a car (and a non-hiking companion) to drop you off, although you could possibly hitch to Hobas if you had enough patience.

The night before the trail you can stay at Hobas campsite or at Ai-Ais, 65km from Hobas at the southern end of the canyon. The trail ends at Ai-Ais which is a well-developed 'resort' (holiday camp) with campsite and accommodation. Facilities include swimming pools, restaurant, petrol station and shop.

Facilities   There are no facilities of any kind on the trail. You can bring a tent but most people find a sleeping bag and mat sufficient. You are allowed to make a fire, but driftwood may be hard to find, so many hikers carry a stove. You need to bring all your food supplies. Water is available from the river and is supposed to be safe to drink, although less hardy hikers may prefer to filter and purify their drinking water.

Throughout the trail, you should not walk too fast because the soft sand, boulders and scorching sun will wear you down. Many hikers recommend an early start, getting more than half the day's walk done by mid-morning. This is followed by a long lunch-break (and cooling swim), then the rest of the stage done in the last three hours before sunset. (Remember that sunset comes earlier when you're at the bottom of a canyon – about 6pm.)

The Trail

The official start of the trail is at Hikers' Viewpoint, 14km from Hobas Camp. A signboard here carries the following message:

Friend, if perhaps in a year or ten,
You may want to walk this path again.
Then fail not to remove the trace
Of synthetic foil, cans and other waste,
Plastics that no living thing can flourish on
Or traps you will not wish to step upon.
Else in times which are soon to come
Instead of beauty you will find a slum.
And perhaps then you will come to understand
How the splendour of our land
Was spoilt by your hand.(Roodepoort Hiking Club)

The first section of the trail drops steeply into the canyon. Chains have been set on the steepest parts. When you reach the floor of the canyon you simply follow the river downstream. After about 12km, a path comes in from the left. This leads out of the canyon up to the Southern Viewpoint and should only be used in an emergency. After 2km you reach the Sulphur Springs, sometimes called Palm Springs. Most groups spend their first night here, and their second night in the area of Table Mountain, on the west bank of the river about 30km from the start.

As you continue down the canyon it is advisable to cross to the inside of bends. This means wading the river but it shortens the distance. After about 45km a path on the right leads away from the river and cuts across a large loop called Bushy Corner. Just beyond this, at about 50km, another path avoids the even larger Three Sisters bend. As you cross the higher ground the impressive Four Finger Rock is visible to the south.

You drop to the river (the third night is usually spent in this area) and leave it again almost immediately on another shortcut path which meets the river once more near the German Soldier's Grave (the soldier was killed in 1905 during a small battle against the local Nama tribe).

The trail leads on to Ai-Ais, with one more short cut and one more night's camp. Just before Ai-Ais you pass a large weir and you don't see the camp until almost the last moment.

The Fish Eagle Backpacking Trail

Just to the north of main Fish River Trail, this new trail follows the Fish River for three days, where it flows through a private conservation area. The canyon here is large and deep, although not quite as spectacular as the main canyon further south. Reservations are required but the trail is not as crowded as the Fish River Canyon, so getting a space is easier.

The base before and after the trail is Augurabies Restcamp, near Holoog, south of Keetmanshoop. (The camp is signposted.) There are simple bungalows and a campsite here, with water, basic shower and toilets, and a small shop. The restcamp can be reached by saloon car, and the landowner drops hikers at the start of the trail in his Land Rover. On the trail there are no facilities, so you need a sleeping bag, stove and food.

If you don't want to do the three-day hike, there are many one-day walks in the area, along tributary gorges or up to the surrounding hills, where zebra, oryx and jackal can be seen.

For more information about the Fish Eagle Trail contact Top Travel in Windhoek (address in *Safari Companies* below). If you don't have a vehicle, Top Travel organise all-inclusive hiking tours in this area.

The Naukluft Mountains

The Naukluft area is a mountain-plateau forming a distinct part of the Namib-Naukluft National Park. There are no roads or tracks through the Naukluft area, so the only way to appreciate it is on foot. The Naukluft Hiking Trail is a 120km circular route around the edge of the plateau, taking eight days. It is also possible to do half the trail, finishing after day four. There are two shorter one-day hikes: the Waterkluft Trail (17km) and the Olive Trail (10km). Both are clearly way-marked and very enjoyable, leading through a variety of landscapes from narrow vegetated ravines to dry open hilltops. The view from the escarpment edge is spectacular, and there's also the chance of spotting some of the shy mountain zebra.

Preparations   The Naukluft Hiking Trail is not as popular as the Fish River Canyon Trail, but it can only be started on the first and third Wednesdays and Sundays of each month between March and October so it is sometimes hard to get a space. You can reserve in advance by writing to the Reservations Office of the Ministry of Tourism (details above). Visitors arriving in Namibia at short notice can visit the office to see if a slot is available. Booking for the campsite can be done at the same time.

Groups must contain a minimum of three and a maximum of 12 hikers, and medical certificates are required (more details on medical certificates in the Fish River section above).

A leaflet describing the eight-day Naukluft Hiking Trail (and its four-day version) is available from the Tourist Office in Windhoek. (Some extracts are reproduced here.) The trail is also fully described in *Discover Southern Africa on Foot* (See page 286).

For the Waterkluft Trail and the Olive Trail no reservations or permits are required and you can do them on any day. Maps are available from the park office.

Approaches   The park office, campsite and start of the hiking trails are in the western corner of the park. To reach the park by car, turn off the Solitaire-Maltahohe road at Bullsport Farm and follow a gravel road southwest for 5km to reach the entrance gate (unguarded). From here to the park office and campsite is another 17km.

It may be possible to reach Naukluft without a car, by hitching to Bullsport, then walking the 22km to the park office. There is also a bus from Mariental to Walvis Bay every Monday (returning every Tuesday) via Bullsport. (Sometimes this bus goes south of Naukluft, via Sesriem, so check before setting out.)

Facilities   There is a small campsite in the park, with water, fireplaces and toilet block. Walkers doing the main Naukluft Trail can stay in a bunkhouse called 'Hikers' Haven'. On the trail itself there are basic shelters so a tent is not required, although you need warm clothes and sleeping bag as nights can be cold. Shelters have water and toilets, but fires are not allowed, so you need a stove, cooking gear and all your food. The park has no shop.

The Naukluft Trail

From Hikers' Haven and the park office the trail keeps to the Naukluft River (usually dry), as it flows southwards out of the mountains. The trail then climbs and follows the edge of the escarpment, with excellent views on the left over the plains, to reach Putte Shelter, 14km (6 hours) from the start.

On the second day the route crosses the rolling plateau to a junction called Bergpos, then drops down the narrow Ubusis Kloof to reach Ubusis Hut, a comfortable cottage (15km, 6 hours).

On day three you retrace to Bergpos then continue across the plateau to Alderhost Shelter (12km, 4 hours). On day four the trail is fairly level at first then drops to the shelter at Tsams Ost (17km, 6 hours). A driveable track leads from here to the Maltahohe-Sesriem-Solitaire road, and hikers doing only four days can be picked up here. It is not allowed to start the hike here.

On day five the trail is steep at first and then fairly undulating, levelling out towards the end where it follows a tributary of the Die Valle River to reach Die Valle Shelter (17 km, 6 hours). On day six the trail climbs up a narrow gorge to reach a high point called Quartz Valley before dropping down the Arbeid Adelt Valley to Tufa Shelter (16km, 6 hours).

On day seven the trail climbs steeply (chains in places) back up to the plateau with excellent views to the left (east) to reach Kapokvlakte Shelter (14km, 5 hours). On the last day the trail descends gradually, then more steeply, to meet the Waterkluft (1-day) Trail and follow the Naukluft River back to the campsite and Hikers' Haven (16km, 5 hours).

Hardy hikers can combine days seven and eight into a stiff 30km walk which requires about 11 hours to complete. An early start is essential, and you should not go beyond Kapokvlakte Shelter if there is less than five hours of daylight left.

The Waterkluft Trail

This trail starts near the campsite. It is 17km long, and you should allow six to seven hours to do it comfortably. White-painted footprints clearly mark the way.

The first part of the trail follows the Naukluft River upstream through the beautiful gorge which gives the area its name (Naukluft means narrow gorge). In the early part of the winter dry season (April-May) the river still flows in some areas and the shady pools are full of frogs and tadpoles.

After about two hours (of slow walking) you reach a painted rock marking the last water point, although you should bring water from the campsite anyway as this source is not reliable. Beyond this point the canyon opens out and you continue for two hours more to reach another painted rock marking the halfway point. From here the trail climbs steeply up to the highest point: a peak of about 600m with fine views of the surrounding area.

The trail winds down through a zone of cactus plants into a large valley, then follows the river (usually dry) downstream, crossing it several times to cut off bends, and keeping left to avoid steep shelves (waterfalls in the wet season). In this area some large cairns mark the route of the old German Cannon Road, which also follows the river valley for a short section before climbing steeply up to the main southern ridge of the plateau.

Below the waterfalls, the trail meets the Naukluft River. You turn left and follow the footprints back to the campsite.

The Olive Trail

This trail starts about 4km to the east of the park office, just north of the track back to the (unguarded) entrance gate. You can walk or drive this first 4km to get to a small parking area at the start of the trail, which is clearly signposted.

The trail is 10km long and takes about four hours to do comfortably. From the parking area, the trail climbs gradually up to the top of a small plateau, then descends, following a series of river valleys and narrow gorges, to meet a driveable track which leads back to the parking area.

The Waterberg Plateau Park

The Waterberg Plateau lies about 300km to the north of Windhoek, and was declared a park in 1972 for breeding and protecting rare animals. The plateau is about 50km long by 20km wide, with mainly broadleafed deciduous vegetation which contrasts sharply with the thornbush savanna of the surrounding plains.

Waterberg's animal population includes rhino, buffalo, leopard, roan and sable antelope, many of which have been translocated from other parts of southern Africa. Animals take priority here, and cars cannot drive around the park, but visitors can explore different parts of the plateau on foot. There is a choice of trails: the four-day Guided Wilderness Trail, led by a park ranger, based in the western part of the park; the four-day circular Unguided Hiking Trail in the southern part of the park; plus several short trails (2 - 4km) around the park restcamp.

Preparation Like all the other long hiking trails in Namibia, the four-day trails at Waterberg can only be done on certain days and groups need to reserve in advance. Visitors arriving in Namibia at short notice can visit the Reservations Office in Windhoek to check for vacant slots.

The long trails are only open from April to November. The guided wilderness trail can be done on the second, third and fourth weekends of every month, and groups must be between six and eight people. The unguided hiking trail can only be started on Wednesdays (ending on Saturdays) and groups must be between three and ten people. Bookings for accommodation or camping at the park restcamp can also be made at the reservations office.

Leaflets describing the longer trails may be available at the Tourist Office in Windhoek. A map of the shorter trails around the restcamp is available from the park office.

Approach Most hikers stay at the park restcamp (called Bernabe de la Bat Camp, after a leading Namibian conservationist) before or after doing a trail. To reach the restcamp, turn east off the main Windhoek-Otjiwarongo road, about 20km south of Otjiwarongo, then follow minor roads for about 50km to reach the restcamp (signposted). It may also be possible to hitch here.

Facilities The Barnabe de la Bat Restcamp has a campsite, rooms and bungalows, plus a restaurant, swimming pool, museum, shop and information centre. The camp is sensitively designed and blends in well with the local surroundings, making it the most pleasant of all the large camps in Namibia.

Both the four-day trails have basic shelters, so all you need is a mat and sleeping bag. (Many hikers prefer to sleep out under the stars.) Firewood is provided on the guided wilderness trail, but fires are not allowed on the hiking trail so you need to bring a stove. For both trails you need to bring your own food. There is a well-stocked shop at the restcamp, which also sells small guidebooks to the flora and animals of the Waterberg area.

The Waterberg Guided Wilderness Trail

This trail starts at the park wildlife administration centre at Onjoka, about 20km from the park office and restcamp. You must arrive here between 2pm and 4pm on the Thursday afternoon. A park nature conservator drives the group up to the top of the plateau.

To reduce pressure on the fragile environment, there are no set paths and the group is led through the bush by the conservator, following natural routes such as game tracks and dry river beds. The conservators are all well-trained and know a great deal about the wildlife, vegetation and even the night stars.

Daily distances depend on the overall fitness of the group, and items of interest found along the way, but generally do not exceed 15km. A variety of birds and animals may be seen, along with dramatic scenery of multicoloured sandstone cliffs surrounding the plateau and a number of hidden springs.

You return to Onjoka on Sunday afternoon with enough time to return to Windhoek, if you are not staying at the restcamp.

The Waterberg Unguided Hiking Trail

This trail starts near the restcamp and is 42km long, taking four days. The days are short and the walking is not strenuous, allowing you to walk slowly and take time to observe the flora, birds and other wildlife.

To reach the start, follow one of the short trails to Mountain View on top of the plateau escarpment. From here the route goes east along the edge of the plateau, then north along the edge of a large ravine to reach Otjozongombe shelter (13km, 6 hours). On the second day, the trail aims east again, keeping to the edge of the plateau to reach Otjomapenda shelter (7km, 3 hours) where you spend two nights, going out to do a 8km circuit on day three. On the last day the trail leads westwards, across less undulating ground back to Mountain View (14km, 6 hours).

The Waterberg Short Trails

Around the restcamp area are nine short trails, designed to take hikers through a variety of landscapes and vegetation types, and past several items of interest such as giant anthills, a grove of aloe trees, and the ruins of a mission dating from German colonial times. Some of the routes lead along the base of the spectacular plateau escarpment, and one leads up to Mountain View, an excellent vantage point overlooking the camp, with clear views along the rocky cliffs and out over the surrounding plains.

Other things to do at Waterberg   The park operates a half-day 'safari' on top of the plateau in a special open-top vehicle. This costs R25 per person and can be booked on the spot. Every Wednesday morning it is also possible to see the park's population of rare Cape vultures being fed.

Other Hiking Areas

The Ugab River Guided Wilderness Trail

The Ugab River is in northwest Namibia, flowing down to the coast north of Swakopmund, and forming the southern boundary of the Skeleton Coast National Park. This is a very dry and barren part of the country, but the river provides water for the vegetation that grows along its course which in turn attracts large numbers of birds and animals. It also provides a natural backpacking route through the desert.

The Wilderness Trail is led by a park conservator and follows the river for three days, covering a distance of about 50 km. The trail can only be done twice each month (starting on the second and fourth Tuesdays) and needs to be reserved in advance, through the Reservations Office in Windhoek. Medical certificates are required and you must provide all your own food and equipment. There are no shelters or any other facilities, but tents are not required. More information is available from the Tourist Office, and in *Discover Southern Africa on Foot*.

The Inselbergs

By Alex Radway

The Inselbergs are isolated intrusions that rise majestically from the barren coastal plains of the Namib Desert to provide some excellent walking terrain. Inselbergs of particular interest include Brandberg ('Burnt Mountain'), Erongo, the Pontoks and Spitzkoppe. All are accessible in a saloon car on gravel roads, although 4WD vehicles will reduce 'walk-in' times.

The Brandberg   The Brandberg Massif includes the Königstein peak, the country's highest point (2,579m). Trips to the Brandberg should be at least three days long, as the ascent to the plateau is a sweat-soaked scramble between huge boulders, best done in the relative cool of early morning or even under the light of a full moon. Walking on the plateau is never easy but is rewarded by spectacular views and unusual boulder-strewn landscapes.

Hikers can visit Brandberg in the dry season, using the water that collects in sheltered pot-holes. However these are extremely difficult to find and not always reliable, so your first visit, at least, should be made with someone with knowledge of their location.

Brandberg has no large game animals but the delicate Bushman 'rock paintings' (engravings) found on cave walls illustrate the wide variety that existed in times of higher rainfall. Giraffe, lion and okapi are just some of the figures depicted. Some paintings are more than 15,000 years old.

For those with insufficient time to reach these remote spots, more accessible rock paintings can be seen on Brandberg's eastern edge. These include the famous 'White Lady', although this has been almost destroyed by visitors, and probably not worth the visit. (Better rock paintings can be seen at Erongo and Twyfelfontein, further north.)

Spitzkoppe   The Klein and Gross Spitzkoppe are two of the most accessible inselbergs, only 30km off the tarred main road between Windhoek and the coast. Rising abruptly 600m above the surrounding Namib gravel plains, these monoliths undergo a fascinating change of colour in the setting sun to enthral any photographer. They provide some of the few recognised climbing routes in a country where there is an abundance of good rock but very few climbers. Climbing equipment is needed to reach the summit of Gross Spitzkoppe although the less impressive Klein Spitzkoppe can be walked up.

Hunsberge

The Hunsberge mountains lie between the Fish and Orange Rivers, and are one of the least explored ranges in Namibia. Although close to the Ai-Ais tourist camp, these mountains are best approached by the Noordoewer-Rosh Pinah road running along the Orange River's northern bank. Waterholes are thought to exist because of the sightings of Hartmann's zebra and leopards, but the location and quality of these sources have yet to be discovered. 'The Shell map was the only one to show a 'road' between Rosh Pinah and Noordoever/Vioolsdrif on the Namibia/RSA border. It follows the Orange River and is very beautiful in parts. It took over three hours to go 60 miles.' (G. & M. Munday)

GAME PARKS AND NATURE RESERVES

Namibia has some excellent and well-managed game parks, and Etosha National Park ranks as one of the best in Africa. The coast also provides some outstanding nature viewing, marine mammals and bird species being varied and plentiful.

The best time to visit most parks is between late April and mid June, and between late September and and early November. These are the dry seasons, when animals congregate around watering places. The season for the coastal parks is October/November (for fur seals) and December to February.

Reservations for accommodation in the national parks must usually be made in advance. For more details see the *Accommodation* section.

Etosha National Park

The heart of this 22,270 square kilometre park is the Etosha Pan, a huge depression that was once a lake but is now waterless and white with salt for much of the year. It fills with water after exceptional rains attracting vast numbers of waterfowl. During the dry winter months wildlife congregates around the various mineral springs around the perimeter of the pan, and this is by far the best time of year to visit the park.

There are three restcamps with lodges and camping facilities: Okaukuejo and Halali, which are only open from March to October, and Namutoni which is open all year round.

Most commonly seen animals include elephant, lion, giraffe and zebra. Other species (which are seldom seen in East Africa) are kudu, a beautiful antelope with spiral horns, the gemsbok, equally lovely with its long straight horns, the black-faced impala, and the little springbok. The largest antelope, the eland, is also found, and the brindled gnu.

'Observation by car over a few days allowed us to see all the large animals except leopard and cheetah. Within minutes of entering the park we saw zebra, giraffe, spingbok and Damaraland dik-dik. At Okaukuejo rest camp there is a waterhole with seats behind a floodlit area; on one night there we saw a rhino, a spotted hyena and several elephant, which in Etosha number over a thousand. A forest of the succulent *Moringa ovalifolia*, a bottle tree unique to Namibia, is found at Spokieswoud (Spook Wood or Haunted Forest near Okaukuejo) its weird shape due to regeneration after extensive browsing in dry periods. The park abounds with birds, chiefly ostrich, bustard, secretary bird, the martial eagle and the pale chanting goshawk among many raptors, and some vultures. The fig tree in the courtyard at Namutoni was filled at evening with screaming grey louries.' (G. & M. Munday)

Namib-Naukluft Park

This enormous park covers nearly five million hectares, and comprises four distinct parts, which can visited relatively easily: the Namib section; the Naukluft section; Sesriem and Sossusvlei; and Sandwich Harbour.

The Namib section in the north is most easily reached from Swakopmund. This area contains fine desert scenery and some of the strange plants for which Namibia is famous, such as the Kokerboom tree and Welwischia. Some main roads pass through this area, and you need a permit to leave these. There are several campsites with minimal facilities which can be booked through tourist offices in Swakopmund and Hardap, as well as Windhoek.

The Naukluft section is a mountain-plateau to the southeast of the Namib section, with springs and streams which support a population of zebra and several other species. (More details in the *Hiking* section above.)

The Sesriem and Sossusvlei section is an area of spectacular sand dunes to the southwest of Naukluft. (More details below.)

Sandwich Harbour is a coastal lagoon, 56km south of Walvis Bay, which attracts tens of thousands of birds (around 100 species). Access is by 4WD only and camping is not allowed. Permits are available from service stations in Walvis Bay and from the Tourist Office in Swakopmund.

Skeleton Coast Park

This park covers a strip of coastal desert in northern Namibia, stretching from the Ugab River to the Angolan border. It has some exceptionally interesting wildlife adapted to living in the harsh, dry environment, making this a marvellous park for serious photographers.

To reach the most interesting section, in the north, you must take a fly-in safari (see addresses below), but the southern part of the park is more accessible with restcamps at the fishing resorts of Terrace Bay and Torra Bay (which also has a campsite – open only in December and January).

The Ugab River Hiking Trail runs along the southern boundary of the park.

Cape Cross Seal Reserve

Cape Cross is about 45km north of the resort town of Henties Bay, and home to tens of thousands of fur seals (actually a very close relative of the sealion, rather than a true seal). The reserve is open from mid December to the end of February, then at weekends and the Easter holidays. From July 1 to December 15 it is only open on Wednesday afternoons. There is a good campsite at Mile 72, halfway between Henties Bay and Cape Cross.

The most interesting time to visit the seal colony is October and November, when the bulls are establishing and defending their territories, the pups are born, and mating takes place for next year's crop of babies. Fur seals are able to give birth, and then mate, at the same time each year even though the gestation period is only nine months. This is achieved through 'delayed implantation' where the fertilised ova remains dormant for three months. Once their harem duties are over the bulls return to the sea to catch up on some much-needed feeding (they can lose up to half their body weight while on land, being too busy gaining and guarding their harem to concern themselves with eating).

Kaudom and Mahango (Popa Falls) Game Reserves

These reserves are in the extreme north-east of the country and very different from other Namibian parks as they protect swamps and flood-plains. These are the habitat of hippo, crocodile, and a variety of buck and antelope including the rare lechwe and sitatunga.

Kaudom is near the Botswana border and has two restcamps and campsites. You must bring all food and water with you. Mahango lies to the north-east; visitors are not allowed to spend the night in the reserve but must go to Popa Falls Rest Camp, 15km away, and on the Okavango River.

'The rest camp gave a powerful sensation of being right in the water; frogs plopping and croaking, otters diving. An area particularly rich in bird life with spoonbills, some of the nine species of kingfishers in the area, African fish eagle, glossy ibis and various egrets. Near to Popa Falls in the dry savannah there are scattered baobabs, including specially massive ones in the Oshakati area.' (G. & M. Munday)

Safari companies

If you prefer not to hire a car, most areas of Namibia can be reached by joining an organised safari. Even if you have your own vehicle, you are recommended to do your more off-the-beaten-track sightseeing on an organised basis. There are several safari companies to choose from, offering a range of camping and game-viewing tours in various parts of Namibia.

SWA Safaris (PO Box 20373, Windhoek, tel: 061 37567/8/9) and Oryx Tours (PO Box 2058, Windhoek, tel: 061 224252) operate a wide range of safaris, travelling by coaches or mini-buses and staying in lodges or bungalows.

Namib Wilderness Safaris (PO Box 6850, Windhoek, tel: 226174) operate more adventurous trips, including camping and walking safaris. An associate company, Namib Travel Shop (same address) can make arrange tours, car-hire, hotel reservations, etc.

Top Travel (PO Box 80205, Windhoek, tel: 061 51975) arrange wildlife safaris, fly-in safaris and also specialise in hiking and backpacking tours in various parts of the country. They also run some good one-day tours of Windhoek and the surrounding area.

Skeleton Coast Safaris (PO Box 20373, Windhoek, tel: 061 37567/8/9) run top quality fly-in safaris to remote parts of the northern Namib.

Desert Adventure Safaris (PO Box 1428, Swakopmund, tel: 0641 4072) specialise in rugged camping trips in the northern region, operating from their base at Palmweg Lodge.

Charly's Desert Tours (PO Box 1400, Swakopmund, tel: 0641 4341) organise a range of trips, from one day to one week, into the Namib desert.

OTHER PLACES OF INTEREST

The Sossusvlei Sand Dunes

The sand dunes at Sossusvlei (part of the Namib-Naukluft Park) stand some 350m above the surrounding salt pan, making them the highest dunes in the world. The orange iron oxide staining of the sand grains is particularly prominent in the early morning or late afternoon sun, giving wonderful photo opportunities, although care must be taken with cameras as mechanisms block and lenses rapidly become sand-blasted. It's a great place to wander around for a few hours, although slogging up the sand ridges can be very tiring.

There is a campsite at Sesriem, 63km from Sossusvlei, although it has only 10 places. You may not spend the night at Sossusvlei itself, but can leave the Sesriem campsite very early to get to the dunes by sunrise.

If you don't have car, you may be able to hitch to Sesriem. You can reach the dunes at Sossusvlei by joining the Land Rover tour which leaves the campsite every afternoon.

Near the Sesriem campsite are some smaller dunes and a deep gorge which can be walked to easily in a few hours, although it gets very hot here around midday.

If the campsite is full, or you want more comfort, the Namib Restcamp, just outside the park to the north of Sesriem, has bungalows for hire. Meals are also available, and tours of the sand dunes by foot or in a 4WD vehicle can be arranged.

The Coastal Dunes

The sand dunes along the coast between Swakopmund and Walvis Bay lack the strong orange colour of their counterparts at Sossusvlei, but provide panoramic views of the Atlantic Ocean. Watching the sun set below the sea is a particularly relaxing way to end the day. Dune 7, outside Walvis Bay, is used for the training of army recruits and its soft, shifting sand is a short but challenging climb even without a pack.

FLORA OF NAMIBIA AND WHERE TO FIND IT

By Gordon and Merlin Munday

To consider the highlights of Namibia's plant life, the country can be divided into three natural regions: the Namib desert to the 'western' mountains; north from Etosha to the Angolan border and Caprivi; and the Kalahari, a sandy internally drained basin.

The Namib Desert   This area, consisting of coastal and inner zones, is typical of sub-tropical desert regions, modified by the cold waters of the Benguela current. Night fogs provide humidity up to an equivalent 40mm/y rain on 100-200 days per year. Sun disperses morning fog, beating on the treeless expanse of high sand dunes, gravelly wastes and rocky outcrops. Vegetation consists of sparsely scattered salt-tolerant bushes, e.g. *Zygophyllum stapfil*, *Z. simplex*, *Arthraerua leubnitziae*, and reddish *Sueda sp.*, two endemic members of succulent genera *Trichocaulon sp.* and *Hoodia sp.* which inhabit rocky crevices where condensate is channelled. Usually less than 10cm high, rather like small maize cobs, with a high volume to surface ratio, they have a knobbly surface of bristles and appear more mineral than plant. They depend on flies to pollinate their foul-smelling flowers.

Many species of lichens (a fungal-algal association) – rare in most deserts – colour the rocks and soil green, orange or black, and are a prominent feature of the fog zone; a little water will revive them from desiccation. Another curiosity is the Nara, *Acanthosicyos horrida*, densely tangled, fiercely spiny and up to one metre high with 'melons', tasting like a cucumber-pineapple mixture, and much appreciated by the locals. Its seeds ('butternuts') are sold in far-off Cape Town.

Probably the world's most unusual tree, *Welwitschia mirabilis*, is found in the intermediate zone between the coastal and inner Namib. Consisting of two heavy, fibrous leaves, torn into strips by wind, the largest specimen is over 2,000 years old and 6m from tip to tip. Intermediate between conifers and flowering plants, the separate male and female plants have cone-like flowers. Yet others, green, small and juicy, are found among grass and are browsed by animals far inland. Survival depends upon a fine network of absorbing roots, anchored by a giant tap root.

All these plants may be seen in the Namib Desert Park near Swakopmund. The Welwitschia Nature Drive provides easy access to many drought-resistant plants.

Many Namibian species are tiny succulents, inhabiting dazzling white quartz patches, e.g. the 'living stones' (Lithops etc.) which flower and seed rapidly, concealed among pebbles (protective mimicry) in the ground into which they retract so avoiding overheating yet optimizing water and light.

Near Keetmanshoop there is a forest of the distinctive tree aloe ('Kokerboom', *Aloe dichotoma*) with dagger-like leaves crisscrossed photogenically against the sky. Kokerboom are also found in the northern section of the Namib-Naukluft Park.

Etosha and the north   Mopane, *Colophospermum mopane*, is the dominant tree of the northwest, and favourite browsing for elephants. It burns well and is suitable for furniture. In strong sunlight the two butterfly-shaped leaves close together vertically to conserve water. It is also the host for caterpillars of *Gonimbrasia belina*, known as 'mopane worms' and dried by the local people as a form of valuable storage food. *Pachypodium leallii* can be found about 50km north of Otavi, at Ruacana Falls and at the southern foot of the Grootberg Pass. Towards Popa Falls in the Caprivi Strip (rainfall 600mm/y) the riverine woodland of the Okavango contains the wild date palm *Phoenix reclinata* accompanied by *Salix subserrata*, *Acacia nigrescens* and *Ahebeclada subsp. chobiensis*.

The Kalahari   East of Windhoek lie the reddish orange Kalahari sands; rainfall is 400mm/y. This is a landscape of dry rivers, their beds indicated by an intensely green vegetation, and large trees, dominant being the camel thorn, *Acacia erioloba,* flourishing on underground water. Dunes formed parallel to the prevailing wind are often clothed with vegetation on their lower slopes but with exposed red tops.

ZEBRA

No one watching a herd of zebra will have any doubt that this is a member of the horse family, although the Grevy's zebra is, in fact, an ass not a horse. Zebra behaviour is instantly recognisable to those that know horses, from mutual grooming (using the teeth), to fighting by rearing, biting and kicking.

Herds are either composed of females and a herd stallion, or bachelor males. The mares are governed by rank (watch the dominant animals displace their subordinates when feeding), as are the bachelors, although their dominance is of a more casual nature.

A zebra's stripes are its unique finger print. No two are exactly alike. The pattern that seems so conspicuous in the zoo is seen to be excellent camouflage in the wide savannah grasslands, where the animal's outline is broken up making it surprisingly hard to see at a distance.

GUIDE BOOKS TO AFRICA AND THE INDIAN OCEAN

Guide to Mauritius by Royston Ellis.
A complete guide to every aspect of Mauritius and its dependency, Rodrigues.

Guide to the Comoro Islands by Ian Thorpe.
Four seldom visited islands lying between Madagascar and Africa.

Guide to Madagascar by Hilary Bradt.
How and where to see the island's spectacular wildlife, rainforests and semi-desert. A complete guide for all budgets.

Guide to South Africa by Philip Briggs.
Budget travel and bird-watching, walks and game parks, beaches and cities, suggested itineraries.

Guide to Namibia and Botswana by Chris McIntyre and Simon Atkins.
Off the beaten track in these sparsely populated countries.

Guide to Zimbabwe & Botswana by David Else
A new edition of the budget traveller's No Frills Guide.

Africa Handbooks: Zaire, Malawi, Senegal, Ivory Coast
Four pocket-sized guides to the less-visited countries of Africa.

Through Africa: the overlander's guide by Bob Swain and Paula Snyder.
Driving, motor-cycling, or mountain-biking through the continent. Preparations, routes, campsites, travellers' tales.

Backpacker's Africa — West and Central by David Else.
Public transport and hitching, walking and exploring.

Camping Guide to Kenya by David Else.
Describes every official campsite in Kenya plus suggestions for camping wild in the mountains.

Guide to Zanzibar by David Else.
A detailed guide to the islands of Zanzibar and Pemba.

Guide to Mozambique by Bernhard Skrodzski
The first guide to this former Portuguese colony.

Guide to Tanzania by Philip Briggs
On and off the beaten track in every corner of the country.

Guide to Uganda by Philip Briggs
Includes gorilla viewing in Rwanda and Zaïre.

And then there's the rest of the world...
Send for a catalogue from Bradt Publications, 41 Nortoft Road, Chalfont St Peter, Bucks SL9 0LA, England. Tel/Fax: 0494 873478.

I NEED YOU!

Please help update the next edition

As you can see, I rely on readers' letters to keep this guide up to date. I expect the next edition to be within a year so please write as soon as you can with your comments and update information. Your remarks don't have to be restricted to travel information – I would be interested to hear your views on the size of print, paper or anything else you feel is worthy of comment.

Please write to Bradt Publications, 41 Nortoft Road, Chalfont St Peter, Bucks SL9 0LA, England. Tel/Fax 0494 873478.

BUFFALO

Mainly notable as being the most dangerous large animal in Africa, the Cape buffalo seldom displays very interesting behaviour, although if you are lucky enough to see two males in serious combat you will understand why they need those massive horns. Herds are mainly composed of females with males forming separate groups.

A healthy adult buffalo's only enemy is lion, whilst spotted hyenas tackle young or sick animals. When attacked a herd will run slowly, keeping in a tight group so making it difficult for the lion to select a victim. Buffalo have been known to kill lions by trampling or goring, and the hunter often finds itself retreating to a tree.

INDEX

Country abbreviations: Sudan (Sud), Eritrea (Eri), Ethiopia (Eth), Kenya (Ken), Tanzania (Tan), Uganda (Uga), Rwanda (Rwa), Burundi (Bur), Zaire (Zai), Malawi (Mal), Zambia (Zam), Zimbabwe (Zim), South Africa (SA), Swaziland (Swa), Lesotho (Les), Namibia (Nam).

Notes

Notes

Notes

Notes

Notes